1980

/

Population Policies and
Growth in Latin America

Population Policies and Growth in Latin America

Edited by
David Chaplin
University of Wisconsin,
Madison

Lexington Books
D.C. Heath and Company
Lexington, Massachusetts
Toronto   London

Table of Contents

List of Tables and Figures

Table

Figure

Preface

In May 1968, a conference was held at the University of Wisconsin on "Population Problems and Development in Latin America," sponsored by the Ibero-American Studies Program, and the Catholic and Presbyterian Student Centers. Its objective was to focus the attention of a wide range of disciplines on this aspect of Latin American development. There have been a number of publications on this theme, but largely from a more specialized demographic perspective. The volume consists of some of the (updated) conference papers supplemented by a selection of the most relevant published works in order to place Latin America in the appropriate historical and world wide context.

I would like to acknowledge the assistance of the Ibero American Studies Program at the University of Wisconsin and the University Graduate School Research Fund for support during the editing of these papers. Invaluable typing services from a frequently illegible manuscript were provided by Janice Hurlbut, Madison, Wisconsin, and Mrs. Gorton, Bishop's Waltham, Hants, England.

Population Policies and
Growth in Latin America

1

Introduction: The Population Problem in Latin America

David Chaplin

The essential population problem in most Latin American countries today is their *rate* of growth. At almost 3 percent, it is the highest regional rate in the world and would, if unchecked, double Latin America's population well before the year 2000. It is approximately twice that of currently developed countries during the comparable stage in their development. The *absolute size* of the population of the Latin American countries today is "excessive" only in relation to the enormous inefficiency with which they develop and distribute the benefits of their resources. Viewing the future optimistically, one may expect that Latin America can some day support a larger population at a higher level of living than at present—but only if, (1) radical changes in their political, economic, social, and cultural institutions occur, and (2) the rate of population growth decreases significantly in the near future.

In Table 1-1, the growth of the twenty "Latin American" republics is compared (the total figure also includes former British West Indian dependencies and Guyana). In this projection, no slackening of the 3 percent growth rate is foreseen by 1980, since, although some countries, (such as Argentina, Uruguay, Cuba, Costa Rica, and Chile) will be growing more slowly, others have yet to reach what one can only hope will be their peak eras of growth—namely; Bolivia, Paraguay, all of Central America (except Costa Rica) including Haiti and the Dominican Republic. Meanwhile most of the other countries will probably experience continued high rates of increase or very minor decreases (Brazil, Colombia, Ecuador, Mexico, and Peru).

Two of the countries in this projection reputedly have quite exaggerated growth rates—namely Chile and Costa Rica. Jiménez estimates that Costa Rica's rate of natural increase peaked in 1959 at 3.9 percent and has fallen sharply ever since (crude birth rates falling from 47.5 in 1960 to 34.5 in 1969). The primary reason for this change is not clear. Family planning programs had just begun to function in 1967. Jiménez offers only a high inverse correlation between the commercial importation of the pill (-.82) and the decline in the crude birth rate.[1] Chile's growth rate has reputedly fallen from 2.6 in the early 60's to 1.9 by 1970.[2] The general picture of population growth in Latin America is that those countries, (1) of overwhelmingly European ancestry—Uruguay, Argentina, Chile and Costa Rica, and (2) Socialist Cuba, have already reduced, or are rapidly reducing their rate of population growth. The problem countries (the majority of Latin America's population) remain those with a substantial Indian population and Brazil.

1

Table 1-1
Population Growth in Latin America 1960-1980*

	Population (millions)	Rate of Natural Increase per 1000			Years in Which Population Would Double if these Rates Continued		
	1970	1960	1970	1980	1960	1970	1980
Argentina	24.3	17	15	14	42	47	50
Bolivia	4.6	22	24	26	31	29	27
Brazil	93.2	29	28	28	24	25	25
Chile	9.7	25	23	22	28	30	32
Columbia	22.1	35	34	34	20	21	21
Costa Rica	1.7	38	38	39	18	18	18
Cuba	8.3	20	20	18	35	35	39
Dominican Rep.	4.3	32	34	36	22	21	19
Ecuador	6.0	35	34	34	20	21	21
El Salvador	3.4	31	33	36	23	21	19
Guatemala	5.1	28	28	29	25	25	22
Haiti	5.2	23	24	26	30	29	27
Honduras	2.5	34	34	38	21	21	18
Mexico	50.7	33	34	34	21	21	21
Nicaragua	2.0	29	29	34	24	24	21
Panama	1.4	32	32	32	22	22	22
Paraguay	2.4	30	34	36	23	21	19
Peru	13.5	29	31	31	24	23	23
Uruguay	2.8	13	12	12	54	58	58
Venezuela	10.7	38	33	32	18	21	22
Latin America**	274.9	29	29	29	24	24	24

*Organization of American States, *Datos Basicos de Poblacion en America Latina 1970*, Departamento de Asuntos Sociales, Washington, D.C., 1970. The 1970 figures are estimated projections from 1960 censuses.
**Also includes Guyana, Jamaica, Trinidad, and Tobago.

The Latin American population growth rate is not only undesirable in terms of its size, but also in terms of its structure. It is the consequence primarily of very high fertility rather than of immigration. (Argentina, Uruguay, Chile, and southern Brazil, to be sure, enjoyed substantial European immigration before World War I, but this "developmental subsidy" has been largely exhausted through the acculturation of this initially economically dynamic element, as well as by subsequent demographic growth in Brazil and Chile.) Growth through immigration was one of the many advantages enjoyed by the overseas English-speaking countries and meant an economic input of young adults, thus saving these receiving countries the cost of childrearing. An additional disadvantage of growth largely through natural increase is that since the most rapid declines in mortality today are in the youngest years, the result is an even younger population (40 percent under fifteen years), thus entailing large increases in the lower levels of education as well as in other childrearing expenses.

The most important aspect of this growth rate is that it runs *ahead of* the rate of economic growth in many areas. It also represents indirectly some of the forces preventing a more rapid development. It is a matter of dispute as to whether the level of living for the lower half or two-thirds of the population is dropping absolutely in terms of real per capita income, but the existence of stagnation, or more often of growing gaps by class and region is more certain.[3] It seems probable that the distribution of income in many countries and areas has become increasingly unequal. Unfortunately, reliable data on this point are almost nonexistent. A United Nations study notes that wage policies are "anti-inflationary" rather than trying to "counteract the regressive nature of the income distribution. Public expenditure has not expanded faster than aggregate product and hence has presumably not had a redistributive effect while the regressive nature of the tax structure has been increased. Land reform as a redistribution of wealth has been of extremely limited importance. The main economic sector which has been benefited by recent economic growth has been the urban middle classes—while the marginal rural and urban sector has increased in size."[4] This report, which is especially relevant to Illich's paper, also notes that "There is no consistent move towards providing equal educational opportunities. Universal primary education is still a distant goal and the highest growth rates generally apply to the secondary and higher levels . . . The high dropout rates at all educational levels suggest that to some extent the new population sector gradually being covered cannot profitably use the services offered for want of equally significant improvements in other aspects of their living conditions : . . A comparison of building rates with overall population growth and urbanization rates suggests that housing levels are deteriorating . . . The resources allocated to education and health already absorb a relatively high proportion of the governmental budget and cannot easily be raised still further."[5] The latter limitation means that more education for women, which generally results in lower fertility, can not be afforded. In addition, with a largely sex segregated system of education, such improvements as are made are likely to go disproportionately to males.

One of the less direct consequences of a heavy dependency burden of youth (the ratio of those under given working ages to those in the working ages) is the demands it raises for elaborate welfare legislation. There are other roots as well for the very generous labor and welfare laws in Latin America, such as a desire to appear "developed" and Western, but the function of these laws of interest in the present context is their cost—even with only very partial enforcement. In the more developed countries such as Chile, the funding of these laws has already become a major drag on development.[6] They represent a diversion of resources into immediate consumption among groups with a low savings capacity and away from investment in long range infrastructure projects. Moreover, they create new urban vested interests (the organized urban factory and white collar workers) with at least as much negative influence on development as the traditional trilogy of the military, the Church and landed "aristocracy." In addition, with only a minority of the urban labor force actually covered by social security, the mass of the poor, through a regressive tax system, are subsidizing those already above them economically. If Allende attempts as full scale a socialization of the Chilean economy as did Castro in Cuba, he will also have to displace many of the leaders of the urban unions and reorganize the social security system on an austerity basis.

Relating fertility reduction directly to economic development, a number of studies have worked out the economic gains to be obtained by varying levels of reduced demographic growth.[7] (However, in all of the economic models which Robinson and Horlacher review, it is always assumed that developing countries will have to finance their own Family Planning Programs. As Epstein's paper (Chapter 7 in this volume) notes, the implementation of family planning in Latin America has been greatly eased by the fact that this cost has been met largely by foreign funds. At the stage of full institutionalization, however, as evidenced by Chile, such funding, especially from the United States, can and should be reduced.) The central point, making conventional assumptions regarding capital/output ratios, is that, just to maintain a stable level of living, there must be at least a 3:1 ratio between investment growth rates and population growth rates. To experience even a 1 percent per capita growth rate in the face of a 2 percent population growth, investment must reach 9 percent of national income; with a 3 percent population growth rate and a goal of 2 percent per capita income growth, investment must increase by 15 percent annually.[8] Viewing the problem from a differing perspective, Berelson notes that it is generally accepted that each prevented birth is worth two to three times the per capita income (see Chapter 5, page 85).

These calculations led to the plausible but highly impolitic assertion by President Johnson, in a 1965 United Nations speech, that less than $5 in population control was worth $100 in foreign aid. This remark was widely quoted in Latin America as indicating that the United States was about to embark on a "cheap" development policy.[9] In fact, United States aid did decrease in the following years, owing to the cost of the Viet Nam War and to increasing demands for attention to welfare problems within the United States. Thus, to the extent that external aid declined, fertility control became all the more imperative, however unjust this decline in aid may seem.

Ideological Opposition

Finally, in detailing Latin America's demographic handicaps it must be observed that not only is it the world's most rapidly growing region, it also has a deeper ideological resistance to recognizing this problem. Initially the assumption has been that Latin American Catholicism was (1) unified and powerful and (2) completely unfavorable to effective fertility control. It now appears that the Catholic Church is no longer united on this issue, nor does it enjoy effective discipline over the demographically critical lower class in this respect as well as many others. [10] The largely formal religious participation of most Latin American Catholics has been especially evident with respect to the use of contraceptives and abortion among urban women. [11] One "cost" of the attempted renaissance of Catholic spiritual influence in Latin America has been the transfer of control to a largely foreign clergy, many of whom are more liberal on the issue of birth control. The main financial support for birth control, even within the Catholic Church, is still from the United States AID, and Ford and Rockefeller funds for church-related research and action groups—initially in Chile and Columbia—but now throughout Latin America.

During the Wisconsin Conference the suggestion was made that, above all, an open controversy with Church officials was to be avoided for fear of damaging the public image of the birth control effort. Ivan Illich, on the basis of the Puerto Rican experience, disagreed sharply with such an assumption. There, when a high church official threatened to excommunicate those voting for Muñoz Marin in 1960, in part because of his support for birth control clinics, the results were: (1) a decisive victory for Muñoz and (2) a flood of requests for birth control devices whose efficacy was "certified" by the Archbishop's condemnation. [12]

The most active clerical efforts with respect to this issue today are those of progressive groups such as CELAP (Latin American Population and Family Center) in Santiago and the International Confederation of Christian Family Movements which, like Ivan Illich, are trying to promote family planning in terms of modern Catholic family ideals instead of "United States middle-class materialism".

The problem of values and apparent motivations greatly complicates the efforts of foreigners—overwhelmingly from the United States—in promoting birth control in Latin America. The greatest obstacle to a recognition of the "population problem" is not primarily the Church, but nationalist and Marxist ideology and a diffuse concern with masculinity (machismo), which, together with Catholicism, covers the spectrum of Latin American orientations on this issue. There remain only a handful of largely United States trained *tecnicos* and some liberal European clergy who are favorably disposed to family planning. Contrary to the assumptions of some Marxists, it should also be noted, the local oligarchies (except possibly in Colombia) do not yet recognize that birth control is really sophisticated conservatism. It must also be admitted, as the cases of Greece, Italy, and Spain suggest, that eliminating the pressure of a population explosion may indeed defuse revolutionary tendencies. Marxist writers, therefore, logically oppose birth control—for United States blacks or colonial peoples—on the grounds that the economic system, not human values and family behavior, should be changed, *prior* to the revolution. For tactical reasons, they argue, immoral economies should be overloaded with people to ensure their collapse. David Epstein, a Marxist critic of United States birth control policies, does recognize, however, the implicit anti-feminist implications of his stance by noting that "Control of their own bodies is a precondition for the liberation of women," but he then goes on to oppose birth control because of the apparent motives United States interests have in promoting it.[13] (Apparently the emancipation of women is a luxury only affluent societies can afford!).

The appropriate response to this ad hominem argument would be that motives for, and consequences of, actions need have little relationship. Many worthy actions have been performed for base reasons. This is especially true in this case where two sets of actions are involved—the first, by North Americans, to promote the awareness and desirability of contraception; the second, the decision by Latin American women to make effective use of birth control devices and techniques. Even the latter's motives are not consciously related to the systemic consequences of a lower fertility, on which so much of United States propaganda mistakenly dwells. (One of the major issues with respect to the politics of population is whether in even the most developed societies the very personal decision to have or not to have children *can* or should be influenced by long run aggregate consequences.) A bold attempt to link women's liberation in the United States with the population-pollution cause was offered by one of *Look's* senior women editors.[14] The bulk of her arguments, however, were still pitched to personal emancipation and the avoidance of unloved children.

It should also be noted that even the most optimistic projections speak only of lowering the growth rate from 3.0 to 2-2.25 in the coming decades—still a very high figure. There is, therefore, little likelihood that this source of revolutionary pressure will decrease. In fact, as Cuba has demonstrated, it is those populations already enjoying a relative improvement who are the most revolutionary—*not* those trapped in traditionally miserable or worsening conditions.

In an excellent treatment of the ideological aspects of the birth control issue in general and with special reference to North East Brazil, Herman Daly notes that "In the North East . . . population growth is more likely to serve the status quo than revolution, since it maintains the masses in a state of hopeless impotent poverty. . . . The middle-class students are the revolutionary force, not the masses. These revolutionary students may exhort the masses to produce more hungry children today in order to have more guerrilla fighters tomorrow, but they (the students) certainly practice birth restriction themselves (by contraception or late marriage) because it is all that keeps them from sinking into the proletariat."[15]

Daly introduced the notion of "Roman Exploitation" as opposed to the Marxist concept of capitalist exploitation as an alternative source of resistance to birth control for the masses. "Encouraging the propogation of 'Wage slaves' is still an attractive policy for oligarchs".[16]

With respect to the Marxist position, the *post*-revolutionary population policies of socialist countries should also be examined. Cuba has welcomed representatives from the Planned Parenthood Federation, and, like other Communist Socialist countries, has presumably experienced a sharp decrease in its demographic growth rate owing to the crash program of advanced training and employment for women—the *two* most effective conditions favoring lower fertility. Communist China went through several cycles of being pro- and anti-natalist, but finally has settled on a firm growth-reducing policy. The point is that *no* economic system can stand 2.5+ percent demographic growth rates arising solely from fertility. Larger populations may mean, other things being equal, greater economies of scale and more political influence in the world, *but* an attempt to get there at 3 percent a year is definitely self-defeating.

Like many Latin American nationalists and Marxists, Paul Baran cites low density figures to prove how much more population Latin America could carry—disregarding the enormous technical and economic problems involved in developing this region's "frontier" land. He then goes on to cite a 1 percent growth rate figure from a book by Josué de Castro (1949). This rate is now much surpassed and, as explained above, the *growth rate* is the essence of the population problem.[17]

An example of the nationalist objections to population control—especially strong among Mexican male politicians—was offered during the May 1968 Wisconsin Conference by Carlos Madrazo, former Governor of Tabasco and ex-director of P.R.I. (the Institutional Revolutionary Party—the monolithic governmental party in Mexico). The population problem will not be acute in Mexico, he observed "until some time after the year 2000 ... The current situation is not due to the increase in population but the ineptitude of our government in solving these problems ... If we can transform the economic system, then enormous possibilities of man as a producer ... will be realized. Mexico is rather like the United States a century ago with its enormous expanse of unoccupied land ... We are working at about an eighth of capacity ... If we develop the resources of the sea, we could feed twice the population ... the great increase in population is a necessary condition for the type of radical social change that is being brought about."

The current president of Mexico, Luís Escheverría Alvarez, declared in May 1970 "We must view objectively and without alarm the new problems and also the social, economic and cultural aspirations that have been generated by rapid population growth which we neither wish to slow nor could slow but, on the contrary, should encourage."[18] Mexico, in spite of its history of populist revolution and anti-clericalism remains more resistant to the mass human need for a reduction in rate of population growth than any other Latin American country.

Neo-Isolationism and United States
Population Policy

A problematic point raised by Stycos (Chapter 6 in this volume) is the effect on

Latin Americans of the recent official United States admission of a need to limit domestic population growth. One could quarrel with Stycos's interpretation that this had much to do with a desire to be consistent with our efforts to persuade others to limit their growth rates, ("what we do unto others"). It would seem to be primarily a reaction to our poverty problem intensified in recent years by heightened racial tension. The other more recent basis for such concern is the environmental pollution issue, which has been linked to the population problem by such groups as Zero Population Growth. But federal action in this latter case is still largely in the birth-control-for-the-poor stage. It seems doubtful that even a greater public dedication to a reduction in the birth rate at *all levels of United States society* would help our efforts in this area in Latin America, since the opposition there is much deeper than merely an objection to the fact that we don't practice what we preach. Non-Chinese Maoists see no need to imitate Communist China's fertility control program, because they view their own situations as radically different. The highly nationalist leaders in most of Latin America likewise do not view their countries as similar to the United States in this respect.

The current neo-isolationist mood in the United State, arising from frustration in Viet Nam, drug addiction, race conflict, poverty, inflation, urban decay and more recently the environment, consumer protection, and Women's Liberation, is indirectly related to the way the government and private groups do or might deal with Latin America, aside from reducing economic aid. The size and growth rate of the United States population has been blamed by Zero Population Growth extremists as a major cause of pollution. Typically it is the physical scientist who takes the extremist position that stopping population growth *now* is a top priority in environmental protection policy.[19] The United States population will of course have to stop growing some day short of "standing room only." The practical issues are: (1) how important is either the *size* or *growth rate* of the United States population *today* compared to the *level* and *growth* of *affluence* in causing pollution, and, (2) what would be the requirements and consequences of *immediate* population stabilization.

It would seem eminently clear that the "per capita increase in production (arising from rising affluence) has been more important than population growth" in causing pollution.[20] The United States "population has increased by about 50 percent in the past thirty years (while) attendence in national parks has increased by more than 400 percent" and the per capita use of electricity has been multiplied several times.[21] The point is that we are already in trouble with our present population. Thus, while an immediate zero population growth rate would help somewhat, primary focus on it as policy goal would: (1) divert public attention from the much more significant, if politically controversial, structural sources of pollution, and (2) be extremely disruptive.

In the United States, zero population growth as a goal will be slowed by the "lump" of young parents produced by the post-World War II baby boom. Thus, even if their completed family size turns out to be the replacement level of 2.25 children per family, their "surplus" status in our currently unbalanced age structure will yield a continuous population growth to about 300 million by the year 2000. Thus to achieve zero population growth with our present age structure we would have to persuade our current parents to drastically reduce childbearing—many necessarily remaining childless; then, later, a renewed pro-natalist policy ("breed for balance!") would have to be instituted to prevent an absolute decline in numbers inevitably accompanied by a heavy burden of aged.

In currently developing countries, even if age-specific birth rates were to drop to the level of replacement, the age structure of these populations creates a "momentum" which would still increase the population by 1.6 before stability could be achieved. If a delay of fifteen years occurred before this replacement level of fertility were reached, the population would still multiply by 2.5. The ultimate population size would in fact be still greater, given assumed continued decreases in mortality.[22] In brief, an immediate zero population growth rate could only be achieved by a politically and socially "impossible" combination of a drastic decline of births and the slowing down of improvements in life expectancy.

It is curious that so many physical scientists, who better understand the technical basis for pollution than do the social scientists, often in radically apocalyptic terms, opt for the "conservative" individual-behavioral-change re-form policy rather than facing up to the obvious need for increased federal control over private business and over local governments. The future of the environment-ecology movement may well founder on the "socialistic" reforms and the inflationary consequences of allocating pollution costs to producers, which a serious attack on pollution would require.

This digression on the United States concern with pollution is relevant to the Latin American population problem in several respects.

1. Even less than in the case of the population issue, the "environment-pollution" issue has aroused little interest in Latin America. From military nationalists to Marxists and radical Catholic humanists the environment is seen, as has been the case until so recently in the United States, as something to be exploited for human prosperity or welfare. One can well imagine a Latin American response to any United States effort to persuade them not to use D.D.T., or not to pollute their own air or water, as a Machiavellian plot to keep them from developing. A United States confrontation in this area, not only with foreign governments but also with the foreign operations of United States firms, seems more likely, or at least called for, since Secretary of State Rogers created an Office of Environmental Affairs in the State Department in February 1970. However, United States agricultural advisors in Latin Amer-ica, so often opponents of ecological "extremists" in the United States, are not pressing Latin American governments on this issue. In fact, United States agricultural firms may well accelerate their efforts to develop food, lumber, and other resources in such countries as Mexico and Brazil, precisely because they can thus escape United States pollution controls. We could thus "use" Latin America as Northern Europe has in effect "used" Italy as the European site in the processing of raw materials at which the largest amount of

pollution takes place.[2 3] Since Latin American governments are anxious to develop through further processing their raw materials we could thus "export" some of our pollution.

2. Latin America's need to disregard pollution and conservation is greater than ours, given their rate of population growth. They presumably feel they can not afford the added costs of developing cleanly. (This does not mean they will not readily pass the most advanced laws against pollution and for consumer protection, as they have already done in the area of social welfare; it means only that they are even less likely to be enforced.) The "poor pay more" not only as individuals but as countries. Most Latin American cities, lacking the capital for efficient mass transit and lower class housing, handle both in a manner which costs less per year or per unit *at present* but will be more expensive in the long run. Their "squatting" poor are allowed to construct "homemade" detached single family dwellings (a luxury for the United States middle and upper classes) which will be extremely expensive to service with roads, water, power, etc., once this population develops the political influence to demand these facilities—compared to high rise apartment complexes. Likewise a transportation system based largely on buses, taxis, *collectivos* (private cars following bus lines), rather than rail commutation has already created Los Angeles style congestion and smog with, of course, the high man-mile cost of such transportation.

Consumer protection is yet another "unexportable" United States domestic concern. United States' attempts to impose its own domestic standards on foreign exporters are typically viewed as a shallow ruse to exclude foreign competition. (Such motives indeed may have been involved in some United States auto safety regulations, which have greatly complicated the ability of British manufacturers to maintain "their share" of U.S. imports.)

All of these issues have indirectly led to a greater United States emphasis on population control in Latin America—by default—since the solution of these problems has led to a reduction in our development aid to Latin America. The total United States commitment to "solving the world's population problem" is now $100,000,000 a year (1970). As a more positive aspect of United States neo-isolationism Latin America is currently enjoying an era of benign neglect which has enabled Peru and Chile to carry out anti-United States "developmental" actions without effective United States reprisals, even where United States law calls for positive action.

The Demographic Transition

Initially Latin America's demographic future was seen in terms of the "demographic transition" model—a highly generalized abstraction from Western experience (see page 222). But, like Rostow's "take-off" scheme, it has been found wanting both as a description of Western history and, especially, as a model of the future of currently developing countries. In its original form it involved a stable traditional population sustained by an inefficient regime of high death and high birth rates. Subsequently, death rates fell before birth rates, thus leaving an era of natural increase growth. Eventually in the model the birth rate falls to the level of modern death rates and thus an efficient demographically "mature" and "developed" population is stabilized.

In terms of Western experience recent historical demographic research suggests deviations from this pattern, which apparently are being repeated today. Both Malthus and contemporary historians agree that a period of even higher fertility is part of the development process.[24] To the extent that the first effects of economic development improve the economic opportunities of a pre-industrial population *within* the context of its high fertility institutions, it should not be surprising that fertility rises even higher. This effect should be all the more prominent in non-Western or marginally Western areas, where industrialization is essentially an alien intrusion. Some Latin American cities, for instance, have reached sizes which far exceed the technical and administrative capacity of the local society. Up to a point and for a limited period of time, the effects of foreign industrialization can be introduced without the corresponding local infrastructure. After this stage, if local industrialization is to succeed, the requisite institutional infrastructure must develop, which in turn is linked to reduced fertility values and behavior.

Heer concludes an analysis of economic development and fertility by observing that investments in health and education have a better chance of hastening fertility reduction than policies which merely raise income within the traditional context.[25] He also asserts that the immediate effect of public health measures is a higher birth rate. Then, by confronting parents with even more children than they need (while simultaneously *not* increasing their income enough to be able to afford this added expense), could a reduction in fertility possibly be brought about. In addition, Heer suggests that the goodwill built up by public health clinics apparently serves as the best basis for the subsequent diffusion of contraceptive methods.

The expectation that economic development reduces fertility, then, refers to its long run effect, not its immediate consequences. The Western transition model is also defective in that it does not account for the unexpected recovery of Western fertility after 1940.

The difference in the mechanism of mortality and fertility reduction in the Latin American case—compared to Western experience—is, however, what most concern us. In the Western case, fewer and later marriages, *coitus interruptus*, and other "traditional" factors helped set the stage for a spontaneous reduction in fertility, i.e., one not aided by modern contraceptive technology or policy, until late in the process. In Latin America, on the other hand, mortality reduction was introduced "artificially" from the outside, rather than by an indigenous rise in the level of living. It also occurred more rapidly and hence gave rise to much higher levels of natural increase. As for fertility reduction, Latin America has not yet experienced significant internal institutional pressure in this direction. In Ireland and Spain a puritan Catholicism and persistently strong family structure *helped* to reduce the birth rate since, with marriage made difficult, and persistently high marital fertility, increasing numbers postponed or avoided marriage, or emigrated. In Latin America, on the other hand, it is the *weakness* of the Church and of the urban lower class family which permits high fertility—by default. In Latin America, since the Church's influence is not sufficient to encourage a high level of sanctioned unions among the lower class, a disorganized family life has led to irresponsibly high fertility. Paradoxically then, faced with traditional obstacles such as a shortage of land, a strictly Catholic peasantry is likely to have a lower birth rate than one that is less strict. Kirk feels that, lacking a stable family organization, birth control programs in Latin America must focus even more on women than is the case in Asia, and should facilitate abortions, which are already common, rather than legitimating a birth control program as a way of reducing the abortion rate.[26] This latter basis for overcoming Church resistance may have been necessary initially, but, once clinics were well established, it is unlikely they would be closed if abortions were made more accessible.

In summary, then, Western demographic history offers little guidance as to the timing or structure of a slackening in the growth rate in Latin America. Therefore, in the absence of firm predictions, both extreme pessimism and optimism pervade the popular and even professional discussions of this issue.

Birth Control Programs

Optimists with respect to a rapid reduction in fertility lean heavily on a few Asian countries.[27] Latin America, on the other hand, does not offer such a promising picture. The most "favorable" evidence available at present relates to: (1) the high abortion rates among women in Lima and Santiago, and (2) attitude and (self-reported) behavior surveys in many Latin American cities with respect to use of, or interest in contraceptives on the part of women.[28] Due to the under-registration of births and deaths in yearly vital statistics reports, only the 1970 censuses will reveal whether any significant reduction in growth has actually been accomplished.

The predominant strategy of the largely United States funded promoters of birth control, or family planning as the more politic term, has been to overcome Church and medical opposition: (1) by enlisting their collaborative support by promising to *reduce* abortions and promote individual health, (2) by not suggesting any radical institutional reforms or changes (which could provide a more effective social pressure for lower fertility), and (3) by stressing the unfavorable aggregate effect of high growth rates for economic development. Most critics fault United States programs for not recognizing the greater appeal of reducing abortion [Chile] or preventing the abandonment of children [Caracas].[29] As Davis's article (Chapter 4 of this volume) effectively argues, this policy (public health-anti-abortion) is a high if not self-defeating price to pay for social acceptability. This approach could be fairly described as technocratic, arising in part from the narrow range of professionals—largely medical doctors and demographers who have been involved in promoting family planning. (A recognition of the overemphasis on the biomedical aspects of the population problem has been the recent creation of a Ford-Rockefeller Program of Research on Law, Social Science, and Population Policy which seeks, as does this volume, a multi-disciplinary approach.)

The primary point seems to be that many countries such as France, Ireland and Spain have *already* reduced their fertility *without* modern contraceptive techniques—hence the seriousness of the expressed interest of many Latin American women may be questioned, except of course in the case of abortions. The reduction of abortions, in fact, could leave the fertility behavior of these women unchanged, since it could merely mean avoiding *that* child in a more efficient manner.

On the other hand, it is not sufficient to wait for the process of industrialization and urbanization to reduce fertility spontaneously, since we cannot be sure that Western history will be repeated in this respect. In addition, as Davis notes, the level of Western population growth is also still too high. Contraception can, however, doubtless accelerate a decline if it is already under way—which *was* its role in a few Asian countries (Japan, South Korea, and Taiwan).

The three most effective fertility-reducing techniques or influences seem to be abortion, female education, and the employment of women of fertile ages. None of these elements seems destined to function in a sufficiently positive direction in Latin America. Current public health-run family planning clinics are working hard to substitute contraception for abortion, while the education and employment of women offer little promise. To be sure, more educated women have fewer children and absolutely more women are being educated. But the increase in and the content of lower-class female education is quite insufficient. Most Latin American primary and secondary schools are sex-segregated, a factor tending to reinforce traditional stereotypes of feminine behavior. In particular, lower-class women receive occupationally less relevant, as well as less, education than men. Moreover, in view of the already large surplus of labor, there seems little reason to accelerate female vocational training as a hopefully positive cost-benefit investment in "human capital." In addition, the extensive labor and welfare laws already on the books discourage the employment of women, a point developed by Chaplin (Chapter 11 in this volume). Thus the suggestions by Blake, Kirk, and others that female employment and abortions be fostered by governments seems highly unlikely in Latin America.

The most effective approach would be to promote all possible techniques of contraception and abortion through both public and private channels in the context of fertility-reducing institutional reforms. Cuba, Puerto Rico, and Trinidad have apparently pursued such a policy and thus presumably are being relieved of this obstacle to successful development. Whether other Latin American countries will take as effective steps remains to be seen. Argentina and Uruguay, partly through a high abortion rate, have already brought their growth rates down (Argentina already imports Bolivians for marginal employment), and have thus graduated into a different set of obstacles to development. Clearly, controlling population growth is only a necessary but not a sufficient condition for development. Moreover, if it is the only step taken, this pressure for broader institutional changes will have been removed, thereby allowing, though not fully explaining, the types of regimes currently ruling Argentina, Greece, and Spain. *Thus institutional reform is not only desirable for purposes of accelerating fertility reduction but also for promoting continued development throughout a society.*

Organization of the Book

In order to place our focus on Latin America in the proper historical and world-wide perspective, we begin, in Section I, with Joseph Spengler's summary of western demographic history. Spengler emphasizes the enormous advantage Northwestern Europe enjoyed compared to the currently developing areas, by having a much slower rate of population growth. The long term average annual growth rate never rose as high as 1 percent. The resulting age structure permitted (but, of course, did not require) a higher savings ratio, and a more productive labor force.

Lincoln Day then deals with the major cultural issue with respect to Latin American fertility: the role of the Catholic Church. As a result of a careful cross-cultural analysis, he concludes that only in a very limited situation does Catholic religiosity *per se* result in high fertility, namely in developed countries where Catholics view themselves as a beleaguered minority (such as in Holland and Switzerland). In Latin America, on the other hand, the Church's effectiveness lies primarily in the political area, where it has often attempted to prevent official support for family planning. Day thus concludes that, even if the Catholic Church officially supported family planning in Latin America, it would make little difference, since other factors are much more important determinants of fertility. The obverse implication does not necessarily follow. Even if clerical pronouncements on family behavior are little heeded (which seems quite evident) the absence of public Church opposition to family planning could facilitate its nation-wide establishment (as the case of Chile and Colombia indicate). At the same time the more formidable opposition of nationalist and Marxist laymen could no longer presume to speak in the name of the church or at least as defenders of the faith. What is certain is that Catholicism *per se* has rarely been primarily responsible for a high level of fertility.

The last part of the first section consists of a public "debate" between eminent demographers on the efficacy of family planning as a solution to the problem of population growth. Kingsley Davis was responding to the optimistically technocratic approach of many Family Planners. His primary points are: (1) The family planning approach at best had worked in only a few Asian countries—and even there its independent efficacy has been difficult to demonstrate, (2) By relying so heavily on the public health approach, which condemns the highly effective technique of abortion, it could not have a significant impact on the birth rate, and (3) This approach provides only the means for fertility control without attempting to affect the motivation for its effective utilization. Specifically it leaves open the classic economic issue of integrating individual decision-making with societal needs. Davis was writing as a professional demographer offering a scientific critique of an action program. Berelson's response was that of both a demographer and a man with official involvement in the research and action aspects of family planning. As such he could only say that family planning was all that was politically acceptable at this stage. He begged off answering Davis's challenge as to the effectiveness of family planning programs, but was quite ready to concede that they must be only the first stage.

The strongest case for a close link between family planning and public health clinics has been offered by Carl E. Taylor.[30] As a medical doctor he also concedes that family planning is only the first stage, but challenges Davis' suggestion that the public health link be broken. Since Davis accepts family planning as the proper first stage, these papers are actually in substantial agreement as to the need for subsequent steps. Unfortunately, both Berelson and Taylor use India as an example of future possible steps, since the Latin American situation is, at present, so unpromising. Berelson's comprehensive evaluation of possible next steps exhibited little of Bogue's optimism,[31] in fact he felt obliged to note that "possibly what would be needed could not be afforded and what could be afforded would not be effective." It would seem useless, for example, to expect conservative authoritarian governments in Latin America to take effective population control measures, since it is just such governments today which are especially in favor of further growth on nationalistic-military grounds.

A further response to Davis' challenge can be found in Bogue's belatedly proposed (1970) "Rapid Feedback for Family Planning Improvement Manual"—designed especially for Korea.[32] Such a feedback evaluation ideally should have been built into the earliest pilot programs, but this is rarely done in any area of planned social change, least of all one carried out in the atmosphere of crisis which has surrounded the population problem in the thinking of the United States Family Planning "establishment." Bogue concedes that "the efficacy of family planning programs have yet to be demonstrated." His critics, such as Davis, do not, as Bogue asserts, all take a gloomy view of the population explosion. They do question whether, where the birth rate has declined, as in South Korea or Taiwan, family planning has done more than accompany a spontaneous trend initiated by the Japanese (their former colonies). As in Costa Rica, such programs have followed rather than preceded the decline in fertility. Bogue underestimates such basic structural changes as urbanization, female employment, and literacy, since he assumes that such gradual changes could not effect the sharp "bend in the trend" observed.[34] In principle, many social science theorists would not agree that all quantitative indicators which shift gradually can only have consequences which change at the same pace. On the contrary, economic and demographic literature reveals many instances of critical absolute sizes which, once reached (and surpassed even at the same rate), have dramatic rather than gradual effects.

Finally, Bogue overstates the dilemma by asserting that the "agnostics" believe Family Planners "are simply indulging in wishful thinking." The alternative is not Family Planning *or* despair, but Family Planning *and* studies of, and action on, those systemic variables which are both favorable to lower fertility and also modifiable by public and/or private actions.

Section II narrows the focus to Latin America. Although the history of the population control movement has yet to be written, J. Mayone Stycos' paper is the best available outline for such a project. Although it neglects the embarrassing remnants of "yellow peril" support and does not do full justice to the actual operations of the private and semi-official public funds which have flowed in this direction, it is an excellent description of the extraordinary complexity and delicacy of the United States-Latin American relationship in this area. Since his paper was written, A.I.D. has increased its population budget and is now willing to go further into the non-medical, socioeconomic aspects of the population control problem. A crucial event will be the completion of the 1970 round of Latin American censuses in order to determine whether any of the family planning programs have had any apparent aggregate effect, or whether again, as in 1960, growth rates are going to be even higher than expected.

The study by Vivian Epstein is one of the first systematic attempts by a political scientist to examine the politics of population control. This paper is especially useful as a detailed description, admittedly at the level of formal legislation and organizations, of what has actually been established up to 1970. As yet we have no hard evidence that any of these programs has had a significant effect on national birth rates. Moreover, Davis' critique of Family Planning would appear to be especially relevant. In none of the few countries where family planning has achieved some level of acceptance do the "acceptors" appear to be ready for subsequent stages of national population control. Only Costa Rica could be said to have an official population policy.

Dr. Ivan Illich, of the Catholic Documentation Center in Cuernavaca, Mexico, one of the Catholic Church's most outspoken internal critics, follows with a critique of the way the United States has promoted birth control in Latin America. He is particularly interested in the relationship between responsible parenthood and responsible citizenship through adult education programs. It is not clear whether he feels that family planning, promoted "American style," *can not* reach the peasant masses because of its "offensive" style of presentation, or *should not* be used for fear it might work all too well. A desire for social and material improvement is quite universal. Appealing to the lowest common denominator of human emotions has worked for advertisers not only in the United States, but in many other very different cultures as well. Given the crisis mentality of advocates of family planning, any sales technique which would "work" might be used regardless of the thereby foregone opportunities to realize a new family ideal in the course of promoting birth control. Yet it may also be presumptuous to attempt to determine why poverty stricken acceptors should adopt contraceptives. They are already in a highly structured and desperate situation in which the range of plausible motives for action is limited.

Ivan Illich has, however, a revolutionary yet perhaps very practical solution—mass adult literacy programs which might ideally create a new sense of responsible citizenship in all areas of life, family planning as well as political participation. "Responsible parenthood," he notes, "cannot be disjoined from the request for power in politics." Although Davis criticized the educational approach to family planning as too slow and moderate to have much effect, he had in mind only conventional propagandistic appeals rather than the radically politicizing type of adult education to which Illich is referring.[35]

In Sections III and IV we move away from explicit population policies into the demographic implications of conventionally "unrelated" policies. William Glade reveals that virtually no governmental attention has been paid to the employment implications of rapid population growth. Moreover, the types of development policies actually pursued do not promise to provide adequate employment opportunities even for current workers. Thus what could be a major source of feedback pressure on government planners, namely the need to enlarge employment opportunities, does not function in Latin America in such a way as to indicate that population growth rates are a related problem.

The November-December 1970 issue of *CERES*, the Food and Agricultural Organization Review, is devoted to the problem of rising unemployment. While several of the contributors cited the population "explosion" as *a* if not *the* major problem, Carlos Alberto de Medina, Director of the Latin American Centre for Research in the Social Sciences at Rio de Janeiro, preferred to interpret the growing urban unemployment as solely the fault of agrarian interests who were mechanizing too rapidly. Like several other writers, he prefers a labor-intensive type of land reform which will hold more peasants on the land.[36] This issue will be taken up in the final section of the book.

Richard Miller's paper carries Glade's focus a step further by showing how certain labor and welfare laws in Latin America actually aggravate the scarcity of employment opportunities. Feedback evaluations of welfare programs are rare enough in Western countries and so are predictably nonexistent in Latin America. The major hoped for source of employment opportunities for rural migrants would be in manufacturing, but due to the factors described in Section III, this sector is actually shrinking. This decline, in turn, is not basically an artifact of changing definitions, nor a sign of progress in terms of the disappearance of artisan handicraft, but is rather a real stagnation (in employment, not in production) which leaves open only the undesirable alternative of marginal traditional service employment such as street vending, prostitution, and domestic service. On the employment problem a United Nations Economic Survey reveals that the factory manufacturing sector has decreased its demand from 10 percent in the 1950s to 7.5 percent in the early 1960s. The major increase in employment has been in marginal urban services which are "to a large extent overt and disguised unemployment." This problem is "created by institutional factors, the rapid population growth and the much faster increase in the urban population . . . Hence the urgent need for an employment policy within the framework of general development plans."[37] Chaplin's paper pursues the topic of *de facto* pro-natalist welfare legislation in terms of the Peruvian experience. His primary attention is devoted to explaining the sharp reduction of women in manufacturing employment, a type of occupation thought to be common for women at this stage of economic development and one generally unfavorable to childbearing. The fact is that the institutional obstacles to population control in Latin America are not merely or even primarily traditional values or organizations, but also modern labor and welfare laws and the large bureaucracies dedicated to enforcing them. Much of this legislation implicitly if not explicitly favors high levels of fertility.

The final section deals with the high-fertility agrarian sector of Latin America in terms of the issues of food production, agrarian reform, and economic development. Without going into the intricacies of the problem at this point, it seems reasonable to assert that if radical changes in agricultural technology and economics were made, much larger populations could easily be fed, but just feeding such a mass would hardly constitute economic development. It is already the case that, under current technological and institutional arrangements, many Latin American countries now suffer food shortages even in basic traditional subsistence crops and hence have to spend precious foreign exchange for food rather than for machinery. Of course some countries enjoy such comparative advantages in nonfood crops that it is still economic to import basic foods, but as Thiesenhusen and Fletcher point out, there is still latitude for fairly labor-intensive investments in agriculture to yield high returns in food for local consumption. The authors are not, however, in full agreement on the role of peasant small holdings (which agrarian reform would increase) in keeping surplus labor out of the cities until sufficient employment is available, as was the case in the United States. In this respect the following ECLA evaluation of Agrarian Reform is highly relevant: "Latin American countries have achieved very little in absolute terms and practically nothing in relation to (their) needs or targets . . . most of the reform programmes have constantly been watered down and many of them are now almost at a standstill."[38]

Emil Haney's paper joins the topics of agrarian reforms and employment opportunities with respect to a specific country, Colombia. Here, too, rapid urbanization is shown to be insufficient to the task of absorbing such high growth rates.

Overall the participants in the Conference revealed a high level of consensus on Latin America's population problem, which can be summarized as follows:

1. The *rate of growth* is the major demographic problem. Western countries at comparable stages generally enjoyed a lower rate of growth and often were able to export their surplus populations at crucial points, or had an expanding frontier supplemented by the favorable immigration of young adults.
2. The recognition of "the population problem" on the part of responsible Latin American elites is still extremely low. For reasons of nationalism, Marxist ideology, or piety, high fertility is still viewed as unproblematic, if not desirable. Even where *family* planning has been accepted, the *national* need for a slower rate of growth has been explicitly rejected.

Finally, while the focus of this book has been on Latin America and on the usually unforeseen demographic consequences of "non-population" policies, the same perspective is equally relevant to industrialized nations. A recent British publication asks "that the comparative neglect of demographic considerations in the design of our institutions and policies should be ended . . . . Further, it should be realized that the absence of specific measures in itself constitutes a form of population policy."[39] The failure to act or to see the demographic consequences of policies with non-demographic goals constitutes a *de facto* population policy. In Latin America we are faced with societies whose traditional values favor high fertility and whose welfare laws and development policies encourage a continuously high population growth rate which is undermining their efforts to promote national economic development. The group which is at once the most receptive to the family planning approach and also large enough to effect a significant drop in the national growth rate appears to be lower-class urban women, if males will permit them to realize this expressed goal. Ultimately this version of the "battle of the sexes" may decide whether Latin America can solve its population problem during this century. In this respect it is encouraging to note that while the Marxist Allende regime in Chile will reject direct United States funding for family planning clinics, they will *not* only *not* be closed, but a Ministry of Family Planning will be created as part of a project to legalize abortion and divorce.

In the meanwhile, those countries opting for a high population growth rate *and* an expanding industrial economy can not afford to distribute the benefits of such growth to a large percentage of their population. They will thus have to adopt or maintain undemocratically repressive governments as overt as Brazil's or as sophisticated as Mexico's in order to contain their exploited mass.

Notes

1. Ricardo Jiménez Jiménez, *Estadísticas Demográficas Básicas de Costa Rica* (Asociación Demográfica Costarricense, April 1970), p. 3.

2. Bruce Handler, "Chile's Marxist Regime Plans to Keep Birth Control Program" (Associated Press dispatch from Santiago, December 1970).

3. United Nations, *Economic Survey of Latin America*, 1966, pp. 32-33.

4. Ibid.

5. In this connection read Ivan Illich, Chapters 8 and 9, in *Celebration of Awareness* (New York: Doubleday & Co., 1969).

6. See Tom Davis, "Dualism, Stagnation and Inequality: The Impact of Pension Legislation in the Chilean Labor Market," *Industrial and Labor Relations Review*, April 1964. Charles J. Parrish and Jorge I. Tapia-Videla, "The Politics of Welfare Administration in Chile," (mimeographed, University of Texas). Marshall Wolfe, "Social Security and Development: The Latin American Experience," in Everett Kassalow (ed.), *The Role of Social Security in Economic Development* (Washington, D.C.: U.S. Department of Health, Education and Welfare, 1968).

7. For an excellent "critical review of the literature centering around cost-benefit analysis of population growth," see Warren C. Robinson and David E. Horlacher, *Population Growth and Economic Welfare*, Reports on Population/Family Planning #6, Population Council (New York, February 1971).

8. Joseph M. Jones, *Does Overpopulation Mean Poverty?* (Center for Economic Growth, 1962), p. 14.

9. Thomas G. Sanders, "Family Planning in Chile, Part I: The Public Program," *American Universities Field Staff Report*, Vol. IV, No. 4, December 1967, p. 15.

10. Thomas G. Sanders, "Family Planning in Chile, Part II: The Catholic Position," *American Universities Field Staff Report*, Vol. XIV, No. 5, Dec. 1967, p. 1.

11. Section III, "Research on Abortion and Family Planning in Latin America," in the *Milbank Memorial Fund Quarterly*, Vol. XLVI, No. 3, July 1968, Part 2.

12. A decade later, in 1970, Archbishop Luis Aponte Martinez "broke with precedent and gave 'conditional approval' to government sponsored family planning activities," in Puerto Rico *Population Bulletin*, Vol. XXVI, No. 6, Dec. 1970, p. 24.

13. David G. Epstein, Washington, D.C., January 1969, "Birth Control: A Plot or a Beneficence," *NACLA Newsletter*, Vol. II, No. 1, March, 1968. A more recent NACLA paper shows the increasing influence of its female staff members who reportedly insisted on a greater recognition of women's rights. This latest NACLA attack on "the Population Establishment" describes its structure rather thoroughly, but refuses to deal with the possibility that desirable consequences could flow from actions they view as maliciously motivated. They very justly criticized the lingering racist themes in some birth control ads and the invalid attempt to blame pollution largely on population growth rather than on affluence. However, they specifically avoided dealing with the fact that most socialist countries also find it desirable to reduce their population growth rates. *NACLA* Newsletter, Vol. IV, No. 8, Dec. 1970.

14. Betty Rollin, "Motherhood—Who Needs It?," *Look*, Vol. 34, No. 19, Sept. 22, 1970, p. 15.

15. Herman E. Daly, "The Population Question in Northeast Brazil: Its Economic and Ideological Dimensions," *Economic Development and Cultural Change*, Vol. 48, No. 4, Part I, July 1970, pp. 568-9.

16. Ibid., p. 563.

17. Paul A. Baran, *The Political Economy of Growth* (New York: Monthly Review Press, 1957), p. 239.

18. *Population Bulletin*, Vol. XXVI, No. 6, Dec. 1970, p. 24. In spite of the extreme male Mexican resistance to birth control for the poor (the wealthy all over Latin America have long practiced various methods of limiting procreation), a female Mexican doctor notes that abortion is "the most traditional method of controlling natality in our country—it should cause fear but is better known and understood—and it works." See Blanca Raquel Ordonez, "El Aborto Inducido y

su Problematica Medico Social" in Programas de Poblacion en Central America y Panama (Asociacion Demografica Costarricense) Mexico City, 1970.

19. See Ansley Coale's review of *Population, Resources, Environment* by Paul R. and Anne H. Ehrlich (Freeman, San Francisco, 1970) in *Science*, Vol. 170, 3956, Oct. 23, 1970.

20. Ansley Coale, "Man and His Environment," in *Science*, Vol. 170, 3954, Oct. 9, 1970, p. 135.

21. Ibid.

22. Nathan Keyfitz, "On the Momentum of Population Growth," *Demography*, Vol. 8, No. 1, Feb. 1971, p. 71.

23. *Atlas*, Mar. 1971, pp. 16, 18-19. Reprint of a *Manchester Guardian* article by John Cornwell, and *Time*, Mar. 15, 1971, p. 44.

24. David Heer, "Economic Development and Fertility," *Demography*, Vol. 3, No. 2, 1966, pp. 424-25.

25. Ibid., pp. 443-44.

26. Dudley Kirk, "Population Research in Relation to Population Policy and National Planning Programs," paper presented to the American Sociological Association Meeting in Boston, August 1968, p. 33. "Contrary to some speculations it now seems clear (from Asian experience) that a strong family structure may be an aid, rather than an impediment, to introduction of family planning." It should be added however that this would be so only if (1) the family were confronted by a traditional obstacle to early marriage or marriage at all—such as a shortage of land or of suitable mates or (2) that the family took on new aspirations which conflicted with childrearing. For further evidence on the deviance of Latin American fertility from Western experience, see Eduardo Arriaga, "The Nature and Effects of Latin America's Non-Western Trend in Fertility," *Demography*, Vol. 7, No. 4, Nov. 1970, p. 483.

27. Donald J. Bogue, *The Public Interest*, No. 7, Spring 1967, p. 11. In this paper Bogue asserts (his emphasis) *"that the world population crisis is a phenomenon of the 20th Century and will be largely if not entirely a matter of history when humanity moves into the 21st Century."* Ronald Freedman, "The Transition from High to Low Fertility: Challenge to Demographers," *Population Index*, Vol. XXXI, No. 4, October 1965, pp. 417-18.

28. Carmen Miro, "Some Misconceptions Disproved: A Program of Comparative Fertility Surveys in Latin America," Bernard Berelson, et. al., *Family Planning and Population Programs* (Chicago, 1966).

29. Iêda Siqueira Wiarda, "Family Planning Activities in a Democratic Context: The Case of Venezuela," mimeographed, Mershon Caribbean Seminar, Ohio State University, Columbus, Ohio, Dec. 1970, pp. 103, 136.

30. Carl E. Taylor, M.D., "Five Stages in a Practical Population Policy," *International Development Review*, Dec. 1968, pp. 2-7.

31. Bogue footnote 27.

32. Donald J. Bogue, *Family Planning Improvement Through Evaluation,* Family Planning Research and Evaluation Manual No. 1 (Community and Family Study Center, University of Chicago, 1970).

33. Ibid., "Family Planning and the Demographic Agnostic," pp. 65-66.

34. Ibid., pp. 71.

35. For a good description of the adult education Dr. Illich is referring to, see Thomas G. Sanders, "The Paulo Freire Method," *American Universities Field Staff Reports,* Vol. XV, No. 1, Jan. 1968.

36. *CERES*, Vol. 3, No. 6, Nov.-Dec. 1970, pp. 28-30.

37. United Nations, *Economic Survey of Latin America*, 1966, p. 31.

38. Ibid., p. 353.

39. "Introduction" in "Towards a Population Policy for the United Kingdom," *Population Studies*, May 1970, Supplement.

Part I: The Demographic Transition and Population Policies

2

Demographic Factors and Early Modern Economic Development

Joseph J. Spengler

How slender an initial difference may come to
be decisive of the outcome in case circumstances
give this initial difference a cumulative effect. Thorsten Veblen

Sometime before the seventeenth century, perhaps as early as the fifteenth, a unique marriage pattern began to develop in Western Europe. It apparently did not exist in the fourteenth century, but had become effective by the seventeenth, if not earlier. John Hajnal has described the genesis of this pattern, which seems to have been a product of both the rational elements in Western European culture and the prevailing institutional arrangements associated with that culture.

This pattern consisted of much later marriage than one found in Eastern Europe or outside Europe. It significantly intensified the birth-limiting influence of ecclesiastical and other forms of celibacy. It contributed greatly to the relatively low level of European birth rates which, "so far as we can tell, were rarely over 38 before the spread of birth control." Thus, it impeded the rate of population growth. This slowing down augmented, in turn, per-capita productivity as well as capital formation and cushioned the impact of numbers upon land and resources. It made average income higher than it otherwise would have been and thereby facilitated the emergence and successful launching of the Industrial Revolution, which finally freed Western man, especially the common man, from the trammels of static, catastrophe-prone, and poverty-ridden pain economies.[1]

Population and Income Growth

The course of both population and income growth corresponded rather closely to that of a Malthusian model in Europe until around the sixteenth century, and in most of Asia and Africa almost to the present. Europe's population did not begin to grow continuously and without marked interruptions until the fifteenth century, but thereafter it proceeded at a slowly increasing rate. Europe's population, M.K. Bennett suggests, increased by about three-quarters between the years 1000 and 1300, only to decline by perhaps three-eighths during the

Reprinted by permission from *Daedalus*, Journal of the American Academy of Arts and Sciences, Boston, Massachusetts, Volume 97, Number 2 (Spring 1968), 433-446.

next century, and then to return to the 1300 level by the early-sixteenth century. Thereafter it grew—about one-quarter of 1 percent per year in the sixteenth and seventeenth centuries and somewhat more rapidly in the eighteenth century, especially in the latter part. The long-term annual growth rate averaged about one-half of 1 percent in the eighteenth century and about three-quarters of 1 percent in the nineteenth: This increase in the growth rate seems to have been attributable mainly, if not entirely, to a decline in mortality. Before the nineteenth century, this decline is traceable chiefly to a marked diminution in the incidence of famine and pestilence and the catastrophic mortality associated therewith, especially in such periods as 1349-1470s, aptly described by Sylvia Thrupp as "the golden age of bacteria."

The movement of the per-capita output of goods and services in Europe was long dominated by the course of its population growth, itself often under the empire of unfavorable events and therefore very low over the long run according to modern standards. The countries of Europe were predominantly agricultural, with three-quarters or more of the population being rural. The mode of agricultural production was relatively traditional and unchanging. Supply was quite inelastic, and its increase depended principally upon the extension of cultivation. English and other data suggest that productivity was low and progressed slowly even when population pressure encouraged the abandonment of the three-field system. In Western Europe, as Phyllis Deane and W.A. Cole write: "The significant variable in the long preindustrial secular swings in productivity seems to have been the rate of population growth. When population rose, product per head fell: when population fell, product per head rose." The Malthusian tendency for numbers to keep abreast of agricultural output seems to have been characteristic also of Asia. Despite a generally higher birth rate, the population of Asia supposedly increased only about five-sixths between 1650 and 1800, no more than that of Europe and Russia. Mortality regulated population growth in Asia much more than it did in Europe. As K.W. Taylor concluded: "Long periods of [population] stability are best explained by the Malthusian hypothesis, and the relatively short periods of rapid growth can be explained in terms of major technological or environmental changes." Even distribution of population, A.P. Usher found, was closely associated with the availability of food. This correlation remained constant until the Industrial Revolution converted mineral resources into a major determinant of population location. Density varied, of course, reflecting in part the fact that full maturity of settlement was not achieved in Northwestern Europe until around 1600—sixteen centuries later than in the Mediterranean world, but three centuries earlier than in India and China. In Northern and Western Europe, density varied greatly even before the Industrial Revolution, ranging from 137 inhabitants per square mile in Belgium and parts of Italy through 90 in England and 110 in France to about 5 in Norway.[2]

So long as the numbers of people tended to press closely upon the food supply, average income and output could not increase greatly over the long run. The elasticity in the supply of produce was too low. Average output increased with the extension of settlement, the formation of capital, and the stimulus of the temporary economic upsurges manifest after 1100 and again after the late 1400s, but not much of this gain could be retained. Indeed, if it had been, average income in 1500 might have exceeded subsistence by 300 to 400 percent, rather than the actual, much lower, margin. If average output in the Roman Empire around A.D. 200 had approximated 1.25 times a hypothetical subsistence level and thereafter had grown about one-tenth of 1 percent per year, by 1500 the level of output should have been about 3.5 times as high as it was thirteen centuries earlier, but it was not.

As English data suggest, in and long after the Middle Ages, population pressure tended to develop in the wake of a continuing growth in numbers. It became manifest, for example, in the late-thirteenth and early-fourteenth centuries—after several centuries of growth, much of which was subsequently wiped out by the Black Death. Population pressure was again felt in the sixteenth and seventeenth centuries and resulted in complaints of unemployment as well as calls for the development of colonial outlets to absorb the excess numbers.[3]

Even so, as Deane and Cole state, England and Wales had apparently achieved by the late-seventeenth century a higher level of material welfare than any other country with the exception of Holland, whose average income, according to Gregory King, was slightly above the English average and at least one-fourth above the French average. Deane and Cole add, however, that the seventeenth-century English average did not greatly exceed that of the "rest of the world" or that of fifteenth-century England. They also observe that "change, outside the cataclysms produced by famines and epidemics, was generally small, slow, and easily reversed" in the seventeenth-century world in which King lived.[4]

Three observations may now be made. Although our information in respect to Europe's rate of population growth before 1800 is incomplete, this rate appears to have been low, averaging perhaps one-quarter of 1 percent per year between 1500 and 1700 and about five-twelfths of 1 percent per year between 1700 and 1750. In France population increased somewhat between 1500 and 1600, though not steadily; in the seventeenth-century, Pierre Goubert believes, it oscillated around an equilibrium of about nineteen million, standing nearer the minimum than the maximum in 1700. It grew about one-third of 1 percent per year in the eighteenth century, about .22 percent per year in 1700-55, and about one-half of 1 percent in 1755-1801. In England and Wales, population grew about one-third of 1 percent per year between 1500 and 1700 and between 1700 and 1780. Even if English incomes and wages were not much greater in the late-seventeenth century than in the late-fifteenth, the slowness with which the population grew at least permitted the standards attained in the late-fifteenth century to be retained and perhaps even improved. Given the low rate of natural increase, over-all real output per head could increase something like .3 percent annually in England and Wales between 1700 and the 1770s, even though the aggregate real output grew slowly throughout the eighteenth century.

Despite the slowness with which average output advanced, it rose above the levels encountered in much of today's underdeveloped world. Phyllis Deane estimates that the average income in England and Wales in 1750 (at least one-third above the 1700 level, but about two-fifths below the 1800 level) would have been equivalent to £70 in the 1950s—a figure nearly treble that of India and two-thirds that of Mexico in the 1950s. According to Simon Kuznets, "per worker income in the agricultural sector in today's most populous" underdeveloped countries (China, India, Pakistan, Burma, South Korea, and most of Africa) is only "one-fourth or one-third of per worker income in the currently developed countries in their preindustrialization phase" when six-tenths or more of their labor force remained in agriculture. Accordingly, *total* income per worker in these countries was two to three times as high as it is in today's underdeveloped countries. "By comparison with many present-day preindustrial economies in Africa and Asia," Cole and Deane conclude, "the English economy of the late seventeenth and early eighteenth centuries had reached a relatively advanced stage of economic organization. So too, no doubt, had certain other countries."[5]

Theories of Population and Income Growth

A low rate of population growth may encourage the rate of growth of average income in three ways. These observations are especially true of predominantly agricultural economies that are equipped with an essentially traditional agricultural technique, are not yet subject to economies of scale, and are just beginning to assume a more commercial-industrial form.

If a population is growing slowly, the bulk of the savings which it generates can be devoted to increasing capital per head, thereby easing indirectly the pressure of population upon land and facilitating the growth of nonagricultural enterprises. Capital formation proceeded at a very slow pace in the seventeenth and early-eighteenth centuries. In England around 1700 the annual rate of saving fell within a range of something like 3 to 6 percent of the national income. The French rate was probably lower, and the Dutch rate may have been higher. With such low saving rates, capital per head could increase significantly only if the rate of population growth were negligible and savings were not employed wastefully, as often happened in ancient and medieval times. Were population growth negligible and were only 4 percent saved and invested annually to yield a 10 percent rate of return, average income would rise about .4 of 1 percent per year, enough to increase per-capita income by approximately one-half in about ninety-five years. Were population growing as much as 1 percent per year, this growth would absorb virtually all the savings, should they amount to only 4 or 5 percent of the national income. Not even in Europe, however, was the former option always exercised. According to E.F. Heckscher, population growth in eighteenth-century Sweden absorbed the disposable resources available.[6]

Slowing down population growth decreases the impact numbers and agriculturalists have upon cultivatable land. Accordingly, the ratio of the agricultural labor force to cultivatable land was only 10 to 50 percent as high in pre-industrial European countries as it is in today's underdeveloped countries. Even so, in and before David Ricardo's day, there was strong evidence of a classical diminishing of returns in England and possibly elsewhere. Nevertheless, because numbers had grown slowly, and limits to production had not been reached, time remained during which yields per acre could be increased or manufactures could be developed and exchanged for imports. This time was utilized, moreover, and yields were increased somewhat, certainly in greater measure than they have been today in those underdeveloped countries whose agricultural productivity has increased little over the centuries.[7]

Potential productivity per capita in a population depends markedly upon the size of the fraction of the population that is of working age. Let this group be represented by those fifteen to fifty-nine or fifteen to sixty-four years of age. This fraction varies appreciably. In 1965, for example, the fraction aged fifteen to sixty-four approximated 54 percent in Africa, Latin America, and Southeast Asia, much less than the 64 percent found in Europe. Therefore, under *ceteris paribus* conditions, potential productivity was about 1.185 (64/54) times as high in Europe as in Africa, Latin America, and Southeast Asia. Northern and Western Europe enjoyed superiority in this respect as early as 1850, when the fraction aged fifteen to sixty-four years ranged between 60 and 66 percent. Of course, the increase in potential productivity made possible would be actualized only if there were not offsetting increases in unemployment.

Before we attempt to estimate the magnitude of this fraction in the seventeenth and eighteenth centuries, we may examine a hypothetical stable population to observe how an age structure is generated by past mortality and fertility patterns. The relative number of persons of working age in a stable population rises as fertility (measured by the Gross Reproduction Rate [GRR]) and life expectancy at birth decrease; the relative number falls as fertility and life expectancy rise. If, for example, we hold expectation of life at birth constant at fifty years, the proportion aged fifteen to fifty-nine rises from 45.8 percent with GRR at 4.0 to around 60 percent with GRR at 1.25 to 1.50. If we hold GRR constant at 2.0, the proportion falls from 64 percent with an expectation of life at birth of twenty years to 54.7 percent with a life expectancy of over seventy years (70.2). Thus, declining mortality cancels out a portion of the improvement in age structure associated with a decline in the GRR. For example, combining a life expectancy of thrity years with a GRR of 3 results in a fraction of 0.545 aged fifteen to fifty-nine; a life expectancy of 70.2 with a GRR of 1.5, in a fraction of 0.577 aged fifteen to fifty-nine.

Information on the age composition of the pre-industrial countries of Northern and Western Europe may be found from two sources. The first souce, hypothetical stable populations, furnishes only inferential information. In the body of Table 2-1, I give the percentages aged fifteen to sixty-four in stable populations resulting from combinations of GRR (see column 1) with expectations of life at birth (see line 2 in head of table). This fraction descends from 64 percent when a GRR of 2.25 is combined with a life expectancy of twenty-five

Table 2-1
Proportions Aged 15-64 Years: Rates of Growth

GRR	Expectation of Life at Birth			
	25	30	35	40
2.25	64(−3)	62(3)	61(7)	60(11)
2.5	62(1)	61(7)	59(11)	58(15)
3.0	59(7)	57(13)	56(18)	55(22)

to fifty-five when a GRR of 3.0 is combined with a life expectancy of forty. The numbers in parentheses are rough indicators of the rates of natural increase per 1,000 inhabitants associated with designated combinations of GRR and life expectancy. We see at once how the proportion aged fifteen to sixty-four declines as GRR and life expectancy at birth increase.[8]

The problem confronting us is that of selecting those combinations in the table which most closely approximate fertility and mortality conditions in pre-industrial Western Europe. The rate of population growth must be low. Life expectancy probably did not exceed thirty-five years in whole populations before 1800. Let us suppose the most representative combinations to be those associated with a GRR of 2.25 to 2.5 and a life expectancy of thirty to thirty-five years. We would then expect the proportion aged fifteen to sixty-four to approach 59 to 62 percent or, more likely, 61 to 62 percent, since the rate of population growth was decidedly below 1 percent per year. This proportion is at least 10 to 15 percent greater than levels encountered in many of today's underdeveloped countries.

Extant data relating to fertility and mortality in pre-industrial Europe presumably support the suppositions made in the preceding paragraph. First, the birth rate was much lower in pre-industrial Europe than it is in present-day and pre-1900 Asia and Africa. During the 1700s the rate was around thirty-five, somewhat lower in England and Wales, France, and Scandinavia (exclusive of Finland, which had a rate sometimes just over forty). Between 1776 and 1800, when the Swedish birth rate averaged somewhat below thirty-five, the GRR averaged about 2.1. We find birth rates of roughly thirty-five to thirty-seven associated with a GRR of 2.25 and of roughly thirty-eight to forty-one associated with a GRR of 2.5. Although the birth rates reported for eighteenth-century Europe may be somewhat off the mark, they do suggest that the GRR was close to 2.25 or 2.5.

So far, information on mortality and life expectancy before 1800 is limited. Around 1800, expectation of life at birth may have been as high as thirty-five to forty years in some Western European countries; if so, it was higher than it was during the sixteenth and seventeenth centuries. Life expectancy at birth rose in Sweden between the period 1755-76 and the period 1816-40, increasing from 33.2 to 39.5 years for males and from 35.7 to 43.5 years for females. Female life expectancy at birth, usually somewhat higher than male life expectancy, was

44.7 years in Denmark in 1835-44; 42.18 in England and Wales in 1841; 40.83 in France in 1817-31; 37.91 in Iceland in 1850-60; and 35.12 in the Netherlands in 1816-25. K.F. Helleiner suggests that life expectancy rose during the eighteenth century because "the periodic erosion of growth by epidemic or harvest failure became less marked," especially after 1750. An alternative might be that other changes gave rise to a decline in mortality during this century. Mortality, however, appears to have been greater in the earlier parts of the eighteenth century and in the seventeenth century. Gregory King's data suggest a life expectancy of only thirty-two in England during 1690s, a figure which Peter Laslett finds fitting "in fairly well with what is known for the seventeenth century both in England and France." Studies of localized populations in the first half of the eighteenth century in France yield an estimate of about thirty-three years for expectation of life at birth. According to S. Peller, life expectancy at birth among Europe's ruling families averaged only about thirty-one years in 1600-99, three years less than in the preceding century and six years less than in the eighteenth. Generation life tables of the British peerage suggest that expectation of life at birth was thirty-three years among males born between 1680 and 1729, but almost forty-five years (44.8) among those born between 1730 and 1779. If violent deaths are not included, male life expectancy at birth for those born between 1330 and 1679 remained in the range of thirty or thirty-one years. One may infer from these diverse data that life expectancy at birth probably did not exceed thirty-five years in any country before the late-eighteenth century.

Our second source of information is the statistics available for the age composition of pre-industrial Europe as well as Japan, a country whose people controlled their numbers. Persons aged fifteen to sixty-four constituted 60.5 and 62 percent, respectively, of Sweden's population in 1750 and 1800; 62.2 and 61.4 percent of France's population in 1775 and 1801; and 58.4 and 60.8 percent of Japan's population in the eighth century and 1888. The proportion of the Danish population aged fifteen to sixty-four in 1787 was similar to that in Sweden in 1750. Iceland's population in 1703 included a larger proportion aged fifteen to sixty-four. Data on the age composition of eighteenth-century Europe suggest, when contrasted with those in Table 2-2 discussed below, that this age composition was more favorable to economic production than that now found in much of the underdeveloped world with its high fertility and relatively low

Table 2-2
Proportions Aged 15-64 Years: Rates of Growth

| | Expectation of Life at Birth | | |
GRR	40	50	55
2.5	58(15)	56(22)	56(23)
3.0	55(22)	53(28)	52(31)
3.5	52(27)	50(34)	49(37)

mortality. Although the conditions that made for high mortality and, hence, for a relatively low proportion of persons under fifteen years of age must have debilitated the population in some degree, they could hardly have offset the advantages derived from a low rate of population growth.[9]

Thus, the age composition of populations in Western European countries was favorable to average productivity. It is difficult, of course, to assess the change in age composition that took place after the adoption of the unique Western European pattern of marriage. This may have increased the favorableness of the age composition by at least three units, or about 5 percent. If per-capita productivity rose correspondingly, the rate of saving could have increased by a larger fraction. In any case, until late in the eighteenth century, the slow rate of population growth permitted savings to be devoted almost entirely to improving productive capital per head. This slowness also held down the rate of increase in population pressure, perhaps sufficiently to permit improvement in yields to offset small increases in population.

Yesterday's Europe Versus Today's Africa,
Asia, and Latin America

Today the economic distance separating various parts of the underdeveloped world from various parts of the developed world is many times what it was two to three centuries ago. At one time, this distance might have been easily bridged. Had, as late as 1800, the index of performance in the most advanced lands been four times that in the least advanced, and had this index continued to improve at a rate of 1.5 percent per year in the more advanced countries, the laggard countries might have caught up by the early-twentieth century. This did not happen. The index rose most rapidly in the advanced countries. Today real private consumption per head is between six and thirty-one times as high in Northern and Western Europe as it is in various underdeveloped countries; it is even higher in the United States. This increase in spread is the result of what was done in the European sphere and not done in the underdeveloped world. In the latter category must be included failure to curtail fertility.

Agricultural population density increased faster in Asia than in Europe. By 1948, it was nearly double that in Africa and Europe, exclusive of the Soviet Union (147 per square kilometer of available land in Asia as contrasted with 83 and 86 in Africa and Europe).[10] Over three-fifths of the labor force of Africa and Asia remained in agriculture, although output per agriculturalist and per acre remained low, often too low, to supply minimum nutritional requirements.

Population grew faster during the nineteenth century in Europe than it did in the underdeveloped countries, with their high levels of mortality. This relationship was eventually altered. Mortality declined in European countries, but so did the birth rates. Today the rate of population growth is much higher in the underdeveloped world than elsewhere and is a number of times what it was in pre-1800 Western Europe. Most Gross Reproduction Rates in Africa, mainland

Asia, and Latin America fall within a range of 2.5 to 3.5; expectation of life at birth falls below forty years in Africa, between forty and fifty years in Asia, and between fifty and fifty-five in Latin America. The rate of natural increase per decade between 1970 and 2000 is expected to range from around 20 percent in Asia to around 30 percent in South America and, perhaps Africa. These prospective rates, roughly double what they were in the period 1920-40, reflect declines in crude mortality uncompensated by declines in natality. These high rates of population growth will absorb much of the capital that is formed in the underdeveloped world and hence will greatly retard growth of output per head.

The age composition of the present-day underdeveloped countries is much less favorable to productivity than that encountered in the developed world or in European countries during their pre-industrial stage. As of 1965, the fraction formed by the population fifteen to sixty-four years was as follows: East Asia (exclusive of Japan), 52.5 percent; South Asia, 54.7 percent; Africa, 54.2 percent, ranging from 51.7 percent in West Africa to 56.1 percent in Eastern Africa; Central America, 50.8 percent; Tropical South America, 53.4 percent; Caribbean America, 56 percent. The Phillippines is exemplary, for the current fraction, 53 percent, is much below the 57.2 percent reported for 1903, but is consistent with an estimated birth rate in the upper-forties and a death rate in the low-twenties.

These percentages are compatible with current estimates of gross reproduction (2.5 to 3.0 in Africa and 2.5 to 3.5 in Asia and Latin America) and life expectancy at birth (around or below forty years in Africa; forty to fifty in Asia; fifty to fifty-five in Latin America). In Table 2-2, GRR and life expectancies are combined to yield stable populations and the percentages of the population aged fifteen to sixty-four. (In parentheses, we give the approximate rates of natural increase associated with these combinations.) The data suggest that in Africa the fraction aged fifteen to sixty-four will range between 55 and 58 percent; in Asia, between 50 and 58 percent; and in Latin America, between 49 and 56 percent.

The relatively low rates of fertility and natural increase—in part the result of the unique fertility-regulating pattern of marriage that developed in Europe during the fifteenth or sixteenth centuries—must have contributed greatly to the growth of average income in the seventeenth and eighteenth centuries. The sustained increase in average income did not, of course, give rise to the Industrial Revolution, for this revolution, unlike the minor ones of the twelfth, fifteenth, and seventeenth centuries, was a *revolutionary* transformation of the British and Western European economies. It was the product of many cooperating factors (capital accumulation, inventions, innovations, favorable factor endowments, *laissez faire*, market expansion, earlier experience, and so forth). Among its causes was the relatively low level of fertility existing in Western Europe. Because fertility was low, the relative number of persons of productive age and, hence, the potential productivity per head were high. Natural increase also was low, so that the pressure of population upon agricultural land did not build up rapidly and nearly all savings could be devoted to improving the stock of capital instead of supporting population growth. Average income could rise, albeit slowly and somewhat intermittently, and pave the way for the coming of the Industrial Revolution.

Notes

1. On the marriage pattern, see John Hajnal, "European Marriage Patterns in Perspective," *Population in History*, eds. D.V. Glass and D.E.C. Eversley (Chicago, 1965), pp. 101-40; see also *Population in History*, pp. 46-51, 99, 298-99, 377, 448-85. On the fertility-controlling effectiveness of deferment of marriage, see J.W. Leasure, "Malthus, Marriage, and Multiplication," *Milbank Memorial Fund Quarterly*, Vol. 41, Part 2 (October 1963), pp. 419-35. For the impact of the Industrial Revolution on the standard of living, see discussion by E.J. Hobshawm and R.M. Hartwell, in *Economic History Review*, Vol. 16 (1963), pp. 120-46.

2. This paragraph and the one preceding are based on essays by K.F. Helleiner and the editors in *Population in History*; W.A. Cole and Phyllis Deane, "The Growth of National Incomes," *Cambridge Economic History of Europe*, eds. H.J. Habakkuk and M.M. Postan (Cambridge, 1966), Vol. 6, Chap. 1; D.V. Glass, "World Population, 1800-1950," *Cambridge Economic History*, Chap. 2; M.K. Bennett, *The World's Food* (New York, 1954), Chap. 1; Phyllis Deane and W.A. Cole, *British Economic Growth 1688-1959* (Cambridge, 1962), pp. 38, 65, 78-82; Phyllis Deane, *The First Industrial Revolution* (Cambridge, 1965), pp. 11-13; essays by K.W. Taylor, J.C. Russell, and A.P. Usher in *Demographic Analysis,* eds. J. J. Spengler and O. D. Duncan (Glencoe, 1965); W. Bowden, M. Karpovich, and A. P. Usher, *An Economic History of Europe Since 1750* (New York, 1937), pp. 3, 6-7; chapters by L. Genicot and R. Kobner, *Cambridge Economic History of Europe*, ed. M.M. Postan (2nd ed.; Cambridge, 1966), Vol. 1; Roger J. Mols, S.J., *Introduction à la démographie historique des villes d'Europe du XIVe au XVIIIe siècle* (Louvain, 1955), Vol. 2, pp. 425-34, on mortality, and Vol. 3, pp. 284-87, on natality.

3. Manifestations of population pressure, especially in England, have been discussed frequently in the *Economic History Review*. See articles by M.M. Postan and E.E. Rich, in Vol. 2 (1950), pp. 221-46, 247-65; D.C. Coleman, Vol. 8 (1956), pp. 288-94; W.C. Robinson, with comments by M.M. Postan, Vol. 9 (1959), pp. 63-83; J.Z. Titow, Vol. 14 (1961), pp. 218-23; J.M.W. Bean, Vol. 15 (1963), pp. 423-37; G.S.L. Tucker, Vol. 16 (1964), pp. 205-18; Sylvia L. Thrupp, Vol. 18 (1965), pp. 101-19; D. Herlihy, ibid., pp. 225-44; P.E. Razzell, ibid., pp. 312-32; E.A. Wrigley, Vol. 19 (1966), pp. 82-109. See also Genicot, loc. cit.; J.C. Russell, *British Medieval Population* (Albuquerque, 1948), pp. 156-59, 232, 312-14; *Population in History*, pp. 434-85 and 507-22 passim; J.W. Thompson, *An Economic and Social History of the Middle Ages* (300-1300) (New York, 1928), pp. 391-92; L.D. Stamp, *Man and Land* (London, 1955), pp. 92-94; also, essay by Charles Parain, *Cambridge Economic History of Europe*, Vol. 1, and essays by R.S. Lopez and M.M. Postan, *Cambridge Economic History* Vol. 2; K.F. Helleiner's essay, *Cambridge Economic Histtory,* Vol. 4.

4. Deane and Cole, *British Economic Growth 1688-1959*, pp. 38-39; E.H. Phelps Brown, *The Growth of British Industrial Relations* (London, 1959), p. 2.

5. In this and the preceding paragraph, I draw on S. Kuznets, *Economic*

Growth and Structure (New York, 1965), pp. 176-93; Deane, *The First Industrial Revolution*, pp. 5-13; Cole and Deane, "The Growth of National Incomes," pp. 3-10; Deane and Cole, *British Economic Growth 1688-1959*, pp. 38, 65, 78-80; essays by Glass, G. Utterström, P. Goubert, L. Henry, and J. Meuvret in *Population in History*; J.C. Toutain, *Le produit de l'agriculture de 1700 à 1958* (Paris, 1961), Chap. 7, and *La population de la France de 1700 à 1959* (Paris, 1963), pp. 24-29. See also W.W. Rostow, *The Economics of Take-Off Into Sustained Growth* (London, 1963).

6. Deane and Cole, *British Economic Growth 1688-1959*, pp. 260-64; Cole and Deane, "The Growth of National Incomes," p. 5; E.F. Heckscher's essay in *Economic History Review*, Vol. 2 (1950), pp. 266-77.

7. On the course of yields, see C. Clark, *Conditions of Economic Progress* (2d ed.; London, 1951), pp. 224-27; Deane and Cole, *British Economic Growth 1688-1959*, pp. 64-67; M.M. Postan, in *Economic History Review*, Vol. 12 (1959), pp. 80-81; also M.J.R. Healy and E.L. Jones, "Wheat Yields in England, 1815-59," *Journal of Royal Statistical Society*, Series A, Vol. 125 (1962), Part 4, pp. 574-579; C. Clark and M.R. Haswell, *The Economics of Subsistence Agriculture* (London, 1964), passim.

8. Tables 2-1 and 2-2 are based on Western-type stable populations, described in A.J. Coale and Paul Demeny, *Regional Model Life Tables and Stable Population* (Princeton, 1966). See also on age composition and population prospects, United Nations, *The Aging of Populations and Its Economic and Social Implications*, Population Studies, No. 26 (New York, 1956) and *World Population Prospects*, Population Studies, No. 41 (New York, 1966).

9. Data on natality and mortality in this and the two preceding paragraphs are based upon United Nations, *Population Bulletin*, Nos. 6 and 7; Glass, "World Population 1800-1950," *Population in History*, pp. 14, 52-57, 79-86, 98, 134, 215, 241, 274, 282, 304-07, 358-359, 446, 467, 469, 474-506, 506, 538, 555, 562-87; articles by H. Gille and H. Hyriennius, in *Population Studies*, Vol. 3 (1949), pp. 3-65, Vol. 4 (1951), pp. 421-31; R.R. Kuczynski, *The Balance of Births and Deaths*, Vol. 1 (Washington, 1928), pp. 6-7, 39, 94; L.I. Dublin, A.J. Lotka, and M. Spiegelman, *Length of Life* (2d ed.; New York, 1949), pp. 41-43, 348-51; Peter Laslett, *The World We Have Lost* (London, 1965), pp. 93-94; Irene Taeuber, *The Population of Japan* (Princeton, 1958), pp. 10, 46.

10. United Nations, *The Determinants and Consequences of Population Trends*, Population Studies, No. 17 (New York, 1953), p. 269.

3 Catholicism and Fertility: A Cross-cultural Analysis

Lincoln H. Day

Introduction

At the time of writing, the Roman Catholic Church is engaged in a major re-evaluation of its position on contraception. Judging from newspaper interest, there exists a widespread assumption that Catholic teaching, together with the political and social influence of the Catholic clergy, is an important deterrent to the practice of contraception and, for that reason, to the reduction of human natality.

Certainly, there can be little doubt that, as of now, and despite a number of recent changes,[1] Roman Catholic doctrine concerning the regulation of births is essentially pro-natalist, whatever the intentions of its promulgators. The Church rejects the most effective and reliable means of controlling births and at the same time rejects, with respect to the means it does allow, the essential reason for resort to birth control in the first place: *viz.* the enjoyment of coitus without risk of unwanted pregnancy.[2] This official position of the Church is buttressed by two other pro-natalist conditions: first, a substantial Catholic literature, both lay and clerical, in direct support of high natality and, second, an apparently ready availability of Catholic platforms to the advocates of large families.[3]

But must the pro-natalist doctrine of Roman Catholicism, or the pro-natalist activity of its official—or officially-endorsed—spokesmen, necessarily lead to higher levels of natality? This is no idle question. In a world of rapidly expanding populations, anything likely to raise natality, or keep it at a high level, among some 600 million people (together with additional tens of millions who might be affected by the political activities of a religious organization to which they do not belong) is bound to be of more than purely scientific interest; especially when half of these 600 million people inhabit the very countries most sorely afflicted by the pressures of human numbers.[4]

There are a number of ways in which Catholic (or any other) doctrine or practice *could* support higher natality: ways that are both direct and indirect; with consequences for higher natality possible from both intentional and unintentional responses on the part of individuals to doctrine and action. For example, additional children could be borne intentionally in response to teaching on the desirability of large families, or unintentionally as a consequence of clerical proscription of the more reliable methods of birth control. The same

---

This chapter is a retitled abridgement of a paper entitled, "Nationality and Ethnocentrism: Some Relationships Suggested by an Analysis of Catholic-Protestant Differentials," published in *Population Studies* 22, No. 1 (March 1968). Readers wishing to examine the data on which these findings are based are requested to consult the original article as it appeared in *Population Studies*.

end could be achieved more indirectly by, for example, ideological encouragement of behavior conducive to higher natality (e.g., settlement in rural areas, or—possibly of particular relevance to conditions in Latin America—passive acceptance of one's present conditions in life) and discouragement of behavior conducive to lower natality (e.g., employment of wives outside the home, status-striving, and migration into towns). There is also the possibility of inculcating and reinforcing those values and attitudes that are conducive to higher natality, and ignoring or actively working against those that are conducive to lower natality.[5] And finally, there is the possibility of exerting political pressure. Certainly, Catholic pressure (or the fear of it) has delayed and limited both American and United Nations support for programs of birth control.[6] Closer investigation may show, in fact, that in most populations it is *political*, and not specifically *religious*, activity that has constituted Roman Catholicism's prime support for higher natality.

The assumption that Catholic doctrine itself exerts a strong influence on natality is not without empirical support. Recent American findings show that loyalty to one's Church (as measured by such externals as frequency of church attendance, amount of religious schooling, clerical officiation at marriage ceremonies) bears a positive relationship to natality among Catholics and, contrastingly, a negative or nil relationship to natality among Protestants.[7] Similar relationships seem also to obtain in the Netherlands.[8] Moreover, within any particular society, the natality of Catholics, as a group seems invariably to exceed that among Protestants[9] (which is not to deny the existence of unusually high natality among certain socially isolated Protestant groups, such as the orthodox Calvinists of the Netherlands and the Hutterites, Southern Mountain whites, and Pennsylvania Dutch of the United States).

However, there are two questions to be asked concerning this higher natality among Catholics: (1) To what extent might it be a function, not of doctrine, but of other determinants, instead: differences in patterns of marriage, for example, or in the comparative social positions of Catholics and non-Catholics?; and (2) If doctrine is, in fact, relevant, is it so invariably? Concerning the first question, we can note that *taking* these other variables into account (e.g., for proportions marrying, age at marriage, duration of marriage, residence, schooling, occupation, ethnicity) *has* not only failed to remove the Catholic-Protestant differential, but *has*, in some instances, actually increased it. The second question is more difficult to answer. Certainly group differences in receptivity to religious doctrine and example could reasonably be expected; but just what these differences are, and what accounts for them, is not readily ascertainable. S. Groenman has suggested that, at least so far as the Netherlands is concerned, the crucial factor may be religious heterogeneity.[10] But van Heek, also discussing the situation in the Netherlands, has concluded that, more important than mere heterogeneity is the fact that Dutch Catholics are a minority—particularly a minority with a history of discrimination at the hands of the majority—that has led to their having substantially higher natality.[11] It is to a discussion of some findings along these lines, for several countries in addition to the Netherlands, that this article is devoted.

Catholic doctrine and official action may be pro-natalist, but whether this is of much actual importance to natality is another matter. All over the world, Catholics—and others—have managed to reduce their natality without the help of family planning centers, and without the encouragement of government or religious leaders. In fact, among populations of European ancestry, control over childbearing has usually been undertaken, at least initially, not only without the concurrence of governments and churches, but in the face of their active opposition. Certainly if entire populations are studied there is little more than inferential evidence of any causal connection between the Catholic position on birth control and actual practice of family limitation, so far as that practice may have been affected by the establishment or non-establishment of family planning programs. It is possible that the Catholic Church's less direct activities—those that retard, or deflect, social and cultural change—are the more important determinants in this sphere of human activity; but whether or not they have such consequences, the causal connection can only be inferred.

After study of the few available data on the subject, I would suggest that the relationship between Catholic doctrine and Catholic natality has usually been considerably over-simplified, frequency in the press, and occasionally in professional writing as well. Far from being merely a case of pro-natalist teaching leading directly to larger families, the relationship between teaching and practice in the determination of Catholic-Protestant natality differentials, if it exists at all, is a matter of considerable complexity: one in which reference group memberships, and both ethnocentric and out-group feelings, would appear to play a decisive role.

Although, within particular societies, Catholic natality invariably exceeds that of Protestants, there is no denying the fact that Catholic natality has itself undergone substantial declines in every country in which control over births has been achieved. In fact, in certain predominantly Catholic countries—France, Austria, Luxembourg, Italy and Hungary, for example—natality has at times dropped to levels as low as anywhere in the world.[12] Moreover, a variety of studies, in the United States,[13] Puerto Rico,[14] Australia,[15] Switzerland,[16] Ireland[17] and Latin America,[18] bear testimony to the existence of substantial natality differentials along socioeconomic lines *within* Catholic populations themselves; even when, as in the study of Australian data, there is standardization for all the purely demographic variables that could have given rise to such differences (i.e., proportion marrying, age at marriage, duration of marriage). In the Australian study, further standardization by year of birth and residence reveals very considerable natality differences among Catholics according to country of birth: whether Australia, the British Isles (including Ireland), Italy, Poland or the Netherlands.[19] In addition, interview studies in both Puerto Rico and the United Kingdom have found only very small proportions (of any faith) offering religion as a reason for not practicing birth control; or, among those practicing it, for not using appliance methods.[20] Finally, there is a growing body of evidence to show that large proportions of Catholics do, in fact, resort to methods of birth control forbidden them by their Church.[21]

Quite obviously, more than Catholic doctrine is at work. But just what is at work, and how it works, remains obscure. Findings of higher natality among Catholics, or among one group of Catholics contrasted with another, are all limited in some degree by failure to separate out one or another variable of conceivably greater relevance than religion—whether this variable operates by itself or in combination with other variables (religion included).

Method of Analysis

Within any particular population, what is at work *in the aggregate* is the whole cultural matrix within which are determined: (1) the extent to which control will exist over childbearing and (2) the range of 'acceptable' family size. My own analysis suggests that what is at work *specifically among Catholics* within this cultural matrix is this group's relative numerical and social position. Whereas the larger culture determines what is possible, and also what is the range of acceptable behavior with respect to family formation, the particular level of Catholic natality within this 'acceptable' range is determined by where Catholics stand relatively to other groups within the society, particularly with respect to the percentage they form of the total population. Thus, my findings on a large number of countries support those of van Heek concerning the Netherlands.

I base this conclusion on an analysis of data concerning aggregate levels both of natality and of economic and social conditions in Christian countries. Natality is indicated by the total fertility rate;[a] social and economic conditions by a variety of measures: average income, consumption of energy per head, daily newspaper circulation, proportion of employed males outside agriculture, proportion illiterate among adult women. These data are presented in Table 1.[b]

None of these economic and social indicators, either singly or in combination with the others, happens, however, to be very strongly correlated with natality. The reason for this lies in the heterogeneity of those countries in which there exists a fair measure of control over natality (this degree of control taken to be indicated by a total fertility rate of less than 4,500). Whereas the countries *without* this degree of control over natality are generally to be found at the lower end of the scale on the various measures of income, schooling and industrialization, it is not the case that the countries *with* this degree of control are always to be found at the high end. Were we to graph the economic and social indicators in Table 1 in their relation to the total fertility rates, we would see that there are always countries in three quadrants, but seldom in the fourth.

---

[a] The total fertility rate is simply the sum of the age-specific birth rates and represents the number of children who would be born per 1,000 women passing through the childbearing ages if (1) there were no deviation from current age-specific birth rates and (2) all women entering the childbearing period survived to its conclusion. A total fertility rate of 3,200, for instance, means that the average woman would (under the conditions specified) bear 3.2 children during her period of reproduction.

[b] Readers wishing to examine the data on which these findings are based are requested to consult the original article as it appears in *Population Studies*.

This would hold for Catholic countries as much as for Protestant ones. The relationship would be, at most, loosely L-shaped.

However, an interesting relationship emerges if analysis is restricted to countries meeting each of two criteria: (1) natality is subject to a fair measure of control and (2) social conditions are such as to justify the presumption that Catholic doctrine on the family has a wide potential dissemination.

As before, the maximum cut-off point for the first is taken as a total fertility rate of 4,500. A rate as high as this by no means denotes low natality, but it does seem to differentiate those populations in which natality *could* be substantially reduced in very short order[c] from those in which it *could not*—i.e., countries in which there is not yet enough control exercised over natality to permit rapid reductions to low levels.

As the cut-off point for the second I have taken an adult female illiteracy rate of 10%. Such a criterion involves considerable guesswork and arbitrariness. Nevertheless, despite the difficulty that must surround any attempt to determine actual levels of literacy, this particular measure does seem in this instance not only to be quite highly correlated with the other social and economic indicators, but also to differentiate well between the countries that on these indicators are quite consistently on one or the other side of the ledger.

Findings

Restricting analysis to countries meeting these two criteria (i.e., total fertility rate <4,500; percentage of adult women 'illiterate' <10) removes the relationship between natality and the various indicators of living levels altogether. Whatever the reason for the differences in natality among these countries where natality is subject to a fair measure of control, there is no relation between those social and economic indicators ordinarily used. However, within this group of countries, Catholic natality not only seems invariably to exceed Protestant (whatever other variables are taken into account), but, with only two definite exceptions (Poland and the Republic of Ireland),[d] to which I shall return presently, and one possible exception (Argentina vis-à-vis Switzerland), the natality of Catholics in countries where they constitute a disinguishable minority

---

[c]For example, the total fertility rate of U.S. non-whites—which was 4,392 in 1962—had been as low as 3,420 in 1948 and 2,317 in 1940: levels which could doubtless be quickly attained once again—with proper motivation. (1962 rate from U.S. Department of Health, Education and Welfare, *Vital and Health Statistics*, Series 21, No. 1, 'Natality Statistics Analysis—U.S., 1962', Table 32, p. 41; 1948 rate calculated from U.S. National Office of *Statistics Rates in the United States: 1900-1940* (Washington: U.S. Government Printing Office, 1943), p. 669.

[d]As will be noted presently, when viewed in context, Poland and Ireland are probably not really exceptions after all.

of the population[e] exceeds that of Catholics where they constitute a majority. On the basis of the available evidence, it appears, in short, that the natality of Catholic *minorities* in Australia, New Zealand, the United States, Canada, the United Kingdom, The Netherlands and Switzerland exceeds that of Catholic *majorities* in Argentina,[f] France, Belgium, Luxembourg, Italy, Austria, Czechoslovakia and Hungary. Poland, an exception in the late 1950s, the period to which these calculations refer, has, since then, experienced a steady decline in its birth rate and, by 1962 (the only year for which the data necessary to its calculation are available), had ceased to be an exception by having a total fertility rate of 2,700.[g] Now, it can be argued that Catholic and Protestant natality go together: that Catholic natality is high where Protestant natality is high. This is true. However, the amount of the Catholic excess varies. Moreover, the natality of *Protestant* majorities is both higher and lower than the natality of *Catholic* majorities, whereas the natality of Catholic *minorities* invariably exceeds that of Catholic *majorities*.

In all this, West Germany is of particular interest; for here is a situation in which Protestants were a majority which has been superseded, as a consequence of political partition, by one in which Protestants and Catholics are numerically equal—and in which (of real importance to this discussion) Catholics are dominant politically. Among those marriages for which childbearing would have occurred before partition—i.e., when Protestants were in the majority—Catholic natality substantially exceeds Protestant. But moving forward to those marriage cohorts in which progressively more childbearing occurs during the period of numerical equality between Catholics and Protestants (and during the period when Catholics are the dominant group, politically), we find this differential steadily diminishes, and also some evidence that it may disappear altogether.

Admittedly, all this is based on rather limited evidence. Only for Australia are the coverage and character of the data sufficient to remove any doubt on the matter.[h] For the other Protestant countries this conclusion derives from an estimate of the level of Catholic natality that has had to be based on findings from various partial surveys (census and otherwise) conducted in each of them. Unfortunately, in some instances Catholic-Protestant differential rates have had to be calculated on the basis of data for married persons only; and for all the countries except Australia there is a potentially biassing lack of *control for the influence of other variables.*

---

[e]"Distinguishable" is defined as amounting to at least 8% of the total population.

[f]Except for the possibility of Switzerland—as noted above.

[g]Calculated from United Nations, *Demographic Yearbook 1964*, Tables 5 and 17.

[h]So far as I know, Australia is the only country for which it has been possible to employ data with these standardizations for a sample large enough (in this instance a 20% national random sample of married women living with their husbands) to permit a wide variety of statistically meaningful cross-tabulations.

Conclusions

Limited as they are, however, these data on Catholic childbearing do strongly suggest that although Catholic pro-natalism serves to increase natality, it does so only under two conditions—when:

1. there exists a high level of economic development; that is, a climate in which one could reasonably expect both the predisposition and the opportunity for effective natality control to be most widespread: and
2. the persons at whom the pro-natalist teaching is directed define themselves as members of a group constituting a numerically and politically important, but not dominant, *minority* of the population.

In the absence of these two conditions, pro-natalist doctrine in itself seems unlikely to have much effect on natality. If Catholic teaching on the family is of any direct consequence to natality, it would appear to be only in predominantly non-Catholic countries of controlled natality and fairly high material levels of living (e.g., the English-speaking countries, the Netherlands and Switzerland). Only in these countries does it seem likely that any very extensive decline in natality might follow upon a change in Catholic teaching. The direct influence of Catholic teaching elsewhere appears to have been decidely overrated, so far as it relates either to countries of high natality and low material levels of living (e.g., most of the countries of Latin America) or to predominantly Catholic countries of controlled natality where material levels of living are either high (e.g., France, Belgium, Austria, Luxembourg), or medium (e.g., Italy, Czechoslovakia, Hungary, Poland).

If there is, in fact, a causal connection between Catholic doctrine and Catholic natality, it would seem to work through an intervening variable: a variable the presence of which is indicated by the two national attributes of a relatively high level of economic development and a minority status for the Catholic population. I suggest that this intervening variable is ethnocentrism coupled with the feeling of being threatened as a group. In countries where nearly everyone else is at least nominally Catholic, there is no particular deviancy in being a Catholic oneself, and scant likelihood of real or imagined threats to Catholics as such—in contrast to threats that might be directed against persons in their capacities as industrial workers, or democrats, or shopkeepers, or physicians, for example. In short, where Catholics are a majority there is no need to feel threatened or at bay *as a Catholic*, and hence, no particular incentive either to seek out co-religionists for support and example, or to attach oneself more closely to the Church and its teachings on account of the slights (or worse) one feels oneself to have suffered on its behalf. The case of Ireland, which was earlier noted as a statistical exception, is probably not really an exception at all, but rather, an instance of a sovereign people still thinking of themselves as a beleaguered minority *vis-à-vis* a recently dominant majority (the English).

In this respect, then, there does seem to be a kind of Catholic sub-culture (the existence of which has on occasion been adduced to explain higher Catholic natality[22]), one effect of which is the encouragement or maintenance of higher natality among its adherents. But it is a sub-culture that develops and has pro-natalist consequences only when Catholics, as such, feel themselves to be in a disadvantaged, threatened position in the society. I suggest that the presence of this feeling is most readily indicated (and possibly directly caused) by Catholic occupancy of a numerical minority position; that, other things being equal, the natality differential in favor of the Catholic members of any particular group will vary directly with their consciousness of minority status. Bringing the matter closer home, I should suggest that such feelings might go a long way toward accounting for the comparatively higher natality of rich *vs.* poor Catholics in the United States (and possibly in other countries, as well); for almost by definition, contacts outside his own ethnic or religious group will be more frequent for the rich person than for the poor. From these contacts will come a greater awareness of being different, of being an outsider; one possible consequence of which could be that the person affected becomes more receptive to the values and attitudes associated with membership in his group. It is possible that, on this account, American Catholics have, today, a greater feeling of separateness at the very time when, as a group, they occupy a position of greater equality and power.

Are there any non-Catholic groups whose natality might have been similarly influenced by this consciousness of minority status, by this feeling of being threatened or at bay? This is a difficult question to answer. Probably such feelings account for a part of the higher natality of the Canadian Doukhobors and American Mormons, and, in contrast with most of their co-religionists in the United States, also of the Jews in Israel (who presumably have the surrounding Arab majority to worry about). All three of these groups have some recent experience with pro-natalism, though among the Israeli Jews this is not likely to have been very prominent. The case of the American Jews, a notably low-natality group, and one virtually free of pro-natalist appeals, whether formal or informal, suggests the importance of pro-natalist doctrine itself to the causal matrix surrounding higher natality among minority groups. It demonstrates that there is no necessary connection between minority status and higher natality; that in the absence of pro-natalism, minority status can actually lead to anti-natalist practices as a means to strengthening the social position of the members of the group (in the case of American Jews, largely by way of higher education and higher average incomes).

Practical Implications

There is at least one possibly practical conclusion to emerge from this analysis: so far as Catholic natality in predominantly Catholic countries is concerned, there seems little reason to attach much weight to the efficacy of any future liberalization of the Church's position on birth control. The frequently voiced hope that the Church will change this position, and thereby help solve the population problem in areas like Latin America, appears largely irrelevant— certainly in any direct sense, and quite possibly in any indirect sense, as well. If what has happened in both Catholic and non-Catholic countries elsewhere is any guide, populations currently experiencing high natality will reduce their natality when, and only when, their other conditions of life are conducive to it. And they will do so largely unaffected by any opposition (or support—which in the case of Catholicism seems unlikely in the extreme) from a religious body. Were a change in the Catholic position on birth control to have any effect on the natality of these populations, it would presumably be only indirect as, for example, in removing some of the political barriers currently impeding education in the practice of family planning. Apart from possibilities like this, which seem essentially limited (after all, extensive programs elsewhere have met with little success, even in the absence of formal opposition), there seems little to expect, so far as the worst 'population trouble-spots' are concerned, from any possible change in Catholic doctrine—whether this doctrine concerns contraception in particular, or family planning in general.

The force of Catholic teaching on the family appears from the data to have been decidedly overrated, so far as it relates either to countries of high natality and limited economic development, or to predominantly Catholic countries of controlled natality and moderate to extensive economic development. But in predominantly non-Catholic countries of controlled natality and moderate to extensive economic development the situation may be quite otherwise.[i] Only in this group of countries does it seem possible that any very extensive decline in natality might follow upon a change in Catholic teaching. Yet, the question remains: In those countries where Catholic minorities are outbreeding non-Catholic majorities, to what extent is the factor of Catholicism, so far as it relates at all to natality, essentially religious in nature, and to what extent is it ethnic (i.e., arising in a strong group awareness and feeling of separateness), instead? Does the typical minority-status Catholic have more children because of the Church's teaching or because of a desire (conscious or unconscious) to preserve the identity of his own group in the face of the numerical and social

---

[i]Rather dramatic indication of the possible effect of Catholic doctrine in such a context is provided by two Detroit Area Surveys: one taken in 1955, the other in 1958. Both samples were randomly drawn in the same way and asked the same questions about expected family size. However, the 1955 survey focused on family and kinship relations, while the 1958 survey focused instead, on religious behavior. Between the two surveys, the average number of children expected by Protestant couples rose only from 2.91 to 3.00. But among Catholic couples, who—as did the Protestant couples—answered the natality questions after some 30 minutes of questions reminding them of their religious affiliation, this average rose almost three-fourths of a child: from 2.95 to 3.65. (D. Goldberg, H. Sharp and R. Freedman, 'The stability and reliability of expected family size data', *Milbank Memorial Fund Quarterly*, v. 37 (1959), pp. 382-84.

domination of another?[j] In short, is it doctrine, or ethnocentrism and the desire for group survival, that is the actual 'religious' factor in Catholic natality? To the student of human behavior the evolution of the Catholic position on birth control may be an absorbing study; but the current excitement over the possibility of a liberalization of that position appears to be largely a result of misplaced blame and undue attribution of social power.

Notes

1. These are well summarized in Philip Appleman, *The Silent Explosion* (Boston, 1965), Chaps. 4 and 5.

2. See, e.g., Lincoln H. Day and Alice Taylor Day, *Too Many Americans* (Boston, 1964), Chap. 4; William J. Gibbons, 'The Catholic value system in relation to human fertility, in George F. Mair (ed.), *Studies in Population* (Princeton, 1949); John T. Noonan, *Contraception: A History of its Treatment by the Catholic Theologians and Canonists* (Cambridge, Mass., 1965); Norman St. John-Stevas, 'A Roman Catholic view of population control', *Law and Contemporary Problems*, v. 25 (Summer, 1960), pp. 445-69; Norman St. John-Stevas, *Birth Control and Public Policy* (Santa Barbara, Calif., 1960); and Alvah W. Sulloway, *Birth Control and Catholic Doctrine* (Boston, 1959).

3. See, e.g. Eunice Kennedy Shriver, 'An answer to the attacks on motherhood', *McCall's*, June 1965 (originally the featured address at Georgetown University's 'Women's Day,' 1965); and Anthony F. Zimmerman, *Catholic Viewpoint on Overpopulation* (Garden City, N.Y., 1961), Chaps. 9 and 10.

4. Figures from *National Catholic Almanac* (Paterson, N.J.; St. Anthony's Guild, 1963), p. 376.

5. On this point, see the more extended discussion in Day and Day, op. cit., Chap. 5. Also see Gerhard Lenski, *The Religious Factor* (Garden City, N.Y., 1962), Chaps. 5 and 6.

6. See, e.g., Day and Day, op. cit., pp. 95-97, 100-101; John Rock, *The Time Has Come* (New York, 1963), pp. 75-89, 103, 120; and Jack Zlotnick, 'Population pressure and political indecision', *Foreign Affairs*, v. 39 (1961), pp. 685, 687.

7. T.F. Coogan, 'Catholic fertility in Florida', Catholic University of America, *Studies in Sociology*, v. 20 (1946), p. 83; J.C. Flanagan, 'A study of factors determining family size in a selected professional group', *Genetic Psychology Monographs*, v. 25 (1943) (cited in Coogan, op. cit.); R. Freedman, P.K. Whelpton and A.A. Campbell, *Family Planning, Sterility, and Population*

[j]In this connection it is interesting to note the following conclusion from a study of African data: 'An important aspect of the relation of religion to fertility in many primitive societies is its intensification of personal identification with the members of one's lineage, clan or society as distinct from all others . . . Intensified competition with other societies [is] conducive to the maintenance of fertility.' Frank Lorimer, *Culture and Human Fertility*, (Paris, 1954), pp. 183-84.

Growth (New York, 1959), pp. 107-8, 183-84; P.K. Whelpton, A.A. Campbell and J.E. Patterson, *Fertility and Family Planning in the United States* (Princeton, 1966), pp. 73, 82-91; C.F. Westoff, R.G. Potter, Jr., P.C. Sagi and E.C. Mishler, *Family Growth in Metropolitan America* (Princeton, 1961), pp. 181, 194-211.

8. J.D.D. Derksen, 'Recent demographic changes in the Netherlands', mimeo, 1946 (cited in Frank Lorimer, *Culture and Human Fertility*, Paris, 1954, p. 193); and F. van Heek, 'Roman Catholicism and fertility in the Netherlands', *Population Studies*, v. 10 (1956), pp. 131-32.

9. See, e.g., T.K. Burch, 'The fertility of North American Catholics: A Comparative Overview , *Demography*, v. 3 (1966), pp. 174-87; Enid Charles, *The Changing Size of the Family in Canada*, Census Monograph No. 1, *Eighth Census of Canada: 1941* (Ottawa, 1948), Chap. 4; Lincoln H. Day, 'Family and fertility', in A.F. Davies and S. Encel (eds.), *Australian Society: A Sociological Introduction* (Melbourne, 1965); R. Freedman, D. Goldberg and Doris Slesinger, 'Current fertility expectations of married couples in the United States', *Population Index*, v. 29 (1963), pp. 366-91; R. Freedman, P.K. Whelpton and A.A. Campbell, op. cit., pp. 102, 106-8, 156, 183, 403; R. Freedman, P.K. Whelpton and J.W. Smit, 'Socio-economic factors in religious differentials in fertility', *American Sociological Review*, v. 26 (1961), pp. 608-14; D. Kirk, 'Recent trends of Catholic fertility in the United States', *Current Research in Human Fertility* (New York, 1955), p. 93; C.V. Kiser, 'Differential fertility in the United States', National Bureau of Economic Research, *Demographic and Economic Change in Developed Countries* (Princeton, 1960), pp. 108-10; E. Lewis-Faning, 'Report on an Inquiry into Family Limitation and Its Influence on Human Fertility during the Past 50 Years', *Royal Commission on Population, Papers*, v. 1 (London, 1949), Table 60, p. 81; K. Mayer, *The Population of Switzerland* (New York, 1952), p. 106; H. Peters, 'Die Geburtenhäufigkeit nach der Religions-zugehörigkeit', *Wirtschaft und Statistik*, v. 10 (1958), pp. 24-25; S.A. Stouffer, 'Trends in the fertility of Catholics and non-Catholics', *American Journal of Sociology*, v. 41 (1935), pp. 143-66; F. van Heek, loc. cit., pp. 125-38; C.F. Westoff, G. Potter, Jr., and P.C. Sagi, 'Some selected findings of the Princeton fertility study: 1963', *Demography*, v. 1 (1964), pp. 130-35; Westoff, Potter, Sagi and Mishler, op. cit., Chaps. 11 and 12; P.K. Whelpton and C.V. Kiser, 'Social and psychological factors affecting fertility. I. Differential fertility among 41,498 native-white couples in Indianapolis', *Milbank Memorial Fund Quarterly*, v. 21 (1943), p. 229; P. deWolfe and J. Meerdink, 'La Fécondité des Mariages à Amsterdam selon l'Appartenance Sociale et Réligieuse', *Population*, v. 21 (1957), pp. 289-318.

10. Cited by F. van Heek, loc. cit., p. 126.

11. F. van Heek, loc. cit., pp. 136-137.

12. See, e.g., Lee Jay Cho, "Estimated refined measures of fertility for all major countries of the world," *Demography*, v. 1 (1964), pp. 359-74.

13. Coogan, op. cit.; Freedman, Goldberg and Slesinger, op. cit.,; Stouffer, op. cit.; Westoff, Potter and Sagi, op. cit.; P.K. Whelpton, 'Trends and

differentials in the spacing of births', *Demography*, v. 1 (1964), pp. 83-93; and Whelpton and Kiser, op. cit.

14. P.K. Hatt, *Background of Human Fertility in Puerto Rico* (Princeton, 1952); Hill, Stycos and Back, op. cit.; and J.M. Stycos, *Family and Fertility in Puerto Rico* (New York, 1955).

15. L.H. Day, 'Fertility differentials among Catholics in Australia', *Milbank Memorial Fund Quarterly*, v. 42 (1964), pp. 57-63.

16. Mayer, op. cit.; and J.W. Nixon, 'Some demographic characteristics of Protestants and Catholics in Switzerland', International Population Conference, New York, 1961, *Papers II* (1963), pp. 43-51.

17. D.V. Glass, 'Malthus and the limitation of population growth', in D.V. Glass (ed.). *Introduction to Malthus* (London, 1953), pp. 34-35.

18. D.M. Heer, 'Fertility differences between Indian and Spanish-speaking parts of Andean countries', *Population Studies*, v. 18 (1964); Carmen A. Mirò, 'The population of Latin America', *Demography*, v. 1 (1964), pp. 37-38; and J.M. Stycos, 'Culture and Differential fertility in Peru', *Population Studies*, v. 16 (1963).

19. Day, 'Fertility differentials among Catholics in Australia', op. cit., pp. 66-74, 76-79.

20. Hill, Stycos and Back, op. cit., pp. 137-39; and Lewis-Faning, op. cit., pp. 175-76, 82.

21. R. Armijo and T. Monreal, 'Epidemiology of Provoked Abortion in Santiago, Chile', *Fourth Conference of the International Planned Parenthood Federation, Western Hemisphere Region*, San Juan, Puerto Rico, 1964; Freedman, Whelpton and Campbell, op. cit., pp. 182-86; D.V. Glass, *Population Policies and Movements in Europe* (Oxford, 1940), pp. 162-65; Dorothy Good, 'Some aspects of fertility change in Hungary', *Population Index*, v. 30 (1964), pp. 137-171; Hill, Stycos and Back, op. cit., p. 139; Lewis-Faning, op. cit., p. 81; W. Parker Mauldin, 'Fertility control in communist countries: Policy and practice.' Milbank Memorial Fund, *Population Trends in Eastern Europe, the U.S.S.R. and Mainland China* (New York, 1960); H. Rozada, 'National Problems and Plan in Family Planning in Uruguay', *Second Family Planning Seminar for Latin American Leaders*, New York, 1963; V. Srb, M. Kucera and D. Vysusilova, 'Une Enquête sur la Prévention des Naissances et le Plan Familial en Tchécoslovaquie', *Population*, v. 19 (1964), pp. 79-94; Stycos, *Family and Fertility in Puerto Rico, op. cit.*, pp. 198-202; C. Tietze, 'The demographic significance of legal abortion in eastern Europe', *Demography*, v. 1 (1964).

22. See, e.g., A.A. Campbell, 'Concepts and techniques used in fertility surveys', Milbank Memorial Fund, *Emerging Techniques in Population Research*, 1963; Freedman, Whelpton and Smit, op. cit.,; and Westoff, Potter, Sagi and Mishler, op. cit., p. 326.

4

Population Policy: Will Current Programs Succeed?

Kingsley Davis

Throughout history the growth of population has been identified with prosperity and strength. If today an increasing number of nations are seeking to curb rapid population growth by reducing their birth rates, they must be driven to do so by an urgent crisis. My purpose here is not to discuss the crisis itself but rather to assess the present and prospective measures used to meet it. Most observers are surprised by the swiftness with which concern over the population problem has turned from intellectual analysis and debate to policy and action. Such action is a welcome relief from the long opposition, or timidity, which seemed to block forever any governmental attempt to restrain population growth, but relief that "at last something is being done" is no guarantee that what is being done is adequate. On the face of it, one could hardly expect such a fundamental reorientation to be quickly and successfully implemented. I therefore propose to review the nature and (as I see them) limitations of the present policies and to suggest lines of possible improvement.

The Nature of Current Policies

With more than thirty nations now trying or planning to reduce population growth, and with numerous private and international organizations helping, the degree of unanimity as to the kind of measures needed is impressive. The consensus can be summed up in the phrase "family planning." President Johnson declared in 1965 that the United States will "assist family planning programs in nations which request such help." The prime minister of India said a year later, "We must press forward with family planning. This is a programme of the highest importance." The Republic of Singapore created in 1966 the Singapore Family Planning and Population Board "to initiate and undertake population control programmes."[1]

As is well known, "family planning" is a euphemism for contraception. The family planning approach to population limitation, therefore, concentrates on providing new and efficient contraceptives on a national basis through mass programs under public health auspices. The nature of these programs is shown by the following enthusiastic report from the Population Council:

Judith Blake's critical readings and discussions have greatly helped in the preparation of this article.

Reprinted by permission of the author and publisher from *Science*, Journal of the American Academy for the Advancement of Science, Vol. 158, Nov. 10, 1967, pp. 730-739.

No single year has seen so many forward steps in population control as 1965. Effective national programs have at last emerged, international organizations have decided to become engaged, a new contraceptive has proved its value in mass application, . . . and surveys have confirmed a popular desire for family limitation . . .

An accounting of notable events must begin with Korea and Taiwan . . . Taiwan's program is not yet two years old, and already it has inserted one IUD (intrauterine device) for every 4-6 target women (those who are not pregnant, lactating, already sterile, already using contraceptives effectively, or desirous of more children). Korea has done almost as well . . . has put 2,200 full-time workers into the field, . . . has reached operational levels for a network of IUD quotas, supply lines, local manufacture of contraceptives, training of hundreds of M.D.'s and nurses, and mass propaganda . . .[2]

Here one can see the implication that "population control" is being achieved through the dissemination of new contraceptives, and the fact that the "target women" exclude those who want more children. One can also note the technological emphasis and the medical orientation.

What is wrong with such programs? The answer is, "Nothing at all, if they work." Whether or not they work depends on what they are expected to do as well as on how they try to do it. Let us discuss the goal first, then the means.

Goals. Curiously, it is hard to find in the population-policy movement any explicit discussion of long range goals. By implication the policies seem to promise a great deal. This is shown by the use of expressions like *population control* and *population planning* (as in the passages quoted above). It is also shown by the characteristic style of reasoning. Expositions of current policy usually start off by lamenting the speed and the consequences of runaway population growth. This growth, it is then stated, must be curbed—by pursuing a vigorous family-planning program. That family planning can solve the problem of population growth seems to be taken as self-evident.

For instance, the much-heralded statement by twelve heads of state, issued by Secretary-General U Thant on December 10, 1966 (a statement initiated by John D. Rockefeller III, Chairman of the Board of the Population Council), devotes half its space to discussing the harmfulness of population growth and the other half to recommending family planning.[3] A more succinct example of the typical reasoning is given in the Provisional Scheme for a Nationwide Family Planning Programme in Ceylon: "The population of Ceylon is fast increasing . . . . The figures reveal that a serious situation will be created within a few years. In order to cope with it a Family Planning programme on a nationwide scale should be launched by the Government."[4] The promised goal—to limit population growth so as to solve population problems—is a large order. One would expect it to be carefully analyzed, but it is left imprecise and taken for granted, as is the way in which family planning will achieve it.

When the terms *population control* and *population planning* are used, as they frequently are, as synonyms for current family-planning programs, they are misleading. Technically, they would mean deliberate influence over all attributes of a population, including its age-sex structure, geographical distribution, racial composition, genetic quality, and total size. No government attempts such full control. By tacit understanding, current population policies are concerned with only the *growth* and *size* of populations. These attributes, however, result from the death rate and migration as well as from the birth rate; their control would require deliberate influence over the factors giving rise to all three determinants. Actually, current policies labeled population control do not deal with mortality and migration, but deal only with the birth input. This is why another term, *fertility control*, is frequently used to describe current policies. But, as I show below, family planning (and hence current policy) does not undertake to influence most of the determinants of human reproduction. Thus the programs should not be referred to as population control or planning, because they do not attempt to influence the factors responsible for the attributes of human populations, taken generally; nor should they be called fertility control, because they do not try to affect most of the determinants of reproductive performance.

The ambiguity does not stop here, however. When one speaks of controlling population size, any inquiring person naturally asks, What is "control?" Who is to control whom? Precisely what population size, or what rate of population growth, is to be achieved? Do the policies aim to produce a growth rate that is nil, one that is very slight, or one that is like that of the industrial nations? Unless such questions are dealt with and clarified, it is impossible to evaluate current population policies.

The actual programs seem to be aiming simply to achieve a reduction in the birth rate. Success is therefore interpreted as the accomplishment of such a reduction, on the assumption that the reduction will lessen population growth. In those rare cases where a specific demographic aim is stated, the goal is said to be a short-run decline within a given period. The Pakistan plan adopted in 1966[5] aims to reduce the birth rate from 50 to 40 per thousand by 1970; the Indian plan[6] aims to reduce the rate from 40 to 25 "as soon as possible"; and the Korean aim[7] is to cut population growth from 2.9 to 1.2 percent by 1980. A significant feature of such stated aims is the rapid population growth they would permit. Under conditions of modern mortality, a crude birth rate of 25 to 30 per thousand will represent such a multiplication of people as to make use of the term *population control* ironic. A rate of increase of 1.2 percent per year would allow South Korea's already dense population to double in less than sixty years.

One can of course defend the programs by saying that the present goals and measures are merely interim ones. A start must be made somewhere. But we do not find this answer in the population-policy literature. Such a defense, if convincing, would require a presentation of the *next* steps, and these are not considered. One suspects that the entire question of goals is instinctively left vague because thorough limitation of population growth would run counter to national and group aspirations. A consideration of hypothetical goals throws further light on the matter.

Industrialized Nations as the Model. Since current policies are confined to family planning, their maximum demographic effect would be to give the underdeveloped countries the same level of reproductive performance that the industrial nations now have. The latter, long oriented toward family planning, provide a good yardstick for determining what the availability of contraceptives can do to population growth. Indeed, they provide more than a yardstick; they are actually the model which inspired the present population policies.

What does this goal mean in practice? Among the advanced nations there is considerable diversity in the level of fertility,[a] At one extreme are countries such as New Zealand, with an average gross reproduction rate (GRR) of 1.91 during the period 1960-64; at the other extreme are countries such as Hungary, with a rate of 0.91 during the same period. To a considerable extent, however, such divergencies are matters of timing. The birth rates of most industrial nations have shown, since about 1940, a wavelike movement, with no secular trend. The average level of reproduction during this long period has been high enough to give these countries, with their low mortality, an extremely rapid population growth. If this level is maintained, their population will double in just over fifty years—a rate higher than that of world population growth at any time prior to 1950, at which time the growth in numbers of human beings was already considered fantastic. The advanced nations are suffering acutely from the effects of rapid population growth in combination with the production of ever more goods per person.[8] A rising share of their supposedly high per capita income, which itself draws increasingly upon the resources of the underdeveloped countries (who fall farther behind in relative economic position), is spent simply to meet the costs, and alleviate the nuisances, of the unrelenting production of more and more goods by more people. Such facts indicate that the industrial nations provide neither a suitable demographic model for the nonindustrial peoples to follow nor the leadership to plan and organize effective population-control policies for them.

Zero Population Growth as a Goal. Most discussions of the population crisis lead logically to zero population growth as the ultimate goal, because any growth rate, if continued, will eventually use up the earth. Yet hardly ever do arguments for population policy consider such a goal, and current policies do not dream of it. Why not? The answer is evidently that zero population growth is unacceptable to most nations and to most religious and ethnic communities. To argue for this goal would be to alienate possible support for action programs.

Goal Peculiarities Inherent in Family Planning. Turning to the actual measures taken, we see that the very use of family planning as a means for implementing population policy poses serious but unacknowledged limits on the intended reduction in fertility. The family-planning movement, clearly devoted to the improvement and dissemination of contraceptive devices, states again and again

---

[a]As used by English-speaking demographers, the word *fertility* designates actual reproductive performance, not a theoretical capacity.

that its purpose is that of enabling couples to have the number of children they want. "The opportunity to decide the number and spacing of children is a basic human right," say the twelve heads of state in the United Nations declaration. The 1965 Turkish Law Concerning Population Planning declares: "Article I. Population Planning means that individuals can have as many children as they wish, whenever they want to. This can be ensured through preventive measures taken against pregnancy . . . ."[9]

Logically, it does not make sense to use *family* planning to provide *national* population control or planning. The "planning" in family planning is that of each separate couple. The only control they exercise is control over the size of *their* family. Obviously, couples do not plan the size of the nation's population, any more than they plan the growth of the national income or the form of the highway network. There is no reason to expect that the millions of decisions about family size made by couples in their own interest will automatically control population for the benefit of society. On the contrary, there are good reasons to think they will not do so. At most, family planning can reduce reproduction to the extent that unwanted births exceed wanted births. In industrial countries the balance is often negative—that is, people have fewer children as a rule than they would like to have. In underdeveloped countries the reverse is normally true, but the elimination of unwanted births would still leave an extremely high rate of multiplication.

Actually, the family-planning movement does not pursue even the limited goals it professes. It does not fully empower couples to have only the number of offspring they want because if either condemns or disregards certain tabooed but nevertheless effective means to this goal. One of its tenets is that "there shall be freedom of choice of method so that individuals can choose in accordance with the dictates of their consciences,"[10] but in practice this amounts to limiting the individual's choice, because the "conscience" dictating the method is usually not his but that of religious and governmental officials. Moreover, not every individual may choose: even the so-called recommended methods are ordinarily not offered to single women, or not all offered to women professing a given religious faith.

Thus, despite its emphasis on technology, current policy does not utilize all available means of contraception, much less all birth-control measures. The Indian government wasted valuable years in the early stages of its population-control program by experimenting exclusively with the "rhythm" method, long after this technique had been demonstrated to be one of the least effective. A greater limitation on means is the exclusive emphasis on contraception itself. Induced abortion, for example, is one of the surest means of controlling reproduction, and one that has proved capable of reducing birth rates rapidly. It seems peculiarly suited to the threshold stage of a population-control program— the stage when new conditions of life first make large families disadvantageous. It was the principal factor in the halving of the Japanese birth rate, a major factor in the declines in birth rate of East-European satellite countries after legalization of abortions in the early 1950s, and an important factor in the reduction of fertility in industrializing nations from 1870 to the 1930s.[11] Today, according to *Studies in Family Planning*, "abortion is probably the foremost method of birth control throughout Latin America,"[12] Yet this method is rejected in nearly all national and international population-control programs. American foreign aid is used to help *stop* abortion.[13] The United Nations excludes abortion from family planning, and in fact justifies the latter by presenting it as a means of combating abortion.[14] Studies of abortion are being made in Latin America under the presumed auspices of population-control groups, not with the intention of legalizing it and thus making it safe, cheap, available, and hence more effective for population control, but with the avowed purpose of reducing it.[15]

Although few would prefer abortion to efficient contraception (other things being equal), the fact is that both permit a woman to control the size of her family. The main drawbacks to abortion arise from its illegality. When performed as a legal procedure, by a skilled physician, it is safer than childbirth. It does not compete with contraception but serves as a backstop when the latter fails or when contraceptive devices or information are not available. As contraception becomes customary, the incidence of abortion recedes even without its being banned. If, therefore, abortions enable women to have only the number of children they want, and if family planners do not advocate—in fact decry—legalization of abortion, they are to that extent denying the central tenet of their own movement. The irony of anti-abortionism in family-planning circles is seen particularly in hair-splitting arguments over whether or not some contraceptive agent (for example, the IUD) is in reality an abortifacient. A Mexican leader in family planning writes: "One of the chief objectives of our program in Mexico is to prevent abortions. If we could be sure that the mode of action [of the IUD] was not interference with nidation, we could easily use the method in Mexico."[16]

The questions of sterilization and unnatural forms of sexual intercourse usually meet with similar silent treatment or disapproval, although nobody doubts the effectiveness of these measures in avoiding conception. Sterilization has proved popular in Puerto Rico and has had some vogue in India (where the new health minister hopes to make it compulsory for those with a certain number of children), but in both these areas it has been for the most part ignored or condemned by the family-planning movement.

On the side of goals, then, we see that a family-planning orientation limits the aims of current population policy. Despite reference to "population control" and "fertility control," which presumably mean determination of demographic results by and for the nation as a whole, the movement gives control only to couples, and does this only if they use "respectable" contraceptives.

The Neglect of Motivation. By sanctifying the doctrine that each woman should have the number of children she wants, and by assuming that if she has only that number this will automatically curb population growth to the necessary degree, the leaders of current policies escape the necessity of asking why women desire so many children and how this desire can be influenced.[17,18] Instead, they claim that satisfactory motivation is shown by the popular desire (shown by opinion surveys in all countries) to have the means of family limitation, and that therefore the problem is one of inventing and distributing the best possible contraceptive devices. Overlooked is the fact that a desire for availability of contraceptives is compatible with *high* fertility.

Given the best of means, there remain the questions of how many children couples want and of whether this is the requisite number from the standpoint of population size. That it is not is indicated by continued rapid population growth in industrial countries, and by the very surveys showing that people want contraception—for these show, too, that people also want numerous children.

The family planners do not ignore motivation. They are forever talking about "attitudes" and "needs." But they pose the issue in terms of the "acceptance" of birth control devices. At the most naive level, they assume that lack of acceptance is a function of the contraceptive device itself. This reduces the motive problem to a technological question. The task of population control then becomes simply the invention of a device that *will* be acceptable.[19] The plastic IUD is acclaimed because, once in place, it does not depend on repeated *acceptance* by the woman, and thus it "solves" the problem of motivation.[b]

But suppose a woman does not want to use *any* contraceptive until after she has had four children. This is the type of question that is seldom raised in the family-planning literature. In that literature, wanting a specific number of children is taken as complete motivation, for it implies a wish to control the size of one's family. The problem woman, from the standpoint of family planners, is the one who wants "as many as come," or "as many as God sends." Her attitude is construed as due to ignorance and "cultural values," and the policy deemed necessary to change it is "education." No compulsion can be used, because the movement is committed to free choice, but movie strips, posters, comic books, public lectures, interviews, and discussions are in order. These supply information and supposedly change values by discounting superstitions and showing that unrestrained procreation is harmful to both mother and children. The effort is considered successful when the woman decides she wants only a certain number of children and uses an effective contraceptive.

In viewing negative attitudes toward birth control as due to ignorance, apathy, and outworn tradition, and "mass-communication" as the solution to the motivation problem,[c] family planners tend to ignore the power and complexity of social life. If it were admitted that the creation and care of new

---

[b]"From the point of view of the woman concerned, the whole problem of continuing motivation disappears, . . ." [D. Kirk, in *Population Dynamics*, M. Muramatsu and P.A. Harper, Eds. (Baltimore: Johns Hopkins Press, 1965)].

[c]"For influencing family size norms, certainly the examples and statements of public figures are of great significance . . . also . . . use of mass-communication methods which help to legitimize the small-family style, to provoke conversation, and to establish a vocabulary for discussion of family planning." [M.W. Freymann, in *Population Dynamics*, M. Muramatsu and P.A. Harper, Eds. (Baltimore: John Hopkins Press, 1965)].

human beings is socially motivated, like other forms of behavior, by being a part of the system of rewards and punishments that is built into human relationships, and thus is bound up with the individual's economic and personal interests, it would be apparent that the social structure and economy must be changed before a deliberate reduction in the birth rate can be achieved. As it is, reliance on family planning allows people to feel that "something is being done about the population problem" without the need for painful social changes.

Designation of population control as a medical or public health task leads to a similar evasion. This categorization assures popular support because it puts population policy in the hands of respected medical personnel, but, by the same token, it gives responsibility for leadership to people who think in terms of clinics and patients, of pills and IUD's, and who bring to the handling of economic and social phenomena a self-confident naiveté. The study of social organization is a technical field; an action program based on intuition is not more apt to succeed in the control of human beings than it is in the area of bacterial or viral control. Moreover, to alter a social system, by deliberate policy, so as to regulate births in accord with the demands of the collective welfare would require political power, and this is not likely to inhere in public health officials, nurses, midwives, and social workers. To entrust population policy to them is "to take action," but not dangerous "effective action."

Similarly, the Janus-faced position on birth-control technology represents an escape from the necessity, and onus, of grappling with the social and economic determinants of reproductive behavior. On the one side, the rejection or avoidance of religiously tabooed but otherwise effective means of birth prevention enables the family-planning movement to avoid official condemnation. On the other side, an intense preoccupation with contraceptive technology (apart from the tabooed means) also helps the family planners to avoid censure. By implying that the only need is the invention and distribution of effective contraceptive devices, they allay fears, on the part of religious and governmental officials, that fundamental changes in social organization are contemplated. Changes basic enough to affect motivation for having children would be changes in the structure of the family, in the position of women, and in the sexual mores. Far from proposing such radicalism, spokesmen for family planning frequently state their purpose as "protection" of the family—that is, closer observance of family norms. In addition, by concentrating on *new* and *scientific* contraceptives, the movement escapes taboos attached to old ones (the Pope will hardly authorize the condom, but may sanction the pill) and allows family planning to be regarded as a branch of medicine: over-population becomes a disease, to be treated by a pill or a coil.

We thus see that the inadequacy of current population policies with respect to motivation is inherent in their overwhelmingly family-planning character. Since family planning is by definition private planning, it eschews any societal control over motivation. It merely furnishes the means, and, among possible means, only the most respectable. Its leaders, in avoiding social complexities and seeking official favor, are obviously activated not solely by expediency but also by their own sentiments as members of society and by their background as persons attracted to the family-planning movement. Unacquainted for the most part with technical economics, sociology, and demography, they tend honestly and instinctively to believe that something they vaguely call population control can be achieved by making better contraceptives available.

The Evidence of Ineffectiveness. If this characterization is accurate, we can conclude that current programs will not enable a government to control population size. In countries where couples have numerous offspring that they do not want, such programs may possibly accelerate a birth-rate decline that would occur anyway, but the conditions that cause births to be wanted or unwanted are beyond the control of family planning, hence beyond the control of any nation which relies on family planning alone as its population policy.

This conclusion is confirmed by demographic facts. As I have noted above, the widespread use of family planning in industrial countries has not given their governments control over the birth rate. In backward countries today, taken as a whole, birth rates are rising, not falling; in those with population policies, there is no indication that the government is controlling the rate of reproduction. The main "successes" cited in the well-publicized policy literature are cases where a large number of contraceptives have been distributed or where the program has been accompanied by some decline in the birth rate. Popular enthusiasm for family planning is found mainly in the cities, or in advanced countries such as Japan and Taiwan, where the people would adopt contraception in any case, program or no program. It is difficult to prove that present population policies have even speeded up a lowering of the birth rate (the least that could have been expected), much less that they have provided national "fertility control."

Rising Birth Rates. Let us next briefly review the facts concerning the level and trend of population in underdeveloped nations generally, in order to understand the magnitude of the task of genuine control.

In ten Latin-American countries, between 1940 and 1959,[20] the average birth rates (age-standardized), as estimated by our research office at the University of California, rose as follows: 1940-44, 43.4 annual births per 1000 population; 1945-49, 44.6; 1950-54, 46.4; 1955-59, 47.7.

In another study made in our office, in which estimating methods derived from the theory of quasi-stable populations were used, the recent trend was found to be upward in 27 underdeveloped countries, downward in six, and unchanged in one.[21] Some of the rises have been substantial, and most have occurred where the birth rate was already extremely high. For instance, the gross reproduction rate rose in Jamaica from 1.8 per thousand in 1947 to 2.7 in 1960; among the natives of Fiji, from 2.0 in 1951 to 2.4 in 1964; and in Albania, from 3.0 in the period 1950-54 to 3.4 in 1960.

The general rise in fertility in backward regions is evidently not due to failure of population-control efforts, because most of the countries either have no such effort or have programs too new to show much effect. Instead, the rise is due, ironically, to the very circumstance that brought on the population crisis in the first place—to improved health and lowered mortality. Better health increases the probability that a woman will conceive and retain the fetus to term; lowered mortality raises the proportion of babies who survive to the age of reproduction and reduces the probability of widowhood during that age.[22] The significance of the general rise in fertility, in the context of this discussion, is that it is giving would-be population planners a harder task than many of them realize. Some of the upward pressure on birth rates is independent of what couples do about family planning, for it arises from the fact that, with lowered mortality, there are simply more couples.

Underdeveloped Countries with Population Policies. In discussions of population policy there is often confusion as to which cases are relevant. Japan, for instance, has been widely praised for the effectiveness of its measures, but it is a very advanced industrial nation and, besides, its government policy had little or nothing to do with the decline in the birth rate, except unintentionally. It therefore offers no test of population policy under peasant-agrarian conditions. Another case of questionable relevance is that of Taiwan, because Taiwan is sufficiently developed to be placed in the urban-industrial class of nations. However, since Taiwan is offered as the main showpiece by the sponsors of current policies in underdeveloped areas, and since the data are excellent, it merits examination.

Taiwan is acclaimed as a showpiece because it has responded favorably to a highly organized program for distributing up-to-date contraceptives and has also had a rapidly dropping birth rate. Some observers have carelessly attributed the decline in the birth rate—from 50.0 in 1951 to 32.7 in 1965—to the family-planning campaign,[d] but the campaign began only in 1963 and could have affected only the end of the trend. Rather, the decline represents a response to modernization similar to that made by all countries that have become industrialized.[23] By 1950 over half of Taiwan's population was urban, and by 1964 nearly two-thirds was urban, with 29 percent of the population living in cities of 100,000 or more. The pace of economic development has been extremely rapid. Between 1951 and 1963, per capita income increased by 4.05 percent per year. Yet the island is closely packed, having 870 persons per square mile (a population density higher than that of Belgium). The combination of fast economic growth and rapid population increase in limited space has put parents of large families at a relative disadvantage and has created a brisk demand for abortions and contraceptives. Thus the favorable response to the current campaign to encourage use of the IUD is not a good example of what birth-control technology can do for a genuinely backward country. In fact, when the program was started, one reason for expecting receptivity was that the island was already on its way to modernization and family planning.[24]

At most, the recent family-planning campaign—which reached significant

---

[d]"South Korea and Taiwan appear successfully to have checked population growth by the use of intrauterine contraceptive devices" [U. Borell, *Hearings on S. 1676 op. cit.*, p. 556].

proportions only in 1964, when some 46,000 IUD's were inserted in 1965 the number was 99,253, and in 1966, 111,242) e[25]—could have caused the increase observable after 1963 in the rate of decline. Between 1951 and 1963 the average drop in the birth rate per 1000 women was 1.73 percent per year; in the period 1964-66 it was 4.35 percent. But one hesitates to assign all of the acceleration in decline since 1963 to the family-planning campaign. The rapid economic development has been precisely of a type likely to accelerate a drop in reproduction. The rise in manufacturing has been much greater than the rise in either agriculture or construction. The agricultural labor force has thus been squeezed, and migration to the cities has skyrocketed.[f] Since housing has not kept pace, urban families have had to restrict reproduction in order to take advantage of career opportunities and avoid domestic inconvenience. Such conditions have historically tended to accelerate a decline in birth rate. The most rapid decline came late in the United States (1921-33) and in Japan (1947-55). The Japanese and Taiwanese birth rates evolved in the same pattern, despite a difference in level. All told, one should not attribute all of the post-1963 acceleration in the decline of Taiwan's birth rate to the family-planning campaign.

The main evidence that *some* of this acceleration is due to the campaign comes from the fact that Taichung, the city in which the family-planning effort was first concentrated, showed subsequently a much faster drop in fertility than other cities[g][26] But the campaign has not reached throughout the island. By the end of 1966, only 260,745 women had been fitted with an IUD under auspices of the campaign, whereas the women of reproductive age on the island numbered 2.86 million. Most of the reduction in fertility has therefore been a matter of individual initiative. To some extent the campaign may be simply substituting sponsored (and cheaper) services for those that would otherwise come through private and commercial channels. An island-wide survey in 1964 showed that over 150,000 women were already using the traditional Ota ring (a metallic intrauterine device popular in Japan); almost as many had been sterilized; about 40,000 were using foam tablets; some 50,000 admitted to having had at least one abortion; and many were using other methods of birth control.[27,28]

---

[e]Before 1964 the Family Planning Association had given advice to fewer than 60,000 wives in ten years and a Pre-Pregnancy Health Program had reached some 10,000, and, in the current campaign, 3,650 IUD's were inserted in 1965, in a total population of 2½ million women of reproductive age. See *Studies in Family Planning*, No. 19 (1967), p. 4, and R. Freedman *et al., Population Studies* 16, 231 (1963).

[f]During the period 1950-60 the ratio of growth of the city to growth of the noncity population was 5:3; during the period 1960-64 the ratio was 5:2; these ratios are based on data of Shaohsing, Chen, *J. Sociol. Taiwan* 1, 74 (1963) and data in the United Nations *Demographic Yearbooks*.

[g]Taichung's rate of decline in 1963-64 was roughly double the average in four other cities, whereas just prior to the campaign its rate of decline had been much less than theirs. R. Freedman, *Population Index* 31, 434 (1965).

The important question, however, is not whether the present campaign is somewhat hastening the downward trend in the birth rate but whether, even if it is, it will provide population control for the nation. Actually, the campaign is not designed to provide such control and shows no sign of doing so. It takes for granted existing reproductive goals. Its aim is "to integrate, through education and information, the idea of family limitation *within the existing attitudes, values, and goals* of the people (italics mine).[29] Its target is *married* women who do not want any more children; it ignores girls not yet married, and women married and wanting more children.

With such an approach, what is the maximum impact possible? It is the difference between the number of children women have been having and the number they want to have. A study in 1957 found a median figure of 3.75 for the number of children wanted by women aged 15 to 29 in Taipei, Taiwan's largest city; the corresponding figure for women from a satellite town was 3.93; for women from a fishing village, 4.90; and for women from a farming village, 5.03. Over 60 percent of the women in Taipei and over 90 percent of those in the farming village wanted four or more children.[30] In a sample of wives aged 25 to 29 in Taichung, a city of over 300,000, Freedman and his co-workers found the average number of children wanted was four; only 9 percent wanted less than three, 20 percent wanted five or more.[31] If, therefore, Taiwanese women used contraceptives that were 100 percent effective and had the number of children they desire, they would have about 4.5 each. The goal of the family-planning effort would be achieved. In the past the Taiwanese woman who married and lived through the reproductive period had, on the average, approximately 6.5 children; thus a figure of 4.5 would represent a substantial decline in fertility. Since mortality would continue to decline, the population growth rate would decline somewhat less than individual reproduction would. With 4.5 births per woman and a life expectancy of seventy years, the rate of natural increase would be close to 3 percent per year.[h]

In the future, Taiwanese views concerning reproduction will doubtless change, in response to social change and economic modernization. But how far will they change? A good indication is the number of children desired by couples in an already modernized country long oriented toward family planning. In the United States in 1966, an average of 3.4 children was considered ideal by white women aged twenty-one or over.[32] This average number of births would give Taiwan, with only a slight decrease in mortality, a long-run rate of natural increase of 1.7 percent per year and a doubling of population in forty-one years.

Detailed data confirm the interpretation that Taiwanese women are in the process of shifting from a "peasant-agrarian" to an "industrial" level of reproduction. They are, in typical fashion, cutting off higher-order births at age thirty and beyond.[i] Among young wives, fertility has risen, not fallen. In sum,

---

[h]In 1964 the life expectancy at birth was already 66 years in Taiwan, as compared to 70 for the United States.

[i]Women accepting IUD's in the family-planning program are typically thirty to thirty-four years old and have already had four children. *Studies in Family Planning* No. 19 (1967), p. 5.

the widely acclaimed family-planning program in Taiwan may, at most, have somewhat speeded the later phase of fertility decline which would have occurred anyway because of modernization.

Moving down the scale of modernization, to countries most in need of population control, one finds the family-planning approach even more inadequate. In South Korea, second only to Taiwan in the frequency with which it is cited as a model of current policy, a recent birth-rate decline of unknown extent is assumed by leaders to be due overwhelmingly to the government's family-planning program. However, it is just as plausible to say that the net effect of government involvement in population control has been, so far, to delay rather than hasten a decline in reproduction made inevitable by social and economic changes. Although the government is advocating vasectomies and providing IUD's and pills, it refuses to legalize abortions, despite the rapid rise in the rate of illegal abortions and despite the fact that, in a recent survey, 72 percent of the people who stated an opinion favored legalization. Also, the program is presented in the context of maternal and child health; it thus emphasizes motherhood and the family rather than alternative roles for women. Much is made of the fact that opinion surveys show an overwhelming majority of Koreans (89 percent in 1965) favoring contraception,[33] but this means only that Koreans are like other people in wishing to have the means to get what they want. Unfortunately, they want sizable families: "The records indicate that the program appeals mainly to women in the 30-39 age bracket who have four or more children, including at least two sons . . ."[34]

In areas less developed than Korea the degree of acceptance of contraception tends to be disappointing, especially among the rural majority. Faced with this discouragement, the leaders of current policy, instead of reexamining their assumptions, tend to redouble their effort to find a contraceptive that will appeal to the most illiterate peasant, forgetting that he wants a good-sized family. In the rural Punjab, for example, "a disturbing feature . . . is that the females start to seek advice and adopt family planning techniques at the . . . end of their reproductive period."[35] Among 5,196 women coming to rural Punjabi family-planning centers, 38 percent were over thirty-five years old, 67 percent over thirty. These women had married early, nearly a third of them before the age of 15; some 14 percent had eight or more *living* children when they reached the clinic, 51 percent six or more.[j]

A survey in Tunisia showed that 68 percent of the married couples were willing to use birth-control measures, but the average number of children they considered ideal was 4.3.[36] The corresponding averages for a village in eastern Java, a village near New Delhi, and a village in Mysore were 4.3, 4.0, and 4.2,

---

[j]Sixty percent of the women had borne their first child before age nineteen. Early marriage is strongly supported by public opinion. Of couples polled in the Punjab, 48 percent said that girls should marry before age twenty (H.S. Ayalvi and S.S. Johl, *Journal of Family Welfare* 12, 60 (1965), p. 57). A study of 2380 couples in sixty villages of Uttar Pradesh found that the women had consummated their marriage at an average age of 14.6 years [J.R. Rele, *Population Studies* 15, 268 (1962)].

respectively.[37,38] In the cities of these regions women are more ready to accept birth control and they want fewer children than village women do, but the number they consider desirable is still wholly unsatisfactory from the standpoint of population control. In an urban family-planning center in Tunisia, more than 600 of 900 women accepting contraceptives had four living children already.[39] In Bangalore, a city of nearly a million at the time (1952), the number of offspring desired by married women was 3.7 on the average; by married men, 4.1.[40] In the metropolitan area of San Salvador (350,000 inhabitants) a 1964 survey showed the number desired by women of reproductive age to be 3.9, and in seven other capital cities of Latin America the number ranged from 2.7 to 4.2.[41] If women in the cities of underdeveloped countries used birth-control measures with 100 percent efficiency, they still would have enough babies to expand city populations senselessly, quite apart from the added contribution of rural-urban migration. In many of the cities the difference between actual and ideal number of children is not great; for instance, in the seven Latin-American capitals mentioned above, the ideal was 3.4 whereas the actual births per women in the age range 35-39 was 3.7.[42] Bombay City has had birth-control clinics for many years, yet its birth rate (standardized for age, sex, and marital distribution) is still 34 per 1000 inhabitants and is tending to rise rather than fall. Although this rate is about 13 percent lower than that for India generally, it has been about that much lower since at least 1951.[43]

Is Family Planning the "First Step" in Population Control? To acknowledge that family planning does not achieve population control is not to impugn its value for other purposes. Freeing women from the need to have more children than they want is of great benefit to them and their children and society at large. My argument is therefore directed not against family-planning programs as such but against the assumption that they are an effective means of controlling population growth.

But what difference does it make? Why not go along for awhile with family planning as an initial approach to the problem of population control? The answer is that any policy on which millions of dollars are being spent should be designed to achieve the goal it purports to achieve. If it is only a first step, it should be so labeled, and its connection with the next step (and the nature of that next step) should be carefully examined. In the present case, since no "next step" seems ever to be mentioned, the question arises, Is reliance on family planning in fact a basis for dangerous postponement of effective steps? To continue to offer a remedy as a cure long after it has been shown merely to ameliorate the disease is either quackery or wishful thinking, and it thrives most where the need is greatest. Today the desire to solve the population problem is so intense that we are all ready to embrace any "action program" that promises relief. But postponement of effective measures allows the situation to worsen.

Unfortunately, the issue is confused by a matter of semantics. "Family *planning*" and "fertility *control*" suggest that reproduction is being regulated according to some rational plan. And so it is, but only from the standpoint of the individual couple, not from that of the community. What is rational in the light of a couple's situation may be totally irrational from the standpoint of society's welfare.

The need for societal regulation of individual behavior is readily recognized in other spheres—those of explosives, dangerous drugs, public property, natural resources. But in the sphere of reproduction, complete individual initiative is generally favored even by those liberal intellectuals who, in other spheres, most favor economic and social planning. Social reformers who would not hesitate to force all owners of rental property to rent to anyone who can pay, or to force all workers in an industry to join a union, balk at any suggestion that couples be permitted to have only a certain number of offspring. Invariably they interpret societal control of reproduction as meaning direct police supervision of individual behavior. Put the word *compulsory* in front of any term describing a means of limiting births—*compulsory sterilization, compulsory abortion, compulsory contraception*—and you guarantee violent opposition. Fortunately, such direct controls need not be invoked, but conservatives and radicals alike overlook this in their blind opposition to the idea of collective determination of a society's birth rate.

That the exclusive emphasis on family planning in current population policies is not a "first step" but an escape from the real issues is suggested by two facts: (1) No country has taken the "next step." The industrialized countries have had family planning for half a century without acquiring control over either the birth rate or population increase, and (2) Support and encouragement of research on population policy other than family planning is negligible. It is precisely this blocking of alternative thinking and experimentation that makes the emphasis on family planning a major obstacle to population control. The need is not to abandon family-planning programs but to put equal or greater resources into other approaches.

New Directions in Population Policy

In thinking about other approaches, one can start with known facts. In the past, all surviving societies had institutional incentives for marriage, procreation, and child care which were powerful enough to keep the birth rate equal to or in excess of a high death rate. Despite the drop in death rates during the last century and a half, the incentives tended to remain intact because the social structure (especially in regard to the family) changed little. At most, particularly in industrial societies, children became less productive and more expensive.[44] In present-day agrarian societies, where the drop in death rate has been more recent, precipitate, and independent of social change, motivation for having children has changed little.[45] Here, even more than in industrialized nations, the family has kept on producing abundant offspring, even though only a fraction of these children are now needed.

If excessive population growth is to be prevented, the obvious requirement is somehow to impose restraints on the family. However, because family roles are reinforced by society's system of rewards, punishments, sentiments, and norms, any proposal to demote the family is viewed as a threat by conservatives and liberals alike, and certainly by people with enough social responsibility to work for population control. One is charged with trying to "abolish" the family, but what is required is selective restructuring of the family in relation to the rest of society.

The lines of such restructuring are suggested by two existing limitations on fertility: (1) Nearly all societies succeed in drastically discouraging reproduction among unmarried women, and (2) Advanced societies unintentionally reduce reproduction among married women when conditions worsen in such a way as to penalize childbearing more severely than it was penalized before. In both cases the causes are motivational and economic rather than technological.

It follows that population-control policy can de-emphasize the family in two ways: (1) by keeping present controls over illegitimate childbirth yet making the most of factors that lead people to postpone or avoid marriage, and (2) by instituting conditions that motivate those who do marry to keep their families small.

Postponement of Marriage. Since the female reproductive span is short and generally more fecund in its first than in its second half, postponement of marriage to ages beyond twenty tends biologically to reduce births. Sociologically, it gives women time to get a better education, acquire interests unrelated to the family, and develop a cautious attitude toward pregnancy.[46] Individuals who have not married by the time they are in their late twenties often do not marry at all. For these reasons, for the world as a whole, the average age at marriage for women is negatively associated with the birth rate: a rising age at marriage is a frequent cause of declining fertility during the middle phase of the demographic transition; and, in the late phase, the "baby boom" is usually associated with a return to younger marriages.

Any suggestion that age at marriage be raised as a part of population policy is usually met with the argument that "even if a law were passed, it would not be obeyed." Interestingly, this objection implies that the only way to control the age at marriage is by direct legislation, but other factors govern the actual age. Roman Catholic countries generally follow canon law in stipulating twelve years as the minimum *legal* age at which girls may marry, but the actual average age at marriage in these countries (at least in Europe) is characteristically more like 25 to 28 years. The actual age is determined, not by law, but by social and economic conditions. In agrarian societies, postponement of marriage (when postponement occurs) is apparently caused by difficulties in meeting the economic prerequisites for matrimony, as stipulated by custom and opinion. In industrial societies it is caused by housing shortages, unemployment, the requirement for overseas military service, high costs of education, and inadequacy of consumer services. Since almost no research has been devoted to the subject, it is difficult to assess the relative weight of the factors that govern the age at marriage.

Encouraging Limitation of Births within Marriage. As a means of encouraging
the limitation of reproduction within marriage, as well as postponement of
marriage, a greater rewarding of nonfamilial than of familial roles would
probably help. A simple way of accomplishing this would be to allow economic
advantages to accrue to the single as opposed to the married individual, and to
the small as opposed to the large family. For instance, the government could pay
people to permit themselves to be sterilized;[47] all costs of abortion could be
paid by the government; a substantial fee could be charged for a marriage
license; a "child-tax" could be levied;[48] and there could be a requirement that
illegitimate pregnancies be aborted. Less sensationally, governments could
simply reverse some existing policies that encourage childbearing. They could,
for example, cease taxing single persons more than married ones; stop giving
parents special tax exemptions; abandon income tax policy that discriminates
against couples when the wife works; reduce paid maternity leaves; reduce
family allowances;[k] stop awarding public housing on the basis of family size;
stop granting fellowships and other educational aids (including special allowances for wives and children) to married students; cease outlawing abortions
and sterilizations; and relax rules that allow use of harmless contraceptives only
with medical permission. Some of these policy reversals would be beneficial in
other than demographic respects and some would be harmful unless special
precautions were taken. The aim would be to reduce the number, not the
quality, of the next generation.

A closely related method of de-emphasizing the family would be modification
of the complementarity of the roles of men and women. Men are now able to
participate in the wider world yet enjoy the satisfaction of having several
children because the housework and childcare fall mainly on their wives. Women
are impelled to seek this role by their idealized view of marriage and motherhood and by either the scarcity of alternative roles or the difficulty of
combining them with family roles. To change this situation women could be
required to work outside the home, or compelled by circumstances to do so. If,
at the same time, women were paid as well as men and given equal educational
and occupational opportunities, and if social life were organized around the
place of work rather than around the home or neighborhood, many women
would develop interests that would compete with family interests. Approximately this policy is now followed in several Communist countries, and even the
less developed of these currently have extremely low birth rates.[1]

That inclusion of women in the labor force has a negative effect on
reproduction is indicated by regional comparisons.[49,50] But in most countries
the wife's employment is subordinate, economically and emotionally, to her
family role, and is readily sacrificed for the latter. No society has restructured

---

[k]Sixty-two countries, including twenty-seven in Europe, give cash payments to people for
having children U.S. Social Security Administration, *Social Security Programs Throughout
the World*, 1967 (Washington, D.C.: Government Printing Office, 1967), pp. xxvii-xxviii.

[1]Average gross reproduction rates in the early 1960s were as follows: Hungary, 0.91;
Bulgaria, 1.09; Romania, 1.15; Yugoslavia, 1.32.

both the occupational system and the domestic establishment to the point of permanently modifying the old division of labor by sex.

In any deliberate effort to control the birth rate along these lines, a government has two powerful instruments—its command over economic planning and its authority (real or potential) over education. The first determines (as far as policy can) the economic conditions and circumstances affecting the lives of all citizens; the second provides the knowledge and attitudes necessary to implement the plans. The economic system largely determines who shall work, what can be bought, what rearing children will cost, how much individuals can spend. The schools define family roles and develop vocational and recreational interests; they could, if it were desired, redefine the sex roles, develop interests that transcend the home, and transmit realistic (as opposed to moralistic) knowledge concerning marriage, sexual behavior, and population problems. When the problem is viewed in this light, it is clear that the ministries of economics and education, not the ministry of health, should be the source of population policy.

The Dilemma of Population Policy

It should now be apparent why, despite strong anxiety over runaway population growth, the actual programs purporting to control it are limited to family planning and are therefore ineffective. (1) The goal of zero, or even slight, population growth is one that nations and groups find difficult to accept. (2) The measures that would be required to implement such a goal, though not so revolutionary as a brave new world or a Communist utopia, nevertheless tend to offend most people reared in existing societies. As a consequence, the goal of so-called population control is implicit and vague; the method is only family planning. This method, far from de-emphasizing the family, is familistic. One of its stated goals is that of helping sterile couples to *have* children. It stresses parental aspirations and responsibilities. It goes along with most aspects of conventional morality, such as condemnation of abortion, disapproval of premarital intercourse, respect for religious teachings and cultural taboos, and obeisance to medical and clerical authority. It deflects hostility by refusing to recommend any change other than the one it stands for: availability of contraceptives.

The things that make family planning acceptable are the very things that make it ineffective for population control. By stressing the right of parents to have the number of children they want, it evades the basic question of population policy, which is how to give societies the number of children they need. By offering only the means for *couples* to control fertility, it neglects the means for societies to do so.

Because of the predominantly pro-family character of existing societies, individual interest ordinarily leads to the production of enough offspring to constitute rapid population growth under conditions of low mortality. Childless or single-child homes are considered indicative of personal failure, whereas having three to five living children gives a family a sense of continuity and substantiality.[m]

Given the existing desire to have moderate-sized rather than small families, the only countries in which fertility has been reduced to match reduction in mortality are advanced ones temporarily experiencing worsened economic conditions. In Sweden, for instance, the net reproduction rate (NRR) has been below replacement for thirty-four years (1930-63), if the period is taken as a whole, but this is because of the economic depression. The average replacement rate was below unity (NRR = 0.81) for the period 1930-42, but from 1942 through 1963 it was above unity (NRR = 1.08). Hardships that seem particularly conducive to deliberate lowering of the birth rate are (in managed economies) scarcity of housing and other consumer goods despite full employment, and required high participation of women in the labor force, or (in freer economies) a great deal of unemployment and economic insecurity. When conditions are good, any nation tends to have a growing population.

It follows that, in countries where contraception is used, a realistic proposal for a government policy of lowering the birth rate reads like a catalogue of horrors: squeeze consumers through taxation and inflation; make housing very scarce by limiting construction; force wives and mothers to work outside the home to offset the inadequacy of male wages, yet provide few child-care facilities; encourage migration to the city by paying low wages in the country and providing few rural jobs; increase congestion in cities by starving the transit system; increase personal insecurity by encouraging conditions that produce unemployment and by haphazard political arrests. No government will institute such hardships simply for the purpose of controlling population growth. Clearly, therefore, the task of contemporary population policy is to develop attractive substitutes for family interests, so as to avoid having to turn to hardship as a corrective. The specific measures required for developing such substitutes are not easy to determine in the absence of research on the question.

In short, the world's population problem cannot be solved by pretense and wishful thinking. The unthinking identification of family planning with population control is an ostrich-like approach in that it permits people to hide from themselves the enormity and unconventionality of the task. There is no reason to abandon family-planning programs; contraception is a valuable technological instrument. But such programs must be supplemented with equal or greater investments in research and experimentation to determine the required socio-economic measures.

Notes

1. *Studies in Family Planning*, No. 16 (1967).
2. Ibid., No. 9 (1966), p. 1.

---

[m]Roman Catholic textbooks condemn the "small" family (one with fewer than four children) as being abnormal J. Blake, *Population Studies* 20, 27 (1966).

3. The statement is given in *Studies in Family Planning* (No. 16, p.1), and in *Population Bull.* 23, 6 (1967).

4. The statement is quoted in *Studies in Family Planning* (No. 16, p. 2).

5. *Hearings on S. 1676, U.S. Senate, Subcommittee on Foreign Aid Expenditures, 89th Congress, Second Session, April* 7, 8, 11 (1966), pt. 4, p. 889.

6. B.L. Raina, in *Family Planning and Population Programs*, B. Berelson, R.K. Anderson, O. Harkavy, G. Maier, W.P. Mauldin, S.G. Segal, Eds. (Univ. of Chicago Press, Chicago, 1966).

7. D. Kirk, *Annals of the American Academy of Political and Social Science* 369, 53 (1967).

8. K. Davis, *Rotarian* 94, 10 (1959); *Health Education Monographs* 9, 2 (1960); L. Day and A. Day, *Too Many Americans* (Boston: Houghton Mifflin, 1964); R.A. Piddington, *Limits of Mankind* (Bristol, England: Wright, 1956).

9. *Official Gazette* (15 Apr. 1965); quoted in *Studies in Family Planning* (No. 16, p. 7).

10. J.W. Gardner, Secretary of Health, Education, and Welfare, "Memorandum to Heads of Operating Agencies" (Jan. 1966), reproduced in *Hearings on S. 1676* op. cit., p. 783.

11. C. Tietze, *Demography* 1, 119 (1964); *Journal of Chronic Diseases* 18, 1161 (1964); M. Muramatsu, *Milbank Memorial Fund Quarterly* 38, 153 (1960); K. Davis, *Population Index* 29, 345 (1963); R. Armijo and T. Monreal, *Journal of Sex Research*, 1964, 143 (1964); Proceedings World Population Conference, Belgrade, 1965; Proceedings International Planned Parenthood Federation.

12. *Studies in Family Planning*, No. 4 (1964), p. 3.

13. D. Bell (then administrator for Agency for International Development), in *Hearings on S. 1676* op. cit., p. 862.

14. *Asian Population Conference* (New York: United Nations, 1964), p. 30.

15. R. Armijo and T. Monreal, in *Components of Population Change in Latin America* (New York: Milbank Fund 1965), p. 272; E. Rice-Wray, *American Journal of Public Health* 54, 313 (1964).

16. E. Rice-Wray, in "Intra-Uterine Contraceptive Devices," *Excerpta Med. Intern. Congr. Ser. No. 54* (1962), p. 135.

17. J. Blake, in *Public Health and Population Change*, M.C. Sheps and J.C. Ridley, Eds. (Pittsburgh: Univ. of Pittsburgh Press, 1965), p. 41.

18. J. Blake and K. Davis, *American Behavioral Scientist* 5, 24 (1963).

19. See "Panel discussion on comparative acceptability of different methods of contraception," in *Research in Family Planning*, C.V. Kiser, Ed. (Princeton: Princeton Univ. Press, 1962), pp. 373-86.

20. O.A. Collver, *Birth Rates in Latin America* (Berkeley, Calif: International Population and Urban Research, 1965), pp. 27-28; the ten countries were Colombia, Costa Rica, El Salvador, Ecuador, Guatemala, Honduras, Mexico, Panama, Peru, and Venezuela.

21. J.R. Rele, *Fertility Analysis through Extension of Stable Population Concepts.* (Berkeley, Calif.: International Population and Urban Research, 1967).

22. J.C. Ridley, M.C. Sheps, J.W. Lingner, J.A. Menken, *Milbank Memorial Fund Quarterly* 45, 77 (1967); E. Arriaga, unpublished paper.

23. K. Davis, *Population Index* 29, 345 (1963).

24. R. Freedman, *Population Index* 31, 421 (1965).

25. R.W. Gillespie, *Family Planning on Taiwan* (Taichung: Population Council, 1965), p. 45.

26. Gillespie, *Family Planning*, p. 69.

27. Ibid., p. 18.

28. Chen, *Journal of Sociology Taiwan* 1, 74 (1963).

29. Gillespie, *Family Planning*, p. 8.

30. S.H. Chen, *Journal of Social Science Taipei* 13, 72 (1963).

31. R. Freedman et al., *Population Studies* 16, 227 (1963); Ibid., p. 232.

32. J. Blake, *Eugenics Quarterly* 14, 68 (1967).

33. Y.K. Cha, in *Family Planning and Population Programs*, B. Berelson et al., Eds. (Chicago: Univ. of Chicago Press, 1966), p. 27.

34. Ibid., p. 25.

35. H.S. Ayalvi and S.S. Johl, *Journal of Family Welfare* 12, 60 (1965).

36. J. Morsa, in *Family Planning and Population Programs*, B. Berelson et al., Eds. (Chicago: Univ. of Chicago Press, 1966).

37. H. Gille and R.J. Pardoko, in *Family Planning and Population Programs*, B. Berelson et al., Eds. (Chicago: Univ. of Chicago Press, 1966), p. 515; S.N. Agarwala, *Med. Dig. Bombay* 4, 653 (1961).

38. *Mysore Population Study* (New York: United Nations, 1961), p. 140.

39. A. Daly, in *Family Planning and Population Programs*, B. Berelson et al., Eds. (Univ. of Chicago Press, Chicago, 1966).

40. *Mysore Population Study.*

41. C.J. Gomez, paper presented at the World Population Conference, Belgrade, 1965.

42. C. Miro, in *Family Planning and Population Programs*, B. Berelson et al., Eds. (Chicago: Univ. of Chicago Press, 1966).

43. *Demographic Training and Research Centre (India) Newsletter* 20, 4 (Aug. 1966).

44. K. Davis, *Population Index* 29, 345 (1963). For economic and sociological theory of motivation for having children, see J. Blake [Univ. of California (Berkeley)], in preparation.

45. K. Davis, *American Economic Review* 46, 305 (1956); *Scientific American* 209, 68 (1963).

46. J. Blake, *World Population Conference [Belgrade, 1965]* (United Nations, New York, 1967), Vol. 2, pp. 132-36.

47. S. Enke, *Review of Economics and Statistics* 42, 175 (1960); S, Enke, *Economic Development and Cultural Change* 8, 339 (1960); Ibid. 10, 427 (1962); A.O. Krueger and L.A. Sjaastad, Ibid., p. 423.

48. T.J. Samuel, *Journal of Family Welfare India* 13, 12 (1966).

49. J. Blake, in Ridley and Sheps, *Milbank Memorial Fund Quarterly*, p. 1195.

50. O.A. Collver and E. Langlois, *Economic Development and Cultural Change* 10, 367 (1962); J. Weeks, Univ. of California (Berkeley), unpublished paper.

5 Beyond Family Planning

Bernard Berelson

This paper rests on these propositions: (1) among the great problems on the world agenda is the population problem; (2) that problem is most urgent in the developing countries where rapid population growth retards social and economic development; (3) there is a time penalty on the problem in the sense that, other things equal, anything not done sooner may be harder to do later, due to increased numbers; and accordingly (4) everything that can properly be done to lower population growth rates should be done, now. As has been asked on other occasions, the question is: what is to be done? There is a certain agreement on the general objective (i.e., on the desirability of lowering birth rates, though not on how far how fast), but there is disagreement as to means.

The 1960s have witnessed a substantial increase of awareness and concern with population matters throughout the world[1] and of efforts to do something about the problem, particularly in the developing countries. That something typically turns out to be the establishment of national family planning programs, or rough equivalents thereof. There are now 20 to 25 countries with efforts along this line, on all three developing continents, all of them either set up or revitalized in this decade. Thus, the first response to too high growth rates deriving from too high birth rates is to introduce voluntary contraception on a mass basis, or try to.

Why is family planning the first step taken on the road to population control? Probably because from a broad political standpoint it is the most acceptable one: since, because it is closely tied to maternal and child care, it can be perceived as a health measure beyond dispute; and, since it is voluntary it can be justified as a contribution to the effective personal freedom of individual couples. On both scores, the practice ties into accepted values and thus achieves political viability. In some situations, it is an oblique approach, seen as the politically acceptable way to start toward "population control" on the national level by promoting fertility control and smaller family size among individual couples. Moreover, it is a gradual effort and an inexpensive one, both of which contribute to its political acceptability. Though the introduction of family planning as a response to a country's population problem may be calculated to minimize opposition, even that policy has been attacked in several countries by politicians who are unconvinced and/or see an electoral advantage in the issue.

How effective have family planning programs been as a means toward

71

population control? There is currently some controversy among qualified observers as to their efficacy[2] and this is not the place to review that issue. But there is sufficient agreement on the magnitude and consequence of the problem that additional efforts are needed to reach a "solution," however that is responsibly defined.

For the purpose of this paper, then, let us assume that today's national family planning programs, mainly via voluntary contraception, are not "enough"—where "enough" is defined not necessarily as achieving zero growth in some extended present but simply as lowering birth rates quickly and substantially. "Enough" begs the question of the ultimate goal and only asks that a faster decline in population growth rates be brought about than is presently in process or in prospect—and, within the range of the possible, the faster the better.[3] Just to indicate the rough order of magnitude, let us say that the proximate goal is the halving of the birth rate in the developing countries in the next decade or two—from, say, over 40 births per thousand per year to 20-25.[4] For obvious reasons, both emigration and increased death rates are ruled out of consideration.

What is to be done to bring that about, beyond present programs of voluntary family planning?[5] I address that question in two ways: first, by listing the programs or policies more or less responsibly suggested to this end in recent years; and second, by reviewing the issues raised by the suggested approaches.

Proposals: Beyond Family Planning

Here is a listing of the several proposals, arranged in descriptive categories. (There may be a semantic question involved in some cases: when is a proposal a proposal? Are "suggestions" or "offers for consideration" or lists of alternatives to be considered as proposals? In general, I have included all those cases presented in a context in which they were readily perceived as providing a supplementary or alternative approach to present efforts. The list may include both proposals for consideration and proposals for action.)

A. *Extensions of Voluntary Fertility Control*

1. Institutionalization of maternal care in rural areas of developing countries: a feasibility study of what would be required in order to bring some degree of modern medical or paramedical attention to every pregnant woman in the rural areas of five developing countries with professional back-up for difficult cases and with family planning education and services a central component of the program aimed particularly at women of low parity (Taylor & Berelson[6]).
2. Liberalization of induced abortion (Davis[7], Ehrlich,[8] Chandrasekhar[9]).

B. *Establishment of Involuntary Fertility Control*

1. Mass use of "fertility control agent" by government to regulate births at

acceptable level: the "fertility control agent" designed to lower fertility in the society by 5 percent to 75 percent less than the present birth rate, as needed; substance now unknown but believed to be available for field testing after 5-15 years of research work; to be included in water supply in urban areas and by "other methods" elsewhere (Ketchel[10]); "addition of temporary sterilants to water supplies or staple food" (Ehlich[11]).

2. "Marketable licenses to have children," given to women and perhaps men in "whatever number would ensure a reproduction rate of one," say 2.2 children per couple: for example, "the unit certificate might be the 'deci-child', and accumulation of ten of these units by purchase, inheritance or gift, would permit a woman in maturity to have one legal child" (Boulding[12]).

3. Temporary sterilization of all girls via time-capsule contraceptives, and again after each delivery, with reversibility allowed only upon governmental approval; certificates of approval distributed according to popular vote on desired population growth for a country, and saleable on open market (Shockley[13]).

4. Compulsory sterilization of men with three or more living children (Chandra-sekhar[14]); requirement of induced abortion for all illegitimate pregnancies (Davis[15]).

C. *Intensified Educational Campaigns*

1. Inclusion of population materials in primary and secondary schools systems (Davis[16], Wayland,[17] Visaria[18]): materials on demographic and physiological aspects, perhaps family planning and sex education as well; introduced at the secondary level in order to reach next waves of public school teachers throughout the country.

2. Promotion of national satellite television systems for direct informational effect on population and family planning as well as for indirect effect on modernization in general: satellite broadcasting probably through ground relays with village receivers (Ehrlich,[19] Meier and Meier,[20] UNESCO,[21] Schramm & Nelson[22]).

D. *Incentive Programs*: This term requires clarification. As used here, it refers to payments, or their equivalent, made directly to contracepting couples and/or to couples not bearing children for specified periods. It does *not* refer to payments to field workers, medical personnel, volunteers, *et al.*, for securing acceptance of contraceptive practice; that type of payment, now utilized in many programs, is better called a fee or a stipend in order to differentiate it from an incentive as used here. Beyond that distinction, however, the term is fuzzy at the edges: is the provision of free contraceptive consultation and supplies to be considered an incentive? or free milk to the infant along with family planning information to the mother? or free transport to the family planning service, which then provides general health care? or a generous payment in lieu of time off from work for a vasectomy operation? or even a financial burden imposed for undesirable fertility behavior? In the usage here, I try to limit the term to direct payment of money (or goods or services) to members of the target population in return for the desired practice. This usage is sometimes referred to as a "positive" incentive in distinction to the "negative" incentive inherent in tax or welfare penalties for "too many" children (E below).

1. Payment for the initiation or the effective practice of contraception: payment or equivalent (e.g., transistor radio) for sterilization (Chandrasekhar,[23] Pohlmann,[24] Samuel,[25] Davis[26]) or for contraception (Simon,[27] Enke,[28] Samuel[29]).
2. Payment for periods of non-pregnancy or non-birth: a bonus for child spacing or non-pregnancy (Young,[30] Bhatia,[31] Enke,[32] Spengler,[33] Leasure[34]); a savings certificate plan for twelve-month periods of non-birth (Balfour[35]); a lottery scheme for preventing illegitimate births among teenagers in a small country (Mauldin[36]); "responsibility prizes" for each five years of childless marriage or for vasectomy before the third child, and special lotteries with tickets available to the childless (Ehrlich[37]).

E. *Tax and Welfare Benefits and Penalties*: i.e., an anti-natalist system of social services in place of the present pro-natalist tendencies.

1. Withdrawal of maternity benefits, perhaps after N(3?) children (Bhatia,[38] Samuel,[39] Davis[40]) or unless certain limiting conditions have been met, like sufficient child spacing, knowledge of family planning, or level of income (Titmuss and Abel-Smith[41]).
2. Withdrawal of children or family allowances, perhaps after N children (Bhatia,[42] Titmuss and Abel-Smith,[43] Davis[44]).
3. Tax on births after the Nth (Bhatia,[45] Samuel,[46] Spengler[47]).
4. Limitation of governmentally provided medical treatment, housing, scholarships, loans and subsidies, etc., to families with fewer than N children (Bhatia,[48] Davis[49]).
5. Reversal of tax benefits, to favor the unmarried and the parents of fewer rather than more children (Bhatia,[50] Titmuss and Abel-Smith,[51] Samuel,[52] Davis,[53] Ehrlich,[54] David[55]).
6. Provision by the state of N years of free schooling at all levels to each nuclear family, to be allocated by the family among the children as desired (Fawcett[56]).
7. Pensions for poor parents with fewer than N children as social security for their old age (Samuel,[57] Ohlin,[58] Davison[59]).

F. *Shifts in Social and Economic Institutions*: i.e., broad changes in fundamental institutional arrangements that could have the effect of lowering fertility.

1. Increase in minimum age of marriage: through legislation or through substantial fee for marriage licenses (David,[60] Davis[61]); or through direct bonuses for delayed marriage (Young[62]); or through payment of marriage

benefits only to parents of brides over 21 years of age (Titmuss and Abel-Smith[63]); or through a program of government loans for wedding ceremonies when the bride is of a sufficient age, or with the interest rate inversely related to the bride's age (Davis[64]); or through a "governmental 'first marriage grant' . . . awarded each couple in which the age of both (sic) partners was 25 or more" (Ehrlich[65]); or through establishment of a domestic "national service" program for all men for the appropriate two-year period in order to develop social services, inculcate modern attitudes including family planning and population control, and at the same time delay age of marriage (Berelson, Etzioni[66]).

2. Promotion or requirement of female participation in labor force (outside the home) to provide roles and interests for women alternative or supplementary to marriage (Hauser,[67] Davis,[68] David[69]).

3. "Direct manipulation of family structure itself—planned efforts at deflecting the family's socializing function, reducing the noneconomic utilities of offspring, or introducing nonfamilial distractions and opportunity costs into people's lives"; specifically, through employment of women outside the home (Blake[70]); "selective restructuring of the family in relation to the rest of society" (Davis[71]).

4. Promotion of "two types of marriage, one of them childless and readily dissolved, and the other licensed for children and designed to be stable"; the former needs to be from 20-40 percent of the total in order to allow the remainder to choose family size freely (Meier and Meier[72]).

5. Encouragement of long-range social trends leading toward lower fertility, e.g., "improved and universal general education, or new roads facilitating communication, or improved agricultural methods, or a new industry that would increase productivity, or other types of innovation that may break the 'cake of custom' and produce social foment" (Hauser[73]); and improved status of women (U.N./ECOSOC[74]).

6. Efforts to lower death rates even further, particularly infant and child death rates, on the inference that birth rates will follow them down (Revelle,[75] Heer and Smith[76]).

G. *Approaches via Political Channels and Organizations*

1. U.S. insistence on "population control as the price of food aid," with highly selective assistance based thereon, and exertion of political pressures on governments or religious groups impeding "solution" of the population problem, including shifts in sovereignty (Ehlich[77]).

2. Re-organization of national and international agencies to deal with the population problem; within the United States, "coordination by a powerful governmental agency, a Federal Department of Population and Environment (DPE) . . . with the power to take whatever steps are necessary to establish a reasonable population size" (Ehrlich[78]); within India, creation of "a separate Ministry of Population Control" (Chandrasekhar[79]); development of an

"international specialized agency larger than WHO to operate programs for extending family limitation techniques to the world . . . charged with the responsibility of effecting the transfer to population equilibrium" (Meier and Meier[80]).

3. Promotion of zero growth in population, as the ultimate goal needed to be accepted now in order to place intermediate goals of lowered fertility in proper context (Davis[81]).

H. *Augmented Research Efforts*

1. More research on social means for achieving necessary fertility goals (Davis[82]).
2. Focused research on practical methods of sex determination (Polgar[83]).
3. Increased research toward an improved contraceptive technology (NAS[84]).

Proposals: Review of the Issues

Here are 29 proposals beyond family planning for dealing with the problem of undue population growth in the developing world. I naturally cannot claim that these are all the proposals made more or less responsibly toward that end, but my guess is that there are not many more and that these proposals are a reasonably good sample of the total list. In any case, these are perhaps the most visible at the present time and the following analysis is limited to them.

Since several of the proposals tend in the same direction, it seems appropriate to review them illustratively against the criteria that any such proposals might be required to meet. What are such criteria? There are at least six: (1) scientific/medical/technological readiness. (2) political viability, (3) administrative feasibility, (4) economic capability, (5) moral/ethical/philosophical acceptability, and (6) presumed effectiveness. In other words, the key questions are: is the scientific/medical/technological base available or likely? will governments approve? can the proposal be administered? can the society afford the proposal? is it morally acceptable? and finally, will it work?

Such criteria and questions have to be considered against some time scale. As indicated at the outset of this paper, I suggest the next decade or two on the double grounds that the future is dim enough at that point let alone beyond and that in any case it is difficult to develop plans and programs now for a more remote future. National economic plans, for example, are typically limited to five years and then a new one made in accord with the conditions existing at that time. In any case, long-run social goals are normally approached through successive short-run efforts.

Since the population problem in the developing world is particularly serious in its implications for human welfare, such proposals deserve serious consideration indeed. What do the proposals come to, viewed against the indicated criteria? (I use India throughout as the major illustrative case since it is the key example of the problem; disregarding Mainland China, India has a much larger population than all the other countries with population programs combined.)

Scientific/Medical/Technological Readiness. Two questions are involved: (1) is the needed technology available? and (2) are the needed medical or para-medical personnel available or readily trainable to assure medical administration and safety?

With regard to temporary contraception, sterilization, and abortion, the needed technology is not only available now but is being steadily improved and expanded. The IUD (intrauterine device) and the oral pill have been major contraceptive developments of the past decade, and several promising leads are now being followed up[85]—though it cannot be said with much confidence that any of them will eventuate for mass use within the next few years.[a] Improved technologies for sterilization, both male and female, are being worked on; and there has been a recent development in abortion technique, the so-called suction device now being utilized in Eastern Europe and the U.S.S.R.[86]

However, neither Ehrlich's "temporary sterilants" nor Ketchel's "fertility control agent" (B-1) is now available or on the technological horizon—though that does not mean that the research task ought not to be pursued against a subsequent need, especially since such substances could be administered voluntarily and individually as well as involuntarily and collectively. In the latter case, if administered through the water supply or a similar source, the substance would need to be medically safe and free of side effects for men and women, young and old, well and ill, physiologically normal and physiologically marginal, as well as for animals and perhaps plants. As some people have remarked, such an involuntary addition to a water supply would face far greater difficulties of acceptance simply on medical grounds than the far milder proposals with regard to fluoridation to prevent tooth decay.

Though a substantial technology in fertility control does exist, that does not mean that it can be automatically applied where most needed, partly because of limitations of trained personnel. In general, the more the technology requires the services of medical or para-medical personnel (or, what is much the same, is perceived as requiring them), the more difficult it is to administer in the

---

[a]In passing it is worth noting that such expectations are not particularly reliable. For example, in 1952–1953 a Working Group on Fertility Control was organized by the Conservation Foundation to reivew the most promising "leads to physiologic control of fertility," based on a survey conducted by Dr. Paul S. Henshaw and Kingsley Davis. The Group did identify a lead that became the oral contraceptive (already then under investigation) but did not mention the intrauterine device. The Group was specifically searching for better ways to control fertility because of the population problem in the developing world, and considered the contraceptive approach essential to that end: "It thus appears imperative that an attempt be made to bring down fertility in overpopulated regions without waiting for a remote, hoped-for transformation of the entire society . . . It seems plausible that acceptable birth control techniques might be found, and that the application of science to developing such techniques for peasant regions might yield revolutionary results." (*The Physiological Approach to Fertility Control, Report of the Working Group on Fertility Control*, The Conservation Foundation, April 1953, p. 69.)

developing countries. For example, such traditional contraceptives as condoms or foams can be distributed freely through a variety of non-medical channels, including commercial ones, though that network is not without limitations in the poorer countries. Oral contraceptive pills *are* now distributed in large numbers without substantial medical intervention in a number of countries—sold by pharmacies without prescription—but not with medical sanction; and most qualified medical specialists here and abroad believe that the pills should be given only after proper medical examination and with proper medical follow-up. IUDs were first inserted only by obstetricians, then by medical doctors, and now, in a few situations where female medical personnel are unavailable in sufficient numbers, by specially trained para-medical personnel (notably, on a large scale, in Pakistan).

In the case of sterilization and abortion, the medical requirement becomes more severe. For example, when the policy of compulsory vasectomy of men with three or more children was first being considered in India (see footnote 14), an estimate was made that the policy would affect about 40 million males: "one thousand surgeons or para-surgeons each averaging 20 operations a day for five days a week would take eight years to cope with the existing candidates, and during this time of course a constant supply of new candidates would be coming along"[87]—at present birth rates, probably of the order of 3.5 million a year. Large-scale abortion practice, assuming legality and acceptability, might additionally require hospital beds, which are in particularly short supply in most developing countries. Just as an indication of order of magnitude, in India, for example, there are approximately 22 million births annually; to abort five million would require the equivalent of about 800 physicians, each doing 25 a day five days a week fifty weeks a year, which is approximately 10 percent of the obstetrical/gynecological specialists in India, or perhaps 25 percent of the female specialists; and about 10 million bed days, which is over half the estimated number of maternity bed days in the country at present.[b] However, the newer abortion technique might not require hospitalization—theoretically, the abortion "camp" may be feasible, as was the vasectomy "camp," except perhaps for the greater sensitivities attaching to the status of women, though it is not medically desirable—and para-medical personnel may be acceptable as well. Reportedly, the newer technique does not involve hospitalization in some parts of Eastern Europe and Mainland China.

In short, the technology is available for some but not all current proposals, and the same may be the case for properly trained personnel.

Political Viability. As mentioned earlier, the "population problem" has been

[b]These are only illustrative magnitudes. Actually, the five million does not really represent 5/22nd of the birth rate since an aborted woman could again become pregnant within a period of months, whereas a newly pregnant woman would not normally become so for over a year. Thus it may be that abortion needs to be combined with contraceptive practice and used mainly for contraceptive failures or "accidents" in order to be fully effective as a means of fertility limitation in the developing countries.

increasingly recognized by national governments and international agencies over the past decade, and favorable policies have been increasingly adopted: national family planning programs in some 20-25 countries, positive resolutions and actions within the United Nations family, large programs of support by such developed countries as United States and Sweden, the so-called World Leaders' Statement. There is no reason to think that that positive trend has run its course.

At the same time, the political picture is by no means unblemished. Some favorable policies are not strong enough to support a vigorous program even where limited to family planning on health grounds; in national politics "population control" can become a handy issue for a determined opposition; internal ethnic balances are sometimes delicately involved, with political ramifications; national size is often equated with national power, from the standpoint of international relations and regional military balances; the motives behind the support and encouragement of population control by the developed countries are sometimes perceived as politically expedient if not neo-colonialist or neo-imperialist; and on the international front, as represented by the United Nations, there is still considerable reluctance based on both religio-moral and political considerations. In short, elite ambivalence and perceived political liability are not absent even in the favoring countries. That state of affairs may not be surprising looked at historically and given the sensitive religious, military, and political issues involved, but it does not provide maximum support for energetic measures directed at the "necessary" degree of population control.

The question of political acceptability of such proposals becomes in effect two questions: what is presumably acceptable within the present situation? and what might be done to enlarge the sphere of acceptability (as, for example, in proposals G-1 and G-2)?

In the nature of the political case, population measures are not taken in isolation—which is to say, they are not given overriding claim upon the nation's attention and resources even though they have been given special authority in a few countries. They must thus compete in the political arena with other claims and values, and that kind of competition accords with the political bases of an open society.

Any social policy adopted by government rests on some minimum consensus upon goals and means. They need not be the ultimate goals or the final means; as noted above, the socio-economic plans of developing countries are typically five-year plans, not 20- or 40- or 100-year plans. Indeed, an ultimate goal of population policy—that is, zero growth—need not be agreed upon or even considered by officials who can agree upon the immediate goal of lowering growth by a specified amount or by "as much as possible" within a period of years. And since there are always goals beyond goals, one does not even need to know what the ultimate goal is, only the direction in which it will be found (which is usually more likely of agreement). Would the insistence *now* on the acknowledgment of an *ultimate* goal of zero growth advance the effort or change its direction?

The means to such ends need not be final either. Indeed, at least at the outset of a somewhat controversial program, the means probably must fit within the framework of existing values, elite or mass, and preferably both—for example, a family planning program for maternal and child health and for preventing unwanted births even though the resultant growth rate may still remain "too high" by ultimate standards.

Specifically, against this background, how politically acceptable do some of the proposals appear to be?

To start with, the proposal of involuntary controls in India in 1967 (B-4) precipitated "a storm of questions in Parliament,"[c] was withdrawn, and resulted in a high-level personnel shift within the family planning organization. No other country has seriously entertained the idea. Leaving aside other considerations, political instability in many countries would make implementation virtually impossible.

Social measures designed to affect the birth rate indirectly—e.g., tax benefits, social security arrangements, etc.—have been proposed from time to time. In India, there have been several such proposals: for example, by the United Nations mission,[88] by the Small Family Norm Committee,[89] by the Central Family Planning Council (e.g., with regard to age of marriage, the education and employment of women, and various social welfare benefits),[90] and in almost every issue of such publications as *Family Planning News, Centre Calling*, and *Planned Parenthood* (illustrative recent headings: "Tax to Reduce Family Size," "Relief for Bachelors Urged," "Scholarships for Children, Family Planning for Parents"). As Samuel reports, with accompanying documentation, "the desirability of imposing a tax on births of fourth or higher order has been afloat for some time. However, time and again, the suggestion has been rejected by the Government of India."[91] In some cases, action has been taken by either the Central Government (e.g., income tax "deductions for dependent children are given for the first and second child only"[92]) or certain states (e.g., "Maharashtra and Uttar Pradesh have decided to grant educational concessions and benefits only to those children whose parents restrict the size of their families . . ."[93] and the former state is reportedly beginning to penalize families with more than three children by withholding maternity leave, educational benefits, and housing privileges, though in the nature of the case only a small proportion of the state's population is affected by these disincentives[94]). As an indication of political sensitivity, an order withdrawing maternity leave for non-industrial women employees with three or more living children—at best a tiny number of educated women—was revoked before it really went into effect.[95] There is a special political problem in many countries, in that economic constraints on fertility often turn out in practice to be selective on class, racial, or ethnic grounds, and thus exacerbate political tensions.

---

[c]Report in *The New York Times*, November 17, 1967. The then-Minister had earlier suggested a substantial bonus (100 rupees) for vasectomy, the funds to be taken from U.S. counterpart, "but both Governments are extremely sensitive in this area. Yet in a problem this crucial perhaps we need more action and less sensitivity" (S. Chandrasekhar, in *Asia's Population Problem, op. cit.*, p. 96).

As another example, promoting female participation in the labor force runs up against the political problem that such employment would be competitive with men in situations of already high male un- and under-employment. One inquiry concludes: "The prospective quantitative effect of moves in this direction seems very questionable. The number of unemployed in India has been rising by approximately 50 percent every five years, and this is a well-known and very hot political issue. The government can hardly be blamed for being reluctant to promote female employment at the expense of male employment, which the great bulk of female employment almost surely would be."[96]

Given the present and likely political climate both within and between countries, whether programs for lowering population growth and birth rates are politically acceptable or not appears to depend largely upon whether they are perceived as positive or negative: where "positive" means that they are seen as promoting other social values as well as population limitation and where "negative" means that they are seen as limited *per se*. For example, family planning programs, as noted above, are often rationalized as contributing both to maternal and child health and to the effective freedom of the individual family; a large-scale television network would contribute to other informational goals (though it is also politically suspect as providing too much power to the government in office); promotion of female participation in the labor force would add to economic productivity at the same time that it subtracted from the birth rate; extension of MCH services to rural areas is clearly desirable in itself, with or without family planning attached; incorporation of population material in school systems can be justified on educational grounds as well as population ones; a pension for the elderly would have social welfare benefits as well as indirect impact upon the large family as a social security system; contraceptive programs in Latin America are promoted by the medical community as a medical and humanitarian answer not to the population problem but to the extensive illegal and dangerous practice of abortion. On the other hand, imposing tax liabilities or withdrawing benefits after the Nth child, not to mention involuntary measures, can be attacked as a punitive means whose only purpose is that of population limitation.

It would thus require great political courage joined to very firm demographic convictions for a national leader to move toward an unpopular and severe prescription designed to cure his country's population ills. Indeed, it is difficult to envisage such a political move in an open society where a political opposition could present a counter view and perhaps prevail. Witness the views of two strong advocates of additional measures beyond family planning:

A realistic proposal for a government policy of lowering the birth rate reads like a catalogue of horrors .... No government will institute such hardship simply for the purpose of controlling population growth.[97]

If a perfected control agent were available now, I am certain that it would not be utilized in any democratic country, for no population would be likely to vote to have such agents used on itself. This means that the effects of overpopulation are not yet acute enough for people to accept an unpleasant alternative.[98]

The political problem of population control, like many political matters of consequence, is a matter of timing: in the 1950s nothing much could be done but in the 1960s a number of countries and international agencies moved at least as far as family planning programs. Political accommodation is typically a matter of several small steps with an occasional large one; and in this case it rests upon the seriousness with which the population problem is viewed. That is growing, hence political acceptability of added measures may also grow. Regardless of what the future may bring in this regard, several social measures like those in the list of proposals have been made from time to time and have encountered political obstacles. At least for the time being, such obstacles are real and must be taken into account in any realistic proposal.

The governmental decisions about measures taken to deal with undue population growth must be taken mainly by the countries directly involved: after all, it is their people and their nation whose prospects are most centrally affected. But in an interconnected world, with peace and human welfare at issue, others are properly concerned from both self-interested and humanitarian standpoints—other governments from the developed world, the international community, private groups. What of the political considerations in this connection?

A recommendation (G-1) that the United States exert strong political pressures to effect population control in developing countries seems more likely to generate political opposition abroad than acceptance. It is conceivable that such measures might be adopted by the Congress, though if so certainly against the advice of the executive agencies, but it is hardly conceivable that they would be agreed to by the proposed recipients. Such a policy is probably more likely to boomerang against a population effort than to advance the effort.

The proposal to create an international super-agency (G-2) seems more likely of success, but not without difficulty. WHO, UNICEF, and UNESCO have moved some distance toward family planning, if not population control, but only slowly and against considerable political restraint on the international front.[99] A new international agency would find the road easier only if restricted to the convinced countries. Certainly the present international organizations at interest would not be expected to abdicate in its favor. If it could be brought into being and given a strong charter for action, then almost by definition the international political climate would be such as to favor action by the present agencies, and then efficiency and not political acceptability would be the issue.

Administrative Feasibility. Given technical availability and political acceptability, what can actually be done in the field? This is where several "good ideas" run into difficulties in the developing world, in the translation of a theoretical probability into a practical program.

One of the underdeveloped elements of an underdeveloped country is administration: in most such countries there is not only a limited medical infrastructure but also a limited administrative apparatus to be applied to any program. Policies that look good on paper are difficult to put into practice—and that has been true in the case of family planning efforts themselves, where the simple organizational and logistic problems of delivering service and supplies have by no means been solved in several large countries after some years of trying. Again, this is one of the realities that must be dealt with in any proposals for action.

It is difficult to estimate the administrative feasibility of several of the proposals listed above, if for no other reason simply because the proponents do not put forward the necessary organizational plans or details. How are "fertility control agents" or "sterilants" to be administered on an involuntary mass basis in the absence of a central water supply or a food processing system? How are men with three or more children to be reliably identified in a peasant society and impelled to undergo sterilization against their will; and what is to be done if they decline, or if the fourth child is born? What is to be done with parents who evade the compulsory programs, or with the children born in consequence? How can an incentive system be honestly run in the absence of an organized network of offices positioned and staffed to carry out the regulatory activity? How can a system of social benefits and penalties, including marriage disincentives, be made to work under similar conditions?

Such questions are meant only to suggest the kinds of considerations that must be taken into account if proposals are to be translated into program. They are difficult but perhaps not insurmountable: somewhat similar problems have been addressed in the development of family planning programs themselves, as with the availability of medical and para-medical personnel. But it would seem desirable that every responsible proposal address itself to such administrative problems in the attempt to convert a proposal into a workable plan.

Some proposals do move in that direction. The plan to institutionalize maternal care in rural areas with family planning attached (A-1) is currently under study in several developing countries with regard to feasibility in administration, personnel, and costs. The plans for a national television system for informational purposes (C-2) have worked out some of the administrative problems, though the basic question of how to keep a television set working in a non-electrified area of a non-mechanical rural culture is not addressed and is not easy (as in the parallel case of keeping vehicles in working order under such conditions). The plan to build population into the school curriculum (C-1) has been carried forward to the preparation of materials and in a few cases beyond that.[100] The plans for incentive programs sometimes come down to only the theoretical proposition that people will do things for money, in this case refrain from having children; but in some cases the permissible payment is proposed on the basis of an economic analysis, and in a few cases an administrative means is also proposed.[101] The plan for wedding loans tied to the bride's age appreciates that a birth registration system might be needed in order to control against misreporting of age.[102]

Thus the *why* of population control is easy, the *what* is not very hard, but the *how* is difficult. We may know that the extension of popular education or the increase of women in the labor force or a later age of marriage would all contribute to population control in a significant way. But there remains the administrative question of how to bring those developments about. For example, the proposal (F-1) to organize the young men of India into a social service program, directed toward later age at marriage and general modernization of attitudes, is extremely difficult from an administrative standpoint even if it were acceptable politically and financially: consider the administrative, supervisory, and instructional problems in the United States of handling nine to ten million young men (the number affected in India), many of them unwilling participants easily "hidden" by their families and associates, in a series of camps away from home.[d] As has been observed, if a country could administer such a program it could more easily administer a family planning program, or perhaps not need one.

In short, several proposals assume administrable workability of a complicated scheme in a country that cannot now collect its own vital statistics in a reliable manner. Moreover, there is a near limit to how much administrative burden can be carried by the typical developing country at need: it cannot carry very many large-scale developmental efforts at the same time, either within the population field or overall. For population is not the only effort: agriculture, industry, education, health, communications, the military—all are important claimants. And within the field of population, a country that finds it difficult to organize and run a family planning program will find it still harder to add other programs along with that one. So difficult administrative choices must be made.

Economic Capability. From the standpoint of economic capability there are two questions: is the program worthwhile when measured against the criterion of economic return? and can it be afforded from present budgets even if worthwhile?

Most of the proposals probably pass the second screen: if scientifically available and politically and administratively acceptable, an involuntary fertility control agent would probably not be prohibitive economically; incorporation of population materials into the school curriculum is not unduly expensive, particularly when viewed as a long-term investment in population limitation; imposition of taxes or withdrawal of benefits or increased fees for marriage licenses might even return a net gain after administrative cost.

But a few proposals are costly in absolute if not relative terms. For example, the institutionalization of maternal care (A-1) might cost the order of $500 million for construction and $200 million for annual operation in India, or respectively $25 million and $10 million in a country of 25 million population[103] (although later estimates are substantially lower). The plan for a "youth

---

[d]In effect, Israel has a program of this general character, though not for population control purposes, but it is a highly skilled society especially from an administrative standpoint. I understand that the Ceylon Government has a program of "agricultural youth settlements," aimed jointly at youth unemployment and agricultural production but not population control. Of the 200,000 unemployed youth aged 19-25, the Government plans to settle 20-25,000 in the 1966-70 period.

corps" in India would cost upwards of $450 million a year if the participants were paid only $50 annually. The plan for pensions to elderly fathers without sons could cost from $400 million to $1 billion a year, plus administrative costs.[104] The satellite television system for India would cost $50 million for capital costs only on a restricted project,[105] with at least another $200 million needed for receiving sets, broadcast terminals, and programming costs if national coverage is to be secured (depending largely on distribution of sets); or, by another estimate, $30-35 million a year over 20 years (or $700 million—$440 million in capital outlay and $250 million in operating costs) in order to cover 84 percent of the population by means of nearly 500,000 receiving sets.[106] All of these proposals are intended to have beneficial consequences beyond population and hence can be justified on multiple grounds, but they are still expensive in absolute amounts.

The broad social programs of popular education, rationalization of agriculture, and increased industrialization (F-4) already absorb even larger sums though they could no doubt utilize even more. Here, however, the better question is a different one. Presently less than one percent of the total funds devoted to economic development in such countries as India, Pakistan, South Korea, and Turkey are allocated to family planning programs—in most cases, much less. Would that tiny proportion make a greater contribution to population control, over some specified period, if given over to education or industrialization or road-building, for their indirect effect, rather than utilized directly for family planning purposes?[107] From what we now know, the answer is certainly No.

Still other proposals, particularly those concerned with incentives and benefits, are more problematic, and unfortunately no clear directions are apparent. For comparative purposes, let us start with the generally accepted proposition that in the typical developing country today, one prevented birth is worth one to two times the per capita income, on economic grounds alone. In that case, the typical family planning program as currently operated is economically warranted in some substantial degree.[108] The per caput annual income of the developing countries under consideration range, say, from $75 to $500. In similar order of magnitude, the typical family planning program operates annually at about six cents per head, and in Taiwan and South Korea, where the programs are more effective, "each initial acceptor costs about $5; each acceptor continuing effective contraception for a year costs about $7-$10; each prevented birth costs, say, $20-$30 (at three years of protection per averted birth); and each point off the birth rate at its present level costs . . . about $25,000 per million population."[109]

This order of cost is not certified in all other situations, so even the economic value of family planning programs is not yet altogether clear[110] although most indications to date are that it is strongly positive.[e] Beyond family planning, the

[e]Even in the United States, where a recent study concluded that "Altogether, the economic benefits (of family planning programs) alone would be at least 26 times greater than the program costs": Arthur A. Campbell, "The Role of Family Planning in the Reduction of Poverty," *Journal of Marriage and the Family*, vol. 30, 1968, p. 243.

situation is still less clear. Assuming that some level of incentive or benefit would have a demographic impact, what would the level have to be to cut the birth rate by, say, 20 percent? We simply do not know: the necessary experiments on either administration or effectiveness have not been carried out. There is, of course, the possibility that what would be needed could not be afforded and that what could be afforded would not be effective.

For guidance, let us review what has been proposed with respect to incentives. Again we take the Indian case; and for comparative purposes, the present budget of the Indian family planning program is about $60 million a year, far higher than in the recent past (only about $11 million in the 1961-1966 Plan) and not yet fully spent.

On the ground that incentives for vasectomy are better than incentives for contraception-easier to administer and check on a one-time basis and likely to be more effective in preventing births[111]–Pohlman proposes for India a range of money benefits depending upon parity and group acceptance: from $7 to a father of four or more children if half the villagers in that category enter the program, up to $40 to a father of three children if 75 percent accept. If the 50 percent criterion were met in both categories throughout India, the current plan would cost on the order of $260 million in incentives alone, omitting administrative costs (based on these figures: 90 million couples, of whom about 40 percent are parity four and above, and 15 percent are parity three; or about 36.0 and 13.5 million respectively; half of each times $7 and $20 respectively). The decline in the birth rate would be slightly over one-fourth, perhaps a third, or of the order of $35-$40 a prevented birth by a rough estimate.[f]

Simon proposes an incentive of half the per capita income "each year to each fertile woman who does not get pregnant."[112] Here a special problem arises. In a typical developing population of 1000, about 25-30 percent of the married women of reproductive age (MWRA) give birth each year: 1000 population means from 145-165 MWRA, with a birth rate of, say, 40. Thus, incentives could be paid to about three-fourths of the women with no effect on the birth rate—since they would not be having a child that year under normal circumstances—so that the cost could be three to four times larger than "needed" for any desired result. Even if the incentive were fully effective, and each one really did prevent a birth, a cut of ten points in the Indian birth rate would cost of the order of $250 million (or 5 million prevented births at $50 each)—and substantially larger if the anyway non-pregnant, including the non- or semi-fecund, could not be screened out efficiently. (Compare this level of incentive with Spengler's suggestion of "rewards to those who prevent births—say $5-$10 per married couple of reproductive age each year they avoid having offspring."[113] In the typical case, the couple could collect for three years and then, as before, have the child in the fourth year; or, if an incentive of this size were effective, the cost would be four times the indicated level.)

Enke addresses himself to this problem by suggesting a system of blocked

---

[f]Mr. Pohlman has under preparation a major MS on this subject, entitled *Incentives in Birth Planning*.

accounts for Indian women who would have to remain non-pregnant for three to four years with examinations thrice yearly.[114] Here again the cost could be high: about $100 for three to four years of non-pregnancy at his proposed rates, or perhaps $500 million a year to effect a similar cut in the birth rate (i.e., over 20 million prevented births over four years at $100 each). And on the administrative side, the plan requires not only a substantial organization for management and record-keeping, but also the dubious assumption that the Indian peasant is sufficiently future-oriented and trustful of governmental bureaucracy.

Finally, Balfour has suggested an ingenious scheme for providing national saving certificates to married women in the reproductive ages who remain non-pregnant for three, four, five, or more years at the rate of about $3-$4 a year.[115] He estimates that this plan in action would cost about $200 per year per thousand population, which comes to about $100 million for all India.

But these are only speculations: to date we simply do not know whether incentives will lower a birth rate or rather, how large they would have to be in order to do so. These illustrations show only that an incentive program could be expensive. In any case, incentive systems would require a good amount of supervision and record-keeping; and presumably the higher the incentive (and hence the greater the chance of impact), the greater the risk of false reporting and the greater need of supervision—which is not only expensive but difficult administratively.

Moral/Ethical/Philosophical Acceptability. Beyond political acceptability, is the proposal considered right and proper—by the target population, government officials, professional or intellectual elites, the outside agencies committed to assistance?

"One reason the policy of seeking to make voluntary fertility universal is appealing—whether adequate or not—is that it is a natural extension of traditional democratic values: of providing each individual with the information he needs to make wise choices, and allowing the greatest freedom for each to work out his own destiny. The underlying rationale is that if every individual knowledgeably pursues his self-interest, the social interest will best be served."[116] But what if "stressing the right of parents to have the number of children they want . . . evades the basic question of population policy, which is how to give societies the number of children they need?"[117] Thus the issue rests at the center of political philosophy: how best to reconcile individual and collective interests.

Today, most observers would acknowledge that having a child is theoretically a free choice of the individual couple—but only theoretical in that this freedom is principled and legal. Many couples, particularly among the poor of the world, are not effectively free in the sense that they do not have the information, services, and supplies to implement a free wish in this regard. Such couples are restrained by ignorance, not only of contraceptive practice but of the consequences of high fertility for themselves, their children, and their country; they are restrained by religious doctrine, even though they may not accept the doctrine; they are restrained legally, as with people who would abort a pregnancy if that action were open to them; they are restrained culturally, as with women subject to the subordination that reserves for them only the child-bearing and child-rearing role. Hence effective freedom in child-bearing is by no means realized in the world today, as recent policy statements have remarked.[118]

Where does effective freedom lie? With the free provision of information and services for voluntary fertility limitation? With that plus a heavy propaganda campaign to limit births in the national interest? With that plus an incentive system of small payments? large payments? finders fees? With that plus a program of social benefits and penalties geared to the desired result? Presumably it lies somewhere short of compulsory birth limitation enforced by the state.

One's answer may depend not only on his own ethical philosophy but also upon the seriousness with which he views the population problem: the worse the problem, the more one is willing to "give up" in ethical position in order to attain "a solution." As usual, the important and hard ethical questions are those involving a conflict of values. In some countries, for example, people who are willing to provide temporary countraception as a means for population control under present circumstances are reluctant to extend the practice to sterilization and firmly opposed to abortion[g]—though again the wheel of history seems to be moving the world across that range under the pressure of population growth. But in some groups, notably religious groups, morality in this connection is absolute and no compromise with social need is to be tolerated, as for example in the case of Pope Paul's encyclical of July 1968.

How much in ethical values should a society be willing to forego for the solution of a great social problem? Suppose a program for population control resulted in many more abortions in a society where abortion is not only morally repugnant but also widely unavailable by acceptable medical standards: how much fertility decline would be "worth" the result? What of infanticide under the same conditions? How many innocent or unknowing men may be vasectomized for a fee (for themselves or the finders) before the practice calls for a moral restraint? How large an increase in the regulatory bureaucracy, or in

---

[g]The issue was sufficiently alive in classical times to prompt the great philosophers to take account of the matter in their political proposals. In Plato's *Republic*, "the number of weddings is a matter which must be left to the discretion of the rulers, whose aim will be to preserve the average of population (and) to prevent the State from becoming either too large or too small"—to which end certain marriages have "strict orders to prevent any embryo which may come into being from seeing the light; and if any force a way to the birth, the parents must understand that the offspring of such a union cannot be maintained, and arrange accordingly" (Modern Library edition, p. 412-414). In Aristotle's *Politics*, "on the ground of an *excess* in the number of children, if the established customs of the state forbid this (for in our state population has a limit), no child is to be exposed, but when couples have children in excess, let abortion be procured before sense and life have begun . . ." (Modern Library edition, p. 316).

systematic corruption through incentives, or in differential effect by social class to the disadvantage of the poor,[h] is worth how much decrease in the birth rate? How much association of childbearing with monetary incentive is warranted before "bribing people not to have children" becomes contaminating, with adverse long-run effects on parental responsibility?[i] How much "immorality," locally defined as extramarital sex, is worth importing along with how much contraceptive practice (assuming the association)? How much withholding of food aid is ethical, judged against how much performance in fertility decline? If it were possible to legislate a later age of marriage, would it be right to do so in a society in which young women have nothing else to do, and against their will? In countries, like our own, where urbanization is a serious population problem, is it right to tell people *where* to live, or to impose heavy economic constraints that in effect "force" the desired migration? Is it right to withdraw educational benefits from the children in "too large" families?—which is not only repressive from the standpoint of free education but in the long run would be unfortunate from the standpoint of fertility control. In the balance—and this is a question of great but neglected importance—what weight should be given to the opportunities of the next generations as against the ignorance, the prejudices, or the preferences of the present one?

These are not light questions, nor easy ones to answer. And they have not been seriously analyzed and ventilated, beyond the traditional religious concern about the acceptability of contraception and abortion. Most official doctrine in the emerging population programs is conservative—as is only to be expected at the outset of a great social experiment of this character.

Guidance on such ethical questions is needed. As an offer toward further consideration, these propositions are put forward: (1) "an ideal policy would permit a maximum of individual freedom and diversity. It would not prescribe a precise number of children for each category of married couple, nor lay down a universal norm to which all couples should conform";[119] correlatively, it would move toward compulsion only very reluctantly and as the absolutely last resort; (2) "an ideal program designed to affect the number of children people want

---

[h]After noting that economic constraints have not been adopted in South Asia, though often proposed, Gunnar Myrdal continues: "The reason is not difficult to understand. Since having many children is a main cause of poverty, such measures would penalize the relatively poor and subsidize the relatively well off. Such a result would not only violate rules of equity but would be detrimental to the health of the poor families, and so of the growing generation." *Asian Drama: An Inquiry into the Poverty of Nations*, Pantheon, 1968, vol. 2, pp. 1502-3.

[i]Frank W. Notestein, "Closing Remarks," in Berelson *et al.*, editors, *op. cit.*: "There is a real danger that sanctions, for example through taxation, would affect adversely the welfare of the children. There is also danger that incentives through bonuses will put the whole matter of family planning in a grossly commercial light. It is quite possible that to poor and harassed people financial inducements will amount to coercion and not to an enlargement of their freedom of choice. Family planning must be, and must seem to be, an extension of personal and familial freedom of choice and thereby an enrichment of life, not coercion toward its restriction." (pp. 828-29).

would help promote other goals that are worth supporting on their own merits, or at least not conflict with such goals";[120] correlatively, it would not indirectly encourage undesirable outcomes, e.g., bureaucratic corruption; (3) an ideal program would not burden the innocent in an attempt to penalize the guilty—e.g., would not burden the Nth child by denying him a free education simply because he was the Nth child of irresponsible parents; (4) an ideal program would not weigh heavily upon the already disadvantaged—e.g., by withdrawing maternal or medical benefits or free education from large families, which would tend to further deprive the poor; (5) an ideal program would be comprehensible to those directly affected—i.e., it should be capable of being understood by those involved and hence subject to their response; (6) an ideal program would respect present values in family and children, which many people may not be willing to bargain away for other values in a cost-benefit analysis; and (7) an ideal program would not rest upon the designation of population control as the final value justifying all others; "preoccupation with population growth should not serve to justify measures more dangerous or of higher social cost than population growth itself."[121]

Presumed Effectiveness. If proposals are scientifically ready, politically and morally acceptable, and administratively and financially feasible, to what extent will they actually work in bringing population growth under control? That is the final question.

Again we do not know the answer. We are not even sure in the case of family planning programs with which we now have some amount of experience. But as an order of magnitude and as a kind of measuring rod for other proposals, the impact of family planning programs, when conducted with some energy at the rate of investment indicated above, ranges roughly as follows: in situations like Singapore, South Korea, and Taiwan, they have recruited 20-33 percent of the married women of reproductive age as contraceptive acceptors within 3-4 years, and in difficult situations like India and Pakistan, from 5-14 percent of the target population.[j] In other settings, like Malaysia or Ceylon or Turkey or Kenya or Tunisia or Morocco, either it is too early to tell or the program has been conducted under political or other restraints so that it is difficult to say what an energetic program could have achieved; as it is, family planning is being introduced into such situations at a pace politically acceptable and administratively feasible. Overall, it appears that a vigorous program *can* extend contraceptive practices by an economically worthwhile amount wherever conducted.[122]

---

[j]Figures based on monthly reports from national programs. Since most of the Indian achievement is in sterilization, it may have a more pronounced effect. For a sophisticated analysis of the Taiwan effort that concludes, "What we are asserting with some confidence is that the several hundred thousand participants in the Taiwan program have, since entering the program, dramatically increased their birth control practice and decreased their fertility," see Robert G. Potter, Ronald Freedman, and L.P. Chow, "Taiwan's Family Planning Program," *Science*, vol. 160, 24 May 1968, p. 852.

What of the proposals beyond family planning? How well might they do, given administrative implementation?

To begin with, the compulsory measures would probably be quite effective in lowering fertility. Inevitably in such schemes, strongly motivated people are ingenious enough to find ways "to beat the system"; if they were numerous enough the system could not be enforced except under severe political repression.[k] Otherwise, if workable, compulsion could have its effect.

What about the proposals for the extension of voluntary contraception? Institutionalizing maternal care in the rural areas with family planning attached does promise to be effective over, say, five to ten years, particularly in its potential for reaching the younger and lower parity women. The International Postpartum Program did have that effect in the urban areas, [123] and presumably the impact would extend to the rural areas though probably not to the same degree because of the somewhat greater sophistication and modernization of the cities. The importance of the particular target is suggested in this observation: "The objective in India is to reach not the 500 million people or the 200 million people in the reproductive ages or the 90 million married couples or even the 20-25 million who had a child this year—but the 5 million women who gave birth to their first child. And this may be the only institutionalized means for reaching them."[124] The total program is costly, but if it could establish family planning early in the reproductive period in a country like India, and thus encourage the spacing of children and not just stopping, it could have great demographic value in addition to the medical and humanitarian contribution.

A liberalized abortion system, again if workable, could also be effective in preventing unwanted births, but it would probably have to be associated with a contraceptive effort: otherwise there might be too many abortions for the system as well as for the individual woman (who might need three a year to remain without issue; in Mainland China, where abortion on demand is available, it is reported that a woman may have only one a year[125]). Free abortion for contraceptive failures would probably make for a fertility decline, but how large a one would depend upon the quality of the contraceptive program. With modern contraception (the IUD and the pill) the failure rates are quite small, but women who only marginally tolerate either method, or both, would be available for abortion. Free abortion on demand has certainly lowered fertility in Japan and certain Eastern European countries,[l] and where medically feasible would do

---

[k]In this connection, see the novel by Anthony Burgess, *The Wanting Seed*, Ballantine Books, 1963. At the same time, a longtime observer of social affairs remarks that "the South Asian countries . . . can, to begin with, have no other principle than that of voluntary parenthood . . . State direction by compulsion in these personal matters is not effective . . ." (Myrdal, *op. cit.*, p. 1501).

[l]For example, the repeal of the free abortion law in Rumania resulted in an increase in the birth rate from 14 in the third quarter of 1966 to 38 in the third quarter of 1967. For an early report, see Roland Pressat, "La suppression de l'avortement légal en Roumanie: premiers effets," *Population*, vol. 22, 1967, pp. 1116-18.

so elsewhere as well; as a colleague observes, in this field one should not underestimate the attraction of a certainty as compared to a probability. Abortion for illegitimate pregnancies, whether voluntary (A-2) or required (B-4), would not have a large impact on the birth rate in most developing countries since known illegitimacy is small (assuming that the children of the numerous consensual unions and other arrangements in Latin America are not considered "illegitimate").

The educational programs, whether in the school system or in the mass media, would almost certainly have an effect over the years though it will be difficult for technical reasons to determine the precise or even approximate degree of impact. Anything that can be done to "bring home" the consequences of undue population growth to family and nation will help reach the goal of fertility decline, but in the nature of the case education alone will have a limited effect if life circumstances remain stable.

The large question of the effect of the various incentive and benefit/liability plans (D and E) simply cannot be answered: we have too little experience to know much about the conditions under which financial factors will affect childbearing to any substantial degree. Perhaps everyone has his price for everything; if so, we do not know what would have to be paid, directly or indirectly, to persuade people not to bear children.

Such as it is, the evidence from the *pro*-natalist side is not encouraging. All the countries of Europe have family allowance programs of one kind or another,[126] most of them legislated in the 1930s and 1940s to raise the birth rate; collectively they have the lowest birth rate of any continent. The consensus among demographers appears to be that such programs cannot be shown to have effected an upward trend in the birth rate where tried. A recent review of the effect of children's allowances upon fertility concludes:

It would be helpful to be able to state categorically that children's allowances do or do not increase the number of births among families that receive them. Unfortunately, there is no conclusive evidence one way or the other . . . To argue that the level of births in the United States or anywhere else depends upon the existence, coverage, and adequacy of a set of family allowances if certainly simplistic. Such a conclusion can and ought to be rejected not only on logical grounds but also on the basis of the demonstrated complexity of the factors producing specific birthrates . . . Recent fertility statistics show no relation between the existence or character of a family allowance program and the level of the birthrate. In specific low-income agricultural countries with such programs, fertility is high. In specific high-income modernized nations with such programs, fertility is low . . . Whether the less developed countries have any form of family or children's allowances appears wholly unrelated to the level of fertility.[127]

As in the case of abortion for illegitimate pregnancies, several of the benefit/liability proposals would affect only a trivial fraction of people in much of the developing world: for example, again in India, programs for governmental employees who make up perhaps 5 percent of the labor force, tax or social security systems where the rural masses are not regularly covered, maternity benefits since so few women are covered, fees for marriage licenses, control of public housing which is insignificant, denial of education benefits to married students who are trivially few and not now covered in any case. Such measures are probably more relevant to the developed than the developing countries. However, because the impact of incentive and benefit/liability plans is uncertain and may become important, the field needs to become better informed on the possibilities and limitations, which information can only come from experimentation under realistic circumstances and at realistic levels of payment.

A higher age of marriage and a greater participation of women in the labor force are generally credited with effecting fertility declines. In India, average female age at marriage has risen from about 13 to about 16 in this century, or about half a year a decade, although the age of marital consummation has remained rather steady at 17 years (since most of the rise is due to the decrease in child marriages). In a recent Indian conference on raising age at marriage, the specialists seemed to differ only on the magnitude of the fertility decline that would result: a decline of 30 percent in the birth rate in a generation of 28 years if the minimum female age of marriage were raised to 20[128] or a decline of not more than 15 percent in 10 years[129]—"seemed to" since these figures are not necessarily incompatible. In either case, the decline is a valuable one. But the effectiveness of increased age of marriage rests in the first instance on its being realized; here are the perhaps not unrepresentative views of knowledgeable and committed observers:

. . . In the absence of prolonged education and training, postponing the age of marriage becomes a formidable problem (Chandrasekhar).
. . . Legislation regarding marriage can rarely be used as a measure of fertility control in democratic countries. The marital pattern will mostly be determined by social circumstances and philosophies of life and any measure by government clashing with them will be regarded as a restriction on freedom rather than a population policy (Dandekar)[131]

Similarly, an increase in the proportion of working women—working for payment outside the home—might have its demographic effect,[m] but could probably come about only in conjunction with other broad social trends like education and industrialization, which themselves would powerfully affect fertility (just as a fertility decline would assist importantly in bringing them

---

[m]However, see David Chaplin, "Some Institutional Determinants of Fertility in Peru," in this volume for some evidence that welfare and labor regulations in Peru discourage the employment of women in low-fertility occupations (factory work) by making them more expensive to employ than men. Laws thus designed to promote maternity do so only by default since the higher fertility of the disemployed women will occur outside the protection of adequate medical and welfare institutions.

about).[n] Both compulsory education and restrictions on child labor would lower the economic value of children and hence tend toward fertility decline: The question is, how are they to be brought about?

Finally, whether research would affect fertility trends depends of course upon its nature and outcome, aside from the general proposition that "more research" as a principle can hardly be argued against. Most observers believe that under the typical conditions of the developing society, any improvement in the contraceptive technology would make an important difference to the realization of present fertility goals and might make an important contribution to turning the spiral down. Indeed, several believe that this is the single most important desideratum over the short run. Easy means for sex determination should have some effect upon the "need for sons" and thus cut completed family size to some extent. Research on the social-economic side would probably have to take effect through the kinds of programs discussed above.

The picture is not particularly encouraging. The measures that would work to sharply cut fertility are politically and morally unacceptable to the societies at issue, as with coercion, and in any case unavailable; or they are difficult of attainment in any visible future, as with the broad social trends or shift in age of marriage. The measures that might possibly be tried in some settings, like some version of incentives or benefit/liability plans, are uncertain of result at the probable level of operation. Legalization of abortion, where medically available, would almost certainly have a measurable effect, but acceptability is problematic.

Conclusion

Where does this review leave us with regard to proposals beyond family planning? Here is my own summary of the situation.

(1) There is no easy way to population control. If this review has indicated nothing else, it has shown how many obstacles stand in the way of a simple solution to the population problem—or a complicated one for that matter. By way of illustrative capitulation, let us see how the various proposals seem to fit

---

[n]Actually, recent research is calling into question some of the received wisdom on the prior need of such broad institutional factors for fertility decline. If further study supports the new findings, that could have important implications for present strategy in the developing countries. See Ansley J. Coale, "Factors Associated with the Development of Low Fertility: An Historic Summary," *Proceedings of the United Nations World Population Conference,* 1965, vol. 2, pp. 205-9; and his paper, "The Decline of Fertility in Europe from the French Revolution to World War II," prepared for University of Michigan Sesquicentennial Celebration, November 1967.

the several criteria, in the large (Table 5-1).° That is only one observer's judgment of the present situation, but whatever appraisal is made of specific items it would appear that the overall picture is mixed. There is no easy way.

(2) Family planning programs do not compare unfavorably with specific other proposals—especially when one considers that any *actual* operating program is disadvantaged when compared with any competitive *ideal* policy. (As any practical administrator knows, when an "ideal" policy gets translated into action it develops its own set of realistic problems and loses some of the shine it had as an idea.) Indeed, on this showing, if family planning programs did not exist, they would have to be invented: it would appear that they would be among the first proposals to be made and the first programs to be tried, given their generally acceptable characteristics.

In fact, when such proposals are made, it turns out that many of them call for *more* family planning not less, but only in a somewhat different form. In the present case, of the proposals listed above, at least a third put forward in effect simply another approach to family planning, often accepting the existing motivation as to family size. In any case, family planning programs are established, have some momentum, and, importantly, would be useful as the direct instrument through which other proposals would take effect. So that, as a major critic acknowledges, "there is no reason to abandon family-planning programs."[132]

What is needed is the energetic and full implementation of present experience; this is by no means being done now. Much more could be done on the informational side, on encouragement of commercial channels of contraception, on the use of para-medical personnel, on logistics and supply, on the training and supervision of field workers, on approaches to special targets ranging from post-partum women to young men under draft into the armed forces. If the field did well what it knows how to do, that in itself would in all likelihood make a measurable difference—and one competitive in magnitude with other specific proposals—not to mention the further impetus of an improved contraceptive technology.

(3) Most of the proposed ideas are not new; they have been around for some time. So if they are not in existence, it is not because they were not known but

---

°As the roughest sort of summary of table 5-1, if one assigns values from 5 for High to 1 for Low on each of the 6 dimensions, the various proposals rank as follows:

Family Planning Programs	25
Intensified Educational Campaigns	25
Augmented Research Efforts	24
Extension of Voluntary Fertility Control	20
Shifts in Social and Economic Institutions	20
Incentive Programs	14
Tax and Welfare Benefits and Penalties	14
Political Channels and Organizations	14
Establishment of Involuntary Fertility Control	14

Table 5-1
Illustrative Appraisal of Proposals by Criteria

	Scientific Readiness	Political Viability	Administrative Feasibility	Economic Capability	Ethical Acceptability	Presumed Effectiveness
A. Extension of Voluntary Fertility Control	High	High on maternal care, moderate to low on abortion	Uncertain in near future	Maternal care too costly for local budget, abortion feasible	High for maternal care, low for abortion	Moderately high
B. Establishment of Involuntary Fertility Control	Low	Low	Low	High	Low	High
C. Intensified Educational Campaigns	High	Moderate to high	High	Probably high	Generally high	Moderate
D. Incentive Programs	High	Moderately low	Low	Low to moderate	Low to high	Uncertain
E. Tax and Welfare Benefits and Penalties	High	Moderately low	Low	Low to moderate	Low to moderate	Uncertain
F. Shifts in Social and Economic Institutions	High	Generally high, but low on some specifics	Low	Generally low	Generally high, but uneven	High, over long run
G. Political Channels and Organizations	High	Low	Low	Moderate	Moderately low	Uncertain
H. Augmented Research Efforts	Moderate	High	Moderate to high	High	High	Uncertain
Family Planning Programs	Generally high, but could use improved technology	Moderate to high	Moderate to high	High	Generally high, but uneven on religious grounds	Moderately high

because they were not accepted—presumably, for reasons like those reflected in the above criteria. In India, for example, several of the social measures being proposed have been, it would seem, under almost constant review by one or another committee for the past 10-15 years—withdrawal of maternity benefits, imposition of a child tax, increase in age of marriage, liberalization of legal abortion, incorporation of population and family planning in the school curriculum.[133] In Mainland China, reportedly, later age of marriage is common among party members,[134] and in Singapore a 1968 law restricts maternity privileges beyond the third child for employed women and makes public housing available to childless couples.[135] As for general social development—compulsory education, industrialization, improved medical care, etc.—that is in process everywhere, though of course more can always be done (but not very quickly). So it is not correct to imply that it is only new ideas that are needed; many ideas are there, but their political, economic, or administrative feasibility is problematic.

(4) The proposals themselves are not generally approved by this set of proposers, taken together. All of them are dissatisfied to some degree with present family planning efforts, but that does not mean that they agree with one another's schemes to do better. Thus, Ohlin believes that "the demographic significance of such measures (maternity benefits and tax deductions for children) would be limited. By and large those who now benefit from such arrangements in the developing countries are groups which are already involved in the process of social transformation" and that "changes in marital institutions and norms are fairly slow and could not in any circumstances reduce fertility sufficiently by itself when mortality falls to the levels already attained in the developing world."[136] Ketchel opposes several "possible alternatives to fertility control agents":

Financial pressures against large families would probably be effective only in developed countries in which there are large numbers of middle-class people. In underdeveloped countries practically no financial inducements to have children now exist to be reversed, and the imposition of further taxes upon the many poor people would depress their living standards even further . . . In order to be effective, economic pressures would probably have to be severe enough to be quite painful, and when they reached a level of painfulness at which they were effective, they would probably seriously affect the welfare of the children who were born in spite of the pressures . . . The same objection applies to the use of financial rewards to induce people not to have children because such programs would make the families with children the poorer families . . . The age at which people marry is largely determined by slowly changing cultural and economic factors, and could probably be changed quickly in a population only by rather drastic measures (in which) an inordinately severe punishment for violators would be required . . . Statutory regulations of family size would be unenforceable unless the punishment for exceeding the limit was so harsh that it would cause harm to the lives of the existing children and their parents. Such possible procedures as vasectomizing the father or implanting long-acting contraceptives in the mother would require a direct physical assault by a government agent on the body of an individual.[137]

Meier argues against the tax on children on both humanitarian and political grounds.[138] To the UN Advisory Mission to India, he said "it is realised that no major demographic effects can be expected from measures of this kind (maternity benefits), particularly as only a small proportion of families are covered ... but they could contribute, together with the family planning programme, to a general change in the social climate relating to childbearing."[139] Earlier, in supporting a family planning effort in India, Davis noted that "the reaction to the Sarda Act (the Child Marriage Restraint Act of 1929) prohibiting female marriage (below 14) shows the difficulty of trying to regulate the age of marriage by direct legislation."[140] Myrdal warns against cash payments to parents in this connection, as a redistributional reform, and supports social awards to the children in kind.[141] Kirk believes that "it might prove to be the height of folly to undermine the existing family structure, which continues to be a crucial institution for stability and socialization in an increasingly mobile and revolutionary society."[142] Raulet believes that "Davis' main observation ... that alternatives to the present stress on familism will ultimately be required ... obviously makes no sense for most less developed countries today ... Aside from the repressive tone of some of (the proposed) measures, the most striking thing about these proposals is the impracticality of implementing them ... The application of social security measures and negative economic sanctions ... are so far beyond the present economic capacities of these countries, and would raise such difficult administrative and economic problems, that they are probably not worth serious mention."[143] Finally, Ehrlich is contemptuous of the professors whose "idea of 'action' is to form a committee or to urge 'more research.' Both courses are actually substitutes for action. Neither will do much good in the crisis we face now. We've got lots of committees, and decades ago enough research had been done at least to outline the problem and make clear many of the steps necessary to solve it. Unless those steps are taken, research initiated today will be terminated not by success but by the problem under investigation."[144]

(5) In a rough way, there appears to be a progression in national efforts to deal with the problem of population control. The first step is the theoretical recognition that population growth may have something to do with the prospects for economic development. Then, typically, comes an expert mission from abroad to do a survey and make a report to the government, as has occurred in India, Pakistan, South Korea, Turkey, Iran, Tunisia, Morocco, and Kenya among others. The first action program is in family planning, and most of the efforts are still there. Beyond that, it apparently takes (1) some degree of discouragement over progress combined with (2) some heightened awareness of the seriousness of the problem to move the effort forward. To date those conditions have been most prominently present in India—and that is the country that has gone farthest in the use of incentives and in at least consideration of further steps along the lines mentioned above. It may be that in this respect the Indian experience is a harbinger of the international population scene. It is only natural that on matters of such sensitivity, governments try "softer" measures

before "harder" ones; and only natural, too, that they move gradually from one position to the next to realize their goals. Indeed, some proposals require prior or simultaneous developments, often of a substantial nature: for example a loan system tied to age of brides may require a good system of vital registration for purpose of verification, instruction in population in the schools requires some degree of compulsory education, tying family planning to health programs requires a medical infrastructure.

Finally, it is also worth noting that more extreme or controversial proposals tend to legitimate more moderate advances, by shifting the boundaries of discourse.

(6) Proposals need to be specified—proposals both for action schemes and for further research. It is perhaps too much to ask advocates to spell out all the administrative details of how their plan is to operate in the face of the kinds of obstacles and difficulties discussed above, or even get permission to operate: the situations, settings, opportunities, and personalities are too diverse for that. But it does seem proper to ask for the fullest possible specification of actual plans, under realistic conditions, in order to test out their feasibility and likely effectiveness. The advocates of further research similarly ought to spell out not only what would be studied and how, but also how the results might be applied in action programs to affect fertility. Social research is not always readily translated into action, especially into administrative action; and the thrust of research is toward refinement, subtlety, precision, and qualification whereas the administrator must act in the large. Short of such specification, the field remains confronted with potentially good ideas like "raise the age of marriage" or "use incentives" or "substitute pension systems for male children" without being able to move very far toward implementation.

(7) Just as there is no easy way, there is no single way. Since population control will at best be difficult, it follows that every acceptable step be taken that promises some measure of impact. The most likely prospect is that population control, to the degree realized, will be the result of a combination of various efforts—economic, legal, social, medical—each of which has some effect but not an immediately overwhelming one.[p] Accordingly, it is incumbent upon the professional fields concerned to look hard at various approaches, including family planning itself, in order to screen out what is potentially useful for application. In doing so, on an anyway difficult problem, it may be the path of wisdom to move with the "natural" progression. Some important proposals seem

---

[p]It begins to appear that the prospects for fertility control may be improving over the decades. After reviewing several factors that "favor a much more rapid (demographic) transition than occurred in the West"—changed climate of opinion, religious doctrine, decline of infant mortality, modernization, fertility differentials, grass roots concern, and improved contraceptive technology—Dudley Kirk shows in a remarkable tabulation that the later a country began the reduction of its birth rate from 35 to 20, the shorter time it took to do so: from 73 years (average) in 1831-1860, for example, to 21 years after 1951, and on a consistently downward trend for over a century. (In his "Natality in the Developing Countries: Recent Trends and Prospects," prepared for University of Michigan Sesquicentennial Celebration, November 1967, pp. 11-13.)

reasonably likely of adoption—institutionalization of maternal care, population study in the schools, the TV satellite system for informational purposes, a better contraceptive technology, perhaps even liberalization of abortion in some settings—and we need to know not only how effective such efforts will be but, beyond them, how large a money incentive needs to be to effect a given amount of fertility control and how effective those indirect social measures are that are decently possible of realization. It may be that some of these measures would be both feasible and effective—many observers 15 years ago thought that family planning programs were neither—and a genuine effort needs to be made in the next years, wherever feasible, to do the needed experimentation and demonstration. The "heavy" measures—involuntary means and political pressures—may be put aside for the time being, if not forever.

(8) In the last analysis, what will be scientifically available, politically acceptable, administratively feasible, economically justifiable, and morally tolerated depends upon people's perceptions of consequences. If "the population problem" is considered relatively unimportant or only moderately important, that judgment will not support much investment of effort. If it is considered urgent, much more can and will be done. The fact is that despite the large forward strides taken in international recognition of the problem in the 1960s, there still does not exist the informed, firm, and constant conviction in high circles that this is a matter with truly great ramifications for human welfare.[q] Such convictions must be based on sound knowledge. Here it would appear that the demographers and economists have not sufficiently made their case to the world elite—or that, if made, the case has not sufficiently been brought to their attention or credited by them. Population pressures are not sharply visible on a day-to-day or even year-to-year basis nor, short of major famine, do they lend themselves to dramatic recognition by event. Moreover, the warnings of demographers are often dismissed, albeit unfairly and wrongly, on their record of past forecasts:[145] after all, it was only a generation ago that a declining population was being warned about in the West. It is asking government leaders to take very substantial steps indeed when population control is the issue—substantial for their people as well as for their own political careers—and hence the case must be not only substantial but virtually incontrovertible. Accordingly, the scientific base must be carefully prepared (and perhaps with some sense of humility about the ease of predicting great events, on which the record is not without blemishes). Excluding social repression and mindful of maximizing human freedom, greater measures to meet the problem must rely on heightened awareness of what is at stake, by leaders and masses alike.

What is beyond family planning? Even if most of the specific plans are not particularly new, that in itself does not mean that they are to be disregarded. The questions are: which can be effected, given such criteria? how can they be implemented? what will be the outcome?

---

[q]Nor, often, among the general public. For example, in mid-summer 1968 the Gallup Poll asked a national sample of adults: "What do you think is the most important problem facing this country today?" Less than one per cent mentioned population. (Gallup release, 3 August 1968, and personal communication.)

This paper is an effort to promote the discourse across the professional fields concerned with this important issue. Given the recent stress on family planning programs as the "means of choice" in dealing with the problem, it is natural and desirable that counter positions should be put forward and reviewed. But that does not in itself settle the critical questions. What can we do now to advance the matter? Beyond family planning, what?

Notes

1. As one example, see "Declaration on Population: The World Leaders' Statement", signed by 30 heads of state, in *Studies in Family Planning*, no. 26, January 1968.

2. For example, see Kingsley Davis, "Population Policy: Will Current Programs Succeed?," in this volume. Robert G. Potter, Ronald Freedman, and L.P. Chow, "Taiwan's Family Planning Program," *Science*, vol. 160, 24, May 1968, p. 848-53; and Frank W. Notestein, "Population Growth and Its Control," MS prepared for American Assembly meeting on World Hunger, Fall 1968.

3. See, for example, the section on "Goals" in Davis, op. cit., pp. 50-54, and the 1968 presidential address to the Population Association of America, "Should the United States Start a Campaign for Fewer Births?," by Ansley J. Coale.

4. For current targets of some national family planning programs, see table 8, p. 39, and accompanying text in Bernard Berelson, "National Family Planning Programs: Where We Stand," prepared for University of Michigan Sesquicentennial Celebration, November 1967, which concludes: "By and large, developing countries are now aiming at the birth rates of Western Europe 75 years ago or the United States 50 years ago."

5. For a first effort to outline the matter, see point 12, pp. 46-51, in Berelson, op. cit.

6. Howard C. Taylor Jr. and Bernard Berelson, "Maternity Care and Family Planning as a World Program," *American Journal of Obstetrics and Gynecology*, vol. 100, 1968, pp. 885-93.

7. Davis, op. cit., pp. 52-66.

8. Paul R. Ehrlich, *The Population Bomb*, Ballantine Books, 1968, p. 139.

9. S. Chandrasekhar, "Should We Legalize Abortion in India?," *Population Review*, 10, 1966, 17-22.

10. Melvin M. Ketchel, "Fertility Control Agents as a Possible Solution to the World Population Problem," *Perspectives in Biology and Medicine*, vol. 11, 1968, pp. 687-703. See also his "Should Birth Control Be Mandatory?," *Medical World News*, 18 October 1968, pp. 66-71.

11. Ehrlich, op. cit., pp. 135-36. The author appears to dismiss the scheme as unworkable on page 136 though two pages later he advocates "ample funds" to "promote intensive investigation of new techniques of birth control, possibly leading to the development of mass sterilizing agents such as were discussed above."

12. Kenneth E. Boulding, *The Meaning of the Twentieth Century: The Great Transition*, Harper & Row, pp. 135-36. For the record, I note a statement that appeared too late for consideration but does argue for "mutual coercion, mutually agreed upon by the majority of the people affected": Garrett Hardin, "The Tragedy of the Common," *Science*, 162, 13 December 1968, p. 1247.

13. William B. Shockley, in lecture at McMaster University, Hamilton, Ontario, reported in *New York Post*, 12 December 1967.

14. Sripati Chandrasekhar, as reported in *The New York Times*, 24 July 1967. Just as this paper was being completed, the same author "proposed that every married couple in India deny themselves sexual intercourse for a year . . . Abstinence for a year would do enormous good to the individual and the country" (as reported in *The New York Times*, 21 October 1968). The reader may wish to consider this the 30th proposal and test it against the criteria that follow.

15. Davis, op. cit., p. 66.

16. Ibid.

17. Sloan Wayland, "Family Planning and the School Curriculum," in Bernard Berelson et al., eds., *Family Planning and Population Programs*, University of Chicago Press, 1966, pp. 353-62; his "Population Education, Family Planning and the School Curriculum," MS prepared for collection of readings edited by John Ross and John Friesen, *Family Planning Programs: Administration, Education, Evaluation*, forthcoming 1969; and two manuals prepared under his direction: *Teaching Population Dynamics: An Instructional Unit for Secondary School Students* and *Critical Stages in Reproduction: Instruction Materials in General Science and Biology*, both Teachers College, Columbia University, 1965.

18. Pravin Visaria, "Population Assumptions and Policy," *Economic Weekly*, 8 August 1964, p. 1343.

19. Ehrlich, op. cit., p. 162.

20. Richard L. Meier and Gitta Meier, "New Directions, A Population Policy for the Future," University of Michigan, revised MS, October 1967, p. 11.

21. UNESCO Expert Mission, *Preparatory Study of a Pilot Project in the Use of Satellite Communication for National Development Purposes in India*, 5 February 1968, especially the section on "The Population Problem," pp. 13-14, paras. 61-66.

22. Wilbur Schramm and Lyle Nelson, *Communication Satellites for Education and Development—The Case of India*, Stanford Research Institute, July 1968: "Family Planning," pp. 63-66.

23. Sripati Chandrasekhar, as reported in *The New York Times*, 19 July 1967. Here again I note for the record a very recent "Proposal for a Family Planning Bond," by Ronald J. Ridker, USAID—India, July 1968. This memorandum is a comprehensive and quite detailed review of the issues involved in providing 20-year bonds for couples sterilized after the second or third child. Along this same line, see another late suggestion of a bond linked both to age of marriage and to number of children, in *Approaches to the Human Fertility*

Problem, prepared by The Carolina Population Center for the United Nations Advisory Committee on the Application of Science and Technology to Development, October 1968, p. 68.

24. Edward Pohlman, "Incentives for 'Non-Maternity' Cannot 'Compete' with Incentives for Vasectomy," Central Family Planning Institute, India, MS 1971.

25. T.J. Samuel, "The Strengthening of the Motivation for Family Limitation in India," *The Journal of Family Welfare*, vol. 13, 1966, pp. 11-12.

26. Davis, op. cit., p. 65.

27. Julian Simon, "Money Incentives to Reduce Birth Rates in Low-Income Countries: A Proposal to Determine the Effect Experimentally"; "The Role of Bonuses and Persuasive Propaganda in the Reduction of Birth Rates"; and "Family Planning Prospects in Less-Developed Countries, and a Cost-Benefit Analysis of Various Alternatives," University of Illinois, MS 1966-1968.

28. Stephen Enke, "Government Bonuses for Smaller Families," *Population Review*, vol. 4, 1960, pp. 47-54.

29. Samuel, op. cit., p. 12.

30. Michael Young, in "The Behavioral Sciences and Family Planning Programs: Report on a Conference," *Studies in Family Planning*, no. 23, October 1967, p. 10.

31. Dipak Bhatia, "Government of India Small Family Norm Committee Questionnaire," *Indian Journal of Medical Education*, vol. 6, October 1967, p. 189. As the title indicates, this is not a proposal as such but a questionnaire soliciting opinions on various ideas put forward to promote "the small family norm."

32. Stephen Enke, "The Gains to India from Population Control," *The Review of Economics and Statistics*, May 1960, pp. 179-80.

33. Joseph J. Spengler, "Agricultural Development is Not Enough," MS prepared for Conference on World Population Problems, Indiana University, May 1967, pp. 29-30.

34. J. William Leasure, "Some Economic Benefits of Birth Prevention," *Milbank Memorial Fund Quarterly*, 45, 1967, pp. 417-25.

35. Marshall C. Balfour, "A Scheme for Rewarding Successful Family Planners," Memorandum, The Population Council, June 1962.

36. W. Parker Mauldin, "Prevention of Illegitimate Births: A Bonus Scheme," Memorandum, The Population Council, August 1967.

37. Ehrlich, op. cit., p. 138.

38. Bhatia, op. cit., p. 188.

39. Samuel, op. cit., p. 14.

40. Davis, op. cit., p. 65.

41. Richard M. Titmuss and Brian Abel-Smith, *Social Policies and Population Growth in Mauritius*, Methuen, 1960, pp. 130-31.

42. Bhatia, op. cit., p. 189.

43. Titmuss and Abel-Smith, op. cit., pp. 131-36.

44. Davis, op. cit., p. 65.

45. Bhatia, op. cit., pp. 189-90.

46. Samuel, op. cit., pp. 12-14.

47. Spengler, op. cit., p. 30.

48. Bhatia, op. cit., p. 190.

49. Davis, op. cit., p. 65.

50. Bhatia, op. cit., p. 190.

51. Titmuss and Abel-Smith, op. cit., p. 137.

52. Samuel, op. cit., p. 12-14.

53. Davis, op. cit., p. 65.

54. Ehrlich, op. cit., pp. 136-37.

55. A.S. David, *National Development, Population and Family Planning in Nepal*, June-July 1968, pp. 53-54.

56. James Fawcett, personal communication, September 1968.

57. Samuel, op. cit., p. 12.

58. Goran Ohlin, *Population Control and Economic Development*, Development Centre of the Organization for Economic Cooperation and Development, 1967, p. 104.

59. W. Phillips Davison, personal communication, 4 October 1968. Davison suggests a good pension (perhaps $400 a year) for men aged 60, married for at least 20 years, with no sons.

60. David, op. cit., p. 53.

61. Davis, op. cit., p. 64.

62. Young, op. cit., p. 10.

63. Titmuss and Abel-Smith, op. cit., p. 130.

64. Kingsley Davis, personal communication, 7 October 1968.

65. Ehrlich, op. cit., p. 138.

66. Bernard Berelson, Amitai Etzioni, brief formulations, 1962, 1967.

67. Philip M. Hauser, in "The Behavioral Sciences and Family Planning Programs: Report on a Conference," *Studies in Family Planning*, no. 23, October 1967, p. 9.

68. Davis, op. cit., p. 65.

69. David, op. cit., p. 54.

70. Judith Blake, "Demographic Science and the Redirection of Population Policy," in Mindel C. Sheps and Jeanne Clare Ridley, eds., *Public Health and Population Change: Current Research Issues*, University of Pittsburgh Press, 1965, p. 62.

71. Davis, op. cit., p. 65.

72. Meier and Meier, op. cit., p. 9. For the initial formulation of the proposal, see Richard L. Meier, *Modern Science and the Human Fertility Problem*, Wiley, 1959, chapter 7, esp. p. 171 ff.

73. Philip M. Hauser, " 'Family Planning and Population Programs': A Book Review Article," *Demography*, vol. 4, 1967, p. 412.

74. United Nations Economic and Social Council. Commission on the Status of Women. "Family Planning and the Status of Women: Interim Report of the Secretary-General," 30 January 1968, esp. p. 17 ff.

75. Roger Revelle, as quoted in "Too Many Born? Too Many Die. So Says Roger Revelle," by Milton Viorst, *Horizon*, Summer 1968, p. 35.

76. David M. Heer and Dean O. Smith, "Mortality Level and Desired Family Size," paper prepared for presentation at Population Association of America meeting, April 1967. See also David A. May and David M. Heer, "Son Survivorship Motivation and Family Size in India: A Computer Simulation," *Population Studies*, 22, 1968, pp. 199-210.

77. Ehrlich, op. cit., pp. 161-66, passim. The author makes the same point in his article, "Paying the Piper," *New Scientist*, 14 December 1967, p. 655: "Refuse all foreign aid to any country with an increasing population which we believe is not making a maximum effort to limit its population . . . The United States should use its power and prestige to bring extreme diplomatic and/or economic pressure on any country or organization [the Roman Catholic Church?] impeding a solution to the world's most pressing problem."

78. Ehrlich, op. cit., p. 138. In the earlier article cited just above, he calls for a "Federal Population Commission with a large budget for propaganda," presumably limited to the United States (p. 655).

79. S. Chandrasekhar, "India's Population: Fact, Problem and Policy," in S. Chandrasekhar, ed., *Asia's Population Problems*, Allen & Unwin, 1967, p. 96, citing a Julian Huxley suggestion of 1961.

80. Meier and Meier, op. cit., p. 5.

81. Davis, op. cit., pp. 50-56.

82. Davis, op. cit., pp. 65-67.

83. Steven Polgar, in "The Behavioral Sciences and Family Planning Programs: Report on a Conference," *Studies in Family Planning*, no. 23, October 1967, p. 10. See also the recent suggestion of research on "the possibilities for artificially decreasing libido," in *Approaches to the Human Fertility Problem,* op. cit., p. 73.

84. National Academy of Sciences, Committee on Science and Public Policy, *The Growth of World Population*, 1963, pp. 5, 28-36. This recommendation has of course been made on several occasions by several people: "we need a better contraceptive." For an imaginative account of the impact of biological developments, see Paul C. Berry, *Origins of Positive Population Control, 1970-2000*, Working Paper, Appendix to *The Next Thirty-Four Years: A Context for Speculation*, Hudson Institute, February 1966.

85. For example, see Sheldon J. Segal, "Biological Aspects of Fertility Regulation," MS prepared for University of Michigan Sesquicentennial Celebration, November 1967.

86. Z. Dvorak, V. Trnka, and R. Vasicek, "Termination of Pregnancy by Vacuum Aspiration," *Lancet*, vol. 2, 11 November 1967, pp. 997-98; and D. Kerslake and D. Casey, "Abortion Induced by Means of the Uterine Aspirator," *Obstetrics and Gynecology*, vol. 30, July 1967, pp. 35-45.

87. A.S. Parkes, "Can India Do It?," *New Scientist*, vol. 35, July 1967, p. 186.

88. United Nations Advisory Mission, *Report on the Family Planning*

Programme in India, February 1966. See Chapter XI: "Social Policies to Promote Family Planning and Small Family Norms."

89. Bhatia, op. cit.

90. Central Family Planning Council, Resolution No. 8, January 1967, in *Implications of Raising the Female Age at Marriage in India*, Demographic Training Research Centre, 1968, p. 109; and *Centre Calling*, May 1968, p. 4.

91. Samuel, op. cit., p. 12.

92. United Nations Advisory Mission, op. cit., p. 87.

93. *Planned Parenthood*, March 1968, p. 3.

94. Report in *The New York Times*, September 12, 1968.

95. *Planned Parenthood*, April 1968, p. 2

96. Davidson R. Gwatkin, "The Use of Incentives in Family Planning Programs," Memorandum, Ford Foundation, November 1967, pp. 6-7.

97. Davis, op. cit., pp. 66-67.

98. Ketchel, op. cit., p. 701.

99. For a review of this development see Richard Symonds and Michael Carder, *International Organizations and Population Control (1947-1967)*, Institute of Development Studies, University of Sussex, April 1968.

100. See footnote 17. At present population materials are being included in school programs in Pakistan, Iran, Taiwan, and elsewhere.

101. As, for example, with Balfour, Mauldin, and Pohlman, op. cit.; and for the economic analysis, Enke and Simon, op. cit.

102. Davis, op. cit. (footnote 64).

103. Taylor and Berelson, op. cit., p. 892.

104. Davison, op. cit., and revised figures.

105. UNESCO Expert Mission, op. cit., p. 23.

106. Schramm and Nelson, op. cit., pp. 164-68. passim.

107. For the negative answer, see Enke and Simon, op. cit. Data from family planning budgets and national development budgets contained in five-year development plans.

108. Enke and Simon, op. cit.; see also Paul Demeny, "Investment Allocation and Population Growth," *Demography*, vol. 2, 1965, pp. 203-32; and his "The Economics of Government Payments to Limit Population: A Comment," *Economic Development and Cultural Change*, vol. 9, 1961, pp. 641-44.

109. Berelson, op. cit. (footnote 4), p. 20.

110. Warren Robinson, "Conceptual and Methodological Problems Connected with Cost-Effectiveness Studies of Family Planning Programs" and David F. Horlacher, "Measuring the Economic Benefits of Population Control: A Critical Review of the Literature," Working Papers nos. 1 & 2, Penn State-U.S. AID Population Control Project, May 1968.

111. Pohlman, op. cit.

112. Simon, "Family Planning Prospects . . .," op. cit., (footnote 27), p. 8.

113. Spengler, op. cit., pp. 29-30. The Population Council is just now completing an analysis of the possible effects and costs of incentive programs with differing assumptions as to acceptance and continuation.

114. Enke, "The Gains . . .," op. cit., (footnote 32), p. 179.

115. Balfour, op. cit.

116. Coale, op. cit., p. 2. However, the author does point out, a few sentences later, that "it is clearly fallacious to accept as optimal a growth that continues until overcrowding makes additional births intolerably expensive."

117. Davis, op. cit., p. 65.

118. For example, The World Leaders' Statement, op. cit.; and the Resolution of the International Conference on Human Rights on "Human Rights Aspects of Family Planning," adopted 12 May 1968, reported in *Population Newsletter* issued by the Population Division, United Nations, no. 2, July 1968, p. 21 ff.

119. Coale, op. cit., p. 7.

120. Coale, op. cit., p. 7.

121. Coale, op. cit., p. 6.

122. Berelson, op. cit., pp. 35-38.

123. Gerald I. Zatuchni, "International Postpartum Family Planning Program: Report on the First Year," *Studies in Family Planning*, no. 22, August 1967, p. 14 ff.

124. Howard C. Taylor, Jr., personal communication.

125. Edgar Snow, "The Chinese Equation," *The* (London) *Sunday Times*, January 23, 1966.

126. See U.S. Department of Health, Education, and Welfare, Social Security Administration. "Social Security Programs Throughout the World, 1964."

127. Vincent H. Whitney, "Fertility Trends and Children's Allowance Programs," in Eveline M. Burns, editor, *Children's Allowances and the Economic Welfare of Children: The Report of a Conference*, Citizens' Committee for Children of New York, 1968, pp. 123, 124, 131, 133.

128. S.N. Agarwala, "Raising the Marriage Age for Women: A Means to Lower the Birth Rate," in *Implications of Raising the Female Age at Marriage in India*, Demographic Training and Research Centre, 1968, p. 21.

129. V.C. Chidambaram, "Raising the Female Age at Marriage in India: A Demographer's Dilemma," in *Implications,* op. cit., p. 47.

130. Chandrasekhar, op. cit. (footnote 79), p. 96.

131. Kumudini Dandekar, "Population Policies," *Proceedings of the United Nations World Population Conference*, 1965, p. 4.

132. Davis, op. cit., pp. 66-67. The same critic was a strong advocate of family planning in India, and quite optimistic about its prospects even in the pre-IUD or pill era and with a health base. See Kingsley Davis, "Fertility Control and the Demographic Transition in India," in *The Interrelations of Demographic, Economic, and Social Problems in Selected Underdeveloped Areas*, Milbank Memorial Fund, 1954, concluding:

"Although India is already well-launched in the rapid-growth phase of the demographic transition, there is no inherent reason why she should long continue in this phase. She need not necessarily wait patiently while the forces of urbanization, class mobility, and industrial development gradually build up to the point where parents are forced to limit their offspring on their own initiative and without help, perhaps even in the face of official opposition . . . Realistically appraising her situation, India has a chance to be the first country to achieve a major revolution in human life—the planned diffusion of fertility control in a peasant population prior to, and for the benefit of, the urban-industrial transition." (pp. 87-88).

133. See, for example, Visaria, op. cit., p. 1343; Bhatia, op. cit.; Samuel, op. cit., p. 12; U.N. Advisory Mission, op. cit., Chapter XI; Chandrasekhar, in *Asia's Population Problem, op. cit.; Myrdal, op. cit., p. 1502; Implications* . . ., op. cit.; and "Shah Committee Recommends Liberalization of Abortion Laws," *Family Planning News*, September 1967, p. 23.

134. Snow, op. cit.

135. K. Kanagaratnam, personal communication, August 8, 1968.

136. Ohlin, op. cit., pp. 104, 105.

137. Ketchel, op. cit., pp. 697-99.

138. Meier, op. cit., p. 167.

139. United Nations Advisory Mission, op. cit., p. 87.

140. Davis, op. cit., 1954, p. 86.

141. Myrdal, op. cit., p. 1503.

142. Dudley Kirk, "Population Research in Relation to Population Policy and National Family Planning Programs," paper presented at meetings of the American Sociological Association, August 1968.

143. Harry M. Raulet, *Family Planning and Population Control in Developing Countries*, Institute of International Agriculture, Michigan State University, November 1968, pp. 5-6, 49-50.

144. Ehrlich, op. cit., p. 191.

145. For an old but enlightening review, see Harold Dorn, "Pitfalls in Population Forecasts and Projections," *Journal of the American Statistical Association*, vol. 45, 1950, pp. 311-34.

Part II: Latin American Population Policies

Family Planning and American Goals

J. Mayone Stycos

For a nation which sometimes has trouble getting its priorities straight, the United States has recently shown admirable clarity in focusing on the significance of the population problem. As early as August 1965 Lyndon Johnson put the problem in a new and startling perspective when he announced that, "Second only to the search for peace, it is humanity's greatest challenge." While most proponents of population reacted ecstatically, a few refused to accept even a second billing for population problems. Thus, Raymond Ewell told the National Academy of Science's Agricultural Research Institute that the food-population problem "will in a few years dwarf and overshadow such political problems as Vietnam, Cuba, the Congo, Cyprus, Kashmir, Berlin, and others."[1] Seemingly convinced, President Johnson subsequently announced that "Man's *greatest* problem is the fearful race between food and population [italics added]." Even though he reassigned it "next to the pursuit of peace . . ." in his 1967 State of the Union message, one can only conclude from these and 29 other Johnsonian statements on population that the biggest problems on the mind of the president of the United States over the past two years have been peace and population.

President Johnson could not be accused of having been a man far ahead of his public, and other Washington influentials have emitted powerful echoes to the presidential credoes. Thus, in October 1966, the United States Senate was told by Joseph Tydings that "There can no longer be any doubt . . . that this Congress was determined to defuse the population bomb. The population clock ticks every hour of every day. There is not a moment to lose in dealing with what President Johnson has called the most profound challenge to the future of the world."[2] In March, Senator Fulbright told his colleagues that "population growth is the greatest single obstacle to economic growth in much of the underdeveloped world;"[3] and after 28 public hearings on the population problem, Senator Gruening likened the givers of testimony to the "pioneers [who signed] the Declaration of Independence, and those who ratified the Constitution of the United States."[4]

But heroism of the word appears singularly unmatched by heroism of the deed. As President Johnson was telling the nation that "The time for rhetoric has clearly passed, the time for concerted action is here and we must get on with

Reprinted from *World Population and U.S. Government Policy and Programs*, Franklin T. Brayer, M.D., Editor (Washington: Georgetown University Press) pp. 19-44.

the job,'" AID's top man in population was having difficulty getting his letters typed. In 1965 AID expended on the world's number-two problem an amount equivalent to the cost of seven M-60 tanks; in 1966, the cost of seven attack helicopters, and in 1967, somewhat more than the cost of a B-52 bomber. Even in 1968, a year of potential budgetary triumph for population activity, AID has been allocated for its worldwide program in population considerably less than India has budgeted for its national program.

Money which failed to materialize for foreign programs was rapidly matched by money which failed to materialize for domestic programs. In April 1967 Senator Tydings could complain that "the promise of significantly increased funds for domestic family planning programs has proved illusory . . . even the limited family planning services offered in antipoverty programs are struggling to remain at present funding levels. The prospects that the OEO would expand the services and institute new services . . . which appeared likely a year ago . . . have now virtually vanished . . . the executive branch has completely let us down."[5]

In the Department of Health, Education and Welfare, although the Secretary established family planning as one of "six priority areas," a consultants' report written for the department late in 1967 could state that "none of the DHEW Regional Officers or operating agencies presently places high priority on family planning . . . the actions of the 90th Congress made clear it is considerably ahead of most DHEW officials in recognizing the need for greatly expanded Federal assistance in the delivery of family-planning services. In our view, the department must respond with prompt and vigorous action, not merely on the level of policy, but on the more meaningful level of allocation of resources."[6]

What accounts for so great a discrepancy between talk and action that even seasoned Washingtonians are beginning to note it? If the popular theory be correct that the Johnson barrage has been part of a carefully timed series of "trial balloons," there can be little doubt that Washington's air-corridors are now clogged with suspended spheres which have never been shot down. (The only exception is Johnson's Birth Control Bargain Speech of June 1965 brought down in a single shot by Pope Paul's address at the United Nations, and subsequently trampled on by the bargain-suspicious Latin American press.) To account for the phenomenon, more historical background is necessary.

Americans have always enjoyed the luxury of being the most planless nation in the world. That private property is sacred and inviolate, that waste is fun, and that that government is best which governs least are aspects of the American credo of individual freedom which have enabled us to plunder our natural resources, keep both beauty and function at a minimum in our cities, effect gross inefficiencies in political administration, pay enormous sums for pedestrian education, perpetuate a bizarre system of medical services, etc.—and still be "better off" than any nation. If Americans have paid dearly for the privilege of planlessness, it is a measure of their prosperity that they *have* been able to pay. Thus far, no more efficient society has been rich enough to cause us chagrin at our mindless extravagance, and only the threat of war or being beaten in a cosmic race compels an inward look at the benefits of planning.

There has been, however, a minor but increasingly important goad to national planning in the United States—it is our own insistence to our less affluent brothers that Planning is Necessary, and that Planning is Good. These principles, which appear so self-evident to Americans when looking at foreign countries, are embarrassingly absent from our own way of life. Since it would violate our democratic principles to answer the foreigners' innocent query about American planning by replying honestly that, "We're too rich to need it," we have shown an increasing willingness to consider planning in the United States. Indeed, if underdeveloped nations did not exist, surely American liberal intellectuals would have invented them, to compel careful local introspection about the merits of planning. With respect to population problems, the impact has been excruciating.

Not only has the United States never had a population policy, but for most of its history it has had an ethos favoring population growth. America achieved spectacular additions to its labor force in the nineteenth century virtually without cost. Europe was the manpower factory which bore the costs of producing, rearing, and educating men and women to the point where they could be shipped totally assembled and duty-free to America's burgeoning industries. America's seemingly boundless resources, its vast territories, the expanding world markets, the bargain-rate European labor force, and industry's quest for an ever-increasing number of consumers led to the equation of a growing with a healthy population.

So deeply ingrained was pronatalist thinking in this country that the first serious social-psychological studies of fertility were initiated in the 1930s, and not as a response to the threat of overpopulation, but as a response to the threat of population *decline*. That the United States rate of population growth might be slowed by deliberate national action has, prior to the mid-sixties, never been a matter for serious consideration among United States policy makers.

If a pronatalist, or at best laissez-faire, attitude has been characteristic at the macrodemographic level, at the level of the family, the deliberate restriction of fertility has always been practiced but not preached. (This is to be compared with our current national population policies, which are preached but not practiced.) Foreign Catholics have always marveled at the efficiency and power of the Church-militant in the United States, but the puritanical strains of Protestantism have perhaps been equally influential in the suppression of contraceptive information in this country. While it has always been sinful to utilize contraceptive devices in most states of the Union, as late as 1965 it was both sinful and criminal in the state of Massachusetts. (A tribute to American regional diversity was the fact that what one could go to jail for in Massachusetts was being dispensed free by the state of South Carolina. Another interesting way of looking at it is that the only significant group denied birth control in the North has been the Negroes, while in the South they are the only significant group which gets it free.)

It is true that while Margaret Sanger was being jailed and vilified, the American birth rate continued unperturbedly to decline, but the public reaction to family planning in the United States has varied between disgust and silent resignation to a necessary evil. At best it was viewed as so delicate and risky that it was a matter of "individual conscience." As such, it was a matter so totally private, so sacred (or profane), that no external agents, and certainly not the state, should have anything to do with it. As late as 1958, when the Draper Committee on the Foreign Aid Program recommended to President Eisenhower that the United States "increase its assistance to local programs relating to maternal and child welfare" and "assist these countries . . . on request, in the formulation of their plans designed to deal with the problems of population growth," the president reacted with astonishment and indignation. "I cannot imagine anything more emphatically a subject that is not a proper political or governmental activity," he stormed. "This Government will not . . . . as long as I am here, have a positive doctrine in its program that has to do with birth control. That's not our business."

In short, the United States, which has always been reluctant to plan anything, has been especially loathe to promote planning within a sacred private institution by means sometimes considered obscene, immoral, or criminal. What has caused the abrupt verbal shift from this position? In addition to the change in popular values and in the position of the Catholic Church there has been an accelerating acceptance of at least three principles: (1) that population increase in the underdeveloped areas is impeding their modernization and dissipating the effects of United States economic aid, (2) that it is now technologically feasible to lower national birth rates, and (3) that what we do unto others we must do unto ourselves. None of these beliefs was seriously entertained a decade ago in high government circles, and partly explains the hollowness of many of the recent words emitted in Washington—there is simply no infrastructure to back up the new ideology.

Economic Aid. While the economic development of most of the non-European nations has been disappointingly slow, the evolution of their expectations for possessing the good things of this life has been alarmingly rapid. For example, in Latin America the gains attributable to the Alliance for Progress, while substantial in an absolute sense, fall so far short of the Latin nations' needs and expectations that pressures have built up rapidly to "do something." One obvious answer is more external capital, but with a war abroad and rumblings of economic discontent at home, the United States is in no position materially to increase economic aid. This has led to renewed respect and attention to our foreign-aid dollar. Since it must be stretched, there is not only a greater concern for long-range planning but also a search for new ways of maximizing our developmental investments. This search soon came to rest on a demographic diagnosis and a medical prescription. First, Washington became aware that population increase was consuming much of potential economic and social gains of development, and then began to see that population control investments might have high positive returns. The first phase has been pressed hard by General William Draper, who frequently states unequivocally that "unless and until the population explosion now erupting in Asia, Africa, and Latin America is brought under control, our entire economic aid program is doomed to failure."[7] As early as June 1965 Senator Clark advised the United States Senate to promote family planning for the underdeveloped countries, ". . . thus preventing American aid from being poured down a rat-hole."[8] Moreover, the world agricultural setbacks in the mid-sixties, and the increasing awareness that the United States grain surpluses were rapidly disappearing have produced a return to Malthusian pessimism among many of the Capitol's agricultural experts. According to the New Poetry of the War on Hunger, "the stork is outrunning the plow."

The major economic apologist for direct attack on the population problem has been Stephen Enke, who flatly told the 1965 World Population Conference that " 1 percent of total developmental budgets spent reducing births could be as effective in raising output per head as the other 99 percent altogether." Elsewhere he calculated "the value of permanently preventing a birth in a typical Afro-Asian country is about $250," while the actual cost of doing so is only about one dollar a year per participant.[9] This hardheaded approach to Man's Greatest Challenge has swayed some of the hardest heads in Washington. President Johnson, for example, broke the news to a startled United Nations audience in June 1965 by saying, "Let us act on the fact, that less than five dollars invested in population control is worth a hundred dollars invested in economic growth." While Johnson's experienced budgetary hand had upped the cost ratio substantially, one thing was clearly nailed down: Family Planning was the Bargain of the Development Decade.

Technology. Before the sixties, even those few developmental economists who saw a relation between population growth and economic modernization went little farther than to worry about it, since they believed that population growth rates could never be manipulated in the underdeveloped areas. Aside from the question of religious tabus, birth-control technology was so crude that very high motivation was required to practice it effectively. Without a "technological breakthrough," it was felt it was easier to adjust the economy to the population than to adjust the population to fit the economic situation. The development of the oral progesterones and the intrauterine devices, their acceptance by lower-class populations in pilot projects, and the willingness of a number of governments to allocate significant budgets to their dissemination has caused many of the economists to take a second look at the "controllability" of demographic variables. Others, however, are pinning their hope on a second breakthrough—a morning-after pill, an immunizing injectible, or even mini-pills. Interestingly enough, the basic research in reproductive physiology necessary for rapid technological development in contraception is as highly underdeveloped in the United States as our applied programs of family planning. A succinct indication of the state of our knowledge was given late in 1967 by a distinguished medical researcher at a high-level conference of population experts: "Nobody," he said, "can yet tell me how the IUD works."

What We Do Unto Others. For decades in the United States, small organized groups of courageous women have been insisting that the health and social welfare of the woman depend on the ability rationally to regulate the number and timing of her births. Such arguments received the degree of respect and attention normally accorded to small organized groups of courageous women in the United States. At the same time, however, a handful of less vociferous but more influential men of affairs began to be concerned about the economic and political implications of world population growth, and in particular, about the growth of the underdeveloped areas. Their fears included Starvation, Unrest, War, and Communism. While the means sought by both groups were identical, both the ends desired and the *modi operandi* were entirely different. Not only were there few men among the family planners and few women among the population planners, but their average personalities and methods of working were very different. The women were more concerned with American than with foreign problems, and they wanted to antagonize and do public battle both with the Church and with puritanism. They opened clinics, distributed leaflets, defied laws, and went to jail. The men located the problem beyond American shores, desired scientific study of the problem and discreet programs of public information. They established philanthropic foundations, sponsored international meetings of scholars, set up news bureaus, and endowed chairs. While the two groups avoided each other as much as possible, when thrown together at an occasional conference, they regarded each other with the combined suspicion and hope of exploitation found only at a social function of Ivy League boys and Townie girls.

The successes of the men were evidenced by the creation of such agencies and organizations as the Demographic Division of the United Nations, the Population Reference Bureau, and the Population Council. Before long, considerable numbers of foreigners were trained in the U.S. as demographers, to such an extent that American demographers often complained that the foundations were virtually anti-American in their prejudices. New competence in demography combined with a new orientation toward rational social and economic planning forced upon many developing nations the significance of their newly derived census statistics. While Eisenhower was still insisting that family planning was a private affair, several Asian countries were pressuring the international agencies for technical and financial assistance, and only the assurance of being turned down kept them from requesting aid from the United States.

Meanwhile, the family planners had achieved the important objective of making family planning a more serious public issue which could be openly discussed and debated, but their legal and clinical gains were painfully slow in coming. For example, in 1967, the year in which the United States Department of Health, Education and Welfare proudly appointed a deputy assistant secretary for population and family planning, Title XVIII of the United States Code still prohibited use of the United States mails for contraceptive materials or advertising; and the Tariff Act of 1930 still prohibited the importation to the United States of any contraceptive drug or article. (Should the letter of the law dampen the new assistant secretary's enthusiasm for importing or mailing the contraceptive materials and information she was presumably hired to disseminate, it was also true that she probably would not even be able to *carry* them, since she was having the utmost difficulty in getting clearance to create a small staff to assist her.)

While Americans are accustomed to lagging laws, they are not accustomed to lagging services. Yet, even today, our greatest cities are only beginning to introduce family-planning programs with public funds. "It was only eight years ago," Dr. Hans Lehfeld noted recently, "that the first municipal birth control clinic was opened in New York City. Many other American cities still have no such clinics at all."[10] A recent analysis of family planning services in New York, New Jersey, Pennsylvania, and Delaware led to the conclusion that outside of New York City, "only about 11 percent of the target populations are being served."[11] In 1965, the year in which AID issued its first instruction on population problems to all its missions, less than 5 percent of all United States short-term general hospitals reported the availability of family planning services, and about three-quarters of all local health departments in the United States offered no family-planning services. In that year, probably no more than 300,000 United States women received family planning assistance through hospitals or local health agencies, and an additional 200,000 medically indigent women received assistance from Planned Parenthood agencies. While perhaps a half million are receiving some form of public assistance on family planning, "*it is estimated that as a minimum, five million fertile medically indigent women in the United States are unable to afford contraceptive services.*"[12]

The middle class, of course, has smugly continued to receive contraceptive assistance from private physicians, unaware of the short change they are receiving from a profession hardly better educated about contraception than their patients. According to a recent study, of 78 non-Catholic medical schools, seven include no materials on family planning in their curricula and 17 others offer no clinical observation and practice. Of the schools which offer any instruction at all, half devote no more than *two hours* during the four years of medical school.[13] Nurses probably get even less. "Very little basic knowledge was given to us as students,"[14] complained Nurse Elizabeth Edmands of Johns Hopkins School of Hygiene and Public Health recently, leaving open the question of whether the nurses *ever* learn. As for the doctors, one can only hope that after leaving the medical school they read about family planning, since they apparently fail to talk about it. When a national survey of physicians was asked, "How frequently does the subject of conception control come up for discussion when you are with other doctors?" only 2 percent said "often," and three-quarters said "rarely" or "never." Perhaps it is a blessing that half of them admitted they never introduce the topic of family planning to their patients, even "in situations in which it is appropriate."[15]

("Love-ins" or no, the children of the middle class seem no more enlightened than their parents. Dr. Joseph English, chief psychiatrist of the Peace Corps, recently mused in apparent wonder that "we thought we could assume with this population that comes from the middle class and good colleges that they would know something about family planning. The remarkable things was to hear from our medical consultants, psychiatrists, and health educators around the country, how totally naive a remarkable percentage of this population was about basic things.")[16]

In the face of this massive conspiracy about birds, bees, and IUDs, it is another tribute to the native cunning of the American people that they have been able to keep the national birth rate within reasonable limits. But by what stretch of the imagination can we condescend to other nations about family planning or population control? We can only conclude on the moral side as one honest physician concluded recently on the technical side. "As an assisting nation," said the War on Hunger's deputy administrator ruefully, "our position on the technical side of population work is all too similar to that of the developing countries."[17]

But if the home front was a shambles on birth control facilities, ideologically and organizationally there has been a consolidation of forces of some importance, and the distinction between the family planners and the population controllers has faded markedly. During the summer of 1967, while the head of the Planned Parenthood Federation of America was in Asia advising the Thais and Indonesians on their population problems, the head of the Ford Foundation's population division was in Washington advising on the domestic family-planning program. Around the time that the Population Council added a division on technical assistance, planned parenthood added a division on research, and if the Population Council still employs few women, it is clear that the masculine takeover of Planned Parenthood is nearing completion. As the men began talking to the women, even their conference formats changed. Almost as if a concordat had been signed, all demographic conferences now end with a section on family planning, and all family planning conferences open with a section on demography. Thus, the needs on the world front have forced upon us an awareness of the shabby condition of our own house. Nevertheless, it would be unrealistic to assume that this house will be put in order before we either preach or do unto others. While Senator Tydings has requested $230 million for the domestic program over the next five years, Senator Fulbright has proposed somewhat more for overseas assistance, and the Citizens' Committee on Population at the 1965 White House Conference recommended twice as much for foreign aid, amounting annually to a current day's cost of the Vietnam War. If the half Vietday allocated to AID for 1968 is small in relation to the magnitude of the problem, it is nevertheless large in terms of the trouble it could cause if misspent. So ill prepared at home, what are the dangers involved in our exportation of population control? We turn to Latin America, a region slowly awakening to the population problem, as an example of the hazards ahead.

The Case of Latin America[18]

Although most of the Latin American nations have extraordinarily high rates of population growth, the recentness of this phenomenon plus the existence of vast unsettled land areas in South America have helped to suppress concern about population problems among the region's intellectuals.[19] Because of religious tabus, moreover, public discussion of population and birth control has been muted. So effective was the blanketing of news on these themes that, as late as 1965, former Colombian president and distinguished journalist Alberto Lleras Camargo referred to population control as "el gran tabu" of our century.

Beginning in the early 1960s, however, a combination of circumstances caused the topics of the "population explosion" and contraception to become public issues in most Latin American countries. These circumstances included publication of preliminary results from the 1960 censuses, which generally indicated higher rates of growth than had been supposed; the opening up of the topic for debate on the part of the Vatican; technological innovations such as "the pill," which lent themselves to journalistic treatment; and the promotional activities of North American private and government agencies that had previously written off Latin America as closed to birth-control programs. In 1965, the Cornell International Population Program decided to determine the extent of attention to population problems and family planning in Latin American newspapers and began to collect newspaper clippings on these topics. Through the services of the Burrelle's Press Clipping Bureau, a surprising total of six thousand clippings was obtained in 1965, and over eight thousand were gathered in 1966. Approximately three-quarters of these articles explicitly mentioned birth control or contraceptive methods.

Thus, population and birth control have become public issues in Latin America just at the time when North American official policy with respect to foreign aid on population problems is being crystallized. What have been the Latin American reactions to the emerging North American positions? Publicly, there has been an almost total absence of enthusiasm, at best, and in most cases the reactions have ranged from suspicion to hostility. The expressed opinions have contained little reference to religious questions and have been more likely to impugn North American political or economic motives. Thus, the Chilean ambassador to the United States noted that family planning "is a problem which cannot be used as a lever for the international egotism of the rich nations, in allowing them to evade their duties of assistance and solidarity with the developing nations."[20] In leading the 1965 defeat of a proposal that UNICEF give assistance in the family-planning area, the Peruvian delegate, a former minister of health, "voicing the views of other Latin American delegates, agreed that countries like India and Pakistan have overwhelming population growth. He explained that Latin America, however, has 'empty lands and untapped resources' and if UNICEF gets itself involved in population control, rich nations might be tempted to reduce economic aid and concentrate on birth control assistance instead."[21]

Nationalism. Often fueled by anti-American sentiments, nationalism is a powerful force cutting across political identifications in Latin America. With reference to population, however, its manifestations on the Right are somewhat different from those on the Left. In large countries such as Brazil and Argentina, nationalists of the Right argue that a larger population is needed to develop the vast interior and make the nation strong. For example, during the August debate in Brazil over the possibility of United States aid on population problems, Dr. Fabio Fonseca, president of the Belo Horizonte Regional Council of Medicine, stated that Brazil needs a population twice its present size in order to settle the vast empty spaces of the country. He warned that "the yellow race, which is becoming more and more numerous, needs space to live and will not hesitate to seek uninhabited places like the immense Brazilian regions if this settlement is not promoted."[22]

A representative of the Brazilian Chamber of Deputies charged that population control was being "imposed on us by a country with the dimensions of Brazil but with 300 million [sic] people, giving the impression that the American people with their land already overpopulated is concerning itself with our empty spaces and intends to occupy our territory."[23]

A feature article in the newspaper *O Povo* claimed that the key to Brazilian prosperity lies in her beds and hammocks. It asked for more population so that Brazil's lands will cease to figure in the schemes of Western or Eastern imperialists as reserves of natural resources or vital space. "Brazilians," the article concluded, "let us continue loving and proliferating. God did not give us all this greatness for the installation of abortion or sterilization industries. Onward! To the children!"[24]

On the issue of family planning, nationalism causes the rightists to reject American cultural and moral values while gladly accepting America's dollars. As stated by the Archbishop of Brasilia, Dom José Newton de Almeida Batista, "Give us dollars and we shall be powerful, provided that we also grow in number so that we can take possession of the immense territory God gave us."[25] Even more pointed was the headline in the conservative Catholic Peruvian monthly *ERPA*: "Latin America Needs Dollars, Not Pills." Under a photograph of President Johnson mounted on a horse, it noted, "From his Texas ranch, Johnson directs the control of births in Latin America. What about nonintervention, Mr. President?"[26] The invasion of foreign morality disturbs both religious and secular rightists, for it is a form of "psychic imperialism" that imperils spiritual and cultural values viewed as close to the heart and soul of the nation. The abortion of national growth along with the substitution of alien values is a combination especially unsavory to nationalists of the Right.

While nationalists of the Right want dollars instead of pills, nationalists of the Left feel Latin America can afford neither. *Both* dollars and pills are regarded as ameliorative measures to shore up a crumbling society whose demise had much better be brought about by revolution. Three Colombian university professors expressed the idea this way:

Birth control is dangerous because it can become a distraction, or a justification for the bourgeoisie to reject change. . . . It might prevent the agrarian reform from ever taking place.

With our system of production we can support about ten million. Since we have seventeen million we are overpopulated, but if our pattern of production were altered we could support fifty million or more. The reason why they want birth control is that they don't want a technical revolution. Birth control is a palliative measure which cannot lead to anything.

Birth control is being proposed as a panacea, which is utopian, false, and treacherous.[a]

The following citation from the Brazilian newspaper *Correio de Manhã* of August 10, 1966, illustrates the mix of nationalist and reformist sentiments:

Neo-malthusianism is manipulated by the big laboratories . . . and pharmaceutical houses . . . . The reactionary attitude is not that of the Catholic Church but of the family planners . . . for commercial reasons, out of North American geopolitical interests (so there will not be a prevalence of underdeveloped populations, or Asiatics, or United States Communists), and out of fear of structural reforms . . . . Brazil, lacking in mechanical resources, depends for her economic progress on her working force. It should not be with birth control financed by the National Development Bank and the Alliance for Progress or foreign enterprises that our country will succeed in developing herself, but through drastic modification of the social and economic structures.

Marxist Influence on Latin American Thought. Whether through the writings of Marx himself or through his present-day exponents in Europe and China, Marxist ideology on population continues to have a powerful influence on Latin American intellectuals of all persuasions but the far Right. Consequently, the initial reaction of the typical intellectual to the question of population growth is that the real problems are social and economic and that any other view must be concealing ulterior motives. The need for basic social and economic reform, moreover, is obvious to virtually all persons of influence in Latin America; the Right talks about it, the Center means it, and the Left means it right now. Mass education, industrialization, agrarian reform, more equitable distribution of wealth, health, and happiness are the ingredients, which vary in priority, timing, and means of accomplishment; but nearly everyone is concerned that somehow and sometime they be realized. These needs are so crushing, so obvious, and so imminent that to talk of anything else appears to many only a diversionary tactic.

---

[a]As part of a 1966 summer project in Colombia of the International Population Program, Sergio Sismondo carried out an investigation of the attitudes of Colombian university professors toward economic development and population problems. Fifty-one interviews were completed, divided more or less evenly among the departments of sociology, economics, philosophy and humanities, and psychology in a leading Colombian university. The universe was defined as the total staffs in these departments, except in the cases of economics and psychology, in which certain ranks or groupings were excluded. In only ten instances was an individual selected for the sample not interviewed. However, 198 appointments had to be made in order to obtain the 51 interviews, i.e., an average of four appointments per interview, despite the fact that most interviews were completed in one sitting. The average duration was two hours and forty minutes, with a range of from fifty minutes to six hours. Translated extracts from these interviews have been employed throughout this article.

Nevertheless, there are some stark facts of population growth facing Latin America, rates of growth never experienced by Europe before or after Malthus and Marx. Increasingly, intellectuals are admitting that population growth is a problem, but for some it is just the kind of irritant needed to precipitate basic reforms in the economic and social structure. As phrased by Chile's ambassador to the United States: "Probably the single most important factor promoting the process of modernization in the underdeveloped societies is *precisely* the social pressure created by population growth .... What would the effect be of reducing the social tensions due to population growth, in the semifeudal and oligarchical societies of so many nations of the third world? Could it not be that a successful birth control program carries with it the seeds of self-destruction for its principal objective of modernization?"[27] Or as phrased by a Colombian university professor: "Population growth can have a very positive role because it can break the vicious circle. If the pressures are very large, the society has to feed many people and this need can create something new .... Like the great intellectual advance during the population explosion in classical Athens ... it can force new ideas and can bring about the transformation of the status quo.[28]

While few socialists admit that population growth could be a problem in a socialist state, in the light of the pattern of recent political developments in Latin America, some socialist thinkers are becoming less optimistic about the imminence of revolution. What if the socialist state is a long time in coming? Is population increase really going to accelerate its occurrence? May population control be employed to assuage the misery of the prerevolutionary period? Three other Colombian professors express their points of view:

Given our political system and the small likelihood of change, the conservative theory that you must control fertility because the economic systems can't take care of people's needs makes more sense ... but if we had a good revolutionary government, then we should push for another alternative as was done by Stalin who gave prizes for mothers of large families.

The revolution is not brought about by the increase in numbers but by the consciousness of the people. To try to increase population would be falling into the absurdity of trying to increase misery in order to try to solve it.

Some say that birth control will delay the revolution. This is a simplification of Marxist theory .... The more poverty and misery exist, the greater the probability of revolutions. But it doesn't take into account that the masses of the poor are totally lacking in revolutionary conscience, and that things are not likely to change.[29]

The dilemma is an agonizing one for the leftist thinker, for while he basically disapproves of the birth control solution, he must consider it in some indefinite short run, if only to slow the pace of accelerating misery.

So we have two arguments working: one of them is that we should be working toward the revolution and the more people who want to join the revolution the better. The other is that since the revolution is going to fail, then we should have birth control to avoid the vain suffering of the people.

If all this misery is necessarily going to continue, then it is necessary to opt for birth control, at least to avoid having more people born only to end in misery and starvation. . . .

While the revolution is brewing, it would be only decent to supply the population with the means they need if they want to practice birth control.

I am lecturing to physicians about birth control and I cannot make up my mind on whether we can make policy for everybody or whether this is mainly a problem of the individual and the solution lies in the individual's mind. . . . Can we sacrifice the well-being of a generation or two in order to increase our dubious expectations of the future? We often say, "Let the population grow fast so that pressures of the status quo are increased and change comes about." But do we have the right to make such judgments on the entire population, or should we instead concentrate on curing the problems of the family as an institution itself?[30]

While politicians, social scientists, and clergy are concerned about the population question, the medical profession is doing something about it. The government of Colombia has allocated $300,000 in counterpart funds to the Association of Medical Faculties to train the nation's physicians in family-planning techniques. In Chile, the major hospitals in the large cities supply modern birth control methods, and even in Brazil a private family-planning association is gaining momentum under high-level medical leadership. Indeed, such activities in combination with a relatively permissive stance on the part of Church spokesmen have led various experts and enthusiasts to conclude that the birth-control battle is more or less over in Latin America.

It is quite true that many members of the medical profession in a number of Latin American countries have accepted the principle that the public deserves contraceptive services as a means of preventing illegal abortions and that the Church has not reacted aggressively to such principles or programs. This is a remarkable story in itself and represents a revolutionary change in medical opinion. The change, however, has been much less profound among nonmedical groups, who figure more prominently in policy-making circles in Latin America. It should be pointed out that while medical men in Latin America may generally be to the Left of the American Medical Association, they are generally considered to be politically conservative. Accordingly, the kinds of concerns expressed by the intellectuals quoted in this article are more rarely articulated by physicians and are almost never expressed to American birth control enthusiasts. On the other hand, in those areas where leftist physicians are a powerful force, they can become a particularly potent influence against population control. Thus, the executive committee of the Guanabara Medical Association (Brazil), described by a *New York Times* writer as a group of "left-wing and anti-American physicians," announced in December 1966 that they were preparing draft legislation to prohibit the production and sale of contraceptive pills and devices in Brazil.[31]

Further, a positive stance on the part of the Church would be a mixed blessing. Basic agreement with the Church on population problems and family planning has always been a mild embarrassment to the Left. A move by the Church to a probirth-control policy would help to consolidate leftist opposition to birth control, since such a policy would make consistent the socialist views of the reactionary character of the Church and the reactionary character of population control. In short, the battle is not yet over.

The United States and Population Control in Latin America. Even when widespread birth control services are accepted in Latin America, there will be serious questions about their role in the society and about the role that United States assistance should play. Few of the Colombians interviewed objected to United States aid for research or for purely technical assistance. As one respondent put it: "At the level of research it is very good . . . but the policy to be followed should not be determined by them, the foreigners. They always suggest, and that should not be, because their suggestions are often taken too seriously, and they are very often bad."[32] Or another, who had termed birth control "utopian, false, and treacherous," said with respect to aid on family planning: "We have to learn how to receive gracefully all that is knowledge or the product of culture, all that is science and technology, all that can help us."[33]

It might appear that in reality there is little danger of the United States' determining what policy Latin American nations should follow, but there is evidence that the United States line on population control is becoming not only clearer but harder. As early as mid-1965, Senator Clark told the United States Senate that, "AID should be advocating the institution of voluntary family programs *as a necessary condition* to meeting the rising tide of unfed mouths and unfulfilled aspirations in these countries. . . . AID should move on from its attitude of limited response to initiatives made by aided governments, to an attitude of *active proselytizing of the cause of voluntary family planning*, in the many countries where that would be appropriate."[34]

Was the United States going to enforce birth control by holding up assistance on food, health, and economic development? What did President Johnson mean, many wondered, when he announced on January 20, 1966, that "the hungry world cannot be fed *until* and *unless* the growth in its resources and the growth in its population come into balance," and again in January 1967 when he stated that, "nations with food deficits *must* put more of their resources into voluntary family planning programs [italics added]"? Was a new concept emerging: the compulsory voluntary family-planning program? Senator Robert Kennedy did not exactly put Latin American fears to rest, when in a Senate speech on the Alliance for Progress he told them why we won't compel them to use birth control. "We cannot attempt to compel Latins to practice birth control," he explained, "this would only inflame their suspicions that we seek to keep them underpopulated and weak."[35]

Latin American officials who had seen a withdrawal of North American support for health programs began to wonder if they were being told to stem life rather than to heal it. As the then minister of health of Peru put it, in what the journal *Caretas* termed a "sensational revelation": "The United States is willing to help in a campaign for the control of births but not in one to reduce the rates of death."[36] If health had been cut back, what next? Was not this concern what lurked behind UNCTAD Secretary General Raúl Prebisch's statement that lowering birth rates is not "an alternative to a broad policy of economic development"?[37]

Perhaps the burdens of the space race, hot and cold wars, and the development of nuclear facilities were causing the United States to look to solutions cheaper than economic development. "Heavy investments [for space research, etc.]," pointed out the Peruvian minister of health in explaining the "pessimistic" or Malthusian position of the developed nations, "are part of the struggle for world supremacy. . . . [The developed countries] are concerned about the competing demands for investments involved in this struggle."[38]

United States government economists had for some time been developing elaborate economic rationalizations for the transfer of funds from the "rat-hole" of economic aid to economically rewarding programs of family planning. One bomb-defusing expert soon produced an even more compelling argument, as stated (unofficially) by a social scientist in the Postattack Division of the Office of Civil Defense: "Rapid population growth rates have made economic growth and political stability increasingly difficult to maintain in some parts of the world, thereby adding to the need for programs and forces *to help maintain internal order and to defend against guerilla warfare.*"[39]

The culmination of the utilitarian school of thought was reached in President Johnson's 1965 San Francisco speech affirming that less than five dollars invested in population control was worth a hundred dollars invested in economic growth. The Chilean ambassador to the United States answered the argument on its own terms: "Are we looking for a cheap solution or the best solution?" he asked. ". . . it could be that the optimum return would result from our choosing the ninety dollars for economic development rather than the five for birth control."[40]

Other Latins asked themselves: if birth-control programs are such a good investment, how is the Yankee capitalist, usually so astute in such matters, able to resist such an obvious bargain in the United States? That the United States has been able to point proudly only to Puerto Rico as its birth control showcase has not exactly been its strongest selling point in Latin America. However, the charge that the United States does not practice what it preaches was countered in mid-1965 when, in the triumphant editorial words of the *New York Times*, "American Indians, Eskimos, and natives of the islands the United States holds in trust in the Pacific have just been made beneficiaries of the first Federal program offering direct help in family planning and birth control."[41] (Little noted was the unappreciative reaction of the *Navajo Times*: "We have had Washington's stock-reduction program forced on us. Now it would seem they are trying to sell us a people-reduction program."[42]

Population Control, Birth Control, and Family Planning. In Latin America ideology is important, and subtle conceptual distinctions can be of great significance. Not always clearly articulated, often used interchangeably in argument, but crucially important to distinguish, are the concepts of population control, birth control, and family planning. Population control, that is, state-encouraged contraceptive programs for the purpose of affecting national birth rates, is the most controversial. It is at the nerve center of national self-consciousness, and since it is closely related to questions of national power and national economic well-being, touches the concerns of such influential citizens as politicians, economists, soldiers, and businessmen—in short, the establishment. While most members of the establishment are unconvinced that there is any need for population control, aside from suspicion about its promotion by the United States, they are usually not opposed to the notion of contraception in the service of family welfare. Since they regard family welfare as the province of doctors, priests, and social workers, they are generally indifferent to family planning, but on occasion may even espouse it. Thus, Brazil's first lady, Dona Iolanda Costa e Silva, recently affirmed family planning to be the inalienable right of married couples, but condemned limitation of Brazil's population, "a restriction which would result in weakening a nation of low demographic density . . . and is recommended only by foreign technicians uninterested in our future, who attribute Latin America's hunger solely to the population explosion."[43]

On the other hand, those interested in family welfare, the doctors, priests, and university women are on the fringes of national decision-making groups, and are little concerned with the economic and political implications of national rates of growth. While the doctors have learned to talk a little demography, especially in mixed groups, they do not much believe in it. In Chile, for example, many of them believed (and wished) that their contraceptive program would not affect the national birth rate, but would eliminate illegal abortions. Moreover, while potentially the greatest supporters of family planning, they are divided in their opinions, with large proportions of priests and university women, and small proportions of physicians highly concerned about the moral implications of family planning. Their doubts and hostility are directed less at particular methods than at the concept of birth control, or contraception in the service of *individual* (and therefore "selfish" or "hedonistic") ends. The distinction between birth control and family planning has been drawn most clearly by Dr. Ramiro Delgado, Colombian medical school professor: "One [family planning] is a mode of conduct, the other a mere technique; one is art, the other artifice; one emphasizes quantity, the other quality; one stresses love, understanding, and responsibility, the other selfishness and egotism; one, the spirituality of man, the other, his animal nature."[44] What may seem a mystical distinction to many North Americans is precisely the source of conflict among many Latin Americans, and between them and their Northern advisers. That it is more than an academic distinction was proved recently in a debate in the Bogota municipal assembly, when the secretary of health, after a vigorous political attack was made against his probirth-control policies, replied chillingly to his opponent, "It is absolutely necessary to distinguish between birth control and family planning, which are completely different. I never spoke of birth control."[45]

Latin Americans have had enough experience with economic and political controls, internal and foreign, to know they do not need any more. Instead of control they want freedom, liberty of spirit, and human dignity. When family planning is seen in this positive light, opposition to it fades. The following quotations from three Colombian professors show the simultaneous objection of population control and birth control, along with an acceptance of the concept of planned parenthood as a way of increasing freedom of choice and action.

Birth control should represent an increase in the free will of the people. It should add one dimension to their possibility of choice. It should be free and available to everybody.... The Malthusian thesis that population growth increases misery is nothing but a comfortable way to justify the existing structures.

The government should not interfere directly with family affairs. The only thing it should do is have intensive educational campaigns on family affairs... not to reduce the size of the family ... but to give parents an opportunity to have the children with responsibility, to space them adequately.

It is not necessary to control population in Colombia to reduce the growth rate since the people are not even in possession of their own land. Birth control can be applied only as an increase in the free will of the Colombian people.[46]

It might be thought that since few object to family planning, the United States should stress this aspect and forget about population control. While this would suit the doctors and avoid irritating the economists, it would be a totally inadequate approach; for even if the establishment is unoffended by family planning and generally approving of health and human dignity, these matters do not command a high priority. *For family planning programs to receive the money and organizational talents required to affect national birth rates, the relevance of family planning to economic development and social change will have to be fully accepted by the top levels of government.* Here, indeed, is a problem of the greatest delicacy and importance for the United States.

Some Suggestions. In the sexual sphere, only a narrow *via media* exists between doing too little and doing too much. So, too, with family planning, where the United States could easily slip over from a shameful past to a shameless future. What suggestions can we make in guiding her on this delicate course?

On the domestic front the United States needs to talk less and do more. It should talk less about "problems of motivation" and establish more clinics; it should have fewer conferences on "needed research" and do more research that is clearly needed; it should not relax after appropriating funds and establishing posts, but go on to spend money and give the posts power and efficiency. But if we need to talk less, we also need to think more, for both with respect to national population growth and family welfare, we need more clearly developed policies and ideologies. We should, for example, study the implications of varying rates of population growth for various national, economic, and social goals; and we should decide under what circumstances and in what fashion existing growth rates should be manipulated to reach these goals. We should come to grips with the question of what to do if the "national interest" runs counter to the collective personal preferences of couples concerning the ideal size of family. Once the theologians cease their debate over means, they could assist by clarifying the ends of contraception, by elucidating the positive goal of responsible parenthood, and by specifying the range of conditions under which restrictions of births is permissible, desirable, and morally compelling. They can assist in the quest for a formula of negotiation between state and family, should this be needed.

Government economists must cease regarding population size, growth and distribution as "givens" which can be ignored or taken for granted in analysis and programming. There must be continuing clarification of the costs and benefits of population changes, and *experimentation* with the social and economic costs and benefits of altering birth rates in American communities.

Should the United States be able to muster a defensible ideology and a viable policy and a functioning program, all of which are needed for their own sake, it would greatly simplify the task of international exhortation, for in the international arena, more talk is still needed in many parts of the world. In those areas where action is needed and talk superfluous—India and Pakistan, e.g., the critical problems ahead are those of experimentation, evaluation, and program reformulation. In such countries already committed to the principle of population control, American dollars and American technicians are welcome and may even be useful. It is rather among the nations which have not yet accepted the notion of national population problems—including most Latin American and African nations—that the problem is a delicate one—for United States dollars and organizational genius are useless here, and our notorious ideological and spiritual inarticulateness a particular handicap. While keeping our mouths shut and waiting until such nations make up their minds would perhaps be the most salutary solution, it would represent too radical a break with our traditions to be feasible. Several other suggestions, then, can be made.

1. In addition to technology and money, what the United States should export is not *its* population ideology, but the notion that it is appropriate and necessary for governments to create their own. The United States must recognize that some nations feel themselves too small in number, or for one reason or another, desire higher rates of population growth. This is no less (and no more) rational than the desire to be rich or powerful. We cannot tell a nation what its growth rate should be or penalize it for a rate we do not believe is "healthy." But what we can insist on is that they become fully aware of the relative costs of one rate of population growth rather than another. If they are both aware and willing to pay the price for this rate, we

should cooperate and reallocate our aid accordingly. For example, for an underdeveloped nation which seriously wishes to double its population in 20 years, we might wish to allocate the bulk of our aid to food and medical services, and disproportionately little to education, science, or technology.

The point is that we should assist underdeveloped nations in achieving their ends, rather than establishing the ends for them. But we *can* insist on the rational coupling of means and ends—especially if we have managed by then to do this ourselves.

2. Another crucial requirement is the upgrading of United States personnel working in population control. The complexity and the delicacy of the population problem in such regions as Latin America and Africa would suggest the need for highly skilled United States personnel to deal with it. Unfortunately, there is a severe scarcity of such personnel, and our government seems singularly unsuccessful in tapping the small supply available. AID has part-time "Population Officers" in a large number of countries. These are usually administrators whose dedication, skill, and efficiency pertain to some field other than population, and the few formal efforts by AID to educate them have ranged from inadequate to counterproductive. If the population problem is "next to the search for peace" in priority, surely it deserves better than this.

3. More profound and imaginative collaboration with international agencies is of crucial importance, to depoliticize the aid, add prestige to work in this area, and give member nations a more realistic sense of participation. Many of the violent reactions in Brazil and Colombia to the suggestion of United States aid on population would never have occurred if the aid had been from the United Nations, the Organization of American States or the Pan American Health Organization. It is perfectly true that the wheels grind slowly in such organizations, but they are already grinding, and they grind exceedingly fine. At the moment even the interagency lines of communication are thin and tend to be at lower levels. There is no over-all plan for what it is reasonable to expect from one organization as opposed to another, nor any clear picture of how the United States can help the international agencies in the tasks they should be doing.

4. There must be a truer integration of social and economic planning with population planning. The Latins and Africans keep insisting that we are seeking a "panacea" in population and that we will thereby neglect the "real needs"—economic and social reforms. Our accommodations to this argument have been essentially rhetorical; whenever we remember, we add a phrase which begins, "Of course, family planning alone is not enough. In addition . . ." But while we protest that family planning is only one necessary ingredient in the development process, we do little else, as if it were necessary only to list the ingredients of a cake, without a recipe for their integration. Of course, we are not alone in this. When the World Bank or the Inter-American Bank considers national programs, do they ask for alternative population projections in calculating size, composition, and productivity of the labor

force? Do the "country reviews" of the Committee for Inter-American Planning (CIAP) ask how educational budgets would be affected by varying assumptions about the trend of fertility? Do the AID country reviews encourage the calculation of costs and benefits of family planning programs for various economic and social goals?

If the "population bomb" is truly analogous to the atomic bomb in the gravity of its potential consequences, then we should act accordingly. Big Money is necessary, but so is Big Brainpower. If the international agencies could really take hold of the problem, this would be the best stance for a nation whose past is so undistinguished in planning, in family planning, and in population planning; but in the interim a great nation should surely be able to muster its vast resources, moving rapidly to the rarest but most blissful of all stages, the stage of effective action.

Notes

1. Raymond Ewell, "Population Outlook in Developing Countries," October 10, 1966. Cited in "People in Crisis," Population Crisis Committee (Washington, D.C., no date), p. 20.
2. *Congressional Record*, Vol. 112, 184, October 25, 1966.
3. *Congressional Record*, Vol. 113, 41, March 14, 1967.
4. Senate Speech, May 4, 1967.
5. *Congressional Record*, Vol. 113, 54, April 12, 1967.
6. O. Harkavy, F.S. Jaffe and S.M. Wishik, "Implementing DHEW Policy on Family Planning and Population," Sept. 1967, mimeo.
7. "Foreign Aid for Family Planning," Population Crisis Committee, (Washington, D.C., 1967), p. 17.
8. Speech to the U.S. Senate, June 14, 1965.
9. Stephen Enke, "Economic Growth Through Birth Control," *Challenge* (May/June 1967), p. 41.
10. "Family Planning and Mental Health," Population Crisis Committee and National Institute of Mental Health" (Washington, D.C., January 1966), p. 21.
11. Frederick S. Jaffe, "The United States: A Strategy for Implementing Family Planning Services," *Studies in Family Planning*, 17 (February 1967).
12. G.W. Perkin and D. Radel, "Current Status of Family Planning Programs in the United States," Population Program, Ford Foundation, 1966.
13. Ibid.
14. "Family Planning and Mental Health," p. 17.
15. M.J. Cornish, F.A. Ruderman, and S.S. Spivack, *Doctors and Family Planning*, (New York: National Committee on Maternal Health, Inc., 1963) pp. 67-68.
16. "Family Planning and Mental Health," p. 24.
17. M.M. Merrill, "U.S. Population Program: A Review of Current Activ-

ities." Speech at Georgetown University Symposium on World Population and U.S. Government Policy and Program, July 12, 1967.

18. This section has been adapted from the author's "Politics and Population Control in Latin America," *World Politics*, XX, 1 (October 1967), 66-82.

19. J. Mayone Stycos, "Opinions of Latin American Intellectuals Toward Population and Birth Control," *Annals of the American Academy of Political and Social Science*, CCCLX (July 1965), 11-26.

20. "Observaciones del Exemo. Sr. R. Tomić." Embajada de Chile (Washington, May 5, 1966).

21. Reported in *Survey of International Development*, III (June 15, 1966).

22. *Diário de Minas*, August 5, 1966. For a detailed account of the Brazilian reaction, see Cornell University International Population Program, *Latin American Newspaper Coverage of Population and Family Planning* (Ithaca, 1967).

23. *Diário de Minas*, August 17, 1966.

24. *O Povo*, August 19, 1966.

25. *Correio Brasiliense*, August 6, 1966.

26. *ERPA* (Peru) January 1966.

27. "Observaciones del Exemo. Sr. R. Tomić," op. cit.

28. International Population Program interviews.

29. Ibid.

30. Ibid.

31. Juan de Onis, in the *New York Times*, December 5, 1966. In Chile, prominent leftist physicians are among the leadership of the family planning movement. Nationalism takes a much milder form in Chile, and a more detailed comparison with Brazil might be rewarding.

32. International Population Program interviews.

33. Ibid.

34. Joseph S. Clark, Speech to the U.S. Senate, June 14, 1965 (italics added).

35. Robert F. Kennedy, Senate speech, May 10, 1966.

36. "La Encuesta Hall," *Caretas*, August 28, 1964.

37. Cited in *Alliance for Progress Weekly Newsletter*, February 7, 1966.

38. Speech by Dr. Javier Arias Stella on the inauguration of the Peruvian Center of Population and Development Studies, Lima, January 14, 1965.

39. Robert Lamson, "Needed Research for Population Policy," *American Behavioral Scientist*, IX (February 1966), pp. 23-25 (italics added). It is stated that the article represents the views of the author and not those of the Office of Civil Defense or the Department of the Army.

40. "Observaciones del Exemo. Sr. R. Tomić," op. cit.

41. "More Headway on Birth Control," *New York Times*, June 21, 1965.

42. Cited in *Indian Voices*, October 1965,5

43. *O Globo*, June 23, 1967.

44. R. Delgado, "Planificación Familiar o Control de la Natalidad," *Occidente* (Cali, Colombia, June 12, 1966).

45. *El Siglo*, June 11, 1967.

46. International Population Program interviews.

7

The Politics of Population in Latin America

Vivian Xenia Epstein

Introduction

In the past decade, the rapid rate of population growth has become an increasingly important problem and issue throughout the world, especially in Latin America, the region with the fastest population growth rate. For example, in 1967 the OAS-sponsored Caracas Conference on Population Policies in Relation to Development evidenced hemispheric awareness of the issue by stating:

There is no doubt that much of each country's effort to raise its levels of productivity and employment and to improve social conditions *is eaten up by being extended to a growing population* [emphasis added] that demands the services it has a right to, without the existing population's receiving enough of the benefits of public and private action.[1]

This recent recognition of the population issue in Latin America has elicited a variety of responses. However, no Latin American republic has yet attempted to develop any comprehensive population policy which would fit the definition offered by the Caracas Conference:

A coherent set of decisions making for a rational strategy, adopted by the public sector in accordance with the needs and desires of the community, to develop, conserve, and use human resources by influencing the probable size and growth of the population, its age make-up, mortality rates, the formation and composition of families, the regional or rural-urban distribution of the people and their admission to the labor force and to education, in order to facilitate the achievement of the objectives of economic growth and enable the people to share in the responsibilities and benefits of progress.[2]

Such an inclusive approach to population policy has largely been limited to debates within the confines of international conferences and professional meetings. By contrast, the climate of opinion within most Latin American nations, with several significant exceptions, has just recently reached the stage where governments permit provision of family-planning services within public health facilities. Thus, the politics of population in Latin America have tended to arise from differences between advocates and opponents of official support for family-planning programs; the more complex question of adopting comprehensive demographic policies has generally not even been at issue.

In light of these policy trends, the purpose of this paper will be to analyze how family-planning programs were able to attain legitimacy in some Latin American countries (in contrast to other nations where such programs have not yet gained political acceptance).

In the context of this study, the term "legitimate" will be applied to family-planning and population programs when both the government and the general public have accepted the provision of family-planning services and information as a normal responsibility of public authorities. In other words, when family-planning programs become legitimate they attain the status held by the other health and welfare services provided by the government (and also often supplemented with supporting endeavors in the private sector). Thus, classifying a program as legitimate does not mean that political differences will cease to arise about the way in which a program is implemented or about the role of foreign assistance; it only indicates that opposition is not likely to endanger commitment to the program's continuing operation.

Since this is a study focusing on policy formation, the intention is to evaluate how a policy or program becomes established and whether the activities necessary to implement the program's purposes become legitimized. Consequently, the aim is *not* to measure the demographic effectiveness of the policy's implementation, which would require recourse to factors beyond the scope of this paper. (As indicated in Chapter I, even recourse to demographic techniques has not been able to conclusively document any aggregate demographic consequences of family-planning programs.)

Furthermore, this analysis of policy formation and legitimation certainly does not seek to imply that family planning programs are a sufficient response to the social, economic and political injustices of the Latin American nations or of any other societies. My normative position is that all persons should have free access to family planning services because control of reproduction is necessary for human dignity and liberation (which includes women's rights). Thus, family planning programs should be seen as a complement to social revolution not as a substitute for it.

Firstly, before we can examine *how* policies have been formulated, it is useful to outline the spectrum of alternatives from which policymakers could *theoretically* choose. These possible gradations will be briefly outlined below with the presentation of a theoretical agenda of principal options.

Secondly, we will indicate the *types* of policies and programs that have *actually* emerged in Latin America during the past decade. The tables will summarize the development of policy and program orientations in the twenty republics.

Thirdly, a political analysis of selected cases of policy formation will try to elucidate the strategies which helped or hindered acceptance of program legitimacy.

Finally, from these specific insights a model will be formulated to summarize the approaches apparently most effective in developing legitimate programs within the Latin American context.

Approaches to Population Policy:
A Theoretical Agenda of
Principal Options

The spectrum of alternatives from which policymakers could choose is theoretically quite extensive. However, in reality, choices are limited by a variety of constraints, from personal and religious ethics through political, economic, social and technical feasibilities. In order to provide a broader perspective on the issue, let us outline the principal policy options. The options can be divided into three principal approaches characterized according to focus of concern, extent of private and/or public role, and proportion of population covered.

1. No explicit birth control or anti-natalist policies. This approach obviously does not consider population policy an area of concern, unless it is a case of encouraging growth. With such an implicit or explicit option, the entire population is affected, except for those who have recourse to private sources of information and services for family planning.
2. The Family-Planning Approach
   A. Private Programs
   B. Public Programs
   C. Mixed Efforts

In this case the focus is directly on the family (and only indirectly on the nation) as the object of policy. The manifest orientation is toward the consequences at the micro-level rather than the macro-level, although, of course, the aggregate of individual choices will affect the national situation. The family-planning approach also emphasizes prevention primarily through contraceptives rather than abortion or sterilization, although these methods may be utilized somewhat as supplementary means.

In theory the family-planning programs could be undertaken entirely by the private or the public sector; although once a certain level of activity is reached it is expected that efforts will be mixed in varying degrees. Private clinics and practitioners (often supported by the International Planned Parenthood Federation) would initiate services and could feasibly obtain sufficient training, supplies, and distribution to reach the entire population. On the other hand, government agencies could also play the initiator role and then develop the program with little interaction from private associations or physicians.

The option which seems to have predominated in Latin America is initiation of private services and information followed by involvement of public health facilities and related agencies. Then a division of labor is evolved between private and public sectors. The mixed sector approach is likely to cover the

broadest proportion of the population.
3. "Beyond Family Planning"—The Population Control Approach[3]
  A. Extension of voluntary fertility control
  B. Establishment of involuntary fertility control
  C. Intensified educational campaigns
  D. Incentive programs
  E. Tax and welfare benefits and penalties
  F. Shifts in social and economic institutions
  G. Political channels and organizations
  H. Augmented research

In this approach, the general objective is lowering the national birth rate quickly. Naturally the ultimate justification for this is to better the lives of the individuals and families who compose the nation, but the immediate objective would presumably be control of the population growth rate for purposes of economic development.

While the private sector could play a significant role in fomenting several of these options (e.g., extension of voluntary control, intensified education and research), most of these alternatives necessitate vigorous and varied involvement of the government. In his article about the alternatives "beyond family planning," Bernard Berelson also discusses the various limitations which should be used as criteria for determining the likelihood of success of the suggested alternatives.[4] However, for our purposes we merely seek to overview the theoretical options; then we shall discuss the choice of agenda within the Latin American framework.

Thus, theoretically speaking, the population control approach offers policy options which would have the broadest coverage and the strongest impact. Its various facets, if combined, would provide a total, if not totalitarian, policy posture.

Synoptic Inventory of Trends In
Latin American Population
Policies and Family-Planning
Programs

The inventory presented on the following tables offers a synopsis of Latin American governments' positions towards population policy and family planning programs. The reality portrays a more modest range of measures than those included in the theoretical agenda. However, reality also has been changing at a very rapid pace and the current picture may be altered in the near future. For example, in 1967, the general status of population policies in Latin American was characterized as follows:

In Latin America as a whole, over 80% of the population lives in countries without nation-wide family planning services and probably well over 90% of the population in actuality has no access to family planning services.[5]

Yet just a few years later, in 1969 and 1970, the Population Council published Factbooks on Population and Family Planning Programs in which they classify twelve Latin American governments as giving "support of family planning activities but no official policies."[6]

The inventory of countries is categorized according to two dimensions of their positions: (1) government policy toward population growth rate and (2) government support of family-planning programs.[7] These dimensions must not be confused or lumped together, otherwise it is difficult to understand the often complex situation of a specific nation. Thus, government policy towards population growth trends presumably reflects its interpretation of the role of demographic variables in affecting the economic, political and social situation of the nation. On the other hand, support of family-planning programs refers to *action* programs which provide information and services at the individual level. Latin American experience shows that a country whose government has not defined a position toward the growth rate of its population may nevertheless have an active action program in family planning. This situation might appear somewhat incongruent if family-planning programs are considered only as a policy response to demographic pressures. However, family-planning programs are generally policy responses to "personal" problems of abortion and high rates of maternal and infant mortality. Table 7-1 illustrates the variety of combinations of these two dimensions (government attitudes toward population growth

Table 7-1
Positions of Latin American Governments Toward Family-Planning Programs and Population Growth Rate (as of 1970)

Government Support of Family Planning Programs	Government Attitudes Toward Population Growth Rate		
	Official Concern	Undefined	Favor Rapid Growth
Active Support	Colombia Costa Rica Dominican Republic	Chile Cuba Ecuador El Salvador Guatemala Honduras Nicaragua Panama Venezuela	
Laissez-faire		Paraguay	Argentina Brazil Mexico Peru Uruguay
Symbolic Support		Bolivia Haiti	

rate and government support of family planning programs) throughout Latin America. The inventory gathered in Table 7-2 presents a more detailed explanation of these positions in each of the twenty republics.

Political Analysis of Selected
Cases of Policy Formation

From the policy formation experiences outlined in the charts, we can draw some generalizations about trends in attaining political legitimacy and government support for programs. For the purposes of analysis, let us focus on the following factors: (1) sources of economic support, and (2) goals of the programs and ideological identification.

As the review of twenty countries indicates, the prevalent trend in policy formation is that almost all activities have been generated first in the private sector. The private national family-planning associations began to organize in the early 1960s (with support from the International Planned Parenthood Federation). Clinics were usually first created by these private associations with predominant leadership emanating from the medical profession or from individuals or groups based in medical schools or hospitals. Research and training have been primarily financed by grants from international organizations, private foundations or the United States Agency for International Development (AID).

Consequently, in terms of the allocation of economic resources, sources of support have come from outside the public treasuries of Latin American countries. This reliance on the private sector and foreign input relieves the government from having to further divide limited funds among competing demands—many with a more powerful political base than that of population groups. This laissez-faire attitude appears to have been the predominant pattern in the first phase of population policy evolution in Latin America. Thus, as long as government decision-makers do not have to appropriate funds for population programs in the early stages, such efforts have been more likely to reach the "take-off" stage without encountering some potentially debilitating political opposition. In accordance with this trend, in those countries where the government has allocated some financial resources to family-planning programs, it has been to supplement endeavors that were already under way, and most allocations were made just by increasing the budget of the established maternal-child care services.

It should be noted, however, that these consequences of private and foreign financial support have been observed in relation to the *initial* stages of policy formation. Once early efforts to provide family-planning services have developed, continued lack of government financial participation may be counterproductive to achieving broad-based legitimacy. Nationalists may then claim that such programs serve alien purposes because they have not developed from within the political system but are maintained by private or foreign interests.

In attaining government and popular acceptance of program legitimacy, the

Table 7-2

Inventory of Trends in Latin American Population Policies and Family-Planning Programs

	Argentina
Population (estimate for 1970) Rate of Natural Increase (1968)	24.3 million 1.4%
Principal Centers of Demographic Research and Training	University of Buenos Aires, Instituto Torcuato di Tella, National Univ. of Córdoba 1968—1st Argentine Congress on Family-Planning. Demography and Prevention of Abortion
Family Planning Program Activities A. Role of the Medical Profession	Doctors take the lead in organizing Family Planning Association; School of Public Health at Univ. of Buenos Aires provides month-long concentrated courses on population and family planning.
B. Private Family Planning Association & Date of Origin	1966—Asociación Argentina de Protección Familiar
C. Training Programs in Family Planning & Population Dynamics	The Asociación Argentina de Protección Familiar gives monthly courses for medical personnel and other courses for social workers and educators. The Asociación also sponsors regional and provincial seminars on family planning.
D. Existence of Units Providing Family Planning Services—1970	The Asociación assists 42 centers of family planning services in private and public clinics and hospitals throughout the country.
Involvement of Government	Strong sentiment in government for large increase in population. Some interest in question of demographic distribution throughout the country. Little support for official involvement in providing family planning services.
Major International Influences and Assistance	IPPF: continuing assistance to Asociación Argentina de Protección Familiar Ford Foundation: grants to Univ. of El Salvador in Bs.As. to carry out studies on anovulatory drugs, and training and research in reproductive biology and demography. Population Council: grants to support research on the physiology of reproduction. National Institute of Health: grants for biomedical research at the Institute of Medical Research in Córdoba.

Table 7-2 *(cont.)*

	Bolivia
Population (estimate for 1970) Rate of Natural Increase (1968)	4.6 million 2.4%
Principal Centers of Demographic Research and Training	Centro de Estudios de Población (CEP) has completed a study on "Socio-Cultural Factors Conditioning Fertility in Bolivia."
Family Planning Program Activities A. Role of the Medical Profession	University of San Andrés Medical School has recently established a Department of Preventive Medicine which includes courses on family planning.
B. Private Family Planning Association & Date of Origin	
C. Training Programs in Family Planning & Population Dynamics	University of San Andres, Department of Preventive Medicine has courses in practical training in community medicine, demography, population and family planning.
D. Existence of Units Providing Family Planning Services–1970	National Family Center (CENAFA) plans to initiate family planning services. Two privately sponsored clinics already in operation. Department of Family Protection in Ministry of Health will initiate maternal-child services including family planning.
Involvement of Government	1968–Presidential decree establishes National Family Center (CENAFA) as autonomous agency with members from Ministries of Health and Planning, university medical schools and Chamber of Commerce. 1968–Department of Family Protection established within Ministry of Health to initiate maternal and child care services including family planning.
Major International Influences and Assistance	AID: gives financial and technical support to CEP, CENAFA and university programs. Population Council: supported demographic studies. UNICEF: funds for extension and rehabilitation of health services of Ministry of Health. Other sources of international assistance: World Neighbors, Church World Services, Pathfinder Fund.

Table 7-2 *(cont.)*

	Brazil
Population (estimate for 1970) Rate of Natural Increase (1968)	93.2 million 3.0%
Principal Centers of Demographic Research and Training	University of São Paulo, Faculty of Hygiene & Public Health: intensive 3 month course in demography and research programs in population; Ministry of Planning, Institute of Research in Applied Economics: recently established Department of Demography.
Family Planning Program Activities A. Role of the Medical Profession	While some groups and individuals have been active in providing family-planning services, there is a lack of unified support within the medical profession.
B. Private Family Planning Association & Date of Origin	1965–Sociedade de Bemestar Familiar (BEMFAM)
C. Training Programs in Family Planning & Population Dynamics	BEMFAM conducts monthly training course for medical and paramedical personnel and other interested groups.
D. Existence of Units Providing Family Planning Services–1970	BEMFAM has 60 clinics distributed throughout the country (including 28 pilot clinics within universities).
Involvement of Government	1967–At the request of the Minister of Health, the Federal Council of Medicine renders favorable judgment of family-planning activities as an ethical endeavor, but Minister of Justice does not sign the court's opinion. 1968–President Costa e Silva sends telegram to Pope Paul VI strongly supporting the Encyclical *Humanae Vitae*. 1970–President Garrastazu Medici makes statement recognizing that "our reality is a demographic explosion" but does not see role for the government in controlling natality; thus Brazilian government continues its position favorable to rapid population growth in order to populate the nation.
Major International Influences and Assistance	IPPF: continuing assistance to BEMFAM. Ford Foundation: grants to University of Bahia for research in reproductive biology and to Federal University of Rio de Janeiro for research on effects of contraception. Population Council: grants to University of São Paulo and University of Rio de Janeiro. Other sources of international assistance: Swedish International Development Agency (SIDA), Pan American Health Organization (PAHO), World Neighbors, Church World Services.

Table 7-2 *(cont.)*

	Chile
Population (estimate for 1970)	9.3 million
Rate of Natural Increase (1968)	1.9%
Principal Centers of Demographic Research and Training	University of Chile School of Public Health. CELADE (Latin American Demographic Center).
Family Planning Program Activities A. Role of the Medical Profession	Widespread concern with high abortion rates; Prominent medical leadership in founding
B. Private Family Planning Association & Date of Origin	APROFA and initiating services in SNS (National Health Service) and university training; Private practitioners have been providing contraceptives since 1938. 1962—Asociasión Chilena de Protección de la Familia (APROFA)
C. Training Programs in Family Planning & Population Dynamics	Latin American Training Course on Family Planning at Center of Human Fertility, Barros Luco Hospital in Santiago; Medical School instruction.
D. Existence of Units Providing Family Planning Services—1970	Family-planning services integrated into maternal and child care program of SNS (approx. 200 clinics). Post-partum program.
Involvement of Government	1962—Director of SNS forms advisory committee on family planning services. 1963—Advisory committee distributes contraceptive information to various clinics. 1963—Advisory committee transfers to private status becomes forerunner of APROFA. 1966—SNS officially incorporates family planning services in its national maternal and child health services. 1967—President of the Republic and Minister of Health address IPPF Eighth International Conference. 1968—SNS delineates priorities in family planning treatment and imposes ceiling on percent of women to receive such services.
Major International Influences and Assistance	IPPF: Chile hosts the Eighth International Conference in 1967; APROFA receives continuing assistance since its founding from IPPF. AID: assistance to Ministry of Health and Ministry of Education. Rockefeller Foundation: grants to Univ. of Chile for family planning research and post-partum program. Ford Foundation: grants to Univ. of Chile for research and training in reproductive biology.

Table 7-2 *(cont.)*

	Population Council: grants to Univ. of Chile and Univ. Católica. UN agencies: CELADE (demographic training and research), CEPAL (Economic Commission for Latin America). DESAL/CELAP: research and conferences on population and development. Pathfinder Fund: distrib. of contraceptives and literature.

Colombia	
Population (estimate for 1970) Rate of Natural Increase (1968)	22.1 million 3.2%
Principal Centers of Demographic Research and Training	Colombian Association for the Scientific Study of Population and ASCOFAME Univ. of the Andes demographic training and research program
Family Planning Program Activities A. Role of the Medical Profession	ASCOFAME (Colombian Association of Medical Schools) created its Division of Population Studies in 1964 and pioneered family-planning activities by extensive medical research and professional conferences.
B. Private Family Planning Association & Date of Origin	1966—Asociación Pro Bienestar de la Familia Colombiana (PROFAMILIA)
C. Training Programs in Family Planning & Population Dynamics	ASCOFAME plans and coordinates training of medical and paramedical family-planning workers; Population Dept. in medical schools of 8 universities; Univ. of Valle—Population Studies Center.
D. Existence of Units Providing Family Planning Services—1970	Ministry of Health includes family-planning in public health clinics; family planning in clinics at all 8 medical schools; Post-partum program in 18 univ.-affiliated hospitals and social security hospitals; PROFAMILIA—26 clinics.
Involvement of Government	1966—President of the Republic inaugurates Operational Committee on Population (bi-weekly meetings of government officials with ASCOFAME Division of Population Studies). 1966—Ministry of Health and U.S. AID each contribute $320,000 toward research and training programs in family planning and population. 1967—President Lleras Restrepo is one of two Latin American presidents to sign United Nations Declaration on Population. 1969—Ministry of Health includes family-planning services in expanded maternal-infant care in rural areas.

Table 7-2 *(cont.)*

Major International Influences and Assistance	IPPF: continuing assistance to PROFAMILIA. AID: continuing assistance to the Ministry of Health. Rockefeller Foundation: aid to Univ. of the Andes and Univ. of Valle. Ford Foundation: grants to ASCOFAME. Population Council: technical assistance to ASCOFAME since 1964. PAHO: technical and financial assistance to clinics. Population Reference Bureau-regional office in Bogotá. Other international linkages: Panamerican Federation of Associations of Medical Schools, Pathfinder Fund, Church World Services, World Neighbors, Cornell University, Univ. of Chicago.

Costa Rica

Population (estimate for 1970) Rate of Natural Increase (1968)	1.8 million 3.4%
Principal Centers of Demographic Research and Training	CELADE (Latin American Demographic Center) Central American regional sub-center University of Costa Rica: CESPO (Center for Social and Population Studies)
Family Planning Program Activities A. Role of the Medical Profession	Early 1960s several physicians provide IUDs (First L.A. country to have initial activity in rural area—Turrialba). Participation of pioneering physicians in creating and expanding ADC.
B. Private Family Planning Association & Date of Origin	1966—Asociación Demográfica Costarricense (ADC)
C. Training Programs in Family Planning & Population Dynamics	CESPO: training course for medical and paramedical personnel from Costa Rica and Central America; community leadership course for Costa Ricans (includes information on family planning and population.) Costa Rican Medical School includes family planning in its curriculum.
D. Existence of Units Providing Family Planning Services—1970	Ministry of Health clinics (85) and rural mobil health units—Social Security clinics and hospitals initiated services in 1970 on a pilot basis; Clinica Biblica in San José, ADC clinic Turrialba.
Involvement of Government	1967—President Trejos decrees establishment of Office of Population in Ministry of Health. 1968—Initiation of family planning services in national maternal and child health program. 1969—Decision of autonomous Social Security agency to include family planning in its health services. 1970—Presidential decree establishes program for sex education in schools under Ministry of Education.

Table 7-2 *(cont.)*

	1969—Formation of national committee to coordinate population and family-planning activities (CONAPO)—representation from public and private sectors.
Major International Influences and Assistance	IPPF: continuing assistance to ADC. AID: contributes to ADC, Ministry of Health, CESPO. Ford Foundation: helped original financing of CESPO at the Univ. of Costa Rica. Episcopal Church: helps finance Family Orientation Center. SIDA (Sweden): ADC, Ministry of Health CELADE: technical assistance. Pathfinder fund: literature contraceptives.

Cuba

Population (estimate for 1970) Rate of Natural Increase (1968)	8.3 million 2.7%
Principal Centers of Demographic Research and Training	
Family Planning Program Activities A. Role of the Medical Profession	
B. Private Family Planning Association & Date of Origin	No private family planning association—program entirely under government supervision.
C. Training Programs in Family Planning & Population Dynamics	Three gynecologists were trained in Chile at the Latin American Training course on Family Planning.
D. Existence of Units Providing Family Planning Services—1970	Family planning services are included in maternal and child care in National Medical Services.
Involvement of Government	Government representatives have explicitly indicated that there is no attempt to promote family-planning programs or population policy; nevertheless contraceptive services are included as part of the maternal-child health program.
Major International Influences and Assistance	IPPF: 1966 Chairman of IPPF Medical Committee visits Havana IPPF, CELADE and Chilean Association for Protection of the Family sponsor a week-long seminar on family planning in Cuba. SIDA provides assistance to Cuban program.

Table 7-2 *(cont.)*

	Dominican Republic
Population (estimate for 1970)	4.3 million
Rate of Natural Increase (1968)	3.4%
Principal Centers of Demographic Research and Training	Since 1968 the National Council on Population and Family Planning is responsible for determining national population and family-planning policy; this sets official priorities concerning demographic factors.
Family Planning Program Activities A. Role of the Medical Profession	
B. Private Family Planning Association & Date of Origin	1966–Asociación Dominicana Pro-Bienestar de la Familia
C. Training Programs in Family Planning & Population Dynamics	Association for Family Welfare and National Council offer joint training courses for medical, paramedical and administrative personnel for government and private clinics.
D. Existence of Units Providing Family Planning Services–1970	Family-planning services are an integral part of public maternal-infant care program and have reached approximately 25 clinics; the Association has 2 pilot clinics.
Involvement of Government	1967–President Balaguer is one of only two Latin American presidents to sign the United Nations Declaration on Population. 1967–Secretary of Health integrates family-planning services into national maternal-infant care program. 1968–National Council on Population and Family Planning is established; the national policy goal announced is to reduce the crude birth rate to 28 per 1,000 in 10 years and to provide family-planning services through government maternal-child health system.
Major International Influences and Assistance	IPPF: continuing assistance to Asociación Dominicana Pro-Bienestar de la Familia. AID: financial and technical assistance to population program; $7.1 million loan in 1969 to Secretariat of Health to expand maternal-infant care program; also advisory services for 1970 census. Population Council: support for development of the National Council on Population and its evaluation of government family planning program. Peace Corps: volunteers work in family-planning program. CELAP: (Centro Latinoamericano de Población) sponsored conference on development,

Table 7-2 *(cont.)*

	population and the family along with the Dominican Roman Catholic hierarchy in December, 1968. Other sources of international influence and assistance: Pathfinder Fund, SIDA, Church World Services, UN Fund for Population Activities.

Ecuador

Population (estimate for 1970) Rate of Natural Increase (1968)	6.0 million 3.4%
Principal Centers of Demographic Research and Training	The Ecuadorian Institute of Planning for Social Development studies and analyzes the effects of population growth on socioeconomic development.
Family Planning Program Activities A. Role of the Medical Profession	Ecuadorian Association of Medical Faculties has assisted the 3 public schools of medicine in developing population study centers to carry out studies in demography and family planning and to teach in medical curricula.
B. Private Family Planning Association & Date of Origin	1965 – Asociación Pro Bienestar de la Familia Ecuatoriana
C. Training Programs in Family Planning & Population Dynamics	The Family Planning Association provides training to physicians and Ministry of Health personnel; Association of Women Doctors has established a clinical and educational program; family planning included in medical school curricula.
D. Existence of Units Providing Family Planning Services – 1970	28 public health clinics currently offer family planning. Association operates 20 clinics.
Involvement of Government	1969 – Ministry of Health has organized a Department of Rural Health-Population to extend clinical family-planning services within five years to all existing government health centers and to establish new rural centers. 1970 – Armed Forces have established 7 family planning clinics in military hospitals.
Major International Influences and Assistance	IPPF: Asociación Pro Bienestar de la Familia receives continuing support from IPPF. AID: supports Ministry of Health and Universities population programs. Ford Foundation: 1970 grant to Assoc. of Ecuadorian Medical Schools to support their Division of Population Studies. Population Council: supported population studies and publication of study on Quito. Other sources of international assistance: Pathfinder Fund, World Neighbors, Y.M.C.A.

Table 7-2 *(cont.)*

El Salvador

Population (estimate for 1970) Rate of Natural Increase (1968)	3.4 million 3.3%
Principal Centers of Demographic Research and Training	1964-65: Population Council sponsors a KAP[a] survey; National Planning Council has an office of Human Resources which does demographic research and analysis; ADS sponsors Regional Training and Educational Center with courses for social leaders (clergy, labor unions, educators).
Family Planning Program Activities A. Role of the Medical Profession	Medical school gives technical assistance for course on population dynamics and physiology of reproduction.
B. Private Family Planning Association & Date of Origin	1962–Asociación Demográfica Salvadoreña (ADS)
C. Training Programs in Family Planning & Population Dynamics	ADS carried out active educational and training program through its Regional Training Center: Monthly courses for medical and paramedical personnel and leaders from other sectors; ADS has public information campaign "PATER."
D. Existence of Units Providing Family Planning Services–1970	Family-planning services have been integrated with maternal-child health programs at 50 public health centers, and in the services of the Salvadorian Institute of Social Security. Maternity hospital in San Salvador also offers family-planning services. There are also 32 private clinics.
Involvement of Government	1968–Ministry of Public Health integrates family planning services within maternal-child health program. Social Security Institute also includes family planning services.
Major International Influences and Assistance	IPPF: continuing assistance to ADS. AID: Regional Office for Central America and Panama (ROCAP) supports ADS' Regional Training Center. Population Council: supported 1964-65 KAP study of San Salvador, gives fellowships and technical assistance to Regional Training Center. Other sources of international assistance: SIDA, Pathfinder Fund, Church World Services.

[a]KAP (knowledge, attitudes, practice) is a standardized Family Planning questionnaire.

Table 7-2 *(cont.)*

	Guatemala
Population (estimate for 1970) Rate of Natural Increase (1968)	5.1 million 2.8%
Principal Centers of Demographic Research and Training	The Central American Institute for Family and Population (ICAPF), located in Guatemala, has completed a KAP survey on Guatemala and published 3 studies.
Family Planning Program Activities A. Role of the Medical Profession	The Guatemalan Medical Society sponsored a Seminar on Family Planning in 1968.
B. Private Family Planning Association & Date of Origin	1962–Asociación Pro Bienestar de la Familia de Guatemala
C. Training Programs in Family Planning & Population Dynamics	The Association holds training sessions for medical and paramedical personnel on prevention of induced abortion and contraceptive methods. 1970–Ministry of Health joins with Association in creating integrated Office of Education and Training.
D. Existence of Units Providing Family Planning Services–1970	The Association supervises 18 family-planning centers: 11 in government clinics, 3 in private clinics and 4 in Central Family Planning Centers of the Association. Government supervises operations in 36 clinics.
Involvement of Government	Under Guatemalan law the Ministry of Health is responsible for all family planning services offered in the country. Family planning is being integrated into national health services. There has been strong opposition from many economists in the university and government.
Major International Influences and Assistance	IPPF: assistance to the Asociación Pro Bienestar de la Familia de Guatemala. AID: assistance to family-planning program. Population Council: grants to the Guatemala School of Medical Sciences. Pathfinder Fund: assisting family planning part of Guatemalan Rural Reconstruction Movement and provides contraception. SIDA: has equipped 10 IUD clinics. Other sources of international assistance: World Neighbors, Church World Services, UN.

Table 7-2 *(cont.)*

	Haiti
Population (estimate for 1970) Rate of Natural Increase (1968)	5.2 million 2.4%
Principal Centers of Demographic Research and Training	Institut des Hautes Etudes Commerciales et Economiques offers a training course in demography. The last national census took place in 1970.
Family Planning Program Activities A. Role of the Medical Profession	There is a very low proportion of doctors to the total population; there is a large "brain drain" of medical personnel to other countries.
B. Private Family Planning Association & Date of Origin	1968—Family Planning Association re-established (originally in operation from 1962-64)
C. Training Programs in Family Planning & Population Dynamics	
D. Existence of Units Providing Family Planning Services—1970	Clinical family-planning services are primarily provided by various protestant groups (Unitarian Universalists have one urban and one rural clinic; Church World Services has an IUD clinic in Port au Prince); in 1970 Pathfinder Fund started a program.
Involvement of Government	1964—Government announced that family planning services will be included in government health services, but by 1969 no action had been taken to implement this symbolic support. 1968—President Duvalier requested technical assistance from PAHO.
Major International Influences and Assistance	Population Council: fellowships for studies in demography and family planning. Other sources of international assistance: PAHO, Pathfinder, Church World Services, Unitarian Universalists, Mennonite Central Committee.

Table 7-2 *(cont.)*

Honduras

Population (estimate for 1970) Rate of Natural Increase (1968)	2.6 million 3.4%
Principal Centers of Demographic Research and Training	
Family Planning Program Activities A. Role of the Medical Profession	In 1963 physicians at a hospital in Tegucigalpa started a pilot clinic offering contraceptive services; this helped demonstrate to public health officials the public's need and acceptance of family planning.
B. Private Family Planning Association & Date of Origin	1963–Asociación Hondureña de Planificación Familiar

C. Training Programs in Family
     Planning & Population
     Dynamics
	1969–Seminar of Population, Reproduction, and Maternal Health Care sponsored by the Association, the University and the Minister of Public Health.

D. Existence of Units Providing Family Planning Services–1970	Ministry of Health operates and supports 60 family-planning clinics: 15 in health centers and hospitals and 45 in rural mobile health program (PUMAR). The Association has 3 clinics.
Involvement of Government	1966–Official government support given to family planning programs within public health units' maternal-child care programs. 1966–Five government agencies host Central America and Panama Conference on Population, Economic Development and Family Planning in Tegucigalpa. 1968–Government sponsors the First Regional Seminar on Population and Labor (in cooperation with International Labor Regional Organization and Population Reference Bureau.)
Major International Influences and Assistance	IPPF: assistance to Asociación Hondureña de Planificación Familiar (and to 1966 Conference). AID: supports program in government health facilities. Population Council: technical and material assistance, for post-partum program, travel and study grants. Other sources of international assistance: Pathfinder, Church World Services.

Table 7-2 *(cont.)*

	Mexico
Population (estimate for 1970) Rate of Natural Increase (1968)	50.7 million 3.4%
Principal Centers of Demographic Research and Training	Center for Economic and Demographic Studies at the Colegio de Mexico.
Family Planning Program Activities A. Role of the Medical Profession	Medical leadership in some family-planning pro- gram initiation. Since 1968, 20 medical schools in- clude demography and contraception in their cur- ricula.
B. Private Family Planning Association & Date of Origin	1965–Fundación para Estudio de la Población

C. Training Programs in Family
    Planning & Population
    Dynamics
	The Foundation for Population Studies has a train-
	ing course for medical personnel and social
	workers and seminars for national
	opinion-makers; Center of Investiga-
	tions of the Physiology of Reproduction
	also cooperates in training program;
	Assoc. for Maternal Health has clinical
	and research training.

D. Existence of Units Providing Family Planning Services–1970	The Foundation for Population Studies operates 40 clinics; Medical schools have pilot clinics; Assoc. for Maternal Health has clinics; Post-partum pro- grams at the American British Hospital and Hospi- tal de la Mujer.

Involvement of Government	Early efforts: 1925–President Calles opened a
	    birth control clinic in Mexico City and dis-
	    tributed 200,000 copies of Margaret
	    Sanger's pamphlet "Family Limitation."
	1936–Minister of Education distributed literature
	    on sex education.
	Current situation: Government stresses economic
	    development as response to rapidly growing
	    population; official position is inimical to
	    family planning programs. However, the
	    Foundation for Population studies has been
	    allowed to use some public health facilities
	    for family-planning services.
	1971–President Echeverría indicates strong
	    approval of the rapid population growth.

Major International Influences
and Assistance
	IPPF: continuing assistance to the Fundación para
	    Estudios de la Población.
	Ford Foundation: grants to Colegio de Mexico,
	    Mexican National Institute of Nutrition,
	    Hospital de la Mujer, Mexican Institute for
	    Social Studies.
	Rockefeller Foundation: grants to Center for
	    Economic and Demographic Studies at
	    Colegio de Mexico.
	Population Council: aid for post-partum programs.
	    and rural KAP study.

Table 7-2 *(cont.)*

	Nicaragua
Population (estimate for 1970) Rate of Natural Increase (1968)	2.0 million 2.9%
Principal Centers of Demographic Research and Training	National Social Security Institute (INSS), with technical assistance from CELADE and financial support from AID, carried out a survey on induced abortions.
Family Planning Program Activities A. Role of the Medical Profession	
B. Private Family Planning Association & Date of Origin	1966–Asocación Pro Bienestar de la Familia

C. Training Programs in Family
     Planning & Population
     Dynamics
	Ministry of Health has established a Family Plan-
	ning Orientation and Training Center to provide
	family-planning information and training to profes-
	sionals and lay groups; however most doctors are
	sent to courses in other Latin American nations.

D. Existence of Units Providing Family Planning Services–1970	By 1970, 60 Ministry of Health maternal health centers were offering family plan- ning services; private groups operate 4 clinics.

Involvement of Government	1967–Ministry of Public Health and AID sign an
	      agreement in which Office of Family Wel-
	      fare was established as part of Maternal and
	      Child Program to coordinate family plan-
	      ning services.
	1968–Ministry of Public Health creates Family
	      Planning Orientation and Training Center.

Major International Influences
and Assistance
	AID: supports programs of Ministry of Public
	      Health and National Social Security Insti-
	      tute.
	Pathfinder Fund: assists 8 clinics and IUD research.
	British Government: helps train Nicaraguan physi-
	      cians in family planning methods.
	CELADE: technical assistance.

Table 7-2 *(cont.)*

	Panama
Population (estimate for 1970) Rate of Natural Increase (1968)	1.4 million 3.2%
Principal Centers of Demographic Research and Training	Department of Obstetrics and Gynecology at University of Panama and Panamanian Family Planning Association have conducted a survey of induced abortions.
Family Planning Program Activities A. Role of the Medical Profession	
B. Private Family Planning Association & Date of Origin	1965 – Asociación Panameña para el Planeamiento de la Familia
C. Training Programs in Family Planning & Population Dynamics	
D. Existence of Units Providing Family Planning Services – 1970	Panamanian Family Planning Association operates 3 clinics in Panama City and 3 in rural areas. Ministry of Public Health provides family planning services in 20 public health centers.
Involvement of Government	1967 – Ministry of Public Helath, Family Planning Association and AID signed an agreement to cooperate in a "Health and Population Project" to provide contraceptive services in public hospitals and health centers and permit the Association to utilize public facilities. By mid-1969, services had not yet been implemented. 1970 – Ministry of Health is now actively supporting a family planning program with services in 20 clinics and a full-time program director. Also a National Committee for Demographic Policy has been established in the Ministry of Health.
Major International Influences and Assistance	IPPF: assistance to Asociación Panameña para el Planeamiento de la Familia. AID: assistance to Ministry of Health and the Association. Population Council: fellowships and grants for study on induced abortion. Other sources of international assistance: Pathfinder Fund.

Table 7-2 *(cont.)*

Paraguay

Population (estimate for 1970) Rate of Natural Increase (1968)	2.4 million 3.4%
Principal Centers of Demographic Research and Training	Centro Paraguayo de Estudios de Población
Family Planning Program Activities A. Role of the Medical Profession	National Medical School: has pilot clinic in Department of Gynecology and provides training in family planning.
B. Private Family Planning Association & Date of Origin	1966—Centro Paraguayo de Estudios de Población
C. Training Programs in Family Planning & Population Dynamics	Training Center at National Medical School in Asuncion; Clinica de la Protección de la Familia sponsors one month course on family planning.
D. Existence of Units Providing Family Planning Services—1970	Center for Population Studies operates 12 clinics; Mennonites sponsor clinic providing family planning services for several Indian settlements; Clínica de la Protección de la Familia.
Involvement of Government	Until 1970 there has been no official support for family-planning programs, but three clinics are permitted to operate within Ministry of Health Facilities. 1970—Ministry of Public Health and Social Welfare signed agreements with AID to train Ministry personnel in family planning and form clinics in Ministry health centers.
Major International Influences and Assistance	IPPF: continuing assistance to Centro Paraguayo de Estudios de Población. AID: grants to support training center at National Medical School and assistance to Ministry of Health Program. Population Council: grants to Centro for national seminars on population and sociodemographic survey in Asunción. Other sources of international support: Pathfinder Fund, Mennonite Central Committee, World Neighbors, Church World Services.

Table 7-2 *(cont.)*

	Peru
Population (estimate for 1970) Rate of Natural Increase (1968)	13.5 million 3.1%
Principal Centers of Demographic Research and Training	Centro de Estudios de Población y Desarrollo (CEPD)
Family Planning Program Activities A. Role of the Medical Profession	Medical organizations in Peru are generally weak and not vitally committed to family-planning programs. Except for leaders in current family-planning groups, doctors do not generally focus on public health approach to medicine.
B. Private Family Planning Association & Date of Origin	1967—Asociación Peruana de Protección Familiar (APPF)
C. Training Programs in Family Planning & Population Dynamics	School of Public Health has a grant from PAHO for research and training in family planning and population.
D. Existence of Units Providing Family Planning Services—1970	APPF: 1969, had 3 clinics in operation with more planned. Instituto Marcelino: largest family-planning clinic in Peru (specializes in 3 month contraceptive injections). CEPD: experimental clinic of maternal and child care in Lima slum. Movimiento Familiar Cristiano: sponsors medical program promoting responsible parenthood.
Involvement of Government	1964—Presidential decree established the Center of Population and Development Studies (CEPD), which included representatives from key branches of the government, political parties, professional groups on its board of directors. 1968—Government agreed to initiate a program of maternal-infant care including family-planning services in Lima area, but in January, 1969, these plans were cancelled and pilot projects closed. 1968—With the advent of the military regime government policy stresses large population growth: family planning policies no longer supported. 1970—Government establishes a committee to develop guidelines for use in formulating a national population policy.
Major International Influences and Assistance	IPPF: continuing assistance to the APPF. AID: financial support for training, research and demographic programs.

Table 7-2 *(cont.)*

Ford Foundation: from 1965, grants to CEPD.
Rockefeller Foundation: grant to University of
    Medical and Biological Sciences.
Population Council: grants to Institute of High
    Altitude Studies and to CISM (Center
    for Social Investigation by sampling).
PAHO: grant to School of Public Health.
Other sources: SIDA, World Neighbors, Church
    World Services, Pathfinder.

Uruguay	
Population (estimate for 1970)	2.8 million
Rate of Natural Increase (1968)	1.2%
Principal Centers of Demographic Research and Training	
Family Planning Program Activities A. Role of the Medical Profession	High rate of illegal induced abortions has caused concern of some doctors and motivated the formation of the Uruguayan Family Planning Association.
B. Private Family Planning Association & Date of Origin	1962– Asociación Uruguaya de Planificación Familiar
C. Training Programs in Family Planning & Population Dynamics	October, 1969–The Association organized the first Latin American training course on sex education and family planning–attended by 41 representatives of 20 nations; the Association also gives sex education and family planning courses to medical and education professionals and laymen.
D. Existence of Units Providing Family Planning Services–1970	The Association has 14 clinics and in 1969 opened 11 other clinics in Ministry of Public Health Centers.
Involvement of Government	The government has made equipment and facilities available to the Asociación Uruguaya de Planificación Familiar in public hospitals and health centers. However, with a relatively low rate of national population growth there is no official interest in promoting measures which could slow demographic growth.
Major International Influences and Assistance	IPPF: aid to Asociación Uruguaya de Planificación Familiar. Population Council: supported to IUD study by the Asociación Pro Maternidad Clinica Ginecología and bio-medical research by the Department of Obstetrics at the University of Uruguay.

Table 7-2 *(cont.)*

	National Institute of Health: grant for research in reproductive physiology at the University of the Republic. SIDA: sponsored the 1969 sex education and family planning course. Other sources of international assistance: Path-finder and Church World Services have provided contraceptives.

Venezuela

Population (estimate for 1970) Rate of Natural Increase (1968)	10.7 million 3.5%
Principal Centers of Demographic Research and Training	Venezuelan Center for Studies of Population and Family (CEVEPOF) established in 1965; Central University: Department of Sociology and Anthropology has demographic training and research in its School of Statistics and Actuarial Sciences.
Family Planning Program Activities A. Role of the Medical Profession	1969–AVPF holds First Conference for Family Planning Doctors (80 participants).
B. Private Family Planning Association & Date of Origin	1966–Asociación Venezolana de Planificación Familiar (AVPF)
C. Training Programs in Family Planning & Population Dynamics	Concepción Palacios Maternity Hospital has training program for medical and paramedical personnel; AVPF has an intensive training program for rural doctors and paramedical personnel.
D. Existence of Units Providing Family Planning Services–1970	Major location of family planning services is Concepción Palacios Hospital (the 2nd largest maternity hospital in the world). AVPF maintains a total of 44 clinics and a post partum program.
Involvement of Government	1965–Ministry of Public Health and Welfare creates a Population Division. 1966–Third Venezuelan Congress on Public Health recommends inclusion of family-planning services in official public health units. 1967–Government cooperates in holding the Meeting on Population Policies in Relation to Development in Latin America by hosting the conference in Caracas. 1968–During the First National Family Planning Conference sponsored by the Ministry of Health it was announced that family-planning services would be integrated into the National Health Service.

Table *(cont.)*

Major International Influences and Assistance	IPPF: provides assistance to the AVPF and to Concepción Palacios Hospital. AID: helped formation of the CEVEPOF and provides population training grants. Population Council: supports the post-partum program at Concepción Palacios, also assisted pilot clinic of Ministry of Public Health. Other international assistance: Ford Foundation, Pathfinder Fund, CELAP.

framing of goals and ideological position of population policies is of crucial importance. As the examples of Brazil, Colombia, Mexico, Costa Rica and Chile will illustrate, the most successful political strategy has been to avoid partisan politicization of the issue. In a relatively open political system, this approach does not prevent the entry of the population issue into the public sphere by limiting forums of discussion. On the contrary, the need for feedback in the policy-making process requires stimulation of public information and concern at all levels of society. However, definition of goals has been most successful in fortifying legitimacy when politicization of the issue has been avoided. Latin American society already has many divisive cleavages and shifting political coalitions; it can therefore be hypothesized that if proponents and opponents of population policies polarize along the lines of existent ideological rivalries development of legitimacy would be handicapped. In the 1960s, family-planning programs in several Latin American nations secured government and public acceptance. In these countries population policy did not become a pawn in the power struggle or a symbol of other economic and social grievances. In light of these observations, let us examine several more specific experiences of population policy formation in Latin America, with Brazil, Colombia, Mexico, Costa Rica and Chile illustrating varieties of political situations.

Brazil. Brazil presents a case where attempts to start population policies were hindered by political controversy. The uproar was triggered by Secretary of State Dean Rusk's announcement on August 4, 1966, that the United States had granted Brazil financial assistance for demographic studies preparatory to an eventual family-planning program.[8] Even before this pronouncement, the distribution of opinion in Brazil was not particularly favorable to family-planning services.[9] For example, the medical profession included some sectors very hostile to family planning; on the other hand, there also were strong supporters within medical circles (in 1965, 200 members of the National Gynecological Congress committed themselves to support BEMFAM, the national family-planning association). In addition, several universities and one private organization were involved in research, and the Planning Ministry had established a Demographic Center concerned with all aspects of the population issue.[10] Furthermore, the spectrum of opinion included some Church officials who recognized the validity of national concern about population dynamics.

Within this context of opinion distribution, family-planning proponents might well have been able to work discreetly by incremental implementation of programs. However, the issue became mired in political controversy when Brazilian newspapers reacted with emotion-laden headlines like: "Brazil limits births with Yankee Aid."[11] In the ensuing publicity outburst population policy became linked to other grievances and was equated with United States imperialism, totalitarian infringement on individual liberty, and other ideologically inflammatory issues.

The chief anti-family planning pressure group involved in this publicity campaign was The Association of Doctors of the State of Guanabara.[12] This small, but vocal group, protested to the Minister of Justice that BEMFAM was practicing genocide.[13]

Meanwhile the national legislature was a forum for attacks on family planners as servants of the oligarchy and of national and foreign capitalism who needed to keep population down to the low productivity rate of the present economic system.[14] Once in the national spotlight, population policy became further entangled in political rivalry. Opponents of then-Planning Minister Roberto Campos used the AID program as a weapon against him. One deputy sarcastically criticized the AID support through guilt by association: "This seems to me like the work of the Planning Ministry, which is planning everything now, even births."[15]

In the wake of this political uproar, the government clarified the proposed program's scope' initial AID assistance would only cover technical aid for demographic studies and not extend to the realm of contraceptive services. Furthermore, at the request of the Minister of Health for a judgment, the Federal Council of Medicine (the highest court of medical ethics in the country) gave a ruling entirely favorable to the ethical legitimacy of family planning.[16] However, by this time, the opposition had attained such momentum that even liberal statements by some Catholic clergy were drowned out by the clamor of medical and journalistic criticism; the argument continued well into 1967 with the advent in April and May of new accusations (and official investigations of the charges) that United States missionaries in the Amazon region were inserting IUDs.[17]

This politicization of the population issue, which was most intense in Brazil in 1966 and 1967, proved to be a detriment to subsequent efforts on behalf of family-planning programs. As Stanley Johnson observed upon his visit in 1969, "most of BEMFAM's energies were spent counteracting the bad publicity that family planning had received."[18]

It might appear somewhat superfluous to analyze these political limitations on family-planning programs in a situation like Brazil's, where the military is ruling the nation. One might argue that under a military dictatorship, policy formation and implementation are dependent only on winning the approval of the military rulers with any other opposition automatically overcome by force if necessary. However, in practice the situation is not so simplistic. The military government must also set its priorities and decide which policies will get the most economic and political resources. Moreover, Latin American military dictatorships, however common, are never securely legitimate. Thus, even if the current regime should become convinced of the need for widespread public family-planning programs, it is doubtful that they would attempt to implement such programs against massive public opposition, or antagonism from significant medical groups. Furthermore, they would be especially reluctant to press for family-planning programs, following the ideology of Latin American military rulers (as in Spain and Portugal) of respecting the sanctity of the family. They are not likely to become such partisans of anti-natalist population policies that they would devote many political or economic resources to force program implementation. Therefore, it is relevant to examine the political limitations and opportunities for family-planning programs, for unless the climate of opinion is suitable, not even a military government (especially one with Brazil's nationalistic ambition for great internal expansion) is likely to make any major family planning policy commitments.

The 1966-1967 episodes have narrowed the range of alternatives in population policy implementation that will be considered politically legitimate in the future. Of course, since then, other factors have intervened which either reinforced or alleviated the suspicions aroused during the original acrimonious debate on family planning. For example, in 1968, President Costa e Silva gave an enthusiastic reception to *Humanae Vitae*; this orientation of national leadership reinforcing the difficulties already facing BEMFAM efforts.[19]

On the other hand, by 1970, President Garrastazu Médici publicly acknowledged the problems of the demographic explosion, but hedged his views about the role of the government in providing family-planning services.[20] This is an ambivalent position; however it does permit consideration of the advantages and disadvantages of family planning and broader aspects of population policy in a less polarized context than has formerly existed in Brazil.

Colombia. The Colombian government also became actively involved in controversy over its support of family planning programs. As in the Brazilian case, request for and receipt of USAID assistance for demographic programs provided a focal point for dispute and debate. The opposing politicians were perhaps even more emotionally vehement than in Brazil. For example, in the Senate debate, the Conservatives attacked then Health Minister Ordoñez as "unpatriotic in service to foreign interests . . . proposing preventive genocide and Hitlerian racism."[21] Their oratory of hyperbole extended to predicting that if family planning were further implemented, "in twenty years Colombia will have a generation of impotent men and frigid women."[22]

Despite such attempts to politically inflame the family-planning issue, Colombian population policies did not suffer the debilitating effect of the Brazilian political crisis. The principal reasons for this difference in the political implementation of family planning in the face of a vocal opposition campaign can be analyzed as follows.

Firstly, in contrast to the deep cleavages within the Brazilian medical profession, Colombia's medical schools provided an almost solid base of support for population research and activities. In 1959 the nation's medical schools established the Colombian Association of Medical Faculties (ASCOFAME) which has been judged "as the most important institutional expression of the medical profession" in Colombia.[23] ASCOFAME's Division of Population Studies (founded in 1965) pioneered efforts in relation to population dynamics. Before attempting any clinical work they conducted thorough research on internal migration, growth, urbanization, fertility, attitudes toward family planning and abortion. These preliminary studies defined the nation's socio-demographic situation to permit a rational development of programs and hard data for the defense of such efforts.

In the second place, Former Presidents Lleras Camargo and Lleras Restrepo have each indicated profound concern with problems posed by population. The early recognition of the issue by such prestigious leaders provided a serious basis for discussion. As early as 1965, Lleras Camargo was trying to convince the somewhat hesitant United States government of the relevance of the population explosion to economic and social development.[24] During his term in office President Lleras Restrepo was one of only two Latin American chiefs of state to sign the United Nations Declaration on population. With such forthright presidential support and a base of popular desire for access to family-planning services (according to the findings of ASCOFAME research), the legitimacy of population policy had a strong foundation.

Of course the legitimacy of family-planning programs in Colombia faces continued opposition from some prominent groups—especially powerful Church leaders and anti-United States nationalists. However, even within the Catholic church in Colombia (which has the reputation of being one of the most conservative in Latin America) some clergy have supported population program research and services which enable families to practice "responsible parenthood" (*paternidad responsable*).[25]

Finally, the timing of the Colombian acceptance of USAID assistance was strategically better than that of Brazil; it came *after* other activities had built a respectable foundation of ongoing endeavors and had gained the committed support of various sectors. For example, before the November 1966 announcement of its first financial support for family planning (the equivalent of U.S. $250,000), the government promoted a considerable information program. Publicity was encouraged so that the public would be acquainted with the issue and thus understand the reasons for official involvement.

Mexico. At present, the Mexican government has avoided involvement in any population planning activities. A valuable survey by Arthur Corwin helps explain why leaders of a nation which has at least a 3.4 percent population growth rate per annum have not considered family-planning programs as a legitimate area for government sponsorship.[26]

Firstly, many economic planners consider rapid population growth as a stimulus, not an obstacle, to national progress. According to these planners, Mexico needs a vast internal market in order to develop basic industries and a larger population with greater purchasing power and greater labor power.[27] Thus, any program which could feasibly slow the rate of population increase is perceived as being counter-productive to the predominant goal of stimulating economic development.

The second restraint on legitimizing government intervention in the population area finds its roots in the mystique of the Revolution:

The vested political interests of the Revolution, of course, feed upon the assumption that the Revolution is a success. Thus, there are obvious reasons for political spokesmen not squarely facing the matter of demographic planning. This would smack of defeatism, and it would be an admission that land distribution and other social welfare remedies are no longer an adequate solution to the problem of 'injusticia social.'[28]

In this sense, PRI decision-makers are limited in the range of the policy alternatives open to them, since their political mythology imposes certain constraints. Furthermore, Mexico's historical experience has instilled a high degree of sensitivity concerning race and racial aggrandizement; from this point of view, "population expansion of the 'Mexican Race' is for the sensitive nationalist a kind of ego compensation—a kind of assurance that Mexico shall not be absorbed by alien foes."[29]

Even if the government were to overcome this proclivity of the national ethos to encourage population growth, Corwin's survey indicates that there might be some popular opposition to a family-planning program. This would *not* occur among the lower classes, where abortion attempts are not uncommon, "parents often expressed a pathetic interest in knowledge about the facts of effective family controls."[30] However, the emerging middle-class male would tend to interpret family-planning services as a threat to the Mexican way of life. Since the literate male plays the predominant role in defining the political ideals of the society, "the male psyche is a more formidable obstacle to population planning than the religious psyche of the passive female."[31]

Since Corwin's study was published in 1963, the population issue has become much more prominent in international circles. However, in Mexico, increased research and educational programs have apparently altered the situation somewhat. For example, a more recent survey conducted by Luis Leñero shows that 42 percent of the social and political leaders sampled were in favor of limiting the national population growth rate; 39.4 percent of the same elite group approved of positive action on the part of national government in disseminating contraceptive information and services.[32]

Such surveys and other research indicates that elite opinion is neither uniform nor static. In recent years the Mexican elite may have become more receptive towards consideration of demographic issues and legitimizing government provision of family-planning services. Nevertheless, as the Leñero study suggests and as remarks of newly inaugurated President Echeverría indicate (as quoted in the Introduction), a majority of those in power still do not consider population as a suitable area for government involvement. Before government could implement any significant public family-planning policy it must reconcile the population policy with the Mexican national ethos and its influence in shaping political opinion.

Costa Rica. Costa Rica was one of the first countries in Latin America to implement governmental family-planning programs. Although this nation has a tradition of intense political competition, family-planning services were initiated in government-run health units by 1968 and since then the program's development has not been seriously threatened.

The lack of serious threats to the growing program of services cannot be attributed to accidental good fortune. Costa Rica might have suffered setbacks similar to those we have discussed in the other nations. In the case of Costa Rica some of the principal constraints to implementation of population policy included: (1) lack of knowledge about public needs and attitudes; (2) potential political controversy; (3) opposition from the Catholic Church; and (4) technical and financial limitations.

In order to overcome these constraints various approaches were evolved in the process of policy formation; the variety of activities that were undertaken can be interpreted from the viewpoint of their implicit or explicit strategic purpose.[a]

---

[a]In the case of Costa Rica I had the opportunity to do field work and interviews with most of the leaders involved in the nation's public and private efforts related to family planning programs. Thus, in some cases, I am *inferring* the strategic purpose of a particular activity from my interviews and observations; in other cases, interviews may have given me exact corroboration of the political motivation—however, I do not cite source in order to respect the confidential nature of the communication.

The principal limitations and how they were overcome can be analyzed as follows:

(1) One of the most favorable factors in initiating family-planning programs as the focal point of population policy was that such programs were developed in response to a large latent public demand.[33] However, except for a few pioneers who had already provided family-planning services on an individual basis, there was general lack of knowledge of the majority's approval for such programs.

Therefore, one of the first constraints was the lack of understanding of the public's needs and attitudes. This constraint could have had most serious repercussions in relation to officials whose collaboration (or at least, acquiescence) was necessary for the program to progress.

In face of this initial challenge, the evident strategy was to orient policy toward research and information efforts. *The Survey of Attitudes Related to Costa Rican Population Dynamics* was one of the first efforts to combat the lack of information. Under a contract with USAID, the American International Association for Economic and Social Development conducted a nation-wide probability sample survey (excluding inaccessible rural areas) of 1,500 individuals. The results of the survey, published in 1966, helped inform policymakers and elite opinion of the general favorability of Costa Ricans toward family planning:

With the issue defined in several ways—health, morality, necessity for development, financial costs, appropriateness for others, appropriateness for self, degree of complexity, and general evaluation—sixty (60) percent or more of the sample subjects indicate that their attitudes are favorable ones.[34]

The results of this study were circulated among relevant decision-makers and further informative data rapidly followed in order to publicize the potentially severe implications of Costa Rica's demographic situation. For example, there were visits from family-planning experts from Chile and Mexico, delegates were sent to a Central American regional seminar in Tegucigalpa in 1966, CELADE (the United Nations Demographic Center in Santiago) conducted a fertility survey of metropolitan San José, a large, prestigious delegation was sent to the 1967 IPPF International Congress in Santiago, Chile, mass media were utilized for discussion of the population issue.

Although there was a strategy of information generation and dissemination, it was of a "low profile" nature. The issue was framed in terms of family-planning programs of a *totally voluntary* character. Awareness of the macro-level implications of population growth for social and economic development and discussion of Costa Rica's rank as having the fastest growing population in Latin America were promoted. Nevertheless, any suggestion of a population control type of policy response was *strictly rejected*.

(2) This emphasis on scientific information and research plus the human rights aspects avoided any overambitious or sensationalistic connotations. Such

an approach was very useful in preventing the eruption of political controversy. Population policymakers followed a strategy of avoiding political polarization. Evidently most politicians were quite willing to permit the gradual establishment of family-planning programs to remain in the non-partisan realm. For example, in the campaign for the 1966 elections, the presidential candidate of the Partido Liberación Nacional, Daniel Oduber, included proposals for family-planning services as a part of the Health Programme proposed in his platform. However, the opposition never sought to exploit the issue by treating it in a sensational manner; it was generally ignored and attained a status of implicit consensus.

On later occasions when family-planning services might have been vulnerable to partisan polarization, the polemics never materialized. As one prominent Costa Rican political leader indicated to me, there seems to be a *tacit* "gentlemen's agreement" among most politicians not to become embroiled in such a potentially sensitive issue which might be very difficult to manage.

Political opposition remains a constraint on population policy formation in terms of what can be called "anticipated response." In other words, advocates of various programs often try to defuse the objections of possible opposition *before* it has developed. Since the Ministry of Health, as a public agency of the government, is most dependent on maintaining a non-controversial political climate, it is very careful to define the limited goals of its family-planning program. For example, upon returning from a meeting of Latin American Ministers of Health, Dr. Aguilar Peralta, former Costa Rican Minister of Health, declared that Costa Rica will *not* adopt any direct means of birth control. He stated:

It is each couple, in complete control of its free will that must decide the number of children it desires to procreate. In accordance with this thesis, the State should only intervene in order to provide the necessary information to enable each couple to make a fully conscious and responsible decision.[35] (My translation)

Policymakers in the private sector also clarify their position in such a manner as to aggregate broad support.

(3) In a Catholic nation an obvious constraint on population policy options is the official opposition of the Catholic Church to what it classifies as artificial methods of family planning. In order to assess the nature of this constraint, it is necessary to realize that in Costa Rica the influence of the Church lies more in its capacity to affect public opinion (at both elite and mass levels) than in directly pulling the strings of government. Furthermore, the members of the Catholic clergy in Costa Rica are not always in accord. Consequently, the messages emanating from various pulpits may differ considerably. This diversity of opinion occurs in respect to the population issue.

The strategy of low-keyed implementation of family-planning programs has helped keep Catholic opposition at a minimum by avoiding any "abuses" which might unite diverse opinions. For example, in February 1967, Archbishop

Rodríguez and all the Costa Rican bishops promulgated a conservative pastoral letter on birth control which anticipated Pope Paul VI's position in the 1968 Encyclical *Humanae Vitae*.[36] Nevertheless, in April 1967, President Trejos officially decreed the establishment of the Office of Population in the Ministry of Health. Evidently, the orientation of the Costa Rican Catholic hierarchy was not pervasive enough to change the government's policy decision. Moreover, the government was presented with a *variety* of Catholic viewpoints which broadened its feasible options. While the government's emerging policies concerning family-planning programs diverged from the standards of the Archbishop, they certainly were in accord with the judgment of some prominent Costa Rican Catholic leaders, with the majority opinion of the Pope's Commission on Birth Control, and with the "individual conscience" which had been inferred from Pope Paul VI's *Populorum Progressio* Encyclical.

This range of Catholic opinions in relation to family planning was emphasized by the Costa Rican Demographic Association in order to aggregate support for the national program. For instance, in June 1967, the Demographic Association published a booklet on *La Iglesia y la Planificación Familiar* (The Church and Family Planning) in which they included a spectrum of opinion.[37] They reprinted the conservative February 1967 pastoral letter; articles by the well-known Costa Rican Catholic philosopher, Dr. Claudio Gutiérrez; comments from the national Catholic periodical *Eco Católico*, and extracts from the Papal Commission's liberal study on birth control. Furthermore, all agencies involved in Costa Rican population programs stressed the necessity to inform patients of all means of limiting births, including the rhythm method approved by the Church.

This approach stressed the educational theme of "paternidad responsable" (responsible parenthood). This was entirely in accord with Catholic doctrines and thus support could be aggregated for *common goals* even if there was some disagreement over the means used to attain these goals.

This strategy withstood the test of the negative influence of the *Humanae Vitae* Encyclical in the summer of 1968. Although there was an initial reaction of public hesitation plus efforts by some Catholic Church officials to halt the provision of family planning services by the Ministry of Health, the Encyclical in no way crippled the program. On the other hand, if the Encyclical had followed the recommendations of the Papal Commission to liberalize Catholic doctrine vis-á-vis birth control, policy implementation in Costa Rica would have received a positive impetus. Instead, desire not to arouse further opposition from the Catholic Church still remains a definite limitation on policy options.

(4) The major constraints which have been mentioned—lack of knowledge, political sensitivity, Church doctrine—are external to the family-planning programs in Costa Rica. However, there are some constraints which are an integral part of policy implementation itself. The two most obvious cases were the initial lack of financial resources and lack of sufficient trained personnel.

The strategy that evolved in relation to financing was to utilize a variety of international and foreign sources (both public and private) while seeking to gain incremental support from the Costa Rican government. In this manner, the Costa Rican programs would avoid dependency on any one external source, yet not overwhelm the Costa Rican budget with initial demands.

Another "internal" constraint was the lack of sufficiently trained medical personnel to staff the services that were being initiated. In this case the strategy was to avoid creating an imbalance between public expectations and service capacities, while establishing training courses on an intensive schedule. The Centro de Estudios Sociales y de Población was promoted by the Dean of the Medical School, Dr. Rodrigo Gutiérrez, in order to provide training for health personnel and community leaders.[38] In the interim, the Asociación Demográfica Costarricense granted scholarships for training in other countries.

These internal constraints of financing and training were naturally most acute at the start of population programs. As the policies became operative they created an internal momentum as initial successes attracted further support and participation. By now, the original internal constraints have been transformed more into problems of coordination and providing the most competent personnel at all levels.

Chile. Chile was also one of the first countries in Latin America to initiate public programs in family planning and its progress in this field has been judged as the most advanced in Latin America.[39] Paradoxically as it may seem, despite Chile's effective integration of family-planning services, the nation has never had a population policy of demographic reduction promulgated by any branch of the government. From the earliest days of the program on through present activities, the National Health Service (Servicio Nacional de Salud or S.N.S.) has emphasized that its contraceptive services were *not* designed to promote aggregate reduction of the nation's birth rate. The three main objectives of the program articulated in 1967 are: (1) to lower the rate of maternal mortality mainly attributable to illicit abortions; (2) to lower infant mortality rates prevalent in part of the population with very low living standards; (3) to promote family welfare by providing adequate information for responsible procreation.[40]

This separation of the public health aspects of family-planning programs from questions concerning Chile's demographic growth in policy formation may appear paradoxical from the perspective of current United States research and policies. However, this very factor of separation of the issues seems to be a key variable in explaining the successful implementation of family planning programs in Chile relative to many other Latin American nations. For example, the benefits of the medical approach are supported in the following appraisal of the earlier stages of activity by a Chilean physician:

It seems to me that the population problem because it was discussed, handled and eventually solutions were worked out as a medical problem and mostly at the university level is one of the reasons to explain such a success. That gave prestige to the problem . . .[41]

Of course, such a medical approach can only produce positive advances if the medical profession has a sufficient group of committed and energetic leaders within its ranks. In Chile, the concern and commitment of a prominent group of leading specialists in gynecology and preventive medicine was aroused by the growing evidence of widespread induced abortion. These physicians became aware of the situation from their own work in the S.N.S. and the universities. Further impetus was generated by several pioneering studies on induced abortion.[42]

For example, in a sample survey conducted by Armijo and Monreal of 3,776 women between 20 and 44 years old in Santiago and Concepción, 23 percent declared that they had provoked abortions; of these, 75 percent had experienced three induced abortions, 8 percent had seven or more, and 15 women had a total of 187.[43] Other data showed that 8.1 percent of all hospital admissions in Chile were cases of complicated abortions and add up to 67 for every 100 deliveries; in 1963, illicit abortions were responsible for 39 percent of maternal mortality.[44]

In response to this public health situation, in 1962 Dr. Gustavo Fricke, then director of the S.N.S., formed an advisory committee of prominent medical leaders to suggest remedies for the high rates of illegal abortion and maternal mortality. The committee initiated efforts to distribute contraceptive services throughout Santiago clinics (with financial assistance from the International Planned Parenthood Federation). The same group continued their work within the S.N.S. but were transferred to the private sector in 1963, and were shortly thereafter reorganized as the Asociación Chilena de Protección de la Familia. The setting up of a separate entity was necessitated by the newly installed director of the S.N.S. who feared unfavorable political reaction to public sponsorship of such innovative committee work.[45]

Nevertheless, by 1965 the continuing family-planning services had secured sufficient legitimacy to attain official inclusion within the regular S.N.S. program of maternal and child care; this program covered approximately 70 percent of the nation's population, primarily from lower socioeconomic groups.

The assurance of national leaders that the family-planning program had achieved widespread public support and political legitimacy was evidenced in April 1967, when the International Planned Parenthood Federation held its Eighth International Conference in Santiago, Chile. This meeting brought together about 1,500 delegates, was addressed by President Frei and Minister of Health Valdivieso, and was the first meeting of such international scope ever held in Latin America. It was not an instance of low profile policy and accordingly received broad, and mostly favorable coverage by the media; moreover, no significant controversies resulted.

By 1968, family-planning services were making such progress as to arouse the anxieties of some officials within the S.N.S. itself who had misgivings about the program. This opposition (primarily based on personal religious and political reasons) did not challenge the legitimacy of anti-abortion efforts. Instead they were reacting against the family-planning services for two principal reasons: (1) family-planning work was seen as overshadowing the importance of other health services, and (2) the distribution of contraceptives could help reduce the national rate of demographic growth, which they considered undesirable. Thus, in 1968, the S.N.S. program goals (reaching 100 percent of the women treated in public hospitals for abortion complications, 40 percent of those attended for deliveries and 10 percent of all other women of reproductive age) were modified. The S.N.S. directive of October 8, 1968, warned that the program as a whole should not cover more than 15 percent of all Chilean women of fertile age.[46]

Since 1968, even with the advent of the Marxist-oriented Allende government in 1970, the fundamental legitimacy of providing family-planning services in public health facilities has not been seriously challenged. What has been challenged, however (as the 15 percent rule indicates), is the direction and scope of such activities. Criticism has been especially directed toward the role of foreign assistance. The nationalistic argument (propounded by some conservative Catholics as well as those from radical Leftist persuasions) focuses on the substantial amounts of assistance to family-planning programs and related demographic research from such sources as the U.S. Agency for International Development, Ford and Rockefeller Foundations, and the Population Council.

The Allende government apparently intends to manage the situation by discouraging the large foreign grants to population programs. However, the announcement by the Minister of Justice that the government intends to seek legalization of abortion (along with other social reforms) does indicate an awareness on the part of Dr. Allende (a medical doctor) of the health, humanitarian, and social aspects of the birth control issue.[47]

Thus, the current situation tends to reflect the medical outlook which was instrumental in promoting earlier efforts toward family-planning policy; the health and welfare of the Chilean people are the announced criteria for legitimizing policy goals. The principal differences lie in the divergent attitudes toward utilizing foreign assistance in attempting to implement these aims. Of course, in appraising the relative success of such family-planning policies in Chile, it is important to acknowledge the role of timing in choosing policy responses to a problem once it has been recognized. In Chile, the growth of awareness about the high human and medical costs of illegal abortions coincided with the growth of attitudes and techniques propitious to creating family-planning programs as a policy response. The announced plans of this more revolutionary and social welfare oriented regime to legalize abortion perhaps indicate that public provision of legal abortion services is an effective antidote to the dangers of illegal abortion. Legalized abortion can be viewed as a necessary component of women's rights, the promotion of which was part of Allende's platform. If so, the result may well be another instance of Chile's innovative position in population policy formation within Latin America.

Conclusions: Model of Family
Planning Policy Formation

The model of family-planning policy formation (presented in Table 7-3) is intended to show: (1) how the principal functions are performed in establishing programs, and (2) how this process also influences the manner in which policy is legitimized. The scenario is derived from the inventory and political analysis of various Latin American cases that have been presented in this chapter in the sections "Synoptic Inventory of Trends" and "Political Analysis of Selected Cases."

In the model, the various functions involved have been separated into different stages for analytical purposes; however, they could actually occur simultaneously and may well emanate from the same activity. For example, a meeting of physicians to discuss family-planning issues may help *formulate* certain basic policy goals, may provide a forum for *consultation* which would draw out more knowledge about program feasibilities, might help *aggregate* political support from those who were previously uncommitted, and bring together representatives from both public and private sectors who could lay the foundation necessary for future *collaboration*.

The strategies of implementation have been an implicit if not an explicit component of the process. They do not necessarily represent the actual history of any specific nation, but rather they have been *abstracted* from a variety of cases and are designed to indicate a composite picture of an "ideal type" policy for legitimating family planning within a general Latin American context. Since the purpose of this paper is to increase understanding of the population policy process I have only sought to interpret the approaches to policy formation. Because this is *not* a work of advocacy, I have not tried to make any value judgments about the ethical merits of particular situations, although I believe that such value judgments can and should be made by defenders of particular ethical and ideological persuasions. Thus, for those who wish to support, oppose, or observe, let us summarize the principal insights into current family-planning policy formation and legitimation in Latin America which are indicated in the model.

Firstly, initiation and implementation of programs has been most successful in cases where they have been justified in terms of the benefits of "responsible parenthood" in remedying health and welfare problems (like widespread induced abortion, high rates of maternal and infant mortality, high illegitimacy rates, many abandoned children, etc.) and family well-being. The macro-aspects of aggregate population growth rates on economic development have also been discussed in some cases (e.g., Costa Rica, Colombia, Dominican Republic) as a supplementary reason to favor measures which could feasibly lower the birth rate. However, the key distinction is that the principal justification for the program is *not* made on the basis of economic or political development. The compulsory connotations of a "population control" approach are strictly avoided, and the voluntary nature of all services is continuously emphasized.

Secondly, in the early and mid-1960's when the first clinics in Latin America were being created and the idea of population policy or family-planning programs was just entering the realm of public attention, the private sector (usually receiving financial assistance from abroad) played the role of program initiation. This approach has usually given a firm foundation in legitimating subsequent involvement on the part of the government in integrating family planning services within its health centers and hospitals.

Table 7-3
Model of Family-Planning Policy Formation

	Policy Channels
Initiation (awareness of problem)	—Several scattered physicians provide contraceptives to patients —Small group forms to link efforts, provide information, broaden services —Surveys indicate favorable public attitude toward family planning —High abortion rate and consequent medical costs are made known by Ministry of Public Health —Population becomes focus of international concern (U.S. Resolutions 1962, 1966, Second World Conference on Population in Belgrade 1965, Caracas Conference 1967, etc.)
Formulation (choice of options)	Gradual division of labor emerges: —International and U.S. agencies: finance and research —National University and Medical School: training —Ministry of Public Health: public clinic services —F.P.A.: information, generating social and political support Leadership shared by various sectors Efforts focused on family planning program development
Consultation (test of potential impact)	Informal channels are most utilized; however, several formal meetings permit consultation: —First Training Seminar on Family Planning —Meetings of national officials with visiting medical experts and Catholic clergy from abroad —Large national delegation to IPPF Conference (1967) —Seminar on Demographic Situation in Latin America —Further survey research on public opinion
Aggregation (assembling a favorable political coalition)	Broad Information Dissemination: —Major newspapers print frequent informative articles, reports of seminars, etc. —Several liberal priests take positions favorable to family-planning program goals —Political parties avoid politicization of the issue —Discreet but widespread publicity on T.V., radio, pamphlets, lectures
Collaboration (coordination between public and private sector)	—Division of labor and multiple leadership roles held by a few key persons reinforces public and private coordination —Formal and informal communication at working level —Avoidance of intergroup rivalry
Ratification (legal legitimation)	—Presidential decrees and directives necessary to legalize all Ministerial programs related to population —National Legislature appropriates funds for necessary staff salaries
Feedback	—Ministry of Public Health records details of all patient treatment in clinics and hospitals —Appropriate university faculties coordinate future research and facilitate communication —All participating organizations compile records and provide opportunities for comparison

Primary Participants	Strategy of Implementation
—Small groups of physicians, nurses and concerned citizens —Consultants from International Planned Parenthood Federation —U.S. Agency for International Development —Private researchers (e.g., university groups, U.N. agencies)	Awareness of population issue emanates from concern with medical problems (abortion) and human welfare. There is no connection made with economic or political ideologies. The issue is treated scientifically, not sensationally. Limited number of people involved in initial efforts. Foreign assistance remains in the background. Issue is framed in terms of family planning; broader aspects of population policy are *not* included.
—Family Planning Association (F.P.A.) —Ministry of Public Health (Family Planning and Maternal-Child Division) —National and Private Universities (Medical schools) —US AID —IPPF	Incremental approach: start with pilot projects, research, training efforts so as not to create an imbalance between expectations and service capacity. Gradual introduction of new activities does not threaten or overload the system with innovations. Shared distribution of functions among public and private sectors helps avoid over-reliance on any one group.
—Medical profession —Social workers —Select university officials, political leaders, clergy —Office of Population —Maternal-child public health units —Family Planning Association —Survey research of public opinion	Consultation often serves dual function: (1) to ascertain potential impact on those whose support will be necessary to initiate and conduct family-planning programs; (2) to arrive at an optimal choice of options by adapting original program formulation to subsequent modifications suggested.
—Key groups involved in formulation of population program and their target publics: journalists, relevant interest groups, women of child-bearing age, legislators and administrators.	Family-planning advocates stress: (1) Right to plan family size as a basic human right, surveys indicate favorable public opinion; (2) Health problem—abortions; (3) Sympathetic opinion of select clergy; (4) Consistency with other national goals—family-planning programs are *not* a substitute for economic development and social justice; (5) Concern of famous national and international leaders.
—Core leadership group from F.P.A., Ministry of Public Health, University in frequent contact. Also liaison with AID —Liaison with foreign aid sources —Administrative personnel	Collaboration helps serve symbolic purposes by assembling a prestigious cross-section of leaders from various sectors. Also achieves functional aim of intergroup communication and coordination of efforts. Sense of common goal, helps keep intergroup rivalry at a minimum—avoid duplication and waste.
—President of the Republic —Minister of Public Health —National Legislature	Presentation to national legislature as an operational program so that it is not seen as a radical or vulnerable innovation. Emphasis is placed on accomplishments and public support. Government involvement in population issue is cautious, but firm.
—Patients treated —Medical professionals —F.P.A., Ministry of Public Health, University, CELADE, AID, Ford Foundation, IPPF	Feedback reinforces involvement with success of on-going programs. Evaluation testifies to progress of family-planning programs; helps encourage further assistance from foreign and international sources. Programs evaluated only according to their family-planning goals: broader population problems not used as a standard of judgment.

The issue of foreign financial assistance has proved in some cases to be a major obstacle to full program legitimation, especially in cases where direct aid from the United States government was involved. However, in those cases where private agencies and foreign governments have maintained a low profile and respected the viewpoints of the Latin American family-planning leaders, program formation and implementation was able to aggregate a generally favorable public and governmental response.

Finally, we can conclude that program formation by doctors and public health and welfare officials has proved quite effective in terms of legitimating national programs. It is necessary, of course, to distinguish between effectiveness in reducing demographic pressures (which some North American scholars—notably Kingsley Davis—have contended can be accomplished only through major changes in social and economic policies) and effectiveness in getting a program established which provides family-planning services and information. However, even at the level of public policy, it has been contended that the "medical approach" is ineffectual in forming active programs. This study has shown that, contrary to this hypothesis, the medical approach has been instrumental in legitimating family-planning programs in many Latin American nations and creating a framework for discussion of other aspects of population policy.

Notes

1. Meeting on Population Policies in Relation to Development in Latin America, *Final Report* (Caracas: 1967), p. 8.

2. Ibid.

3. See Bernard Berelson, "Beyond Family Planning," pp. 72—passim.

4. Ibid., pp.

5. Third Pan American Sanitary Bureau Conference on Population Dynamics, *Proceedings* (Washington, D.C.: 1967), p. 64.

6. See Dorothy Nortman, "Population and Family Planning Programs: A Factbook," *Reports on Population/Family Planning*, December 1964 and July 1970.

7. The principal sources of information for this inventory of current trends in Latin American population policy and family planning programs are the following: Federación Internacional de Planificación de Familia, *La Planificación de Familia en Cinco Continentes* (Londres: Julio 1968 y Enero 1969). María Luisa García, *Programas de Planificación Familiar en América Latina: 1969* (Santiago: CELADE, Mayo 1970). Dorothy Nortman, "Population and Family Planning Programs: A Factbook," *Reports on Population/Family Planning*, December 1969 and July 1970. Pan American Health Organization, Population Information Center, *Population Dynamics: Programs of Organizations Engaged in Pan American Cooperation 1965-66*, Document II (Washington, D.C.: Pan American Health Organization, 1967). Unión Panamericana, Secretaria General

de la OEA, Departamento de Asuntos Sociales, *Datos Básicos de Población en América Latina, 1970* (Washington, D.C.: Unión Panamericana, 1970). U.S. Agency for International Development, Bureau for Technical Assistance, Office of Population, *Population Program Assistance* (Washington, D.C.: October 1969 and October 1970). In addition, information has been drawn from interviews I conducted with family planning program leaders in Costa Rica, Chile and Argentina during 1970 as part of my dissertation field research.

8. See J. Mayone Stycos, ed., *Latin American Newspaper Coverage of Population and Family Planning* (Ithaca, New York: Cornell University International Population Program, January 1967).

9. A perceptive analysis of ideological positions on the population issue in Brazil is presented by Herman E. Daly, "The Population Question in Northeast Brazil: Its Economic and Ideological Dimensions," *Economic Development and Cultural Change*, XVIII, No. 4, part 1 (July 1970), pp. 554-74.

10. Stycos, ed., *Latin American Newspaper Coverage*.

11. Ibid.

12. Thomas G. Sanders, "Population Policy in Brazil" (unpublished manuscript of an American Universities Field Staff Report on World Population Problems, 1970), p. 11.

13. Stanley Johnson, *Life Without Birth* (Boston: Little, Brown and Co., 1970), p. 21.

14. Stycos, ed., *Latin American Newspaper Coverage*, quoting Deputy Alfonso Arinas.

15. Ibid., quoting Deputy Gilberto Azevedo.

16. Sanders, "Population Policy in Brazil," p. 11.

17. Daly, "The Population Question in Northeast Brazil," p. 556.

18. Johnson, *Life Without Birth*, p. 21.

19. Ibid., p. 28.

20. Sanders, "Population Policy in Brazil," p. 11.

21. See Stycos, ed., *Latin American Newspaper Coverage of Population and Family Planning* (May 1967).

22. Ibid.

23. Thomas G. Sanders, "Family Planning in Colombia," *Field Staff Reports*, West Coast South America Series, Vol. XIV, No. 3, 1970, p. 2.

24. *Population Crisis: Hearings Before the U.S. Senate Subcommittee on Foreign Aid Expenditures, Committee on Government Operations, 1965-1968* (Washington, D.C.: Socio-Dynamic Publications, 1970), pp. 38-41.

25. See Rev. Gustavo Perez Ramirez, "The Catholic Church and Family Planning," in *Population Dilemma in Latin America*, ed. by J. Mayone Stycos and Jorge Arias (Washington, D.C.: Potomac Books, 1966).

26. See Arthur F. Corwin, *Contemporary Mexican Attitudes Toward Population, Poverty, and Public Opinion* (Gainesville: University of Florida Press, Latin American Monographs, 1963).

27. Ibid., p. 49.

28. Ibid.

176

29. Ibid., p. 40.
30. Ibid.
31. Ibid., p. 48.
32. Luis Leñero Otero, *Investigación de la Familia en México* (México, D.F.: Instituto Mexicano de Estudios Sociales, 1968), pp. 180 and 185.
33. Interview with Ing. Alberto González, Dr. Arturo Cabezas, and Dr. Edgar Brealey in San José, Costa Rica in December 1969, February 1970, and August 1968, respectively.
34. F.B. Waisanen and Jerome T. Durlak, *A Survey of Attitudes Related to Costa Rican Population Dynamics* (San José: American International Association, 1966), p. 48.
35. Alvaro Aguilar Peralta, Press Conference cited in *La República*, October 30, 1968, p. 11.
36. See "Carta Pastoral sobre Paternidad Responsable," *La Nación*, Febrero 26, 1967.
37. See *La Iglesia y la Planificación Familiar* (San José: Asociación Demográfica Costarricense, 1967).
38. See Centro de Estudios Sociales y de Población, *Informe de Labores 1968* (San José: Universidad de Costa Rica, 1969).
39. Evaluation by Dr. Oscar Harkavy of the Ford Foundation, cited by Johnson, *Life Without Birth*, p. 34.
40. Servicio Nacional de Salud, Dirección General, *Política y Programa de Regulación de la Natalidad en el Servicio Nacional de Salud de Chile*, Circular No. 998 (14 de enero, 1967), p. 10.
41. Dr. Juan A. Zañartu quoted in Third Pan American Sanitary Bureau Conference on Population Dynamics, *Proceedings* (Washington, D.C.: 1967), p. 59.
42. Some of the studies often cited as initial documentation of the high level of induced abortion in Chile include: Leon Tabah and Raul Samuel, "Encuesta de fecundidad y de actitudes relativas a la formación de la familia: Resultados preliminares," *Cuadernos Médico-Sociales*, II:2 (Diciembre 1961); Rolando Armijo and Tegualda Monreal, "Epidemiologia del aborto provocado en Santiago," *Revista Médica de Chile* 92 (Julio 1964); Mariano Requena, "Condiciones determinantes del aborto inducido," *Revista Medica de Chile* (Noviembre 1966).
43. Hernán Romero, "Chile," in *Family Planning and Population Programs*, ed. by Bernard Berelson et al (Chicago: University of Chicago Press, 1966), p. 244.
44. Ibid., p. 245.
45. "Reseña Historica de Nuestro Comité," *Boletín del Comité Chileno de Protección de la Familia*, I (Junio 1965), p. 1.
46. Director General Servicio Nacional de Salud, *Resumen de Normas Básicas Sobre Regulación de la Natalidad en el Servicio Nacional de Salud*, Circular A.2.1., No. 3 (8 de Octubre 1968), p. 1.
47. "Chile tras legalización del aborto y el divorcio," *Prensa Libre* (San José, Costa Rica) November 15, 1970, p. 1.

8

Sexual Power and Political Potency

Ivan Illich

In urban areas of Latin America, at least one of four pregnancies terminates in abortion. In many inner city districts the rate is even higher. At the end of their childbearing age, at least two women in five have braved serious damage to their health, and suffered disrepute, and often gruesome guilt, to avoid the birth of another child. Evidently a lot of people do not want to have any more children.

Most of these abortions are performed by midwives, herb-doctors, witches, except in Uruguay and Argentine, where many doctors volunteer their illegal services even to the poor. Abortion is by far the most frequent cause of death among young women. These women need an alternative to the present situation.

The conditions for increased carnage are favorable. Enough girls have already been born to insure a doubling of women of childbearing age in the very early eighties. Neither development nor revolution can prevent growing misery for an exploding and hungry population, which drifts into abulia and passivity. It would be misleading to tell a woman seeking an abortion that a rosy future is on the horizon for her child.

But also, where can politicians afford to take a strong, positive stand for either birth control or legal abortion? Only a strongman could afford simultaneously to dare traditional Catholics who speak about sin, communists who want to out-breed the United States imperialists, and nationalists who speak about colonizing vast unsettled expanses.

The major change in public policy must be initiated at the grass roots. Present programs, semi-clandestine, try to gain acceptance for birth control among the common people. I suggest that a major campaign demanding clear population policies should rise from the grass roots. In the following article, I explain why this campaign must be coupled with a major effort leading to critically increased political awareness.

This paper was written some months before publication of the notorious papal encyclical on birth control. I had hoped that the Pope would speak, but wagered that he would keep silent. I lost my wager, and was disappointed. I had hoped that the Pope would speak about the ambiguity of technology, as well as the need for a more intense consciousness and love on the part of men forced by circumstances to use that technology. I had hoped that the Pope would make all

From *Celebration of Awareness: A Call for Institutional Revolution*, by Ivan Illich (New York: Doubleday & Company, Inc., 1970). Reprinted by permission of the author and publisher.

177

men face the fact that lowered infant mortality must be accompanied by equally lowered birth rates, if we wanted to avoid widespread de-humanization, and that we were obligated as Christians to restrain self-reproduction. The results of modern hygiene's fostering physical life must be countered by the use of modern hygiene to check its cancerous growth.

Instead, the Pope came out with a document written in dead, juridical language, a document into which one can read all this, but one which lacks courage, is in bad taste, and takes the initiative away from Rome in the attempt to lead modern men in Christian humanism. This is sad.

In Latin America the population is exploding. The citizenry of Mexico is growing at 3.4 percent per year, that of Brazil—2.18 percent, and that of Peru—3.1 percent. A swelling of the lower age groups is occurring in countries where, even now, two-thirds of youth cannot complete an elementary education. The result of this is not only inferior education for the great majority, but also the growing awareness of the adult masses that they are being excluded from all the key institutions of middle-class society. The brief education they receive is, in the long run, an education in dissatisfaction.

Birth control programs in Latin America generally fail because they stress the fear of poverty rather than the joy of life. An individual may employ contraception as the only defense against imminent misery—or he can choose it as a constructive means for a more human life. But there is nothing constructive in the present message of family planning. It is addressed to the same audience as the TV commercial and billboard advertising: The minority that is moving into the middle class. Today's clients for consumer goods and contraceptives in Mexico and Brazil form an odd and a marginal lot; they are the very few who will allow their sexual patterns to be affected by an appeal involving constant consumption and material advancement.

Success in modern schools, in modern jobs, or at modern sex seem related. Such success remains the privilege of a minority in Latin America. Although this minority is drawn from all strata of society, it is selected from those "achievers" who know how to maintain the growth rate of their personal income above the national average. And this class of strivers surges into political power, providing further privilege to those already on their way to affluence. Even if family planning were practiced by this small group, it would have little impact on the over-all population growth. The "others" (which in Latin America means most) remain excluded from an equal opportunity to plan their families. Like the legal provisions for social, educational, and political equality, opportunities for the poor to practice birth control are but a mockery.

Within the present political and social context, it is impossible to induce the majority of the people to adopt birth control. Neither seduction nor current efforts at education work. To seduce effectively, the marketing of birth control would have to become more aggressive: twenty-five dollars offered for the insertion of each coil, one hundred dollars for each sterilization. To educate effectively, governments would be promoting their own subversion through sudden and widespread adult education. For it is clear that the education that enables adults to formulate their own dissent risks the loss of all constraints on freedom and imagination.

The double failure of seduction and education is based on a discrepancy between the new message and the style of life common to Latin America's peasant majorities. For most, the idea that sexual technique can prevent conception is incredible; but even less credible to them is the idea that such techniques will produce personal affluence. Both claims seem to invoke magic. Further, the style by which this magical remedy is pushed has an odious smell. It evokes a rich establishment solicitous of teaching the poor how not to reproduce their like.

Even the approach to the individual is frequently brash, involving the tragic moment in a woman's life when, as an alternative to the next abortion, she has become a receptive victim for initiation into the mystery of contraception. Claim, style, and method put the accent on protection against life rather than freedom for it. No wonder they fail.

To be attractive, family planning would have to be embraced as a way to express a deeper sense of life rather than be used as a mere protection against evil.

The appeal to magic, myth, and mystery must be dropped by both the proponents and the opponents of contraception. Obviously this is not easy. The vision of increasing world poverty overwhelms the imagination, and the creation of a myth is one way to escape unbearable anguish. The transformation of hungry persons into a mythical corporate enemy is as old as mankind, but so is the illusion that we can manage the myths we have made.

Once the "poor" have been reduced to a faceless river reaching the high-water mark on a statistical table, birth control campaigns can be credited with magical power and invoked to conjure away further flooding. Such programs give the impression that individuals should recognize themselves as drops in a swelling tide, so that each can do his best to reduce his kind. Not surprisingly, nobody does.

Only professors can delude themselves into the belief that men can be prodded to take for their *personal motives* in family planning the possibly valid *policy reasons* of the economist and the sociologist. One's vital behavior is always beyond the reach of a decision made by others.

Populations are mindless: they can be managed but not motivated. Only persons can make up their minds; and the more they make up their minds, the less they can be controlled. People who freely decide to control their own fertility have new motivations or aspirations to political control. It is clear that responsible parenthood cannot be separated from the quest for power in politics. Programs that aim at such goals are unwelcome under the military governments prevailing in South America, and such programs are not the kind usually financed by the United States.

The development of Latin America as a Western colony requires massive schooling for children, to fit them passively into the acceptance of an ideology that keeps them "democratically" in place. Political order cannot tolerate too much awareness or originality or risk. The kind of education of adults that is analytical and dialectic leads inevitably to a liberation from taboos. Idols cannot be knocked off selectively; the kind of adult education that is aimed at dethroning some idols dethrones them all and is always politically subversive.

Kindred insights usually reinforce each other. The awareness that sex does not have to lead to unwanted motherhood provokes another concept: the insight that economic survival does not have to breed political exploitation. The freedom of the mate and of the citizen lead over the same road. Each taboo left behind means one obstacle less in the change from the social conditions that make all idols necessary.

All those who will give birth before 1984 are now in life. For each I ask: Will this child becomes a passive object, manipulated and sated by a technological milieu that encroaches on his feelings? Or will this child grow into a man who shares in the responsibility for a set of social trends? Will demographers trim his sex patterns to fit the planned population curve, just as industrial designers fit his job behavior to investment needs? Or will his move from the subsistence farm to a sprawling city increase his conscious control over his own life history?

In other words, will the city swallow his life? Or will he live with deeper freedom in the city? This is the question for 300 millions. Two-thirds of the 200-odd million inhabitants of America, below the Rio Grande, now are considered "rural." Yet less than 35 percent of the 350 millions expected in the next generation will make a living from agriculture. Most of those now alive—or those to be born during the next fifteen years—are existing in a world where mind, mores, and myth are rooted in a rural past. This means they come from a milieu in which personal success depends on the struggle for scarce resources, say, limited land, and where survival of one's group had to be ensured by massive procreation against high mortality. Peasants value possession, tradition, and multiple fertility. This taste finds expression in their style of language, symbol, ideology, and religion.

Peasants' culture provides categories that endow even extreme rural privation with dignity. The individual who moves to the city loses this powerful hereditary tool, and awareness and acceptance of this loss becomes a condition for survival. This requires a change in each man: a change both of behavior and of personal bearings.

This necessary change in behavior is the sum total of the change in the many strains of conduct that, like the strands of a rope, make up a human life. Each change in a man's actions (on the job, in the street, or with his girl friend) is the fruit of his personal insight. Either it has freed him for the invention of a new habit, or it has resulted in his deadening submission to the new rhythm of the city.

Even more revolutionary than change behavior, however, are the new moorings the personality must find in the city. Urbanization for the individual means the search for new bearings in a world that assigns new coordinates to his most intimate feelings and drives. Character forces are given new labels and new slogans, and symbols are attached to them, to fit them into a new ideology.

The city, like any other engineered product, is sold to the newcomer with a set of instructions for its use. These instructions mystify the non-believer, the man who has not subscribed to the prevailing beliefs. This city creed has many dogmas. It prizes a medically protracted span of life, scholastic performance and certification, continued advancement and achievement on the job. Production and consumption become measuring sticks for most values, including fertility.

Change in behavior, change in bearings, and change in belief go hand in hand. Only the few capable of this triple change can elbow their way into the tiny islands of affluence.

Within this context, high consumption combined with high fertility is a luxury that few can afford. These few, quite often, are not the old bourgeois, but couples who by good luck rose quickly and established themselves. For most families the speed of social climb depends upon tight control of family size.

The lifelong discipline demanded by such control is hard on any adolescent raised in a hut, untrained as he is for silent deference to the humdrum of schooling, or the monotony of an office, or docility toward clock and schedule. A rare combination of character, circumstances, and peers is necessary to teach a peasant the set of disciplines by which he alone can ensure his climb to the upper reaches of city, business, or family life. The city is a much better selector than teacher.

The personality structure or character that makes for a child's success in school ensures the passing of those who will also fit the corporate structure in the modern city. Those labeled by a certificate and outfitted with a car are presumably those most suited to take the needed precautions to lower their fertility and raise their insurance. The proven correlation of high schooling and low fertility is usually interpreted as a result of a schooling that renders pupils capable of using technical know-how, such as contraceptives. Actually the contrary is probable: schools select those already inclined toward such technical know-how. This is much more true in countries where grammar schools are selective and by that selection exclude more individuals than they accept.

Let me explain: the height of a social pyramid in Kansas and Caracas is about the same. What is different, north and south, is its shape. At best, three men out of one hundred in Caracas take the path corresponding to high school graduation, the family car, private health insurance and corresponding hygiene. I suggest that we distinguish between those who were lifted onto this level by birth and privilege and those who climbed there. These latter are much more carefully selected in Caracas than in Kansas. The steeper the pyramid, the more successfully it bars weakly motivated climbers who would barely even amble to the top of a slightly slanted incline. Those who scale the narrow and steep passage to success in Caracas must be sustained by more common drives and aims than those who are pushed up the broad flight of stairs of the United States college.

We are frequently reminded that family planning was adopted rapidly by certain ethnic groups, for example, Puerto Ricans in New York. Fertility of the entire group declined suddenly as the group moved to the city. This is true of those who made up their minds to go to New York and then "made it" there: those who moved out of Harlem, through school and into jobs that pay more than $7,000 annually. They are the ones who survived the police, drugs, discrimination, and welfare. Indeed, they rose faster than any ethnic group before them, and their fertility, too, fell faster.

Similar groups of leapfrog immigrants to affluence can be spotted all over Latin America. Their members tend to join the Lions Club, Knights of Columbus, the Christian Family movement, and other clubs that allow them to organize for further privilege for their kind. "The Association for the Protection of the Middle Classes" recently formed by Esso employees in Caracas is a good example of their tactics. But the fact that members of such groups do control their fertility is no proof that contraception is, even partially, a result of a more comfortable life. It means more probably that at present in Latin America only a few can be bewitched by the mirage of affluence.

It is revealing that fertility among the United States poor, particularly in the black ghetto, remains near Latin American levels. The common element is not some numerical indicator but a mood. In the United States ghetto, economic averages have been reached that are out of sight for our generation in Latin America. Per capita income, years of schooling, expenditure on health, printed pages read per person—all are beyond the healthy aspiration of 80 percent of all Peruvians or Colombians, for example. But both here and there, political participation is low, power is limited, and the mood bleak. For the United States Negro the signs pointing to integration and affluence have led all too often to a dead-end street.

Recently the United States public has begun, very rapidly, to sympathize with the Negro sentiment against birth control in the ghetto. It is more shocking that the same public considers the poor overseas less sensitive and more gullible than those at home. More free advice in Brazil is supposed to turn the same trick that failed in the United States ghetto. A rebuff at home is to be taken seriously. That same rebuff overseas can be written off as folly and hysteria.

In the spring of 1967 the Roman Catholic bishops and the communists in Brazil combined to arouse public indignation against supposed favors extended by the military government to missionaries who import U.S.-produced "serpents" into Amazonia. The *serpentinas* (coils) were to be "put into women" to render them sterile and to make Amazonia fit for colonization by Negroes imported from the United States, it was said.

The population expert bred around the North Atlantic easily interprets this as an outburst of sick imagination, rather than a symbolic protest against the United States serpent, soliciting tropical Eve to taste the apple of affluence. The economist, the planner, and the doctor tacitly assume that all men are compulsive consumers and achievers yearning for well-paid jobs and wishing themselves in the shoes of those who have made it with fewer babies and more things. Such reasoning is based on a presumed "law of human nature," but that presumption is at least as spurious as that preached by the Catholics. Too often missionaries condescendingly see their own idiosyncrasies as other peoples' natures.

Current American conversation in English about population unwittingly promotes an "imperialist" bias. I suggest that we awaken to this bias and handle it as an acceptable variable in policy-making. But equally I suggest that we beware of joining in the controversy over sin, usually conducted in Latin, or in the conspiracy to outbreed the paleface, which sounds Chinese.

Only for a minority in Caracas or São Paulo could having a small family pay off immediately in higher living standards. For some 90 percent, a meaningful improvement of such standards through birth control is beyond even their own temporal horizon. Most "constructive" reasons peddled to this majority for family control, therefore, are deceptive. They usually imply a subtle indoctrination of "middle-class values." Acceptance of these values should forestall revolution against them. He who has learned to see wealth as the key sign of success, and children the major obstacle to growing rich, might now blame his children for his poverty. Few do, of course, because the argument is outrageous and also untrue.

To obtain the unreasoned assent of the majority all kinds of programs are launched, most of them emphasizing immediate economic gain for the individual: direct rewards for each contraceptive treatment; oblique favors to small families; subtle, persuasive nudges connecting rising levels of expectation with low fertility. None works well enough. Why?

The fear of unattainable affluence does not intimidate the traditionally poor, just as the appeal to Hell has hardly influenced the sexual behavior of devout Catholics. In any case, it is cynical to expect them to forego present enjoyment for the sake of a paradise that is open to others but is beyond, and will remain beyond, their reach. Nowhere do people breed according to White House policies or the Pope's commands. Socioeconomic "reasons" and moral codes are equally ineffective in introducing contraceptives. The use of ideology to push or oppose family planning is always a call to idolatry and, therefore, anti-human.

Ideology can arouse in some persons regressive forces and lead them to the use of contraceptives. Ideology can justify the desire for money, resentment, envy, unwillingness to share, the fear of risk, or the desire to keep up with whatever Joneses. Ideology can explain these tendencies as contributions to political stability and productivity. But such reasoned sex control works only with a few, and they are strange and sick; their ideological motivations more frequently lead to irresponsible aggression than to discipline. Birth control is sold to the great majority under false pretenses; for them, it is a blind alley to enrichment and there it does not decrease fertility. The use of ideology to motivate individual behavior then is not only inhuman but it is also a fallacious policy. In such private matters, an appeal to patriotism, public spirit, or religion is usually a good excuse—but rarely a good reason.

For example, let me compare the documented failure of teachers to turn out readers to the failure of welfare agencies to teach contraception. Teachers try to convince Juanito that he should want to read in order to be able to know, and work, and vote. But Juanito wants none of this, and there is no reason why he should. Reading will hardly lead to college unless he gets help from an uncle who is already there. And his vote in Latin America today is certainly less meaningful than ten years ago when the Alliance for Progress began. The one argument that might convince Juanito to stay in school is the need for a certificate that is supposed to open the door to a job—many years later.

People learn complex skills best if this process of learning affords the learner an opportunity to give clear shape to feelings of images that already exist in his heart. Only he who discovers the help of written words in order to face his fears and make them fade, and the power of words to seize his feelings and give them form, will want to dig deeper into other people's writing. The mere ability to decipher the written message will only lead indoctrinated masses to submit to instruction *by* schools and *for* factories, and at best enable them thereafter to use their leisure time to escape into cheap pulp-reading or make out the dubbed versions of foreign films.

Health workers tend to proceed very much like the teachers, except that they suggest that a pessary rather than a book will serve as the flying carpet into the better life. The product of the druggist, the stationer and the witch are used in the same style. Therefore, women who just swallow contraception are not better off than those who submit to print, or trust love potions or, superstitiously, Saint Anthony.

Schools succeed, at high cost, in producing literacy in a few children: only one out of four, in all of Latin America, go beyond the sixth grade. Welfare clinics have equally modest results in teaching adults contraception: only one out of four who seek advice ceases bearing children. Both agencies help to maintain the mold and the fold of the West. An economic comparison of school and clinic speaks for a shift of resources from literacy to birth control. On a short-term basis (let us say over fifteen years) the savings to a nation from one prevented life is much greater than the rise in productivity resulting from one schooled child.

Classroom and clinic both select better than they teach. If their combined budget were cut, it would probably not very significantly affect over-all fertility. But such a cut in favor of other programs cannot be taken into consideration unless it is understood to what degree the present school and health programs are politically necessary.

Latin American society is regarded as barren even by some of its utopian dreamers. Even educational reformers speak and act as if teachers on this continent are unable to bring forth something truly new in education. Whenever effective adult education programs are conceived and grow and threaten tradition, they are declared spurious and either aborted or ridiculed. Certainly large-scale programs are never financed, the excuse being that on such a scale the methods proposed for them have never been proven.

Military governments must fear Socrates: he must be jailed, exiled, ridiculed, or driven underground. Few great, popular, and respected Latin American teachers are employed in their own countries. If such men join the government, the Church, or an international agency, they will be threatened by corruption through compromise.

There is a profound difference in the character of those who participate in

Latin American educational structures, and this difference makes it difficult for North Americans to understand the reasons fundamental education is both more important and more dangerous in South America than it is in the ghetto. In Latin America the political establishment consists of the less than 3 percent of heads of family who have graduated from secondary school. For this minority, any massive involvement of the unschooled in political argument threatens a profound change. Therefore programs that might ultimately promote such involvement are either written off as self-defeating demagoguery, or quelled, quite understandably, as incitement to riot. Certainly they are not financed.

The prevailing uneven distribution of schooling is usually considered a major obstacle to the spread of technological know-how and to effective political participation. Huge increases of school budgets for children are recommended as the one way of spreading political power and technological know-how, including contraception. This policy, in my opinion, rests on three erroneous assumptions: an overestimation of the educational efficiency of schools; an unrealistic expectation that a geometric increase of resources for schooling could ever become feasible; and a lack of confidence in the educational value of politically oriented education.

Paulo Freire, the exiled Brazilian educator, has shown that about 15 percent of the illiterate adult population of any village can be taught to read and write in six weeks, and at a cost comparable to a fraction of one school year for a child. An additional 15 percent can learn the same but more slowly. For that purpose he asks his team to prepare in each village a list of words that have the greatest intensity of meaning. Usually these words relate to politics and are, therefore, a focus of controversy. His literacy sessions are organized around the analysis of the chosen words. The persons attracted by this literacy program are mostly those with political potential. We must assume that they are interested in dialogue and that learning to read and write its key words means for them a step to carry their political participation to new levels of intensity and effectiveness.

Obviously such education is selective. So are our present schools. The difference is that political potential makes the written page the place of encounter for the potentially subversive elements in society, rather than making it a sieve through which to pass those children who prove tolerant to compliance and qualified failure. Freire's alumni consume a diet that is different from the pulp and trash on which dropouts feed.

I will never forget an evening with Freire's pupils, hungry peasants in Sergipe, in early 1964. One man got up, struggled for words and finally put into one utterance the argument I want to make in this article: "I could not sleep last night . . . because last evening I wrote my name . . . and I understood that I am I . . . this means that *we* are responsible."

Responsible citizenship and responsible parenthood go hand in hand. Both are the result of an experienced relatedness of the self to others. The dicipline of spontaneous behavior is effective, creative, and sustained only if it is accepted with other people in mind. The decision to act as responsible mate and parent implies participation in political life and acceptance· of the discipline this demands. Today in Brazil this means readiness for revolutionary struggle.

In this perspective, my suggestion to orient large-scale formal educational programs for adults intensively toward family planning implies a commitment in favor of a political education. The struggle for political liberation and popular participation in Latin America can be rooted in new depth and awareness if it will spring from the recognition that, even in the most intimate domains of life, modern man must accept technology as a condition. Conducted in this style, education to modern parenthood could become a powerful form of agitation to help an uprooted mass grow into "people."

Part III: Labor and Welfare Institutions in Latin America

The Employment Question and Development Policies in Latin America

William P. Glade

Among the many troublesome aspects of rapid demographic growth in Latin America is its dual impact on the working class, a segment of the social structure which has the slimmest economic, cultural, and other resources for coping with the problems created by an increase in the supply of labor and an increase in the number of consumption claims on aggregate output. As wage earners, workers are necessarily concerned with policies which affect labor-market conditions by influencing the supply of workers (both quantitatively and qualitatively) and the number and types of jobs available for absorbing that supply. Here the labor interest in demographic matters comes to its sharpest focus in questions of employment policy. Since workers generally must share job earnings with other (either unemployed or partially employed) members of their households, the question of how many dependents there are to feed, clothe, and otherwise provide for defines a second dimension of worker concern with population policy, that aspect of it which bears on family size.

The two aspects of worker involvement with population policy are, of course, interrelated. For example, birth control measures would, in time, reduce the pressure of a growing supply of job seekers in labor markets, while a contraction of household size would, in the shorter run, increase the income available for supporting each member of worker households. To the extent that economic rationality is operative in working-class attitudes and behavior, these two dimensions of the population question would presumably find some reflection in the policy preferences of workers as these preferences are articulated in the forum of public discussion by the various institutional channels available to the working class.

This is not to deny that other considerations play a role as intervening variables in shaping an actual labor position on development policies. For instance, particular workers and groups of workers may perceive their self-interest from a perspective which is more limited than that of the working class as a whole; on occasion organized and relatively well-paid groups of workers have endorsed policies which, viewed in their broader impact, are possibly injurious to the welfare of other segments of the labor force. Moreover, to the degree that the real income of at least certain portions of the labor force is composed of supplementary nonwage components (such as benefits provided through social programs and financed through a variety of income transfer mechanisms), there is obviously reason for labor to concern itself with policy

Reprinted from the *Journal of Economic Issues*, Vol. III, no. 3, September 1969, with permission of the author and publisher.

questions that lie somewhat outside the field of employment as such.[a] As a practical matter, too, partisan political considerations may from time to time influence the action orientations of workers and of organizations which presumably express their interests on development issues.[1]

In this chapter, however, we prescind from considerations of this sort, although they may help to explain why spokesmen for Latin American workers have seldom figured in any important way in constructive discussions of the family-planning aspects of demographic policy, despite its clear relevance to the welfare of their worker constituency. (A very few labor organizations, such as the CTM of Mexico, have adopted modest family-planning programs.) But if this basic issue has largely been by-passed, one of its partial derivatives—the conditions which affect employment—has not been altogether ignored, perhaps because the job market is more readily perceived as a matter for worker concern than are the demographic circumstances which underlie the operations of that market. Accordingly, it is of some interest to explore the kinds of employment and employment-related policies which have been considered at various hemi-spheric-level meetings of labor specialists, labor officials, and trade union representatives in the Americas during the 1960s. The aim in so doing is (a) to assess the degree to which employment expansion has figured as a priority in policy-making, and (b) to raise certain questions regarding the efficacy of present policies, given the existing high rate of population increase, for generating a sufficient number of jobs to overcome unemployment and under-employment.

The conferences selected for review are the major hemispheric meetings at which labor policies have been discussed as a component of contemporary development efforts:

1. First Inter-American Conference of Ministers of Labor on the Alliance for Progress, Bogotá, Colombia, May 1963—(hereinafter referred to as Colombia-63).
2. Meeting of the Inter-American Economic and Social Council, São Paulo, Brazil, October 20-November 16, 1963—(hereinafter referred to as Brazil-63).
3. First meeting of the Special Committee on Labor Matters of the Inter-American Economic and Social Council, Lima, Peru, January 30-February 7, 1964—(hereinafter referred to as Peru-64).
4. Second meeting of the Special Committee on Labor Matters of the Inter-

---

[a]A number of these fringe benefits (whether provided through social programs or employment arrangements) represent a type of payment of income-in-kind as contrasted with monetary wages. These payments-in-kind may be favored by workers as offering greater protection than that provided through money wages against the erosion of real value by inflation. Thus, the relatively important role of these supplementary fringe benefits as a portion of worker income in certain Latin American industrial fields may be at least as much a response to the economic circumstances in which organized labor seeks to increase and safeguard its income position as a culturally-engrained preference for paternalistic labor policies. To the extent that this is the case, it provides evidence of abandonment of the money illusion.

American Economic and Social Council, Buenos Aires, Argentina, October 1964—(hereinafter referred to as Argentina-64).
5. Second Inter-American Conference of Ministers of Labor on the Alliance for Progress, Federal District, Venezuela, May 1966—(hereinafter referred to as Venezuela-66).
6. Second meeting of the Permanent Technical Committee on Labor Matters, Viña del Mar, Chile, June 1967—(hereinafter referred to as Chile-67).

The earliest of these meetings coincided, approximately, with a series of discussions of the topic of "Employment Policy, with Particular Reference to the Employment Problems of Developing Countries," sponsored by the International Labor Office.

Expositional Perspective

For better exposition of the issues, it is here assumed that the overriding interest of the working class lies in an expansion of the remunerative employment opportunities to which that group has access. By making this assumption, we are thus deliberately excluding other perspectives which might be taken to assess the appropriateness of alternative development policies. Some, for instance, have argued that employment aspects of developmental investments should be treated as a secondary consideration, that capital-intensive projects might be preferred over more labor-intensive ones on the grounds that the new income generated by the former projects would accrue more to the recipients of profit and interest than, as in the case of the latter, to recipients of wages. On the assumption that the profits-and-interest categories of income are more likely to lead to further savings and reinvestment, whereas wage income more likely goes into consumption, such an investment criterion, it is claimed, would tend to raise the aggregate rate of capital formation and, hence, the long-term growth rate.[2] Another argument which has been adduced to justify the relegation of employment considerations to a secondary position in development policy stems from a more behavioral type of consideration. In this case, the claim is made that an initial choice of capital-intensive production technologies (with a corresponding sacrifice of jobs) reduces the likelihood that an entrenched labor force would be able, at some future date, to resist the introduction of still further labor-displacing technologies. Thus, in this view, the accentuation of job-creating investments in the short run carries with it a risk of blocking technological progress in the future.[3] Moreover, under certain circumstances balance-of-payments considerations may be decisive, at least in the short run, in determining the most desirable pattern of investment allocation, whatever the employment effects of the investments deemed desirable by this criterion. More broadly speaking, comparative international advantage as structured by natural resource endowments (e.g., petroleum or copper deposits) may occasionally point to the desirability of concentrating investments in fields in which the capital/labor ratio is quite high, given the prevailing technical coefficients of production, and in which, correspondingly, the direct employment effects of new investments are likely to be limited.

In any event, we do not wish to enter here into the extensive discussion of investment criteria, nor are we denying that certain possibly crucial development projects (such as hydroelectric power facilities, chemical plants, petroleum refineries) apparently have quite inflexible technical coefficients of production and should, on occasion, be undertaken even though they directly generate little new employment.[b] In these cases, unskilled or semi-skilled labor, however cheap, is not competitive as a factor input because of the very high productivity of modern capital-intensive methods. Instead, the intention here is to leave aside these sorts of issues and to examine the degree to which the development approaches currently *in vogue* in the Americas give some promise of socializing the benefits of growth via employment channels.

The Employment Question in Discussions of Inter-American Policy

A concern, of sorts, with employment aspects of development was incorporated in the Punta del Este Charter with which the Alliance for Progress formally began in 1961, particularly in the clause which stated that the Alliance programs should "assure to workers a just remuneration and adequate conditions of work." Although employment policies were not spelled out in any detail, the general context in which the Punta del Este Charter was conceived—that of framing a policy which would broaden participation in the processes and fruits of development—creates a strong presumption in favor of such policies.

The Charter touched on the employment issue, indirectly, in several points. Paragraph Two of Title One, for example, spoke of designing development so as to achieve a broader distribution of income and raising the living levels of the most necessitous groups in the population. Paragraph Two of the second chapter of Title Two referred to reducing underemployment, while Paragraph Two of the third chapter of the same title emphasized projects which would "benefit directly the greatest number of persons" and would utilize resources, especially manpower resources, then not fully employed.

A year later, at the October 1962 meeting of the Inter-American Economic and Social Council (IA-ECOSOC) in Mexico City, further action, albeit of an indirect sort, in that direction was taken with Resolution A-10, which called for worker representation at various levels of the planning and policy-making organizations of the Alliance program. At the same meeting, however, a report was received from a special international labor mission appointed by the Organization of American States to ascertain the degree of labor involvement in

---

[b]Even in less extreme cases, of course, the productive superiority of more mechanized processes may be so great as to render unfeasible alternative labor-intensive processes; the superiority of the power loom over the hand loom is a frequently cited example.

the economic and social programs of the Alliance. The report indicated that the mission had been unable to find, in the course of its Latin American investigations, any significant worker participation in the formulation of development programs.[4] This being the case, it was to be expected that employment objectives did not figure very centrally in the policy deliberations which had occurred up to that point.

With the Colombia-63 conference, at least a start was made in confronting the employment problem,[5] although even then the participating labor ministers seem to have devoted a great deal of their attention to such matters as export stabilization schemes, foreign aid, minimum wage and salary programs, the harmonization of social and labor legislation among countries, and social benefit programs (i.e., housing and other cooperatives, worker banks, and the like). Under the circumstances prevailing in Latin America, the benefits of a good many of these measures would tend to accrue primarily to that segment of the labor force which was already employed and relatively better off to begin with. Nevertheless, the need to strive for full employment was ostensibly assigned a top priority for the work of the labor ministries, the necessity of compiling more accurate labor market statistics was recognized, vocational training programs were accorded some emphasis, and action was urged in the field of establishing employment exchanges or services. To prepare technicians to carry out these activities, the labor ministers also recommended creation of a multilateral training center for labor ministry personnel—a project which, after lengthy study and negotiation, finally got under way in 1966 with the opening of the Inter-American Center for Labor Administration in Lima.

Later in 1963, at the Brazil-63 conference, the IA-ECOSOC established a Special Committee on Labor Matters to provide continuing supervision of the various efforts then being made to strengthen and expand the use of manpower evaluation, training, and planning activities. It was also recommended that member states carry out, with the assistance of international organizations, national studies evaluating human resources for use in economic and educational planning agencies. This latter point reasserted the importance of preparing current and future manpower supply and demand estimates, a measure which had been recommended at the Conference on Education and Economic Development held in Santiago in 1962. During the same period, 1962-1963, the Pan American Union also put into operation a regional program to support the growth of technical competence in the human resource field.

When, in early 1964, the Special Committee on Labor Matters was convened for its first meeting, the Peru-64 conference, a uniform reporting system was devised for gathering employment and other labor data from the several Latin American republics, and the rather limited accomplishments of these countries in developing more systematic manpower programs and policies were reviewed.[6] Although some headway had been made in setting up vocational training programs (particularly in Brazil, Venezuela, Colombia, Peru, and Chile)[c] as well

[c]The efforts at vocational training were, however, a bare beginning. While, for example, it was estimated that the Peruvian *annual* training requirements for skilled workers would run between 9,400 and 16,000 workers during a five-year period in the mid-1960s, the *total* number of workers trained in the SENATI program by 1968 was approximately 14,000.

as some rather modest employment services, little had yet been done to integrate manpower questions with national development planning. Moreover, on the basis of information reported at Peru-64, it was evident that the informational and organizational basis for incorporating employment objectives more explicitly into development programs was largely absent in the hemisphere—except for some initial efforts being made in Peru and a few other countries. On the other hand, the widespread failure to utilize manpower planning—in either its employment-creation and skills-identification-and-formation aspects—in national development plans should be seen in the light of the nature of those development plans themselves, few, if any, of which possessed more than a remote relationship to what was actually happening in the economies for which they were devised.

By the time of the second meeting of the Special Committee on Labor Matters at Argentina-64, the national reports called for at Peru-64 (under the uniform reporting procedures set up at that meeting) had been received and processed from twelve Latin American countries and the United States.[7] Even in the case of the countries which filed the reports, much of the information requested was unavailable, and a portion of that which was obtained almost certainly consisted of very crude estimates. For the nonreporting countries, it is reasonable to suppose that useful data were still less readily available. In any case, the reports, with their substantial data lacunae, reveal how marginal the whole area of manpower planning and employment policy still was in the Latin American development effort. No country, for instance, was able to report "the existence of a specific policy regarding employment, wages, technological unemployment, or income distribution," and the ministries of labor were found to be "doing very little in the way of analyzing these problems or of planning or coordinating these policies."[8] Few countries made any analysis of their labor markets, and most of those which did restricted their focus to the "most important urban area or areas."[9] In most countries there were no public employment services; where they existed, their activities were largely confined to the capital and a few principal cities. The preparation of studies projecting labor supply and demand was conspicuously absent from the actual functions of labor ministries, while the existing statistical basis for deriving such projections was generally quite inadequate.

In short, two years after the OAS had sent its international labor mission through Latin America to check on labor participation in the Alliance for Progress (and two years after the IA-ECOSOC had initiated action to increase this participation), it was evident that "in general, neither the ministries of labor nor the workers have reached any appreciable degree of participation in the work of the planning agencies. . ."[10] Given this situation and all that it implies for the attention accorded employment policy, it is perhaps remarkable to find that very shortly thereafter, in February 1965, the secretariat of the Inter-American Regional Organization of Workers (ORIT) claimed

The ORIT has advanced along this road [i.e., the granting to trade unionists of an ever-increasing responsibility in the planning and execution of Alliance programs] and has achieved undeniable success, for the representatives of the highest organizations at the hemispheric level have recognized that the presence and action of the workers is indispensable for the success of the Punta del Este Charter program. . . .[11]

The ORIT secretariat, however, was understandably vague in providing details on this success.

At the Venezuela-66 conference, the labor ministers reworked much of the territory covered in previous meetings, the chief novelties being a call for the creation in each country of (a) a national council on income and prices to serve as a mechanism for developing wage policies, and (b) a national council (within the labor ministries) on human resources.[12] The latter organizations were seen as a vehicle for injecting "policies on employment, labor, and human resources into the national planning process." In addition, the conference established a hemispheric Permanent Technical Committee on Labor Matters (composed of labor ministry officials and trade union representatives) to assume essentially the functions previously performed by the IA-ECOSOC Special Committee on Labor Matters, and an appeal was made to the Inter-American Committee on the Alliance for Progress to use its supervisory leverage to encourage more labor participation in national planning processes. All of these steps represented efforts to devise new institutional means to cope with the continuing failure of Latin American countries to incorporate labor interests into their development programs—or at least to stimulate action of that sort.[d] The labor ministers also returned to a theme which had been played in previous meetings and which probably indicates rather accurately the level of actual national commitment to labor interests in development: namely, the notoriously low budgets assigned to supporting the work of labor ministries in most of the countries of the hemisphere.

For the first time, however, at Venezuela-66 the question of employment policy began to receive something more than merely general recognition—nearly five years after the Alliance for Progress was launched. For one thing, the conference participants were able to study a survey report, "Summary of National Reports on the Labor Situation in the Hemisphere," which systematically reviewed what little was being done in various countries to relate employment (and other labor) considerations to the development effort, thereby providing a limited pool of experience and knowledge for discussion and evaluation.[13] Second, the conference took up a more narrowly-focused report on "Aspects of Employment Policy in Latin America," which, based upon a survey of five countries, examined in some detail the problems encountered in devising an employment policy: inadequate statistical records, improvisation and lack of coordination in development planning and policy implementation,

---

[d]Whatever the lack of concern with employment objectives at the national level, it must be said that the organizational proliferation at the international level (including the American Institute for Free Labor Development in addition to the other entities mentioned in this paper) was certainly providing something close to full employment for persons charged with the responsibility of promoting a greater labor participation in development.

characteristics of occupational structures, nonemployment constraints on economic policy.[14] The report also reviewed alternative approaches then being followed in manpower planning and identified certain policy contradictions which worked at cross-purposes to employment objectives. Among other things, the report concluded:

An examination of the consideration given to problems of employment in Latin American countries shows on the whole a negative picture. The development plans drawn up so far are comprehensive fundamentally depending for their cohesion on national accounting systems. In some cases attention has been paid to the feasibility of achieving the implicit increases in manpower productivity; but as a rule the attainment of specific levels of employment constitutes a secondary issue, to be settled by the other measures proposed for stimulating development.

In general there is no clearly defined policy with regard to employment, or any agency with full responsibility for dealing with the different problems that arise in this area. The countries in the sample do not have adequate means of obtaining information on what is being done by the various agencies whose decisions affect the level of employment, and consequently have no way of preventing the development of duplicate or conflicting activities. . . .[15]

Finally, in a third conference report, "The Formulation of Labor Policy for National Development," it was recognized explicitly that identification of specific employment and wage objectives would be essential to ameliorating the lot of the estimated 10 percent of the Latin American labor force which was unemployed and that these objectives would have to be pursued deliberately, not as an eventual by-product of development efforts.[16]

. . . One of the basic factors to be considered, therefore, whenever decisions are made in connection with development activities, both at the level of the national economy and at the local or sectoral level, must be the impact that these decisions will ultimately have on the level of employment.[17]

The report went on to illustrate aspects of the current policy mix which were undesirable from the standpoint of attaining higher employment levels. Modest though it was, the report, along with the other two mentioned previously, at least had the merit of moving towards more specific analysis of the real problems encountered in generating jobs sufficient to meet the growth of the work force and of taking a more forthright position on the importance of integrating employment policy with other policy measures.

If this promising, if belated, confrontation with the employment issue raised hopes that a more concerted effort would follow along this line, then those hopes were in time dispelled. The first meeting of the Permanent Technical Committee on Labor Matters, held in Washington in September 1966, was largely devoted to speechmaking and committee organizational matters, with the usual array of general resolutions or recommendations on a wide variety of matters.[18] The second meeting of the Permanent Technical Committee, the Chile-67 conference, had rather more of a substantive focus, but, even so, the consideration of employment policy was left aside.[19] So far as can be ascertained, it has not yet been accorded a strong priority in any of the development programs currently under way in the Americas.

Thus, resolution of a major problem of demographic growth for Latin American labor remains not much beyond where it was when the Alliance for Progress first set out purportedly to bring a larger share in economic growth to the working-class population of the area. Considering the magnitude of the problem—an estimated 70 percent increase in the Latin American labor force between 1960 and 1980, including a 78 percent increase in the number of women workers and an 80 percent increase in the number of younger, inexperienced workers[20]—there is little reason to feel optimistic that the somewhat desultory attention directed to the question thus far will lead to a satisfactory response in the future. In April 1970, to be sure, the Prebisch report to the Inter-American Development Bank and CIAP identified the employment problem as a central issue for Latin America, but the actual policy response remains to be seen.

The Employment Impact of Current Development Policies

While it might be argued that efforts to promote general economic expansion in the hemisphere contain an ultimate answer for the employment problem, a closer examination of both the general design of development policy and the particular policy instruments which have been used to promote economic growth leads to doubts that a satisfactory relationship between growth of GNP and growth of employment will be obtained automatically. Indeed, there is some basis for believing that a number of policies and institutions tend to influence a nearly economy-wide choice, at the firm level, of relatively capital-intensive techniques, partly because of their effects on relative primary and intermediate input prices.

For one thing, industrialization along import-substitution lines has played a fairly central role in the overall development strategies of many of the larger Latin American countries, and this in itself raises the possibility that a large part of the employment problem originates in the problem of technological dualism which has been discussed by such writers as R.S. Eckaus and Harvey Leibenstein.[21] Moreover, while industrialization was especially rapid in the 1940s and 1950s, there has been a distinct change in the character of industrial development (at least in the relatively more advanced countries) since the late 1950s. In the earlier periods of industrialization, the growth of manufacturing activity was concentrated in such fields as textiles, food and beverages, and other nondurable consumer goods (as well as simpler sorts of durable consumer goods), many of which were, relatively speaking, labor-intensive types of operations. Consequently, as these industries were established and expanded, their growth created jobs for a considerable number of workers, while the income of these workers, in turn, helped to expand the markets for the kinds of simpler consumer goods these industries were producing. To the extent that these types of goods were widely consumed, particularly among the lower-income groups of the population, the rise in the associated marketing or distribution activity also opened up new employment opportunities in the labor-intensive tertiary sector.

By the mid-1950s, however, the major dynamism had gone out of these fields, and industrialization shifted into such activities as the production of more elaborate consumer durable goods and basic industrial goods. For the most part, the production technologies employed in these newer fields have been borrowed almost intact from the industrialized nations in which they were originated, comparatively little attention having been devoted to examining the possibilities of modifying and adapting them to the very different factor endowment and factor prices which obtain in the borrowing milieu. Relatively little use, for example, seemed to be made of the kinds of subcontracting and other practices which enabled Japanese industry to develop on the basis of a technological dualism that tended to enhance the employment aspects of growth.[22] At the same time, however, it must be conceded that the cost of searching for means of adapting imported industrial technologies to the Latin American factor situation may not be negligible, given the dearth of the kinds of engineering and other skills needed for this task. The weakness of competition—because of protectionist policies and the prevalence of monopoloid and oligopoloid structures in domestic markets—has generally served to exempt many of these firms from the necessity of seeking the most efficient types of production technologies for their own production environments. Among a sizable number of these newer firms, however, foreign ownership, in whole or in part, is present, and with it access to the international capital market. Consequently, for these firms the supply price of capital often does not reflect domestic factor market conditions (where capital is relatively scarce and dear) so that their microeconomic-level decisions may even lead rationally in the direction of greater capital intensity on this basis alone.

Particularly may this be the case if we consider that it is not solely the internationally transferred capital (i.e., material or production technology) which contributes to the level of productivity in these foreign-linked enterprises. Of great importance, too, are the concomitant internationally transferred organizational structures—the social technology of management systems and the like, which determine the way one organizes, lays down channels of communication, and arrives at decisions. While there is, admittedly, an insufficient amount of empirical information available on the actual production functions utilized in foreign operations (with production functions defined to include organizational inputs as well as capital and labor inputs), it may well be that one element which contributes strongly to maintaining relatively fixed production functions of higher capital intensity derives from these transferred organizational arrangements which, without conscious adaptation, do not permit greater flexibility in feasible combinations of capital and labor inputs. In other words, a shift to other, less familiar, factor combinations may be perceived as involving high opportunity costs of an organizational nature. (To illustrate one of several possibilities in this respect, the shortage of middle-level supervisory skills required for effective management of a larger labor force [possessing fewer skills] works to bias the choice against relatively labor-intensive techniques.) Something of the sort, for example, does seem to have been involved in the observed preference of the World Bank and similar lending institutions for large capital-intensive projects which, in the context of a given organizational form and an accustomed mode of operations on the part of the loan agencies, are easier to plan and control than less capital intensive projects.[23] More broadly, if it is reasonable to assume that larger sale enterprises may generally (at least in many fields) tend to be more capital intensive than smaller scale ones, the distinct edge which the former usually enjoy over the latter in access to loan capital again leads to an anti-employment bias in the allocation of capital.

In any event, whatever the cause, it appears that that portion of the industrial sector which has exhibited the most dynamism in recent years has had very different implications for the employment situation when contrasted with the earlier phase. To be sure, labor productivity tends to be relatively high (if, partially, artifically so because of administered prices) in these newer fields, and wage levels in them are correspondingly higher than in most of the older industries. Yet, for the most part, they are much more capital-intensive than the earlier types of industries, so that their establishment and subsequent expansion have not increased the employment opportunities in manufacturing at anything like the rate which prevailed up to, say, the mid-1950s. Serving much more limited markets, relatively speaking, the new industries' effect on associated expansion in tertiary-sector employment has probably been less as well. At the same time, the kinds of jobs available in the new industries have skill requirements far higher than those which many of the new entrants into the urban labor market possess, a circumstance which, appropriately (in the absence of much greater social investment in skills development), encourages a resort to increased capital intensity as a means of economizing on skill labor. This situation of course, simply underscores the point that labor is not a homogeneous commodity and that, whereas unskilled labor is abundant, skilled labor (the type of input germane to the choice of factor mix) is scarce. Few governments provide direct subsidies linked to labor-training costs. Since, moreover, many of these newer industries cater to a higher-income clientele, which is augmented only slightly by the employment generated in the industries themselves, they contribute relatively less than did the earlier industrial growth to a general broadening of the national market. For a number of reasons, it may be supposed that many of these newer industries will reach the limits of their rapid growth stage much sooner than did the older industries, so that it would be misleading to expect the new wave of industrialization to provide much of an answer to the employment problem over the years ahead.[24] Indeed, to the extent that regional economic integration should accelerate the process of technological modernization in the older, and hitherto protected, industries, it is conceivable that increased technological unemployment might result in the same period.[e]

A second macrostructural feature of contemporary Latin America which raises problems for the employment level stems from the widespread relative neglect of the agricultural sector. In this case the failure to introduce meaningful institutional and other reforms has apparently been a factor in driving people out of the depressed rural regions into the cities, where they arrive with few skills of the sort which would facilitate their absorption into the urban employment structure. At least a portion of these migrants might well have found productive employment in the countryside had public investment been geared along Nurksian lines to transforming rural labor into rural capital, into raising the production possibilities of the agricultural sector by labor-intensive construction projects to build dams, irrigation and drainage systems, farm-to-market roads, rural schools, erosion control schemes, land-clearing schemes, and the like—some of which projects would also have served to increase the supply of cooperant land factors. At the same time, the institutionally-conditioned distribution of rural income has tended to inhibit the growth of national markets (in the more modest-income segments of those markets) for the kinds of manufactures and services which have generated many of the new jobs in the past several decades (thereby restricting the labor-absorptive capacity of the urban sector), while the neglect of agricultural productivity has apparently been a factor in raising food prices in urban markets producing a consequent upward pressure on industrial sector wages and encouraging employers to respond by replacing men with machinery in an effort to cut the wage bill.

Unfortunately, now that relatively more thought is at last being given to programs for agricultural development, some of the new ideas under consideration seem to offer scant promise of relieving unemployment—particularly those which aim at replicating the large-scale, capital-intensive, corporate style of agriculture practiced in the United States.[25] While this latter approach to agricultural modernization might conceivably be more compatible with the existing land tenure system, at least so far as concerns the large holdings, it is doubtful that it will be politically and socially tolerable or, indeed, really very economic if all social costs be taken into account. More difficult, institutionally speaking, but in the long run probably more feasible even from an economic point of view would seem to be an alternative route of rural modernization patterned somewhat after the Japanese experience, one in which a more progressive, labor-intensive type of agricultural technique would serve both to raise rural productivity and to enhance the employment opportunities of the rural sector.[26]

---

[e]Even without integration and its stimulus to technological modernization, the displacement of artisan production has been a source of technological unemployment. "The relative reduction in artisan employment as against factory employment is one of the factors most responsible for the failure of Latin American manufacturing as a whole to absorb much of the increase in the labor force." United Nations Economic Commission for Latin America, *The Process of Industrial Development in Latin America*, E/CN.12/716/Rev.1, New York: 1966, p. 40.

Related to the emphasis on industrialization and the neglect of the agricultural sector is a third macrostructural policy choice which has tended to compound the difficulties of maintaining reasonable levels of employment, particularly among the unskilled and semiskilled. Where export sector activities have suffered from discriminatory taxation and/or a discriminatory manipulation of exchange rates (as in the Uruguayan case), the result has often been to discourage the expansion of output and employment in fields in which the comparative international advantage has depended, in part, upon extensive use of labor factors.[27] Granted that the adverse employment repercussions stemming from this source are more significant in the case of agricultural exports than in mineral export industries, the importance of the former in the overall pattern of Latin American exports is such that the implications of development policy framed on the basis of export disincentives can hardly be overlooked.

A fourth problem at the macroeconomic policy level, one suggested by the previous reference to Nurkse's concept of capital formation, relates to the general inability or disinclination to institute the kinds of fiscal reforms which would enable the Latin American governments to accelerate public or social investment programs without recourse to inflationary techniques of finance. Any curtailment of the existing levels of conspicuous consumption (with their usual high import component) would probably be justifiable from the standpoint of releasing resources for more productive alternative uses (such as employment-creating outlays), just as a reduction of the possibilities for capital exportation currently enjoyed by the moneyed classes might be desirable on the grounds of fostering greater domestic capital formation. But from an employment perspective, there are even additional values. To the degree that social investment programs redistribute income downwards, they tend to broaden the home market for the kinds of items in which Latin American manufacturing industries have accumulated some production competence already, thereby renewing the dynamism of the industries which formerly played such an important role in adding to the supply of jobs. Beyond this, however, it is clear that a public investment program of the sort which is needed to meet the most pressing economic and social needs of the day in most countries would involve a considerable emphasis on construction activity (the building of roads and highways, education and health centers, popular housing, urban water systems, and so on), in which, it appears, there are considerable possibilities for utilizing labor-intensive production techniques effectively to absorb larger numbers of unskilled and semiskilled workers into the employment structure.

There are, of course, still other developmental values to such a program, among them the ability of the construction industry to draw upon resources which are largely internally available, the external economies generated by infrastructure, the use of construction employment to "prepare" workers for industrial employment in terms of skills and discipline, and the probable usefulness of popular housing as an "incentive good." Further, by expanding and modernizing the educational system, governments could do much to increase the supply of trained workers to industrial and other employers. The failure to do much along this line in the past has forced employers either to assume the additional expense of training their workers on the job (which consequent higher costs of production, higher prices, and narrower markets) or to seek to overcome the skills bottleneck by replacing labor with automated processes of production.

Besides these four general or macrostructural policy questions, the much-discussed problem of Latin American inflation is also germane to the issue because of its effects on the character of investment decisions. Quite apart from the inducement it has provided for capital flights, and the relation it thus has to the consequent lowered rates of national investment (and associated increases in employment), inflation has functioned as a tax on liquid assets. Since labor-intensive methods of production tend to require relatively heavy current assets as contrasted with fixed assets, and since investments in fixed capital may often be financed on credit, the impact of inflationary expectations may well have been that of encouraging firms to incur debts (for investment in material capital) the real burden of which declines through time in a manner which is not available in the handling of labor charges, particularly where the rate of inflation is high. The differential impact of inflation on fixed and variable segments of the cost structures of enterprises, in other words, would seem to be such that employment has suffered from the consequent biasing of investment decisions at the firm level. This in turn leads to a consideration of other policy repercussions which are manifested chiefly at the microeconomic level of operations.

At the microeconomic level of decision-making, one can identify a number of policies which seem inappropriate to a context in which employment objectives should loom large. For example, in most Latin American countries the labor and social legislation is such that "the incidence of fringe benefits on the total labor cost in industry is high in relation to straight hourly wages (as much as 50 percent or more, in some instances)," as a result of which employers "tend to favor the payment of overtime rather than the recruitment of new workers for whom they would have to pay all the fringe benefits."[28] Legally prescribed rules (where not circumvented) which make severance difficult and costly also increase the reluctance of employers to hire workers if, subsequently, it should be desirable to discharge any of them; here, increased capital intensity carries the advantage of a greater flexibility in decision-making.

For that matter, the fringe benefit costs are as high as they are because of the prevailing Latin American practice of financing social programs by what are, in effect, taxes on payrolls rather than through taxes on net business income.[f] While such practices may conceivably be justified on the grounds that employers might directly provide social services where needed more efficiently than could the public administrative apparatus, it is obvious that the policy of tying the tax

[f]A typical example of this may be taken from the Peruvian case in which employers assume responsibility for maternity benefits for female workers and must provide free elementary schools for the children of workers when the workers' families live adjacent to the establishment and when the school-age dependents of the workers number more than thirty. For further details on this and related topics see David Chaplin, *The Peruvian Industrial Labor Force*, Princeton University Press, 1967.

obligation to the size of the wage bill rather than to net income tends to increase, artificially, the supply price of labor while leaving the supply price of capital unaffected. To this extent, therefore, the existing labor and social legislation tends to bias business decisions against the employment of labor factors and to favor their replacement by capital. In all probability, the same set of circumstances also operates to discourage a more widespread use of multiple shifts as a technique of modifying the capital-labor mix in a direction favorable to employment objectives.

Additional distortion of business decisions regarding the factor mix, again in a direction unfavorable to the employment of labor, has been fairly common as a result of other prevalent policies. Very often, for instance, internal inflation (reflected in, among other things, money wages) has coexisted with fixed exchange rates and, from an international point of view, overvalued currencies. Since much of the capital equipment used in Latin American industry is imported, the effect of this foreign exchange policy has generally been to cheapen the supply price of (imported) capital inputs at the very time that labor costs were rising. While this alone would tend to encourage the displacement of labor by capital, the effects have on many occasions been accentuated when, under multiple exchange rate systems, preferentially low (and, in effect, subsidized) rates have been given for the importation of machinery and equipment. To be sure, the practice of favoring importation of capital items through preferential foreign exchange rates has been pursued with the intention of stimulating industrial growth rather than reducing employment, but from the standpoint of employment policy the negative impact of such a policy can hardly be ignored.

It should be noted that the same antiemployment side effects also inhere in a number of the other industrial promotion techniques common to the area. Here and there, for example, tax reduction inducements designed to encourage new investment seem to be based largely, or even entirely, on new investments in fixed capital rather than on new investments in fixed and working capital combined, the latter of which includes the wage bill. Few, if any, of the countries base tax reductions on employment created, while accelerated depreciation rates, where used as an industrial incentive, also lower the cost of fixed capital relative to labor. In the same manner, the low-interest loans frequently offered by development banks to new industries as a technique of subsidizing their inception are, more often than not, extended for the purchase of capital equipment and/or the construction of physical plant; much less frequently is this special low-cost credit made available for working capital purposes such as the financing of payrolls. In both cases—the tax inducements and the development loans—the manner in which the investment incentive is provided tends not only to raise the inducement to invest but also to influence the investment choice regarding factor proportions in a direction prejudicial to the employment of the labor factors of production.

Conclusion

The foregoing is intended to be a suggestive rather than exhaustive listing of the employment aspects of contemporary development policy in Latin America. The fact that employment policy, as such, has been so evidently peripheral to most Latin American policy-making and that, even when it has been mentioned, it has not entailed a systematic examination of the employment consequences of the policies actually being pursued, a number of which are of questionable value in this regard, suggests that serious efforts to moderate the impact of population growth on the working-class population lie almost entirely in the future. Furthermore, little in recent experience would support the view that the existing framework of policy formation in Latin America is adequate to the task. For reasons which lie beyond the scope of this paper, the most salient feature of the policy-making machinery which has functioned in the period under review has been, in plain terms, its rather consistent capacity to dodge the issue, or, perhaps, to bury it amid a preoccupation with other matters.

Notes

1. For a rather murkily expressed but nevertheless useful discussion of considerations of this sort, see Alain Touraine and Daniel Pécant, "Working-Class Consciousness and Economic Development in Latin America," *Studies in Comparative International Development*, Vol. III, No. 4 (1967-1968).

2. W. Galenson and H. Leibenstein, "Investment Criteria, Productivity and Economic Development," *Quarterly Journal of Economics*, Vol. LXIX, No. 3 (August 1955), pp. 343-70. The article makes a number of other relevant points not mentioned here, such as the supposedly superior skills-generating aspect of large, modern industries. See, however, W. Paul Strassmann, "Economic Growth and Income Distribution," *Quarterly Journal of Economics*, Vol. LXX, No. 3 (August 1956), pp. 425-40, in which it is argued that a broader distribution of income favors higher productivity and development.

3. See Walter Phillips, "Technological Levels and Labor Resistance to Change in the Course of Industrialization," *Economic Development and Cultural Change*, Vol. XI, No. 3 (April 1963), pp. 257-66.

4. The special labor mission's findings and recommendations are reproduced in *Revista Interamericana de Ciencias Sociales*, segunda época, Vol. 2, No. 2 (1963), pp. 170-82. In the main, the mission dwelt upon the need to strengthen trade union organizations (in urban and rural fields), to increase technical and vocational training facilities, and to foster such social projects as worker housing, credit cooperatives, and consumer cooperatives (preferably through trade union organizations) rather than an elaboration of programs to multiply employment opportunities. The general impression arises that the mission was somewhat more concerned with improving the lot of the organized workers than with more comprehensive programs which would embrace the unorganized as well.

5. Ibid., pp. 183-268, contains a review of the topics taken up for consideration at the conference, including the recommendations for action adopted by the labor ministers.

6. "Report of the First Meeting of Special Committee VII: Labor Matters," Inter-American Economic and Social Council, Pan American Union, Washington, D.C.: March 24, 1964 (OEA/Ser.H/XIII, CIES/Com.VII/22, Rev. 2-English).

7. "Summary of National Labor Reports on the Labor Situation in the Hemisphere," Special Committee VII: Labor Matters, Second Meeting, Buenos Aires, Argentina, October 19-26, 1964, Inter-American Economic and Social Council, Pan American Union, Washington, D.C.: October 2, 1964 (OEA/Ser. H/XIII, CIES/Com.VII/53-English). Also useful was another report prepared by the OAS General Secretariat for the same meeting: "Information on the Labor Force in Latin America" (OEA/Ser.H/XIII, CIES/Com.VII/52-English, October 1, 1964). The "Final Report of the Second Meeting of the Special Committee of the IA-ECOSOC on Labor Matters" (OEA/Ser.H/XIII, CIES/Com. VII/72, Rev.-English, October 26, 1964) was also used in preparing this paper. A number of other documents from the meeting were consulted but not found germane to the issues here under discussion.

8. "Final Report of the Second Meeting of the Special Committee of the IA-ECOSOC on Labor Matters" (OEA/Ser.H/XIII, CIES/Com.VII/72, Rev.-English, October 26, 1964), p. 13.

9. Ibid., p. 9.

10. Ibid., p. 14.

11. Secretariat of the Inter-American Regional Organization of Workers, "Report to the Sixth Continental Congress of ORIT," Mexico, D.F.: February 2-6, 1965, p. 11. At its Fifth Congress in Rio de Janeiro in August, 1961, the ORIT had emphasized the need to have labor representation in national planning, the CLASC (a christian-oriented labor confederation) had called for this repeatedly, and national labor centrals of every sort had also taken this position. See Geraldo von Potobsky, "Participation by Workers' and Employers' Organizations in Planning in Latin America," *International Labour Review*, Vol. 95, No. 6 (June, 1967), pp. 533-52. Interestingly, at the third meeting of the Trade Union Technical Advisory Committee of the OAS Department of Social Affairs, which was held at Bogota in January 1966, the results of another survey of trade union participation in national development plans were discussed. The findings of the survey indicated that there was still little evidence that trade unions were being brought into participation in the planning structure or in the plan implementation agencies. Neither was there any indication that trade unions were consulted about policies on employment, wages, and income redistribution. Generally speaking, unions were represented chiefly on minimum wage-setting agencies (where these existed) and on vocational training agencies. "The replies under study indicate that the development of trade unions, cooperatives, or other working class institutions is not as a rule among the socioeconomic objectives of the countries, nor are they considered essential to well-balanced development." "Report of the Third Meeting of the Trade Union Technical Advisory Committee," pp. 19-21 (OEA/Ser.H/X.8/CIES/846).

12. A convenient summary of this conference is contained in the *Revista Interamericana de Ciencias Sociales*, Vol. 4, No. 1 (1966).

13. OAS Official Records, OEA/Ser.K/XII.2.1, Dec. 16, April 15, 1966.

14. OAS Official Records, OEA/Ser.K/XII.2.1, Dec. 9, April 26, 1966.

15. Ibid., p. 16.

16. OAS Official Records, OEA/Ser.K/XII.2.1, Dec. 13, April 18, 1966.

17. Ibid., p. 1.

18. "Informe Final de la Primera Reunión del Comité Técnico Permanente Sobre Asuntos Laborales," Washington, D.C.: September 26-28, 1966 (UP/Ser. H/V/COTPAL/I/17, September 29.1966).

19. "Final Report, Second Meeting of Permanent Technical Committee on Labor Matters," Vina del Mar, Chile, June 12-14, 1967 (UP/Ser.H/V/ COTPAL/II/20, July 27, 1967).

20. International Labour Organisation, *Manpower Planning and Employment Policy in Economic Development*, Eighth Conference of American States Members of the International Labour Organisation, Ottawa, September 1966, pp. 35-36.

21. See R.S. Eckaus, "The Factor Proportions Problem in Underdeveloped Areas," *American Economic Review*, September, 1955, and H. Leibenstein, "Technical Progress, the Production Function, and Dualism," *Banca Nazionale del Lavoro Quarterly Review*, December, 1960. To the extent that the advanced industrial sector is characterized by a comparatively high capital intensity and production functions with relatively fixed factor proportions, while the "traditional" sector is characterized by a lower capital intensity and production functions with relatively variable factor proportions, the capacity of the advanced industrial sector to absorb labor is limited by the rate of capital accumulation and the balance of the growing labor force is thrown back upon the traditional sector wherein its marginal product may approach zero.

22. See S. Broadbridge, *Industrial Dualism in Japan: A Problem of Economic Growth and Structural Change* (London: Frank Cass and Co., Ltd., 1966).

23. For a discussion of this point, see Andrew Shonfield, *The Attack on World Poverty* (New York: Random House, 1960), pp. 15-16, 124-30.

24. For two articles examining this development, see "The Growth and Decline of Import Substitution in Brazil," *Economic Bulletin for Latin America*, Vol. IX, No. 1 (March 1964), pp. 1-60; and "Structural Changes in Employment Within the Context of Latin America's Economic Development," *Economic Bulletin for Latin America*, Vol. X, No. 2 (October 1965), pp. 163-87. See also the *Economic Survey of Latin America*, 1966, E/CN.12/767, pp. 50, 63.

25. Typical of the new perspective in agrarian modernization is L.H. Berlin, "A New Agricultural Strategy in Latin America," *International Development Review*, Vol. IX, No. 3 (September 1967), pp. 12-14. That this may be, in part, a function of the particular institutional context of the lending process (as Shonfield observed) through which credit-administration costs are reckoned is suggested by Warren J. Bilkey, "The Dominican Beef Case: Two Approaches to Stimulating Industry in a Developing Country," *International Development Review*, Vol. VIII, No. 1 (June, 1966), pp. 19-22.

26. A provocative discussion of the possibilities of this approach (with reference to India) is found in Morton Paglin, " 'Surplus' Agricultural Labor and Development: Facts and Theories," *American Economic Review*, Vol. LV, No. 4 (September 1965), pp. 815-34. For a cogent argument of the point in reference to Latin America, see Thiesenhusen in this volume and Melvin Burke, "An Analysis of the Bolivian Land Reform by Means of a Comparison between Peruvian Haciendas and Bolivian Ex-Haciendas," Ph.D. thesis, University of Pittsburgh, 1967.

27. For a useful discussion of Uruguayan problems in this connection, see David C. Redding, "Uruguary: An Advanced Case of the English Sickness?," mimeographed paper, Federal Reserve Board of Governors, Division of International Finance, July 28, 1966.

28. The same legislation also tends to impair labor mobility, resulting in the "overcommitment" of workers to particular jobs or firms.

10 Statutory Wages and Employment Stabilization in Latin America

Richard U. Miller

Although the humanitarian ideals embodied in modern social welfare legislation rarely engender controversy, its actual achievements often do. Rather than helping those groups in a society who are exploited by substandard wages, unsafe or unhealthy working conditions, or who are vulnerable to job loss by one means or another, it is frequently argued that the legislation has the opposite effect. Child labor laws are said to lead to high unemployment rates for younger workers; statutory wages cause the discharge of uneconomical, low-skilled workers (both young and old); social security costs induce employers generally to substitute capital for labor; and so on.

That social legislation does have an impact on employment is undenied. Instead the argument is joined first over the magnitude of the employment impact on the one hand and secondly on the value of the benefits received by those employed on the other. Existing empirical data, unfortunately, shed little light on these two questions. Moreover, most of the research carried out has been limited to the developed nations and that particularly to the United States.[1] This is a significant omission when one considers that social welfare programs are quite extensive in most developing countries while concomitantly, employment problems bulk large as major economic and political issues.

It was recently estimated, for example, that total unemployment in Latin America in 1960 reached nearly 26 percent of the economically active population and for individual sectors such as agriculture was 36 percent.[2] The OAS observed that the situation since 1960 has worsened, concluding "[o]bviously, measured by its performance in generating enough jobs to bring about a decline in unemployment and underemployment, Latin America has not turned the corner from 'stagnation or deterioration . . . into sustained growth.' "[3]

It is the premise of this paper that, in particular, two classes of social legislation, statutory minimum wages and employment stabilization policies, are in good part responsible for explaining several observable labor market phenomena in Latin America: stagnation of industrial sector employment; very large wage differentials between agricultural and industrial sectors; and relative uniformity of wage rates within the industrial sector. One is also tempted as well to add to this high rates of urbanization, since this also seems in part traceable to the dysfunctional consequences of wage and employment legislation.

The author wishes to acknowledge his indebtedness to Mr. Juan Viudez for his assistance in formulating the analysis and Professor Donald Schwab for his valuable suggestions for redrafting the original manuscript.

209

The discussion in Part I of the paper will identify certain characteristics predominating in Latin American labor markets as well as relate these characteristics to several generally accepted explanations of labor market structure and functioning in developing countries.

In Part II the statutory wage and job stabilization legislation will be analyzed for their potential employment and wage impact. Here resort will be made primarily to marginal analysis from economics in order to identify causal relationships.

The final section will consider the implications derived from the analysis, indicating briefly the direction to which manpower policy might be channeled in order to alleviate the dysfunctions associated with wage and employment legislation in developing countries.

I. Discussion

In recent years economic science increasingly, albeit grudgingly, has come to accept the proposition that economic growth is a function of human resource development as well as capital accumulation and levels of investment. No longer is it heresy to suggest that "[t]he building of modern nations depends upon the development of people and the organization of human activity. Capital, natural resources, foreign aid, and international trade, of course play important roles in economic growth, but none is more important than manpower."[4] The work of Harbison and Myers,[5] Schultz,[6] Hagen,[7] McClelland,[8] among others, has long since legitimated this position.

The recognition accorded to human resource development and manpower planning has in turn generated theoretical and empirical attempts directed at describing, explaining and predicting the precise causal nexus between economic growth and the quality and quantity of an economy's human resources. On the basis of the "models" as well as data now accumulated, one can generalize Latin American societies to be characterized as (1) dual economies in which small modern industrial sectors exist as enclaves within much larger undeveloped agricultural sectors;[9] (2) rapidly urbanizing populations in which mass migration from rural to urban areas prevail;[10] and surplus labor markets in which visible and disguised unemployment are rampant in both rural and urban areas. (Economically speaking, surplus labor will be defined as those workers whose marginal product is negligible or zero.)[11]

In particular, conventional labor market theory postulates that in the absence of regulatory impediments competitive economic forces will produce a sequential growth of manufacturing and services employment in response to a decline in the agricultural sector.[12]

A study of many countries over long periods reveals certain general principles of growth. As a country increases in per capita income and wealth, the relative importance of different sectors of the economy shifts in a systematic way....

The clearest and strongest tendency is a long run decline in the relative importance of agriculture. The proportion of the labor force engaged in agriculture falls from 70 percent or more in the least developed countries to between 10 and 20 percent in the most advanced... Industries engaged in commodity production—manufacturing, mining, construction—increase sharply in importance as economic growth proceeds, but this increase does not continue indefinitely. After a certain point, the proportion of the labor force engaged in these industries levels off and moves along a plateau.[13]

The plateau is expected to vary between 30 and 40 percent of the labor force although it might possibly reach as high as 50 percent of the labor force.[14] As agriculture declines and commodity production levels off, tertiary or services connected employment then expands to take up the slack. The predominance of this sector in the labor force serves as the hallmark of the wealthiest, most developed countries.

Secondly, average wages paid to workers in the modern or capitalist sector should exceed those paid to subsistence sector workers only by a small amount (that necessary to cover costs of transfer from one sector to the other in addition to higher urban cost of living).[a] And finally, within the industrial or capitalist sector, as economic development advances, wages of skilled workers should increase at a proportionately faster rate than those for unskilled workers. The logic of this generalization is that while there are unlimited supplies of unskilled workers available at a constant wage, the same can not be said for skilled workers. The supply of the latter is much less elastic, hence with upward shifts in the demand for skilled labor, the price must necessarily rise, widening the gap between skilled and unskilled wages in the capitalist sector.

The growth, structure, and pricing of labor factor inputs in response to the course of Latin American economic development thus can theoretically be described in some detail. An impressive amount of evidence is being accumulated in support of the first three sets of generalizations considered above; that is, that Latin American societies are dual economies marked by rapid urbanization and surplus labor. Empirical support for the hypothesized sectoral shifts in employment as well as capitalist subsistence or skilled-unskilled wage differentials, however is much less evident. The paradox posed by confronting Latin American reality with theory will be considered below.

The sectoral expansion of employment: Contrary to Clark, as agricultural employment has declined, manufacturing or industrial employment has not expanded. Rather, as Table 10-1 shows, employment growth has been limited to the services sector.

---

[a]With an unlimited supply of labor from the subsistence sector, employers can hire any quantity of units of labor desired at a constant wage. The labor supply curve thus approximates perfect elasticity with changes in capitalist sector wage levels dependent upon changes in the subsistence sector. W.A. Lewis, "Economic Development with Unlimited Supplies of Labour," *The Manchester School of Economic and Social Studies*, Vol. XXII, No. 2, May 1954, pp. 145-51.

Table 10-1
Distribution of Employment by Economic Sectors Latin America 1925-1960

	Percent of Economically Active Population		
	Agriculture and Mining	Manufacturing	Services[a]
1925	62.3	13.7	24.0
1950	52.2	14.5	31.4
1955	51.1	14.3	34.6
1960	48.3	13.4	37.4

Source: "Structural Change in Employment Within the Context of Latin American Economic Development," *Economic Bulletin for Latin America*, Vol. X, No. 2, October 1965, p. 167.
[a]Includes construction to maintain comparability with Clark.

Individual countries showing a marked decline in the proportion of manufacturing employment in the period 1947-1960 are Chile, Ecuador, Haiti, Panama, Paraguay, and Peru, while most of the remainder were stationary or experienced minimal change.[15] Mexico, for example, employed relatively fewer in its manufacturing sector in 1960 than it did at the advent of its revolution in 1910.[b] While some authors[16] contend that we are merely witnessing "an employment multiplier effect" in which one new manufacturing job creates the need for three or four jobs in the service sector, a more plausible explanation is that rural migrants to urban areas, unable to secure factory employment, are forced into service employment of a predominantly petty nature. In Lewis' terms they come to occupy urban subsistence employment.[17] Thus, in contrast to the United States and Europe, where better than one-half of urban employment is accounted for by industrial work, Latin American urban centers provide one-third or less of their job seekers with industrial work.[18]

The subsistence v. capitalist sector wage differential: It was stated above that W. Arthur Lewis, in what has become a classical work, argued persuasively that so long as productivity was low and the supply of labor unlimited in the subsistence sectors the gap between this sector and wages in the industrial or capitalistic sector would be on the order of 30 percent.[19] Recent research indicates this differential is far greater than assumed by Lewis. For example, the Economic Commission for Latin America concludes that for Brazil industrial wages average 70 percent greater than those in agriculture while in Mexico the capitalist-subsistence differential is 75 percent.[20] The wage disparity is even larger in such countries as Colombia, Costa Rica, Peru, and Chile.[21]

Skilled v. unskilled capitalist sector wage differential: At a recent conference on manpower planning and economic development the ILO pointed out:

[b]Statistics presented in Nacional Financiera, *Statistics on the Mexican Economy*, Mexico, D.F., 1966, p. 26 give a sectoral division of employment to be:

	Agriculture and Extraction	Mfg.	Service and Construction
1910	64.4	15.4	18.7
1960	51.8	13.1	30.5

Shortages of trained manpower available to meet current and foreseeable needs in a wide range of occupations are reported from almost all Latin American countries. . . . The general situation is well known: there is a mass of actual and potential workers lacking partly or wholly the most elementary technical qualifications; as to the more qualified manpower already in employment, the basic training received is often so inadequate that upgrading and retraining are very costly if at all possible. Such shortages of trained manpower have been a serious bottleneck for economic development, particularly for industrialization schemes.[22]

Well known also is the non-technical orientation of the bulk of Latin American educational systems. Thus it is not illogical to conceive of the labor market for skilled workers to be one in which progressive industrialization generates a growing demand for these workers which can not be met. The predicted result would be a growing disparity in wages between skilled workers and the unskilled whose wage remains set by conditions in the subsistence sector.[23]

Evidence, which can be considered as fragmentary at best, seems to indicate that the logic of the situation is not borne out. For those countries for which wage structure data are available, the differential between skilled and unskilled in the industrial sector, has narrowed very greatly, if not disappeared all together. Argentina, for example, has experienced a situation in which a differential in favor of skilled factory workers of 71 percent in 1935-1939 was successively reduced to 26 percent in 1950-1954 and by 1965 stood at a mere 13 percent.[24]

Although evidence is not presented, Fischlowitz indicates that the situation in Brazil parallels that in Argentina, concluding that the former country possesses "an extreme uniformity of wage rates which certainly discourages any great effort to acquire higher vocational skills, with the investment of time, money, and other immediate sacrifices which such an effort would involve."[25]

The third of the ABC countries, Chile, follows the pattern of the first two. A trend toward narrowing of the skill differential is apparent here as well.[26] Moreover, the gap between skilled-unskilled wages is now so small that it would virtually disappear if total remuneration (fringe benefits) were considered.[27] Consequently, the Chilean wage structure is much more like that of the most highly developed countries than its actual counterparts in development elsewhere in the world.[28]

The final country for which pertinent wage data were available was that of Mexico. And here the data are even more restricted in scope, pertaining, unfortunately, only to the steel industry. As can be observed from Table 10-2, however, a narrowing of the differential clearly has occurred over the period 1936-1963 on the order of 18 percent.

From the foregoing, a picture of Latin American labor markets begins to take shape in which the industrial sector holds little potential for absorbing a rapidly expanding urban labor force; that despite an unlimited supply of labor at constant wages the industrial wage has risen far beyond that of the subsistence

Table 10-2
Ratio of Skilled to Unskilled Wages Mexican Steel Industry

1936-1963	
1936	1:65
1948	1:57
1955	1:41
1959	1:35
1963	1:35

Source: Computed by the author from the wage schedule of labor grades negotiated by the Industrial Union of Miners and Metal Workers and La Fundidora Steel Company.

sector; and finally, again, in the face of "irrevocable" laws of supply and demand, the internal wage has become quite narrow and uniform.

In the following section, the question of the relationship of statutory wages and employment stabilization to those characteristics of the labor markets enumerated above will be considered analytically through a conventional tool of economics, marginal analysis. It is hoped that by so doing the variables in the relationship can be more precisely identified, their dependency specified, and the nature of their relationship more clearly understood.

II. The Impact if Statutory Wages and
Employment Stabilization Policies

Statutory Wages

Given an unlimited supply of labor the supply curve is perfectly elastic. The firm can hire as many additional units of labor as it desires without having to pay any more for these additional units. The wage differential is determined by the cost to the worker, both real and psychological, of moving from the agricultural or subsistence sector to the industrial, urban, capitalist sector. This differential was conceived by Lewis to be on the order of 30 percent.

The employer's demand curve for labor is derived from two factors: the productivity of labor; and the price for which the goods produced by labor can be sold. Thus an employer will hire additional units of labor only up to the point where the cost of the last worker equals the value to be received from the sale of what he produces. To hire more units of labor would require the employer to pay more in wages to the worker than could be obtained from selling what this worker produced. Therefore, if a statutory wage increase has been decreed, to keep his marginal labor costs and revenue in balance, the employer must reduce his employment.

In many Latin American countries, such as Mexico, statutory minimum wages have been increased biennially while in others, like Argentina, Brazil, and Chile, this has occurred over even shorter intervals.[29] In addition, the legal minimum wage, even if it applies beyond the industrial sector, which frequently it doesn't, is enforced most effectively and energetically upon the more conspicuous manufacturing firms. These are often the larger, foreign owned companies for whom avoidance is difficult if not dangerous. Finally, it should be noted that the agricultural sector of most Latin American countries has not achieved significant increases in productivity but rather in some instances exhibits declining productivity. Thus the ingredients are at hand for a situation in which the subsistence wage remains fixed, the capitalist sector wage increases periodically, and the differential between the two grows far beyond the 30 percent prophesized by Lewis. "Islands" of high wages occur in which the industrial workers become the elite of the proletariat.

Further, it could be expected that high industrial or capitalist sector wage levels have an acceleration effect on the urbanization of the population on the one hand as well as to urban unemployment on the other. One could argue that workers are pulled out of rural areas by the high wages of the capitalist sector in contrast to the conventional thesis that unemployment or underemployment in rural areas pushes workers out to urban areas in search of employment. And once there, these rural migrants, lacking skills which would offset the "artificially" high cost the employer would have to bear in hiring them, drift into service jobs or become unemployed.[30] Thus urban unemployment or underemployment could exist independent of unemployment in the countryside.

It was indicated above that the employer responded to the wage increase with a reduction in employment. Were he to do this he would have to raise the productivity of his remaining workers in order to prevent the firm's total output of goods from falling. For this reason the employer is provided with an incentive to increase the amount of capital he is using; that is, to substitute capital for labor.

A third possibility is a situation in which, over time, demand for the firm's produce increases but simultaneous increases in the statutory wage have also occurred. If one were to diagram the appropriate changes, it would be depicted by successive upward shifts in the supply curve of labor and outward shifts in the employer's demand curve. The new intersection point for the supply and demand curves would result in increased wages with unchanged or reduced quantities of labor demanded. Therefore, despite greatly expanded industrial production, industrial employment remains stationary, or perhaps even declines, relative to other sectors such as service employment. This phenomenon was noted in the discussion section as characteristic of most Latin American labor markets.

Next is the question of the uniformity of the industrial wage structure. Narrowing of skilled-unskilled wage differentials has occurred in a number of countries contrary to what labor market theory would predict. Again, at least in part, this occurrence seems traceable to statutory minimum wages through the following mechanism. As the minimum wage is raised, workers below the minimum (likely to be the unskilled or semi-skilled) are brought up to it, but workers already at or above minimum are not given corresponding increases.[c] Although only one observer points directly at minimum wage legislation as the major determinant in observed industrial wage uniformity,[31] it nevertheless seems inescapable that a strong relationship exists.

In addition to general employment and wage effects, statutory wage changes also have been observed as related to the special problems of particular segments of the economically active population. Thus, for example, a rapid increase in population has lowered the age structure, producing in many Latin American countries a population averaging under twenty years of age. This, coupled with a school dropout rate reaching 90 percent before a six grade level of education is attained, means that nearly all of this young population is soon in the labor market seeking work.[32] Having few skills and little productivity to offer, industrial employers find young workers uneconomical to hire in view of their legally stipulated cost. Even in those instances where the wage law permits a reduction in the statutory wage for youthful workers there are dysfunctional employment consequences.[d] Illustrative of this fact, a recent report concluded:

. . . When there is an official period of probation during which a wage below the minimum (or even no wage at all) is paid, it often appears that the employer dismisses the young worker as soon as the period is up and brings in another who will suffer the same fate.[33]

Under the circumstances many workers find themselves shuttling around to different employers and different jobs without an opportunity to acquire necessary skills or job security.

Employment Stabilization Legislation[34]

A pervasive concern for affording workers maximum job security is manifested throughout the nations of Latin America in legislation aimed at restricting the employer's power of dismissal. Specifically job security has come to signify "the idea that an employee has a right to keep his job during his whole working life and that he cannot be deprived of it unless there is cause justifying dismissal."[35] In much of the legislation "just cause" is synonymous only with serious misconduct on the employee's part, thus excluding reasons not connected with the worker's behavior (including economic problems of the firm). Recourse is provided through civil or labor court systems which may either order reinstatement or require the payment of compensation of varying amounts to the individual declared unjustifiably dismissed.[e]

---

[c]The U.S. Department of Labor, studying the effects of the 1956 $1.00 minimum wage on seven low wage industries, found this to be a major result of the statutory increase. Norman Samuels, "Effects of the $1.00 Minimum Wage on Seven Industries," *Monthly Labor Review*, March 1957, pp. 323-28.

[d]In Argentina, for example, a minus differential is permitted as follows: Age 17, 10 percent; Age 16, 20 percent; Age 15, 30 percent; and Age 14, 40 percent. Amaldo R. Campaño, "The Minimum Wage Act in Argentina," *International Labour Review*, Vol. 94, Sept. 1966, pp. 237-54.

[e]In Argentina, Bolivia, Brazil, Colombia, Costa Rica, Ecuador, Guatemala, Honduras, Peru, Uruguay, and Venezuela, one month's wages per year of service is the norm. For Mexico,

For many countries the law is quite restrictive as well for those situations in which technological change, market conditions, and related factors necessitate a reduction in force. For example, Ecuador stipulates that the approval of a governmental labor inspector be obtained prior to dismissal and that it is unlawful to dismiss simultaneously two or more workers in a firm of twenty or less employees or to dismiss five or more workers in a firm larger than twenty employees. In other countries, such as Mexico and Chile, suspension or dismissal of personnel for economic reasons also requires prior governmental permission.

Hence, although employment stability legislation does not preclude completely dismissals for either disciplinary or economic reasons it does introduce elements of uncertainty, expense, and delay if this course of action is attempted. As a consequence, incompetent or inefficient workers may be retained, as well as quantities of employees in excess of those optimally required for given levels of production.

The increased inefficiency of the workforce will be reflected in lower physical productivity per worker. In contrast to minimum wage legislation which affects the supply side of the labor market, job security or employment stabilization legislation affects the demand for labor. Given the existence of stabilization legislation, labor's marginal product curve is to the left of what it would otherwise be. Assuming a condition of perfect elasticity in the supply of labor, the employer's response to reduced productivity will be to hire fewer units of labor. The reason for the employer's behavior is not hard to comprehend if it is remembered that the firm, in optimizing, must adjust employment levels to keep the marginal product of its labor input in line with its marginal cost. The latter equals average cost under the circumstances and is constant, while the marginal product is not. Thus the response to reduced productivity must necessarily be lower employment. While they work in different ways, the employment impact of both types of social legislation is the same however: fewer jobs available to employment seekers.

Unfortunately the dysfunctional consequences do not end with reduced levels of employment. To compensate for the inefficiencies and additional costs employment stabilization imposes, the employer will be forced to substitute capital for labor.[f] Capital is thereby diverted from other uses, placing further strains on already capital short economies.[g]

---

the compensation required is three months wages plus twenty days additional indemnity for each year of service. Brazil also requires double indemnity for workers with ten years or more employment.

[f]With productivity reduced the employer would have to employ more units of labor to reach "normal" levels of output in doing so the marginal cost of these additional labor inputs would exceed the value of the product obtained from them. Rather than do this he would raise the productivity of the smaller number of workers by providing them with more capital and raise output to the desired level this way.

[g]It might be suggested that the labor of the remaining units could be used more intensively as through working employees longer hours, raising its output this way. Given restrictions on the number of hours which can be worked in most Latin American countries as well as the existence of high premiums for overtime this would offer only a temporary solution at best.

Further, with output raised by increasing the ratio of capital to labor the total returns to capital would increase while those to labor would diminish. In other words, the amount of national income generated by the industrial sector belonging to profits would grow proportionately larger than that for wages.[h] Wages and salaries as a share of national income would decline proportionately and this in turn would act to dampen consumption and restrict the growth of domestic markets. The characteristic Latin American market situation is then created of overcapitalized firms, producing below efficient levels of operation with attendant high costs and prices.

Upward biases on price levels also can be traced to employment stabilization legislation in another way. Since the employer can not reduce his workforce with any ease in an economic downturn in which a falling volume of sales in turn requires a concomitant lowering of output, a static level of employment will raise unit labor costs. This will act as a floor preventing prices from being adjusted downward to compensate for falling sales. On the other hand, under conditions of increasing volume of product demand an employer will be reluctant to add the additional workers necessary to raise output to meet demand. Therefore, with supply to the market relatively inelastic, the inevitable result will be increased prices.

III. Summary and Conclusions

The generalizations to be made in this section are intended to be only tentative. In the first place, a great many more data are required before the full nature of the relationship of wages and employment to social legislation is understood and predictable. Secondly, the analysis has been limited purposely to only two categories of legislation, statutory wages and employment stabilization. We have omitted any discussion of other categories including pension, family allowance, maternity benefits, and trade union legislation. It is likely, however, that each of these as well has an identifiable and perhaps measurable impact. Support for this assertion is supplied at least for Peru by Chaplin who, in reviewing the effect of social welfare laws regulating the employment of females, concludes: ". . . these laws are seen by employers as being so expensive that, since they have been enforced, especially after 1956 in the larger urban factories. . . . A deliberate policy of hiring as few women as possible has been pursued."[36]

In the foregoing sections it was concluded that:

1. Observed lack of growth of secondary or industrial employment, widening of the wage gap between subsistence and capitalist sectors, as well as narrowing of differentials between skilled and unskilled workers within the industrial sector appear strongly related to governmental minimum wage activity. The

[h]It should also be noted that with productivity raised those units of labor employed in the industrial sector could and, aided by trade union action, probably would be paid higher wages. This would permit the gap between the subsistence and industrial wage to grow even more.

high capitalist wage probably speeds urbanization of rural workers who, unable to find industrial employment, are forced into unemployment or urban subsistence employment. Moreover, as the industrial wage narrows, the incentive for acquiring work skills diminishes reducing further the availability of already scarce higher level manpower.

2. Employment stabilization legislation also gives evidence of contributing to a decline in employment opportunities in the secondary sector. To combat the rigidity in labor use accompanying this legislation employers were observed also to substitute capital for labor. The resulting increased ratio of capital to labor raises total profits and lowers the amount going to the waged sector of the labor force thus dampening the growth of domestic markets. Paradoxically, it was noted that the increased capital raised productivity of the remaining industrial workers permitting their average wages to go up. This contributed to widening further the subsistence-capitalist sector gap. Also identified through governmentally stabilized employment was an upward bias on prices.

It seems obvious from the foregoing that developing countries must integrate investment, employment, and social welfare programs. To neglect this may result in the creation of unforeseen obstacles which cause the programs to cancel each other out. On the one hand, developmental programs which lower the cost of investment capital while raising the price of labor may lead to the growth of industries for which there are no markets. On the other, welfare laws requiring pre-natal care, family allowances, and child care centers result in women being channeled by employer discrimination into occupations in which they have more children than otherwise, but without access to the benefits and services covered employment would have supplied.[37] Thus, at a time when a government may be struggling to dampen its swelling population, its social legislation, by raising the fertility rates of urban females, is encouraging a contradictory result. Other illustrations drawn from governmental agricultural policies, import substitution programs, and the like could be provided, but the above should be sufficient to illuminate the problem.

Economic planning, therefore, must consider simultaneously the setting of employment and investment goals together with those dealing with social welfare if scarce resources are to be allocated optimally and programs are not to be self-defeating. As it stands now, planning is limited to capital investment, employment assumed to flow automatically out of investment, and social welfare programs operated without regard for either employment or investment.[38] The pitfalls of governing a society in this fashion are clearly evident.

Notes

1. The major exceptions to this generalization, at least as far as Latin America is concerned, appear to be: Tom E. Davis, "Dualism, Stagnation, and

Inequality: The Impact of Pension Legislation in the Chilean Labor Market,"
Industrial and Labor Relations Review: Vol. 17, April 1964, pp. 380-98; Lloyd
G. Reynolds, "Wages and Employment in a Labor Surplus Economy," *American
Economic Review*, March 1965, pp. 19-39; and Carlos W. Lastra, *The Impact of
Minimum Wages on a Labor-Oriented Industry*, GovBank Technical Papers, No.
1, Puerto Rico, 1964, among others.

2. "The Unemployment Problem in Latin America," Third Inter-American
Conference of Ministers of Labor on the Alliance for Progress, Organization of
American States, October 1969, Table 6, p. 13.

3. Ibid. p. 14.

4. Frederick Harbison and Charles A. Myers *Education, Manpower, and
Economic Growth*, (New York: McGraw-Hill, 1964), v.

5. Ibid.

6. T.W. Schultz. "Investment in Human Capital," *American Economic
Review*, Vol. 51, No. 1, March 1961.

7. Everett Hagen, *On the Theory of Social Change* (Homewood, Ill., Dorsey
Press, 1962).

8. David C. McClelland, *The Achieving Society* (Princeton, N.J.: Van
Nostrand, 1961).

9. Various authors have dichotomized developing countries in terms of
capitalist vs. subsistence; traditional vs. modern, and so on. Cf. W.A. Lewis,
"Economic Development with Unlimited Supplies of Labour," *The Manchester
School of Economic and Social Studies*, Vol. XXII, No. 2, May 1954, pp.
139-91.

10. A plethora of materials exists for the issue of urbanization in Latin
America, but for two recent efforts see: Glenn H. Beyer, *The Urban Explosion
in Latin America* (Ithaca: Cornell University Press, 1967); and Gerald Breese,
Urbanization in Newly Developing Countries (Englewood Cliffs, New Jersey:
Prentice-Hall, 1966).

11. See Stanislaw Wellisz, "Dual Economies, Disguised Unemployment and
the Unlimited Supply of Labour," *Economica*, February 1968, p. 35.

12. Colin Clark, *The Conditions of Economic Progress*, 3rd edition (London:
MacMillan and Co., 1957), p. 492. According to Clark ". . . as time goes on and
communities become more economically advanced, the numbers engaged in
agriculture tend to decline relative to the numbers in manufacture, which in
their turn decline relative to the numbers engaged in services." (p. 492) See also
Everett E. Hagen, *The Economics of Development* (Homewood, Ill.: Irwin,
1968), pp. 45-49.

13. Lloyd G. Reynolds, *Labor Economics and Labor Relations* 3rd edition
(Englewood Cliffs, New Jersey: Prentice-Hall, 1959), p. 349.

14. Ibid.

15. International Labour Organization, *Manpower Planning and Employment
Policy in Economic Development*, Report II, Eighth Conference of American
States Members of the International Labour Organization, Ottawa 1966, pp.
43-45.

16. See Walter Galenson. "Economic Development and the Sectoral Expansion of Employment," *International Labour Review*, Vol. 87, June 1963. Galensen argues that "Under conditions of modern technology, however, [the manufacturing sector's] role is not likely to be that of a major source of new employment. Rather it will tend to generate the effective demand leading to employment expansion in other sectors." This explanation of the growth of urban service employment is rejected here for reasons which will be outlined below.

17. See Lewis, "Economic Development," p. 141.

18. "Structural Change in Employment Within the Context of Latin American Economic Development," *Economic Bulletin for Latin America*, Vol. X, No. 2, October 1965, p. 182.

19. Lewis, "Economic Development," p. 150.

20. Comision Economica para America Latina, *Estudios Sobre La Distribución del Ingreso en America Latina*, E/CN. 12/770 Add. 1, 21 April 1967, p. 9.

21. International Labour Organization, *The Role of Social Security and Improved Living and Working Standards in Social and Economic Development*, Report III "Remuneration and Conditions of Work," Eighth Conference of American States Members of the ILO, Ottawa, September 1966, p. 3.

22. ILO, p. 80.

23. See Estanislaw Fischlowitz, "Manpower Problems in Brazil, *International Labour Review*, Vol. 79, April 1959, pp. 398-417, on this point. He cites the case of the expansion of the Brazilian auto industry in the early 1960s in which the level of employment jumped from 35,000 to 120,000, necessitating a crash program to upgrade semi-skilled workers.

24. U.S. Department of Labor. *Labor Developments Abroad*, June 1967, pp. 21-22. Cf. also Morris Horowitz, "High-Level Manpower in the Economic Development of Argentina," in Frederick Harbison and Charles A. Myers, (eds), *Manpower and Education* (New York: McGraw-Hill, 1965), pp. 24-25.

25. Fischlowitz, "Manpower Problems," p. 407.

26. H. Günter, "Changes in Occupational Wage Differentials," *International Labour Review*, Vol. 89, February 1964, p. 143.

27. Peter Gregory, *Industrial Wages in Chile* (Ithaca, N.Y.: New York State School of Industrial and Labor Relations, 1967), p. 88.

28. Ibid., p. 90. Gregory lays the blame for wage narrowing at the door of inflation. The effect of statutory wages, social security costs and the like is rather one of reduced employment through encouraging employers to substitute capital for labor.

29. Pan American Union, Inter-American Economic and Social Council, *Summary of National Reports on the Labor Situation in the Hemisphere*, OEA/Ser H/XIII, CIES/Com. VII/53, October 2, 1964, pp. 12-17.

30. See Stanislaw Wellisz. "Dual Economies, Disguised Unemployment and the Unlimited Supply of Labour," *Economica*, February 1968, p. 43.

31. Fischlowitz, "Manpower Problems," p. 407.

32. "Youth and Work in Latin America," Part I, *International Labour Review*, Vol. 90, No. 1, p. 20.

33. "Youth and Work in Latin America," Part II, *International Labour Review*, Vol. 90, No. 2, p. 160.

34. Except where noted, the information for this section of the paper is drawn from International Labour Organization, *Some Aspects of Labour-Management Relations in the American Region* (Geneva: International Labour Office, 1962), pp. 64-94.

35. Ibid., p. 68.

36. David Chaplin, "Some Institutional Determinants of Fertility in Peru," in this volume, p. 225.

37. Ibid., p. 226.

38. See Glade on this point in his, "The Employment Question and Development Policies in Latin America," in this volume, pp. 191-192.

11 Some Institutional Determinants of Fertility in Peru

David Chaplin

There are several established expectations as to the demographic transition in currently developing countries which seem to be contradicted by evidence from Peru. In this respect it is assumed, and in some cases it can be demonstrated, that Peru's experience is similar to the majority of other Latin American countries except for Uruguay, Argentina, and Cuba. (Peru was chosen as the focus for this study because its demographic situation has received far more attention than that of any of the other Andean Latin American countries.)

The first of these expectations is that the current population explosion arises, not from an increase in birth rates, which were initially high and presumably uncontrolled, but only from a decrease in death rates which could be manipulated externally and with relatively little local resistance. Growth then would occur from the resulting natural increase and would continue until the birth rate fell to the level of the death rate.

A detailed examination of Latin American birth rates reveals, however, that most have actually risen in recent decades rather than fallen. Collver notes that "pessimists ... will find cause for alarm in (his) report."[1] As Latin America continues to develop economically it can be assumed that this trend will eventually be reversed—as the dotted line in Figure 11-1 suggests—but in the meanwhile, the transitional stage will be even more difficult than anticipated and the possibility of occasional Malthusian checks (famine, war, and disease) operating in some areas seems fairly likely.

The reasons for this unanticipated increase in birth rates, then, are well worth pursuing. Improved health conditions, and therefore lowered mortality, can have the effect of raising the birth rate since more women live through their fertile years, and are also more fecund during this period.[2] Thus, even if the percent married—or the age specific birth rates[a]—did not rise, large increase in female longevity would raise the annual birth rate. In Peru, the average life expectancy of females only recently exceeded that of the end of the fertile period (fifty years in 1961). After Collver took changes in the distribution of age groups into account, the increase in the crude birth rate between 1940 and 1960 was raised still further.[3]

The author wishes to acknowledge the helpful criticism of Dudley Kirk, Yuan Tien, and Murray Gendell, but accepts, of course, all responsibility for deficiencies.

[a] *Children born to women of a specific age*
   All women of that age

223

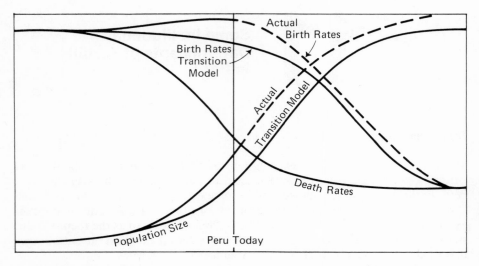

Figure 11-1. The Demographic Transition and Peruvian Population Growth.

   In addition to trends in mortality, which transitionally increase fertility, there are other, more institutional, factors in operation in all societies which should be examined.[4] Two closely interrelated ones are the age-at-marriage of women and the percent married. If age-specific birth rates do not change and fertility takes place within marital unions (their legality is an open question in Latin America), then an increase in the average age-at-marriage will decrease the immediate birth rate as well as the long run level of fertility. This effect is especially relevant to a high fertility population such as that of Peru.[5] Again, even if marital fertility, defined as the size of completed family, remained unchanged, fertility would be reduced by virtue of a wider spacing of generations.[6] In addition, during the shift up of the age-at-marriage there would be a transitional lost birth group which would never be made up. Of course, a population marrying later would probably also have smaller families and thus decelerate growth even further.

   At the same time, this factor, like the others to be discussed, could operate in the opposite direction. If the age-at-marriage fell, an extra "cohort" of children would be added on top of a speeded up reproductive velocity, i.e., a shorter length of generations. Again, while the cited studies on this variable assumed no change in completed family size, in order to measure the effect of changes in age-at-marriage alone, it is likely that the size of completed family would increase if the age-at-marriage fell.

   In Peru in 1961 the mean age of mothers at the birth of their first child was twenty for both urban and rural areas. Unfortunately there are no reliable comparable data for an earlier period. It could be assumed that with an increasing proportion of women in school for longer periods of time, the age-at-marriage would rise—especially as urban areas grow faster than rural. However, the under-age-twenty distribution of the age at the birth of the first child indicates that women bear sooner in urban areas up until age eighteen.

While a younger age-at-marriage favors a higher birth rate and higher completed family size, very young ages of reproduction can have detrimental effects on later fecundity for biological as well as social reasons. Therefore, if the average age-at-marriage rose above these subminimal levels, a rise in fertility could occur but at the higher ages, such as twenty, at which we now find Peru, an increase should have the opposite effect.

The percent married would clearly tend to increase fertility if it rose—as it in fact has done in most Latin American countries.[7] The extensive number of consensual unions is such that one could well discount changes in this index as relevant more to changes in morality than in fertility. However, Collver found a significant relationship between changes in the marriage rate and in the birth rate in Latin America, owing to wars and business cycles.[8] This finding, then, has at least a double importance for present purposes. It establishes changes in the marriage rate as a highly probable cause of fluctuations in the birth rate and it reveals that the birth rate in Latin America has already been "controlled" even if not by means of contraception. That is, the population has voluntarily undertaken an action—postponing or foregoing marriage, which has the effect of reducing the birth rate. We should then examine factors which affect the marriage rate more closely.

Collver found that the marriage rate fell: (1) during depressions—the Great Depression—and in countries, during the world wars, whose exports declined; (2) when mass male emigration occurred—for reasons of employment or war. Economic booms have had the opposite effect. Since 1940 Peru has enjoyed one of the longest and steadiest eras of economic growth of any Latin American country. Consequently, its increase in the percent married is yet another factor accounting for the increase in birth rates. Since such a change is intrinsically transitional (once all marriageable women are married), the more important long run question would be the size of completed family.

Up to this point we have been discussing institutional factors operating directly on fertility. Beyond these, we should also consider several less direct influences, namely urbanization and industrial employment. Each is assumed to reduce fertility spontaneously as a society develops economically.

With respect to urbanization and fertility in Mexico, the Robinsons and Zarate found that fertility was not only *not* decreasing, but even increasing in the larger cities.[9] Urban fertility is still lower than rural, but the gap is being narrowed, primarily by increases in urban fertility. This is especially striking in Monterrey, which is a highly industrialized city. In this chapter we shall not attempt a comparable assessment of the rural-urban fertility differential for Peru, but it seems reasonable to assume a similar pattern, especially when trends in female employment are taken into account.

The depressing effect on fertility of female employment is a well-established pattern for developed nations, with the extremes found in communist countries whose inheritance laws and welfare programs appear to remove the last of the practical advantages of having children.[10] However, with reference to Peru, Puerto Rico, and Turkey, studies suggest that labor market participation does not significantly reduce the fertility of the employed female worker.[11] The essential reason for this finding is that most employed women are in occupations which permit, or at least do not conflict with, high fertility, i.e., agriculture, service occupations, and artisan handicrafts.[12] This absence of a significant differential would presumably change with a shift in the occupational structure in the direction of low fertility occupations. Such a reduction in fertility would, however, require that women should move into these new occupations at an even higher rate than men—if fertility reduction is to be a major goal of employment policy. In Peru, however, the percent of women has been *reduced* in most of the major occupational categories between 1940 and 1961 with the result that their overall labor force participation has actually declined from 27.9 percent in 1940 to 13.6 percent in 1961.[b],[13] These reductions have been heaviest in agriculture, manufacturing, and commerce, which are those occupations with a significant number of females. Women have held their own mainly in services which combine the traditional high fertility domestic service (24.7 percent) and modern low fertility professional (7.0 percent) services. The foreclosure of employment opportunities in the agricultural sector will presumably not have a significant effect on local fertility whereas in the city the lost opportunities are precisely in those occupations associated with the lowest fertility.

The primary reason for the reduction in female employment in manufacturing (the factory sector) is the labor and welfare laws pertaining to female employees. In brief, these laws are seen by employers as being so expensive that, since they have been enforced, especially after 1956 in the larger urban factories (at the most involving only 15 percent of the labor force), a deliberate policy of hiring as few women as possible has been pursued.[c] This is especially striking in the textile industry, which in most countries has a predominantly female labor force. Consequently, the small number of women who remain in factory employment reflect contrary pressures whose relative strength is unknown. On the one hand, employers have hired very few women recently and whenever possible discharge those of childbearing ages. On the other hand, married women

---

[b]It should be noted that this is not due to any changes in censuses definitions, such as the elimination of unpaid family workers in agriculture or artisan handicrafts. This largely female group was included in the 1961 Peruvian Census but has been dropped in some other countries in an apparent effort to present a more developed appearance.

[c]Women in factories with over 25 workers: (1) must receive equal pay for equal work; (2) may not work over 45 hours a week—but must be paid the same weekly wages as their male counterparts who usually work 48 hours a week; (3) receive 60 days of maternity leave at 60% of full pay; (4) enjoy an hour off daily to nurse their children who must be cared for in the factories' day nurseries—which must employ qualified nurses. In addition to these benefits employers also pay for the extensive medical and pension costs which this category of worker enjoys. (Jorge Ramirez Otarola, *Codificacion de la legislacion del trabajo y prevision social del Peru*, 2nd ed., Lima: Editorial Antonio Lulli, 1963, pp. 105-6.)

have every reason to hold on to these favored jobs in the face of such extensive pro-natalist benefits. The only reason for their not having been discharged years ago is that after a worker has been employed for ninety days (in a large unionized factory) it is extremely difficult to discharge him by law and by virtue of the political influence of the urban unions.

The enforcement of labor and welfare laws has been so vigorous in this limited segment of the economy that Peru's organized urban blue collar workers have enjoyed a continuous relative and absolute increase in their real income since 1946.[14] At the same time, white collar workers and the mass of unskilled manual workers have suffered a relative if not absolute decline in the income from their primary occupations. (The actual income of the urban middle class is often maintained through desperate efforts at multiple job holding.)

Before leaving the topic of the potential fertility reduction to be hoped for from female factory employment, Glade's and Miller's explanation of the decline or at least stagnation of this sector should be recalled. This employment trend means then that *even if* the "usual" high percentage of young females *were* employed in factories in Peru, this would involve so few women that their fertility would have no significant impact on the national birth rate. In addition, of course, with the currently pro-natalist labor and welfare laws, it is not at all certain that their fertility would be much reduced by this type of work.

In examining fertility patterns we will also look at the presumably uniformly high fertility rural areas. Here we find that, in fact, there are important variations which could permit both further increases or a decrease in the rural birth rate.

Evidence from peasant societies of a direct relationship between landholdings and fertility is relevant to Latin America. Stys found that in late nineteenth century Poland, average completed family size varied directly with size of farm. Moreover, the higher fertility in the large farms arose from a younger age-at-marriage.[15] It is possible, then, that in land-scarce areas in Latin America, where there are many small holders or sharecroppers rather than wage peons, fertility has been reduced by late or foregone marriages.[d] In the event of a land reform program, whether it took the form of the division of large estates or the colonization of new areas, it is possible that, as occurred in Ireland in the late eighteenth century, the age-at-marriage could drop, the percent married rise, and thus considerable increase in fertility result. This in turn would make such reform efforts of only temporary benefit as a solution to peasant unrest—as the recent reradicalization of once "reformed" areas suggests.[16]

Therefore the rural sector presents the following potential: (1) heavy emigration shrinking its proportion of the national population—especially of young adults of childbearing ages; (2) first generation peasant migrants to the city will

---

[d]Stycos finds that in Peru the highest fertility regions were *not* the predominantly high density Indian rural departments but rather those with a largely Spanish-speaking population in the more prosperous central and Northern regions. (Stycos, "Culture and Differential Fertility in Peru," *Population Studies*, March 1963, p. 262.)

not necessarily have fewer children than they would have had in a land-scarce rural area; and (3) if extensive redistributive agrarian reform and/or colonization were to occur, these peasants would be retained on the land at the expense of a resulting increase in their fertility.[17]

Summing up these observations on the relationship between employment status and fertility, we find that the pro-natalist effect of much of the government's legislation is clearly at odds with a policy of fertility reduction, but not in the direct sense expected. Women who lose or cannot obtain jobs owing to child care costs thereby lose these benefits, since they are not yet available to the general public, but only to the fully employed. But in losing them, non-employed women do not thereby have fewer children than employed women. In fact they have more children, but without benefit of the above-mentioned services at the lower class level. A policy designed to reduce fertility in Peru through employing married, or at least mated, women would not be very successful in the face of such pro-natalist legislation at the blue collar level, to say nothing of the shortage of employment opportunities for males, as explained in the two prior chapters by Glade and Miller.

In conclusion, it has been demonstrated that: (1) current Peruvian birth rates represent an increase over the already high levels existing before death rates were reduced; (2) Recent as well as traditional institutional factors favoring high fertility are found in the urban industrial sector as well as the traditional rural sector; and (3) the era of the highest rate of population growth in Peru is just now underway. As in the case of the total level of employment, the government not only has failed to reduce the excess supply of labor, it has also worsened (even if unintentionally) the efforts of women to obtain such favorable urban employment as is available, both by discouraging the employment of women and by slowing the development of the manufacturing sector.

Notes

1. Andrew Collver, "Birth Rates in Latin America: New Estimates of Historical Trends and Fluctuations." Research Series No. 7, Institute of International Studies, University of California, Berkeley, 1965, pp. 55-56.

2. Eduardo E. Arriaga, "The Effect of a Decline in Mortality on the Gross Reproduction Rate," *Milbank Memorial Fund Quarterly*, July 1967, Vol. XLV, No. 3, Part 1, pp. 333-34.

3. Collver, "Birth Rates," p. 161; Roberts found that in the Caribbean, birth rates rose because, although the size of completed family fell, childlessness decreased even more with a resulting annual growth rate of over 3%. (G.W. Roberts, "Populations of Non-Spanish-Speaking Caribbean," in J. Mayone Stycos and Jorge Arias, *Population Dilemma in Latin America* [Washington, D.C.: Potomac Books, 1966], pp. 81-82.)

4. Kingsley Davis and Judith Blake, "Social Structure and Fertility," *Economic Development and Cultural Change*, April, 1954, Vol. 4, No. 3.

5. Norman B. Ryder, "The Conceptualization of the Transition in Fertility," *Cold Spring Harbor Symposia on Quantitative Biology*, Vol. XXII, 1957; Ansley J. Coale and C.Y. Tye, "The Significance of Age Patterns of Fertility in High Fertility Populations," *Milbank Memorial Fund Quarterly*, Oct. 1961, Vol. XXXIX, No. 4.

6. Coale and Tye, Ibid., p. 645.

7. Collver, "Birth Rates," p. 51. This rise in the marriage rate is striking since the percent married is lower in urban than in rural areas and since Latin America is rapidly urbanizing. In addition, rising birth rates mean younger populations—hence, relatively fewer eligible for marriage. Also, in Peru at least, the Indian rural areas have a lower fertility and a lower percent mated than the Spanish-speaking areas—and the latter are growing at the expense of the former as mass literacy develops. (See pp. 262-63, Stycos, "Culture and Differential Fertility," *Population Studies*, March 1963.)

This ethnic-regional fertility differential has been the subject of a series of demographic analyses. Stycos' original paper was followed by David Heer "Fertility Differences between Indian and Spanish-Speaking Parts of Andean Countries," *Population Studies*, Vol. 18, No. 1, (July 1964), pp. 71-84. Heer reaffirmed Stycos' empirical findings, but challenged Stycos' explanation that marital instability and illegitimacy were the causal factors. William H. James subsequently "The Effect of Attitude on Fertility in Andean Countries," *Population Studies*, Vol. 20, No. 1, (July 1966), pp. 97-101) preferred altitude as the explanation without challenging the differential itself.

Finally Benjamin S. Bradshaw ("Fertility Differences in Peru: A Reconsideration," *Population Studies*, Vol. XXIII, No. 1, (Mar. 1969), pp. 5-19,) attempted to reverse the basic finding through a tortuous correction procedure employed on the same 1940 Census data. The present author prefers to tentatively accept the original finding without agreeing to the various interpretations. Since all of the correlations were based on departmental level aggregated characteristics the "ecological correlation fallacy" is especially likely as much in the case of Bradshaw's corrections as in the preceding works. Therefore, it seems reasonable to accept the original differential on a tentative hypothetical basis pending disaggregated individual data, in view of its plausibility as outlined alone.

8. Collver, "Birth Rates," p. 52.

9. Alvan O. Zarate, "Differential Fertility in Monterrey, Mexico," *Milbank Memorial Fund Quarterly*, April, 1967, p. 93; Zarate "Fertility in Urban Areas of Mexico: Implications for the Theory of the Demographic Transition," *Demography*, Vol. 4, No. 1, 1967, p. 365; Robinson, W.C. and E.H., "Rural-Urban Fertility Differentials in Mexico," *American Sociological Review*, Feb. 1960.

10. Stanley Friedlander and Morris Silver, "A Quantitative Study of the Determinants of Fertility Behavior," *Demography*, Vol. 4, No. 1, 1967, pp. 38, 55.

11. J. Mayone Stycos, "Female Employment and Fertility in Lima, Peru," *Milbank Memorial Fund Quarterly*, Jan. 1965; and Stycos & R.H. Weller,

"Female Working Roles and Fertility," *Demography*, Vol. 4, No. 1, 1967, pp. 210-17; Robert O. Carleton, "Labor Force Participation: A Stimulus to Fertility in Puerto Rico," *Demography*, Vol. 2, 1965, pp. 233-39.

12. Abram J. Jaffee and Koya Azumi, "The Birth Rate and Cottage Industries in Underdeveloped Countries," *Economic Development and Cultural Change*, Vol. IX, No. 1, Oct. 1960, p. 62. Jaffee and Azumi found that in both Puerto Rico and Japan cottage industry employment reduced fertility very little below that of the non-employed.

13. For a fuller explanation of this point see Chapter 7 in David Chaplin, *The Peruvian Industrial Labor Force* (New Jersey: Princeton University Press, 1967).

14. *U.N. Analysis and Projection of Economic Development VI: The Industrial Development of Peru*. Mexico City, 1959, p. 43.

15. W. Stys, "The Influence of Economic Conditions on the Fertility of Peasant Women," *Population Studies*, Vol. XI, No. 2, (November 1957), pp. 136-48.

16. Gerrit Huizer, "On Peasant Unrest in Latin America," Pan American Union, Washington, D.C., June 1967.

17. For further discussion of the role of agrarian reform, see Section IV in this volume.

Part IV: Demographic Implication of Agricultural Policies

12 Agrarian Policies and the Structural Transformation of Latin American Economies

Lehman B. Fletcher

One of the characteristics of less developed countries as compared with the more economically advanced nations is their heavy dependence upon agriculture. A higher percentage of their labor force is engaged in farming and a larger proportion of their national product is contributed by the agricultural sector. In Latin America as a whole approximately 50 percent of the population is now considered urban, but the proportion of rural population varies from as high as 70 percent in some countries to as low as 20 percent in others. The agricultural sector in most countries contributes directly 20 to 30 percent of the national output, ranging from slightly more than 10 percent to slightly less than 50 percent. Thus, it is also true that labor productivity is generally lower in agriculture than in other sectors of the economy.

Economic development basically consists of a transformation of the economy from a state in which labor is abundant, technology static and traditional, and capital scarce to production using modern inputs and methods and a high ratio of capital to labor. Development usually means a shift of resources, especially labor, out of agriculture and into industry and the urban sector. This does not suggest, and indeed the notion should avoided—that industry is superior to agriculture as a means for development. Rather, there is evidence that most Latin American countries have placed too little emphasis on agriculture for the good of their overall economic development.[1]

Because agriculture and the other economic sectors are interdependent, emphasizing industrialization at the expense of agriculture has generally led not to a more rapid rate of economic growth but to the reverse of slow growth in industry as well as in agriculture. Thus, the great push in the past for achieving structural change through diverting resources into industry and neglecting agriculture has frequently backfired. It is now understood that agricultural and nonagricultural development are complementary and not competitive, and that growth policies and programs must place more emphasis on agricultural development as an integral part of the development process.

Agriculture's Contribution to Economic Development

The agricultural sector can make a number of basic contributions to the development process:

233

(1) *Agriculture serves as the main source of labor which industry draws upon as it grows.* In overpopulated countries, the agricultural sector contains some workers who are adding little, if anything, to production. If the necessary labor demand exists elsewhere in the economy, national output can be raised by transferring this labor to productive uses in industry or the service sector. This shift of labor from agriculture to the nonagricultural sector does not necessarily imply geographical movement, since farm workers may start working on the construction of feeder roads or in rural industry on a seasonal or part-time basis. However, in Latin America the growth of industrial output does not seem to generate an equally rapid growth of industry's need for labor. As a result, it is too often true that labor leaves agriculture at a faster rate than it can be productively absorbed elsewhere in the economy. People forced off the land by population pressure often end up as part of a growing contingent of urban underemployed and unemployed. In planning their development, Latin American countries must keep a watch on the numbers of people leaving agriculture relative to the opportunities for their absorption in other sectors. If this problem becomes serious, more attention may have to be paid to the possibility of more labor-intensive investments in urban industry as well as to the possibility of shifting some investment from industry to agriculture, where a given amount of investment usually creates a larger number of jobs than in manufacturing. [The relation of industrial growth to employment and implications for agricultural organization and employment are emphasized by Professor Thiesenhusen in the following paper.] Employment creation in agriculture results when investments are used for new techniques and inputs, such as irrigation, hybrid seeds and fertilizer, which are complementary to labor and increase the amount of labor required for each unit of land cultivated.

(2) *Agriculture can provide capital to finance industrial development.* Since agriculture makes up a large part of the Latin American economies, it is often the main source of domestic finance for their development. Effecting this capital transfer is frequently difficult. There are three main methods: voluntary savings, taxation, and turning the "terms of trade" against the agricultural sector. Each has its problems. In the case of a country with a very poor agricultural sector, voluntary savings are likely to be extremely small. Also, the lack of a well-organized banking system or money market poses a serious obstacle to channeling whatever savings are forthcoming into productive investment elsewhere in the economy. Taxing the agricultural sector in the absence of a strong civil service usually makes collection and enforcement spotty. Taxes which are easy to administer such as export levies, have the disadvantage that they fall heaviest on the most productive producers, thereby discouraging output. Turning the terms of trade against agriculture (i.e., raising prices of things farmers buy relative to prices of things they sell) amounts to taxation, and, like most forms of taxation, it acts as a disincentive to agricultural development. Moreover, returns may be high for well-allocated investment funds in the agricultural sector. Research to develop new varieties, fertilizer, pesticides, irrigation, credit and marketing facilities have all proven to be potentially

productive claimants on capital.[2] Thus, tax, price, and investment policies must be carefully considered and there may well be an initial period in which investment funds on a net basis should flow into agriculture. In Mexico, for example, there is evidence that capital inflows to agriculture have consistently exceeded outflows, but also that the returns in increased output and productivity have been high.

(3) *Agricultural development, through "linkages" with other sectors, stimulates growth elsewhere in the economy*. It does this by providing a market for certain domestic industries and a source of raw material supply for others. As agricultural output and income grow, an expanding market is created for manufactured consumer goods (processed foods, radios, bicycles, etc.); for agricultural inputs (fertilizers, pesticides, and herbicides); and, in time, for agricultural equipment (tractors and other machines). At the same time, agricultural expansion supplies food for urban workers and foodstuffs and raw materials for domestic manufacturing and processing industries. Exports of agricultural products, which provide foreign exchange for imports of intermediate goods needed in industry and construction, is another important linkage. Through such forward and backward linkages, agricultural growth can contribute substantially to the development of new industry and to the rise of GNP overall. These linkages also help explain why it can be so hard for GNP to rise if agriculture is stagnant.

Agricultural Production, Food Supply and Trade

Agricultural production is not increasing rapidly enough in many countries to provide an adequate diet for the growing population nor the exports needed to earn foreign exchange. Poor nutrition, food scarcity, rising food prices and imports are the result. Low productivity in agriculture is the basic cause. Land is not always fully utilized and the men who work the land are not given the opportunity to improve their farming and earn higher incomes. This reduces the rural demand for consumer goods and farm supplies produced by industry and the possibility of expanding national markets by effectively integrating the large rural population into the market economy. Overcoming this problem of low productivity in agriculture is crucial to the economic development of Latin America. Rural poverty and the lack of employment opportunities are the manifestations of the productivity problem.

During the last decade agricultural output in Latin America increased slightly more than 3 percent annually. Most of the increase resulted from expansion in the cultivated area rather than from increased yields per unit of land cultivated. Yields have been increasing recently at about 1 percent per year, suggesting that area changes have accounted for some two-thirds of the production increases and yield improvements only one-third.

Trends in food production over the last decade indicate that supplies have at least kept pace with population growth and may well have increased at a slightly higher rate. Food production seems to have increased at a rate slightly in excess of total agricultural production which, in turn, was slightly in excess of the rate of population growth. Food imports have also been increasing. Even so, food supplies per capita in the mid-1960s were only about 6 percent above 1947 levels.[3] Thus, there appears to have been little improvement in the average diet of Latin Americans since the 1940s.

Agricultural production has risen somewhat more rapidly during the 1960s. Increases in production of some products have been especially rapid in several Latin American countries. Mexico, for example, has substantially increased its production of wheat. Such developments indicate that production may be "taking off," at least in a few isolated cases, in response to new technology and improvements in policies and institutions.

Livestock production, which accounts for about 35 percent of the value of total agricultural output in Latin America, has lagged behind crop production. Little increase in livestock production was registered in the last decade. As a result, per capita livestock production actually declined. This poses a serious obstacle to upgrading diets through providing more high-protein and protective foods such as meat, milk, fats and oils, fruits and vegetables to offset widespread deficiencies in consumption.

General statements about Latin American agriculture conceal substantial differences among sub-regions and countries. Yudelman recently reviewed and analyzed the production data on a more disaggregated basis and concluded that:

(1) Total agricultural output is rising more rapidly in the tropical areas than in the temperate zones. The absolute level of per capita production and consumption is higher in the temperate sub-regions, however.

(2) On a country-by-country basis, considering an annual compound rate of growth of agricultural output of 5 percent or more to be "high," 3 to 5 percent to be "medium," and less than 3 percent to be "low," the following classification can be made:

"High Growth"	—	Mexico, Venezuela, Nicaragua, Guatemala, El Salvador
"Medium Growth"	—	Brazil, Colombia, Ecuador, Peru, Bolivia, Costa Rica, Honduras, Panama, Dominican Republic
"Low Growth"	—	Argentina, Chile, Haiti, Paraguay, Uruguay[4]

Agricultural Exports and Imports. Agricultural products constitute the largest single category of exports from Latin America. They account for nearly two-thirds of the value of total exports from about half of the Latin American countries. Export earnings from agricultural products have fluctuated recently between $3 and $4 billion per year. Agriculture's share of total export earnings declined from 48 percent in 1955 to 35 percent in 1965, even though the physical volume of agricultural exports increased.[5] (The relative importance of agricultural exports is greatly increased if petroleum exports from Venezuela are excluded from total exports.)

Although the absolute levels of agricultural imports are low relative to total consumption, the volume and value of imports have been rising.[6] Cereal and livestock products are the most important import categories. Brazil, Chile, Peru, and the Central American countries have all suffered from pressures to import more food. These imports have the immediate and direct effect of using scarce foreign exchange needed for the importation of investment goods and industrial raw materials.

The growing requirement for foreign exchange which confronts Latin America is drawing attention to the need to increase exports of agricultural products. The uncertain prospects for traditional Latin American agricultural exports suggests that emphasis on exports of beef, oilseeds, feedgrains, and fruits and vegetables is needed. Substantial investments will be required, however, to increase the production of these products, to improve and standardize their quality, and to improve the internal marketing systems for these products.

Most Latin American countries are emphasizing the production of import-substitutes to promote self-sufficiency in food production. Policies to promote self-sufficiency in food production can, in some cases, weaken the basis for the development of common markets in Latin America and may slow economic growth. Unfortunately, regional studies designed to determine the comparative advantages of different crops in different Latin American countries are not yet available. Policies of total national self-sufficiency could weaken the basis of trade between temperate and tropical zones in the region, reduce exports, and lower productivity. Intra-regional trade is likely to increase most if conscious and coordinated policies are established to reduce trade restrictions, improve marketing and communications, and broaden consumption of nontraditional products.

Outlook for Demand for Latin American Agricultural Products. It was shown above that agricultural output in Latin America in recent years has not fully kept pace with demand changes resulting from rapid population growth, increases in per capita income, rural-urban migration, and improvement in the quality of diets. An extraordinary production effort will be required if Latin American agriculture is to meet the demands for its products in the future. Not only must the total magnitude of agricultural output increase but the composition of agricultural output must respond to changes in demand resulting from urbanization, growth of incomes, changes in distribution of income, the need to improve diets, and the necessity to diversify agricultural exports.

Population and Demand: The high rate of population growth in Latin America, which exceeds 3.0 percent—and even 3.5 percent—in some countries, is the single most important factor affecting the demand for food. If this rate of population growth continues, a minimal increase in output of almost 3 percent per year will be required just to feed and clothe the additional people at the same low average level of today.

Income and Food Demand: As incomes rise, people tend to consume more and better food. For Latin America as a whole, it seems reasonable to assume that a 1 percent increase in income will lead to at least a one-half percent increase in expenditures on foodstuffs. Thus if incomes were to increase at the rate of 2.5 percent per year, as postulated by the Alliance for Progress, then the income effect would increase food demand by 1.25 percent per year. Adding this income effect to the population growth effect indicates that demand for food will grow by more than 4 percent per year. In other words, food production (or imports) will have to increase annually by more than 4 percent in order to maintain consumption levels for the larger population, provide for increased food expenditures per person, and prevent rapid increases in food prices. As income levels increase, the desire to consume more food will decline, but the tendency to upgrade the quality of the diet will continue to strengthen the income-food expenditure relationship.

This estimate does not provide for any significant change in income distribution. While it is obvious that shifts of income to poorer groups will raise food demand, little is known about existing income distribution in Latin America and there is no basis for anticipating the extent to which redistribution may actually take place in the future. Certainly, the extent to which nutrition can be improved for the 50 percent of the population that now has deficient diets will depend not only on agricultural growth and how fast development takes place, but also on social and economic policies affecting income distribution. It seems likely that some redistribution of income in favor of low income groups will occur in the future. As this redistribution takes place, the demands for protective foods such as meat, milk, fats and oils, fruits and vegetables will rise at a faster rate than the demands for carbohydrate foods such as cereals, sugar, and potatoes.

Urbanization and Demand: The phenomenon of urbanization is a normal and necessary aspect of the development process. The out-migration of the rural population to the cities has been especially rapid in Latin America and has created severe social and economic problems. While rural population is increasing in some countries by as much as 1.5 percent annually, high rural birth rates and heavy emigration to the cities is causing urban population to grow at rates of 5 percent or more per year. Employment has not been available to productively employ the larger number of urban workers. As a result, sizeable belts of extreme poverty have been created around almost every important city. These large groups of urban unemployed or underemployed suffer low levels of living which match, or even surpass, the marginal conditions found in the countryside. The question arises if these migrants improve their welfare by moving to cities, or, if the cost of supplying essential educational and social services are thereby decreased.

Rapid urbanization and agricultural development are closely related. If food supply is not increased in urban markets, increases in food prices can be expected. Political pressures may then lead to price policies which hold prices at levels which discourage production increases. Also, high rates of urban unemployment and underemployment reduce food expenditures and suppress the potential demand for food products. Furthermore, when there is inadequate effective demand, increased output can drive farm prices down to levels which discourage further expansion. These interrelated aspects of urbanization, government price policies and food demand have worked to retard agricultural growth in a number of Latin American countries.

Production Goals: It was indicated above that an increase in agricultural output in Latin America somewhat greater than 4 percent per year will be necessary to meet expected internal demands for food and minimize imports resulting from deficient domestic production. Agricultural exports must also provide part of the foreign exchange needed to finance essential capital goods and non-agricultural raw materials. This will become increasingly difficult, if the terms of trade of traditional exports continue to weaken unless substantial efforts are made to diversify agricultural exports. It seems likely that total agricultural output will have to increase by at least an additional one percent to provide the required expansion in agricultural exports.[7]

Total agricultural output in Latin America will therefore have to increase by more than 5 percent per year to satisfy internal demand and export goals. This rate of increase is substantially higher than the historical rate. Achieving the desired level and composition of agricultural output poses a major challenge to development planners and policymakers in many Latin American countries.

Population Growth, Agricultural
Productivity, and Structural
Transformations

Another implication of high rates of population growth concerns the rate at which an economy undergoes structural transformation, as reflected by an increase in the absolute and relative share of nonagricultural employment. This shift depends on the rates of increase in the total labor force and the nonagricultural labor force and on the existing share of the agricultural sector in total employment. It is obvious that structural change will be slow where 60 to 70 percent of the labor force is in farming, where population is growing at 3 or 3.5 percent annually, and where nonfarm employment is growing quite slowly.

If the nonfarm population of a country increases more rapidly than total population, leading to a decline in the proportion of the population and labor force in agriculture, output per farm worker and/or imports must increase if food supplies per capita are to be maintained. When the farm labor force has declined to 30 or 40 percent of the total, and possibly is decreasing absolutely as well as relatively, the "required" rates of increase in labor productivity in agriculture can be fairly large if major food imports are to be avoided.

Projections of total urban and rural population growth to 1980 by country and area are given in Table 12-1. These recent projections were made by the Economic Commission for Latin America and particular attention is directed to the expected relative changes in urban and rural populations. As seen in the table, urban population as a percent of the total will increase in all countries and regions in Latin America. However, with the exception of Uruguay, the rural population in all countries is expected to increase in *absolute* terms. This increase will be slow in countries having already undergone substantial structural change, such as Argentina and Chile, but much more rapid in Brazil, Central America, and other countries where the rural population still looms large in the economy.

In the context of structural transformation it has been common to view agriculture as the "self-employment" sector whose size is determined as a residual on the basis of exogenous rates of change in the total and nonfarm labor force. It is conspicuously true in much of Latin America that urban population growth greatly exceeds the increase in nonfarm employment. Thus the "self-employment" sector has come to include a large urban population unable to find productive nonfarm employment. This disparity between growth of urban population and growth of employment opportunities poses problems of under-utilization of labor and low productivity very comparable to those that arise with excessive population in the countryside. For agricultural as well as overall development, it is of crucial importance that there be rapid growth of nonfarm employment opportunities. Otherwise, Latin American countries will face the dilemma pointed out by Davis: "If they do not substantially step up the exodus from rural areas, these areas will be swamped with underemployed farmers. If they do step up the exodus, the cities will grow at a disastrous rate."[8] [A most revealing case study of this dilemma, emphasizing the vicious circle of poverty, population growth, and exploitative production techniques which reduce productivity, is given by Haney in Chapter 14 in this volume.]

Another conclusion to be emphasized is that growth of the rural population for a considerable period in the future is a reality that must be reckoned with in development planning. Apart from those countries where the proportion of farm employment has been substantially reduced, Latin American countries are faced with certain and substantial increases in rural population and, in many cases, in their farm labor force. In addition to the need for rapid expansion of agricultural output, for substantial capital formation for infrastructure and industrial investment, population growth will also require agriculture to provide productive employment for more workers. This fact bears meaning for the choice of measures for agricultural development. Thiesenhusen (in Chapter 13 in this volume) uses this point to build a strong case for an emphasis in agriculture on labor-intensive inputs and methods rather than on labor-substituting mechanization. He neglects the degree to which mechanization may be required to increase yields. There is a general lack of empirical information on the extent to which new methods and inputs can increase productivity and income per person while providing employment for more workers. It is obvious that such opportunities

Table 12-1
Total, Urban, and Rural Population by Countries, 1950 to 1980

Country and Area	(Thousands of Persons)						
	1950	1955	1960	1965	1970	1975	1980
Argentina	17,189	19,122	20,956	22,909	24,937	27,068	29,334
Urban	11,038	12,657	14,161	15,767	17,431	19,179	21,043
Rural	6,151	6,465	6,795	7,142	7,506	7,889	8,291
% urban	64.2	66.2	67.6	68.8	69.9	70.9	71.7
Bolivia	3,013	3,322	3,696	4,136	4,658	5,277	6,000
Urban	778	915	1,104	1,345	1,652	2,040	2,514
Rural	2,235	2,407	2,592	2,791	3,006	3,237	3,486
% urban	25.8	27.5	29.9	32.5	35.5	38.7	41.9
Brazil	52,178	60,453	70,309	81,300	93,752	107,863	123,566
Urban	16,083	21,526	28,329	36,026	44,926	55,207	66,779
Rural	36,095	38,927	41,980	45,274	48,826	52,656	56,787
% urban	30.8	35.6	40.3	44.3	47.9	51.2	54.0
Columbia	11,679	13,441	15,468	17,787	20,514	23,774	27,691
Urban	4,253	5,574	7,134	8,958	11,161	13,865	17,193
Rural	7,426	7,867	8,334	8,829	9,353	9,909	10,498
% urban	36.4	41.5	46.1	50.4	54.4	58.3	62.1
Chile	6,073	6,761	7,627	8,567	9,636	10,872	12,300
Urban	3,327	4,005	4,861	5,791	6,850	8,024	9,274
Rural	2,746	2,756	2,766	2,776	2,786	2,848	3,026
% urban	54.8	59.2	63.7	67.6	71.1	73.8	75.4
Ecuador	3,197	3,691	4,317	5,036	5,909	6,933	8,080
Urban	878	1,100	1,423	1,803	2,297	2,898	3,573
Rural	2,319	2,591	2,894	3,233	3,612	4,035	4,507
% urban	27.5	29.8	33.0	35.8	38.9	41.8	44.2
Paraguay	1,397	1,565	1,768	2,007	2,296	2,645	3,065
Urban	392	444	508	583	674	785	920
Rural	1,005	1,121	1,260	1,424	1,622	1,860	2,145
% urban	28.1	28.4	28.7	29.0	29.4	29.7	30.0
Peru	7,969	8,790	10,025	11,650	13,586	15,869	18,527
Urban	2,498	3,003	3,904	5,021	6,345	7,935	9,782
Rural	5,471	5,787	6,111	6,629	7,241	7,934	8,745
% urban	31.3	34.2	38.9	43.1	46.7	50.0	52.8

Table 12-1 *(cont.)*

Uruguay	2,195	2,348	2,491	2,647	2,802	2,960	3,126
Urban	1,734	1,887	2,030	2,186	2,341	2,499	2,665
Rural	461	461	461	461	461	461	461
% urban	79.0	80.4	81.5	82.6	83.5	84.2	85.3
Venezuela	4,974	6,049	7,331	8,722	10,399	12,434	14,827
Urban	2,422	3,414	4,611	5,844	7,300	9,052	11,031
Rural	2,552	2,635	2,720	2,878	3,099	3,382	3,796
% urban	48.7	56.4	62.9	67.0	70.2	72.8	74.4
South America	109,864	125,542	143,988	164,761	188,489	215,695	246,516
Urban	43,403	54,525	68,065	83,324	100,977	121,484	144,774
Rural	66,461	71,017	75,923	81,437	87,512	94,211	101,742
% urban	39.5	43.4	47.3	50.6	53.6	56.3	58.7
Costa Rica	801	984	1,206	1,467	1,769	2,110	2,491
Urban	232	297	377	494	647	836	1,071
Rural	569	687	829	973	1,122	1,274	1,420
% urban	29.9	30.1	31.3	33.7	36.6	39.6	43.0
El Salvador	1,868	2,142	2,490	2,914	3,417	4,022	4,730
Urban	515	595	721	892	1,105	1,378	1,708
Rural	1,353	1,547	1,769	2,022	2,312	2,644	3,022
% urban	27.6	27.8	29.0	30.6	32.3	34.3	36.1
Guatemala	2,805	3,258	3,765	4,343	5,053	5,906	6,942
Urban	674	886	1,124	1,403	1,780	2,262	2,885
Rural	2,131	2,372	2,641	2,940	3,273	3,644	4,057
% urban	24.0	27.2	29.9	32.3	35.2	38.3	41.6
Honduras	1,428	1,660	1,950	2,315	2,750	3,266	3,879
Urban	247	321	432	593	797	1,051	1,367
Rural	1,181	1,339	1,518	1,722	1,953	2,215	2,512
% urban	17.3	19.3	22.2	25.6	29.0	32.2	35.2
Nicaragua	1,060	1,245	1,477	1,754	2,083	2,474	2,938
Urban	297	383	502	638	819	1,047	1,343
Rural	763	862	975	1,116	1,264	1,427	1,595
% urban	28.0	30.8	34.0	36.4	39.3	42.3	45.7
Panama	797	923	1,055	1,209	1,387	1,591	1,823
Urban	282	363	447	548	669	811	975
Rural	515	560	608	661	718	780	848
% urban	35.4	39.3	42.4	45.3	48.2	51.0	53.5

Table 12-1 *(cont.)*

Central Am.	8,759	10,212	11,943	14,002	16,459	19,369	22,803
Urban	2,247	2,845	3,603	4,568	5,817	7,385	9,349
Rural	6,512	7,367	8,340	9,434	10,642	11,984	13,454
% urban	25.7	27.9	30.2	32.6	35.3	38.1	41.0
Cuba	5,508	6,127	6,797	7,523	8,307	9,146	10,034
Urban	2,753	3,261	3,816	4,423	5,083	5,792	6,546
Rural	2,755	2,866	2,981	3,100	3,224	3,354	3,488
% urban	50.0	53.2	56.1	58.8	61.2	63.3	65.2
Haiti	3,380	3,722	4,140	4,645	5,255	6,001	6,912
Urban	340	401	513	683	927	1,274	1,749
Rural	3,040	3,321	3,627	3,962	4,328	4,727	5,163
% urban	10.1	10.8	12.4	14.7	17.6	21.2	25.3
Mexico	26,366	30,612	36,018	42,681	50,733	60,554	72,659
Urban	12,144	15,397	19,741	25,268	32,105	40,626	51,340
Rural	14,222	15,215	16,277	17,413	18,628	19,928	21,319
% urban	46.1	50.3	54.8	59.2	63.3	67.1	70.7
Dominican Rep.	2,243	2,587	3,030	3,588	4,277	5,124	6,174
Urban	482	634	834	1,096	1,435	1,874	2,444
Rural	1,761	1,953	2,196	2,492	2,842	3,250	3,730
% urban	21.5	24.5	27.5	30.5	33.6	36.6	39.6
Latin Am.	156,120	178,802	205,916	237,200	273,520	315,889	365,098
Urban	61,369	77,063	96,572	119,362	146,344	178,435	216,202
Rural	94,751	101,739	114,858	117,838	127,176	137,454	148,896
% urban	39.3	43.1	46.9	50.3	53.5	56.5	59.2

Source: Economic Commission for Latin America, *Statistical Bulletin for Latin America*, Vol II, no. 2, New York, 1965, pp. 9-10.

should be exploited, but we need to be realistic about the longer-term, farm size-technology-income implications. Some observers also believe that adoption of improved practices is discouraged by large supplies of cheap labor in rural areas, especially where large land holdings are involved.

Prospects for Agricultural Development in Latin America

That output *and* productivity in agriculture must increase in Latin America has been stressed. Although there is no Malthusian crisis looming in Latin America as a whole, the rate of population growth, the need to improve nutritional levels in many areas, to expand exports and to provide more jobs and higher incomes leave no room for complacency. In Latin America, as elsewhere, rates of growth in agriculture and the total economy tend to be closely related. The demand stimulus for agricultural growth must come from growth in the general economy in connection with price, tax and distribution policies which make effective consumers out of the mass of the urban population. Agricultural production represents an important and direct component of total output linked to expansion in nonfarm sectors through product and factor markets. Because of these interrelationships, agriculture's role will depend in all countries on raising output and productivity through appropriate economic policies and well-directed public investments and programs.

But growing importance should be attached to increases in rural employment and improvements in income distribution in agriculture as well as increased output. Producing more per hectare and per man is the best way to reconcile output and welfare goals. This means that questions of "where" and "how" output is increased must be considered along with "how much." To achieve a desirable blend of output and income distribution objectives, policies and programs must be matched to the needs of different types of farmers and different geographic areas of the countries.

It has been argued that the payoffs to be obtained from investments in small-scale agriculture are low. This argument is hard to accept. In Guatemala, for example, it appears that returns to corn fertilization by peasant producers in the mountainous central region compare favorable to returns to commercial production in the Coastal area. Moreover, new varieties and a package of improved production practices could sharply increase the return. At the same time, a program to improve yields by small farmers would raise productivity per man, absorb underemployed labor, improve diets, increase income, and enlarge rural markets for production inputs and consumer goods.

Sources of Future Output Growth. It is useful to analyze supply changes in terms of area and yield components. This permits separation of output gains from cultivating additional acres from increases in yield per acre. The latter component will include higher yields per crop, more crops per year and shifts to higher-valued crops.

For Latin America as a whole, area expansion has historically been more important than yield increases as a source of growth in output. It was noted earlier that probably two-thirds of the output expansion in the last decade were due to area changes and only one-third to yield improvement. Although substantial yield increases have occurred in some countries and for some crops, they have not been numerous.

The expansion of land area in Latin America will undoubtedly continue. However, it is not likely that the *rate* of area expansion in the future will be as high as in the recent past. Much of the land remaining to be settled is jungle located where there is no infrastructure and where knowledge to develop intensive crop or livestock production is lacking. Also, irrigation projects remaining to be developed will be more expensive and difficult to implement than those already in operation. It will be expensive to bring such land into production. Thus, more and more of the increased output will have to come from yield-increasing inputs and production practices.[9] Policies and programs must be designed to generate these yield-increasing possibilities and to get them adopted by millions of small low-income farmers. These productivity increases will raise incomes and standards of living in the rural sector as well as meeting the demands for additional agricultural output.

Substantial increases in yields of major crop and livestock products per unit of land and per man are feasible in every country in Latin America. In many cases, average yields are well below those now being obtained by the better farmers and only a fraction of yields from demonstration plots. Progress is being made on the development and introduction of yield-increasing, cost-reducing technology. Thus, the tendency to depend more on yield increase for output growth—already apparent in Mexico and a few other countries—is likely to become more general in the next decade.

Strategy for Agricultural Growth. The essential elements of a strategy designed to achieve the needed expansion in agricultural output and productivity are:

1. *Development of agricultural production technology, extension services and rural education.* Rapid strides are needed in the development of yield-increasing, cost-reducing, technology adapted to established agricultural areas in Latin America. New high-yielding varieties of wheat, rice and corn have already been developed at the International Centers. Work on other crops and on livestock must be expanded. There is continuing need to develop first-class research centers to support extension programs and to invest as heavily as possible in farm people.

2. *Provide modern agricultural inputs and credit necessary to enable producers to purchase them.* It will be necessary to work with a relatively few key inputs. Most countries do not have the financial nor management resources required to assemble, deliver, and utilize a combined "ideal package" of inputs. The inputs selected should be those that will provide the most certain impact on output, will be simple to use, and can be most easily distributed.

3. *Reduce losses, expand markets and improve returns through improvements in the marketing system.* Development of roads and communications is important in this connection. Improved assembly facilities, processing plants, central markets, retail distribution and storage can contribute to lower losses and greater efficiency in marketing.

4. *Provide price and other incentives to producers.* There is much evidence that government policies in Latin America have reduced profitability and discouraged production in agriculture. Industrial development through import substitution has raised the costs of agricultural inputs and consumer goods to farmers. Policies to keep food prices low have depressed prices at the farm

level. Export taxes to raise revenue to support industrialization have placed a low economic value on production of farm products even when the country possessed a strong comparative advantage in their production. Many such policies should be changed.

Security of price and income expectations is also needed. Price fluctuations, weather variations, availability and price of purchased inputs, inflation, devaluation, land tenure conditions and laws, all combine to make investments in agricultural production a risky business. Reducing these risks would promote additional investments in agriculture.

Public Policies and Programs. Provision of even the minimum requirements for agricultural development is likely to tax the will and institutional capabilities of most Latin American countries. More stable and consistent price policies, tax policies, and import-export policies are needed. More and better farm and market information must be gathered and disseminated. Research and extension programs have to be improved. Credit and modern agricultural inputs have to be made more readily available. The efficiency of marketing channels and techniques will have to be increased. In many countries, all of these programs and policies seemingly must be implemented at once. It may well be that the capacity of Latin American governments to support agricultural development through appropriate planning, policies, investments and services will continue to be the most limiting factor in many countries.

Notes

1. T.W. Schultz, "Economic Growth Theory and the Profitability of Farming in Latin America," *University of Chicago Agricultural Economics Paper*, 1967. p. 5.

2. Inter-American Development Bank, *Agricultural Development in Latin America: The Next Decade* (Washington, D.C.: April 1967), p. 176.

3. U.S. Department of Agriculture, *Indices of Agricultural Production for the 20 Latin American Countries*, ERS-Foreign 44 (January 1967), p. 12.

4. M. Yudelman, *Agricultural Development in Latin America: Current Status and Prospects*, (Washington, D.C.: Inter-American Development Bank, October 1966), pp. 18-19.

5. Committee on Foreign Relations, U.S. Senate, *Survey of the Alliance for Progress* (Washington, D.C.: U.S. Government Printing Office, 1967), p. 5.

6. Yudelman, *Agricultural Development: Current Status*, p. 33.

7. Ibid., pp. 37-38.

8. Kingsley Davis, "The Urbanization of the Human Population," *Scientific American*, September 1965, p. 51.

9. Inter-American Development Bank, *Agricultural Development: Next Decade*, pp. 100-104.

13 Population Growth and Agricultural Employment

William C. Thiesenhusen

Benjamin Higgins once summarized the major problem of underdevelopment in three words: "too many peasants."[1] Many social scientists agree and believe the problem can be solved only by a massive rural-to-urban transfer of labor.

Formulating the issue in this manner suggests a familiar sequence of prescriptions: (1) push investment in industry to attract farm people to city jobs; (2) substitute mechanization for displaced workers in agriculture to improve labor productivity; (3) improve production per land unit. While this statement of basic strategy is oversimplified, its gross outline has been followed— often unconsciously, sometimes with planning—in many currently developed countries.

Without disputing the necessity of industrialization and the inevitability of internal migration, we shall argue that in at least some parts of Latin America stopgap policies should be designed to create more jobs for peasants in farming. This employment should provide greater security and higher income earning potential than farm workers now realize as hired hands on large estates. The agrarian reform proposal to be suggested should also give these farm people in situ an opportunity to develop some basic skills needed to raise their productivity in agriculture—or for urban life—while providing some demand stimulus to the nonfarm sectors.

Higgins echoes many contemporary social scientists as he argues against a "more-farm-jobs" development program: ". . . the solution may not be to retard the movement to the cities by making conditions more attractive in the countryside—a policy which is in itself anti-developmental—but rather to accelerate the rate of industrialization and consequently the rate of employment creation outside the agricultural sector."[2] But this point of view leaves several questions unanswered: Who will supply the effective demand to provide impetus for industry, considering that 60 to 80 percent of the Latin American farm population has a yearly cash family income of less than $500?[3] Where will the relatively large amounts of capital come from to create needed jobs in industry and to invest in related social and economic infrastructure? How will industry employ the huge work force that will enter the labor market in the seventies,

The author thanks Professors Peter Dorner, Don Kanel, and Marion Brown, Mr. Lawrence Lynch and Mr. Kenneth Forman, his colleagues at the Land Tenure Center; Dr. Eric B. Shearer, Comité Interamericano de Desarrollo Agrícola; and Professor Lehman Fletcher, Iowa State University, for comments. Reprinted from *American Journal of Agricultural Economics*, Vol. 51, No. 4, November, 1969, pp. 735-752, with the permission of the author and publisher.

considering that it has not even been able effectively to absorb smaller increases in the past? What will be the socioeconomic consequences of more unemployment and underemployment in Latin American cities where many thousands are now without productive work?

Alexander comments on the need for effective demand when import-substituting manufacturing is a primary focus of development policy, as it has been of late in Latin America: "Sooner or later the import-substitution strategy reaches a point of exhaustion. A point is reached at which an economy has installed virtually all those kinds of industries which can produce commodities formerly imported. At this juncture, the nature of the development problem changes. Instead of being the largely physical one of mounting industries for which there is already a market, it becomes one of amplifying existing markets—if the process of development and growth is to continue. . . . [There] are a few Latin American countries—notably Brazil, Chile, Mexico, and Argentina, as well perhaps as Venezuela, Colombia, and Peru—which have completely or nearly exhausted import-substitution possibilities, at least as a major impetus to further development."[4]

Employment, Population Growth, and the Latin American City

Slightly over half of the population of Latin America now lives in rural areas and slightly under half of the work force is employed in agriculture.[5] The rate of over-all population growth between 1950-52 to 1963-65 was 2.8 percent per year.[6] The population growth rate for cities in this period was a phenomenal 4.6 percent, representing a rise from the 3.8 percent rate that prevailed between 1940 and 1950. Between 1925 and 1960 the urban work force tripled, while the economically active farm population increased by 50 percent.[7]

Growth of the urban labor force is caused by the "population explosion" coupled with massive internal migration. Still, off-farm migration has not been sufficient to offset natural increase. To stabilize the agricultural population, the initial annual rate of population growth in the nonfarm sector would have to be about 5.6 percent, approximately one percentage point higher than at present. If agricultural population were to remain stable, nonagricultural population would have to increase at a rate equal to the rate of population growth multiplied by the quotient that results when total population is divided by nonagricultural population. This rate would, of course, be variable over time. To reduce farm population in Latin America would require increasing the rate of farm-to-city migration above this figure or reducing the birth rate.

But even at the present rate, internal migration has strained the facilities of the Latin American city. Approximately 5 million families now live in urban shantytowns and slums. This "marginal" population is estimated to be growing at about 15 percent per year—a rate over 10 percentage points higher than the city population as a whole.[8] And whether the birth rate will slow down in the immediate future in Latin America is an open question. T. Lynn Smith shows that population growth in Latin America between 1950 and 1960 was unprecedented; he believes that there will be some over-all reduction of this rate in the sixties.[9] This contention seems to be borne out by estimates of birth and death rates for a more recent period than the one he examined. Comparing Smith's birth and death rate calculations for 1959-61 with those of the United Nations for 1962-65, one discovers that the crude birth rate in nearly half of the Latin American countries is dropping somewhat faster than the crude death rate.[10] Thus, for the 15 countries Smith analyzed, one finds a drop of between .3 and .6 of a percentage point in natural increase in five countries; a drop of .1 of a percentage point in five countries; a constant rate in three countries; and a rise of between .1 and .2 of a percentage point in two countries.[11]

These data, coupled with Bogue's forecast (based on a few Asian countries) that "it is probable that by the year 2000 each of the major world regions will have a population growth that is either zero or is easily within the capacity of its expanding economy to support,"[12] provide some grounds for cautious optimism about the ability of Latin America to cope with its population explosion. But we must remember the speculative quality of these assertions in view of the provisional nature of the intercensal data on which they (vital statistics) are based.

Moreover, it is sobering to consider that a rapid and immediate decline in the birth rate would have little impact on the size of the labor force for 15 years. Myrdal has further suggested, "Especially since any decrease in the birth rate in an underdeveloped country will ordinarily be a slow and gradual process, we can safely predict that, till the end of the present century and perhaps longer, the labor force . . . in the Latin American countries [will increase] by around three percent . . ."[13]

Supplying more jobs in Latin America will be a formidable task. The economically active population in Latin America more than doubled between 1925 and 1960, a 35-year period in which the average rate of population growth was much slower than presently. An increase in the labor force on a similar scale in the United States took the 60 years of high average annual economic growth between 1900 and 1960.[14]

Thus, whether Latin American economic policy in the foreseeable future succeeds or fails will depend both on increasing average per capita income and on the related (but sometimes quite distinct) matter of creating adequate employment.

Slow Absorption of Workers in Industry

Economists intuitively look to industry and, more particularly, manufacturing as the major job source in the course of economic growth. But it appears that more employment will be needed than Latin America's secondary sector can possibly provide in the short run. Even its manufacturing component has employed labor at a lethargic pace. Myrdal explains the slow absorption of labor early in the contemporary development process by noting that where manufacturing implies rationalization of earlier and more labor-intensive firms, the new factories "... will out-compete craft and traditional production and the net effect on labor demand will be negative..."[15]

This is an overstatement—but not a gross one—of the recent Latin American situation. In 1950, 7.4 percent of the labor force worked in artisan crafts; by 1965 the figure had dropped to 6.3 percent. This slump more than cancelled the slight percentage increase in factory employment, so that the manufacturing sector as a whole (factory work plus artisan industries) employed about 14 percent of the work force in 1950 and only 13.7 percent in 1965. Numbers engaged in manufacturing increased at an annual rate of 2.4 percent from 1950 to 1965, but the rate slowed to 2.1 percent at the end of the period (1960-65).[16]

The participation of manufacturing in nonagricultural employment sharply illustrates the failure of this sector to utilize the labor force moving into urban centers. Between 1925 and 1960, manufacturing was able to absorb only a little over 5 million of the 23 million added to the urban labor force.[17] Put differently, an estimated 35.4 percent of a relatively small nonagricultural labor force were engaged in manufacturing in 1925; but by 1960, as urbanization advanced, the percentage had dropped to 27.1[18] In most developed countries, the ratio of manufacturing jobs to urban employment remained essentially constant over long periods of time—and at a much higher level. Experience in industrialized nations points to two basic features: (1) a relatively high percentage of urban employment is engaged in manufacturing, and (2) this percentage persists over long periods. "Thus, for example, it has been shown that the percentage in the United Kingdom in 1951 (51.9 percent) was practically the same as in 1901 (51.1 percent); in Italy, after a slight decline during the twenties, the percentage remained little below that for the beginning of the century (59.5 percent in 1901; 56.6 percent in 1939; and 53.5 percent in 1954).... In the United States the percentage has been lower, but has also shown very little tendency to decline over the long term (47 percent in 1870; 44 percent in 1900; 45.4 percent in 1920; and 42.3 percent in 1950)."[19]

In sum, a 5.6 percent average annual increase in manufacturing output was associated with a 2.1 percent average annual growth in employment between 1960 and 1965.[20] While it is hoped that investment and effective demand can remain high enough to increase both rates, the output-to-labor ratio will probably become more unfavorable to employment in the future. From a technological standpoint, manufacturing in Latin America is likely to become less rather than more labor intensive. It may be possible to foster economically justifiable policies that retard this trend in a few industries from time to time, but it is difficult to see how enough jobs can be created thereby. For example, income redistribution policies should shift the demand structure for manufactures (in the short run) away from its current emphasis on intermediate and even heavy lines to more labor intensive consumer nondurables, for which markets are presently exhausted in most Latin American countries. This development would also ease balance of payments difficulties. Even so, Barraclough explains, "A new factory in Medellín or São Paulo will generally adopt the labor saving technology of industries in present-day Detroit or Pittsburgh, not that of 19th century Birmingham or Manchester." Glade (Chapter 9) argues that in the initial push toward import substitution in the '40s and '50s, manufacturing activity was concentrated in nondurable consumer goods many of which were, relatively speaking, quite labor intensive. By the mid-fifties, however, major dynamism had gone out of these fields, and the focus of industrialization shifted to consumer durables and basic industrial goods that are less labor intensive. Miller (Chapter 10) shows that employment stabilization policies and, by inference, some other kinds of social legislation have contributed to a decline in employment opportunities and increasing substitution of capital for labor in the secondary sector.[21]

The picture is not much brighter in the industrial sector as a whole (mining, manufacturing, construction, and associated technological services). In 1950-55, it employed 44 percent of the addition to the nonfarm labor force; in 1955-62, only 36 percent.[22]

Because the nonfarm goods-producing sectors have not absorbed a substantially larger percentage of a growing labor force lately, more workers are drifting to the tertiary sector ("other services") and to what the United Nations has called "unspecified activities"—mainly disguised unemployment. In absolute numbers, 1965 employment in these subsectors was nearly double that for 1950—a growth that does not seem to be in line with the need for services engendered by the region's slow rate of economic growth.[23]

The Economic Commission for Latin America recently elaborated on the oversimplified assumption that "other services" and "unspecified activites" provide the only refuge for the nonfarm underemployed by observing that all sectors seem to have high-, medium-, and low-productivity subsectors. It estimates, for example, that in manufactures, construction, and technological services, the work force allocated to each productivity subsector would be about 20, 60, and 20 percent, respectively. As urbanization proceeds at a rate faster than industrialization, new in-migrants—if they are absorbed at all—are employed in the low-productivity subsector.[24] It stands to reason that if the economies of Latin America do not grow much faster and if rural-to-urban migration continues at the present pace, the capacity of this subsector to provide jobs will become saturated, raising open unemployment to very high levels.[25]

One can conclude, therefore, that industrialization must be given as much impetus as scarce resources allow, but that unless Latin America is willing to suffer the massive social unrest that idleness and underemployment may well spark, agriculture must be relied upon not to repel workers to the extent it has in the past. This is not because of any inherent advantages of farm employment, but because the capacity of industry to utilize labor in Latin America is not as rapid as necessitated by the high rate of in-migration.

Farm Financed Social Welfare: the U.S.
North, the South, and Latin America

Even though there are indications that much privately owned farm land is not used to capacity, given present technology,[26] agriculture in most of Latin America does not now provide an adequate haven for underemployed and jobless people. One reason is to be found in the manner in which farming is organized. Large estates (plantations or haciendas) encompass most of the best land—except in Mexico, Bolivia, and Cuba—and are worked by large numbers of hired laborers who have little or no bargaining power.

When farming is structured in this manner, it: (1) does not provide either the security of employment or adequate income necessary to keep workers in farming until a late enough stage of development and (2) does not permit a viable community organization to flourish that would support an educational system capable of developing basic literacy and the skills and attitudes needed for urban employment or for upgrading the rural labor force.

When management is separated from the more-than-ample supplies of poorly-organized labor, as in the estate system in Latin America, resource owners can offer an extremely low wage and are freer than in a family farm system to discharge workers who have few employment alternatives.

On the other hand, while an owner-operator may sell out when the situation becomes acute, he cannot fire himself or his family labor when he is caught in a cyclical cost-price squeeze. Consequently, in a system dominated by the family farm a large proportion of surplus labor takes the form of involuntary underemployment in the countryside rather than involuntary unemployment in town. Even today U.S. agriculture harbors a surprisingly large amount of surplus labor.

As Owen has argued, farming in the United States has thus performed a self-financed social welfare function: redundant labor resources have not only funded their own sustenance, they have also been expected to cover a substantial percentage of their schooling costs and to support a large portion of other necessary social overhead capital.[27]

With each passing year, U.S. agriculture performs this function less adequately. By relying too heavily on farm-financed social welfare, our affluent country has consistently overlooked its rural poor.[28] While liberals may abhor this neglect, they must admit that the "agrarian dualism" which developed throughout this century had some important advantages: one subsector of farming has provided immense production, while the other afforded a stopgap matrix of jobs that retarded premature cityward migration. Through primarily locally financed schools, agricultural communities have helped to prepare farm people to be more productive in agriculture if they remained, and in urban employment if they migrated.

United States agricultural dualism has not been static; land in the welfare subsector constantly "moves" into the growth subsector in response to the dynamic functioning of the market. Labor-saving capital has now become so cheap relative to labor that for the past several decades farming has been caught in an accelerated combination of farm units accompanied by a release of labor. Labor has not always benefited from these land and capital "flows." That some entire communities have been "left behind" is but one indication that farm-financed social welfare has not worked altogether smoothly; this implies that supplementary policies to cope with rural poverty in the United States are long overdue.

But in some parts of the United States—notably much of the South—farm-financed social welfare never was a part of the institutional framework. To the degree that the southern sharecropping system separated ownership-management from labor (that had little countervailing power) and discouraged the education of the farm work force, it can, albeit roughly, be compared to the Latin American hacienda or plantation. Indeed, the southern cropper may be considered as one U.S. analogue of the Latin American hacienda worker. (There are other analogues, like the "company town" poor white from Appalachia and the blacks of the central cities who live in absentee-owned slum units and may be victimized by high rents as well as lack of community control.)

These farming systems seem to have serious urban repercussions. In the United States, the problems of today's ghetto are not due to racial prejudice alone (in boom periods, Negro unemployment in cities does drop somewhat). They are at least partly due to the release of an unskilled and even illiterate labor force that could not be fully hired by industry at the state of development it was passing through. Kain and Persky conclude:

The North's biggest cities attract large numbers of rural Negroes from the Core South. Smaller Northern areas draw disproportionately large numbers of Appalachian whites. Ironically, it is these groups that are relatively the worst prepared for coping with the complexities of the industrial, metropolitan North. The educational achievement of each is inferior to the majority of the Southern population from which they came. Negroes of the Core South are especially disadvantaged in this respect. In analyzing the distribution of poverty in the North Central region of the country, we found that a substantial fraction of the metropolitan North's poor were born and educated in the South. . . . Finally, we have found no evidence to support the widely held view that rural Southern migration to the North will soon abate.[29]

And if the central city problem here has some roots in a remnant plantation system, which represents only a small fraction of U.S. agriculture, one cannot but be alarmed at the potential for social unrest in most Latin American countries where the preponderance of the land is organized along similar lines and where slum settlements are growing faster than ours ever did.

As the peasant was deprived of land from colonial times, so was his U.S. counterpart—especially if he was black. Even the Homestead Act benefited the black little; his pleas for "40 acres and a mule" after the Civil War largely went unheeded.[30] Recent commentators have noted of the immediate *post bellum* period: "The planters still owned the land but they needed a labor supply to farm it. As a result, a new kind of partnership—sharecropping—was formed. The landowners supplied land and work stock and the newly freed Negroes supplied the labor to continue farm production in much the same pattern as before . . ."[31]

Movement of blacks out of the South was slow in the late nineteenth century because of adequate employment possibilities in agriculture and a great deal of competition for northern industrial jobs by recent immigrants—mainly of European stock. But during the early 1920s, "The enormous growth of northern industry, the increasing demand for unskilled labor, and the relatively high wages offered by business enterprise, and above all the curtailment of European and Asiatic immigration multiplied the opportunities available . . ."[32] Subsequently, World War II created unprecedented demand for labor and encouraged a much larger out-migration of farm workers. Now, higher welfare payments in the North than in the South seem to provide an additional attraction.

But out-migration also had its "push" aspects—employment possibilities on large cotton farms began to decline in the '20s: "For a few years the boll weevil caused great panic as millions of acres of cotton were severely damaged and production fell . . . thousands of Negroes emigrated as the landlords turned to livestock and dairying."[33] Soil depletion and erosion were the other major problems, especially in the Piedmont country of Georgia and South Carolina, and impelled thousands to leave. The depression, when "the bottom dropped out of the cotton market," seems to have had similar effects.[34] In later decades mechanized planting and subsequently mechanized harvesting of cotton discharged more southern workers at a time when the labor market was unable to absorb them in sufficient numbers.[35] And in the sixties, as yet uncounted numbers have been pushed off the farm by reductions in cotton allotments,[36] and by employers' response to the 1966 extension of the minimum farm wage legislation.[37]

Had the sharecrop system supported adequate schooling, more blacks doubtless would have gotten urban jobs despite the scourge of discrimination. But at the same time that former sharecroppers were being released from southern farms in ever larger numbers, the ratio of skilled-to-unskilled labor required by industry began to rise in accelerated fashion. The latter day manifestation of this is particularly serious to the U.S. economy. "In [the] word 'skill' lies the answer to the seeming paradox of 3,000,000 unemployed and a concurrent shortage in manpower. The unemployed are chiefly those who are, in various ways, unskilled. It is our national shame that a very large part of the unemployed are Negroes in slum ghettos who have neither the education nor the training in a specific skill to get a job . . ."[38]

Describing the inadequacy of the rural southern educational system to prepare workers for these jobs, one commentator has noted:

In 1960, the average years of schooling completed by the nonwhite farm population 25 years old and over was 5.7 years, compared with 8.9 years for the white farm population and 11.1 years for the total urban population.[39]

This says nothing of the comparable quality of schools educating blacks and whites. Nicholls places blame for this situation squarely on the planters:

In striking contrast to most of the Middle West, the South has been dominated by power groups who, shunning the public schools in the education of their own children, see little reason to tax themselves in order to finance the education of the less privileged classes . . .[40]

Poor farmers who remain today in the planter-dominated parts of the rural South are often nearly destitute and are permitted to remain—in houses they do not own, on land which is not theirs—only because of the paternalistic spirit of large holders. And a high percentage of those who migrated are today living in the ghetto where unemployment—or subemployment—is high. In early 1968, unemployment was as low as it has been in the past decade and a half, 3.5 percent of the labor force. But this rate was twice as high among Negroes and higher still among young Negroes living in the nation's slums. In addition to those who are looking for work and cannot find it—the unemployed—the slums hold those who do not have jobs and are not looking for them and those who are looking for full-time jobs and can find only part-time jobs. When all of these groups are combined, the "subemployment rate" reached 24.2 percent in Boston's Roxbury; 28.6 percent in Harlem; and 34.2 percent in Philadelphia, for example.[41] If jobs in the industrial era of our history have become progressively more scarce for the unskilled, one cannot but be alarmed at what this implies for the dawning technotronic age.

Several Tentative Hypotheses

While retrospective conjecture may result in highly inaccurate representations of history, we may pose several plausible but tentative and overlapping hypotheses from our experience with direct relevance for contemporary Latin America: Had a land tenure system that was labor absorptive over the long run been established in the rural South after the Civil War, recent out-migration would not have been as rapid. When it occurred it would have represented a more genuine response to viable economic opportunities. And if that tenure system had fostered farm-financed social welfare, laborers would have reached the urban labor market more adequately prepared for urban life.

Evidence bearing on this speculation is scanty. But when all rented and sharecropped units in the South—as well as those that are partially or fully owned—are counted as farms, in all but four census periods from 1900 to 1964 either (1) numbers of farms operated by blacks disappeared more rapidly than farms operated by whites, or (2) numbers of Negro units declined while numbers of white units increased.[42] Differences in the opposite direction in the four exceptional periods were slight. Thus, it appears that through most of this century the institutional framework of Negro agriculture has been less able than the white system to hold labor and that this situation becomes steadily more unfavorable to the black as the century wears on.

Looking only at farm consolidation one may, on balance, understate the amount of Negro off-farm migration that occurred. Since rural blacks have families that are larger than the families of rural whites, there are proportionally more people who must leave for other work at some time in their life cycle—even when the family head is not fired. Each 1,000 nonwhite farm women 40-44 years old in 1960 had given birth to an average of 5,618 children; each 1,000 rural white women in this age bracket had borne an average of 2,873 children.[43]

The issue becomes somewhat clearer when race is distinguished from tenure type. In each census period after 1925-30, farm owners in the South (the majority, of course, family farmers) have been far more able than the croppers— whether white or black—to remain in agriculture.[44] Some croppers became hired farm labor in mid-century, but on the average only one hired hand was engaged for each three or four croppers that were discharged.[45] It should be noted that there is more similarity in the trends within the "owner" and the "cropper" categories than within those of "white" and "black." Thus, the plantation sharecrop "system" seems to have contributed importantly to reducing the job opportunities in agriculture; it seems less able than family farming to maintain employment in the face of adverse prices (the '30s) or mechanization (the '40s and '50s).

Race is a lesser complication in much of Latin America, but the hacienda system seems no more viable than the sharecrop system in providing adequate educational facilities or a stopgap matrix of jobs.

Absorption of Labor in Agriculture in Latin America

Like the remnant southern plantation, the hacienda is not noted for its ability to absorb labor. The set of studies by the Inter-American Committee on Agricultural Development,[46] which focuses on seven Latin American countries with a traditional agrarian structure, shows that production per acre is inversely related to farm size; and while *latifundios* are 400 times larger than *minifundios* on the average, they employ only 15 times more workers.

As in the U.S. South, a variant of noblesse oblige has been some substitute for self-financed rural welfare on family farms—owners who feel responsibility for their workers' protection have not fired resident labor even after the factor is in surplus.[47] But in Latin America, as in southern United States, this spirit is no longer widespread.

More serious than the issue of resident labor, proportionally fewer seasonally hired workers (who make up the bulk of the rural labor force) are now being contracted. A noticeable shift in some countries is being made from cash crops—which require a substantial amount of labor—to livestock. Then, too, pressures for the adoption of labor-saving farm technology in Latin America are similar, if not yet as pervasive, as those in industry. Minimum agricultural wage legislation is making labor more expensive in relation to capital. In some countries, notably Venezuela, those who mechanize are often able to obtain machinery at relatively low cost with cheap credit and long term repayment arrangements. While sometimes necessary to increase product per unit of land, the effect of mechanization on production—which is primarily labor displacing— is usually not as great as would be equivalent expenditures on yield-increasing inputs such as fertilizers, hybrid seeds, and protective chemicals.

Even if land taxes that cannot be evaded are utilized as a means to modernize agriculture, large landowners may find it profitable—at least as long as inflation continues—to dislodge workers and substitute capital for labor to meet this new fixed cost, instead of selling out.

Education of the Rural Labor
Force in Latin America

Landlords who dominate Latin American economies and politics usually send their children to urban schools. Hence, those with investable funds have little interest in improving rural education. In Chile, generally considered to have one of the most progressive school systems in Latin America, only four of ten urban first graders ever advanced through the sixth and final elementary grade; of every ten rural students who enter primary school, only one is graduated. The dropout rate is higher in the countryside than in town because of longer distances to school, more illness, greater labor needs at home, poorer facilities, and fewer books. Most dropouts leave before they learn to read and write.[48]

Primary school graduates are only slightly better off. The curriculum in the grades is largely unrelated to the background of the students or to the occupational role they might play if they migrated to town. Furthermore, teachers are usually poorly prepared. For example, in Brazil there are 90,000 employed teachers who have not finished their primary education.[49] In Colombia, 41 percent of the urban primary teachers, but 78 percent of the rural, have no more than a primary education.[50] Needless to say, if the products of this system migrate to town, they are ill-equipped to even take unskilled jobs.

By contrast, in Mexico, where the hacienda system has been abolished, one observer recently noted:

There is an upsurge in the literacy level among the young and there are some signs of improvement among the older generation as well. . . . It is not easy to estimate how far the investment in human resources will go, but the course has been charted and the vision of the future quoted below [by Frank Tannenbaum in 1950 from a conversation with President Calles] may not prove to be an idle dream: "in the past Mexico was divided into *latifundios*, with a big house (*casco*) in the center; in the future we will organize it around the village, with a school in the center."[51]

Citing the experience in Bolivia since haciendas were broken up as part of the revolution of 1952, Hobsbawm states, "The first thing any peasant community does when it can is to build a school."[52] In 1964, Mexico allocated nearly a quarter of her annual budget to education, a figure exceeded only by Costa Rica among the 19 Latin American republics. Bolivia spent 17.9 percent of her budget in education; only the aforementioned and El Salvador, Panama, and Honduras had better records.[53]

Implications for Agricultural Development Policy in Latin America

Unless other policies intervene, one impact of agricultural "modernization" now occurring in most of Latin America may be that workers will leave the farms for cities at an increasing rate in the next decade. This argument implies that a concerted effort should be made to slow the rate of farm-to-city migration until industry is able to absorb labor at a faster rate. Unfortunately, colonization of new lands in Latin America may be too slow and expensive and some measure of land reform may be the only alternative for the task at hand, in spite of the understandable opposition of the landed. Especially since the writings of Ragnar Nurkse, the possibility of a capitalistic system providing the rural under-employed with productive work through rural public works projects has been recognized. (See a late advocacy of this position in Millikan and Hapgood.[54]) The present author does not argue with the desirability of this policy alternative but doubts that it is sufficient for the task at hand.

To partially meet immediate employment needs, "contrived dualism," which has parallels in the historic development of agriculture in our North and West, might be considered by development planners in Latin American countries with a traditional land tenure structure:[55]

(a) *Subsector that emphasizes growth in marketable surplus.* It would seem as though the progressively managed large farm and plantation subsector should be stimulated to greater productivity through the application of more yield increasing inputs, since these are the farms that feed the city and provide export earnings. At the same time, as much employment and income security as possible should be encouraged in this subsector without creating disincentives for management.

(b) *Subsector that emphasizes growth in employment.* The existing subsector of very small farms can probably continue to absorb some population increase until development-created employment begins to catch up with population growth. If technology can be adapted to their needs (as in Japan and Taiwan) and if markets and credit can be made available to them, these small farms might employ even more people and make a greater contribution than presently to marketable surplus.

Programs to provide secure and legal title for present occupants may be inexpensive and are of great importance in some areas. Most Latin American countries have farmers who are "squatters" on public lands; there are several hundred thousand farmers who do not have title to the land they farm.[56] This is not conducive to employment stability, nor does it offer the security required for long-term investments in agriculture.

Since underutilized and poorly managed land on traditional large-scale farms contributes little to production, and since its absentee ownership and paternalistic labor patterns are vulnerable to labor unrest and consequent worker eviction, it should be transformed into new peasant farms. Past performance gives no indication that large investments in the traditional subsector of agriculture would result in either enough increased production or rural employment to meet the needs of the growing population.

As with existing small farms, attempts should be made to move reform-created farms as rapidly as possible toward commercial agriculture with limited mechanization, more use of yield-increasing inputs, and improved extension-type services. Given the exceedingly scarce supply of resources available, however, this may need to be regarded as a long-term goal rather than a present possibility. Even if, for the time being, reform does no more than provide sustenance for large numbers of rural people, it will contribute to economic and political stability and buy time for industrial development to catch up with population growth. As the labor market tightens, land and capital should be freed for the "primarily marketable surplus" subsector. That this will happen only over the long run because of the current high rate of population growth should not surprise us.

A high cost colonization program will be counterproductive; if it costs more to settle farmers on the land than to secure a job in manufacturing (as unfortunately it has in some countries), land reform will soon grind to a halt. If "agrarian reform" actually displaces labor—as it also may have done in some countries—it will not have fulfilled its prime objective.[57] Whatever program is adopted, settlement cost per family must be low.

Furthermore, the need is for flexible agrarian policies and more research on an exceedingly complex situation. Doctrinaire and ideological solutions are inappropriate, not only because conditions vary from country to country, but also because the policy needs of a given country vary over time. Thus, the post-reform tenure system may or may not take the form of the family farm.[a] In

---

[a]Even though a type of cooperative farming known as the *asentamiento* is being utilized in the early stages of the current Chilean reform, research on eight such farms the year after incorporation into the program shows that both employment and production practically doubled from the pre-form situation. Whether this type of organization is too expensive relative to output, whether it will be viable over the long run, whether it is adversely influencing the existing commercial subsector of agriculture, and even whether it can survive the serious 1968 drought are matters for further research and observations. Over time, it is conceivable the *asentamiento* may have the problems that have plagued the proportional profit farm in Puerto Rico. Relieving unemployment had been one avowed intent of this land tenure arrangement. Now, 16 Unions bargain with the Land Authority, the government agency vested with most management functions. They have pursued a militant wage policy coupled with featherbedding techniques that have increased operating expenses and caused consistent negative profits on some farms. FAO-ICIRA, Evaluación Preliminar de los Asentamientos de la Reforma Agraria de Chile, Santiago, Ediciones ICIRA, 1967. FAO, "Puerto Rican Land Reform," Documents of the World Land Reform Conference, Rome, 1966. Stahl, John Emery. "Economic Development Through Land Reform in Puerto Rico," unpublished PH.D. thesis, Iowa State University, 1966.

general, however, the emphasis should be on increasing production at low cost through yield-increasing technology along with maximum employment and employment security. A cue—but no recipe—can be taken from U.S. history, and emphasis should be placed on creating a milieu in which farm-financed social welfare can become part of the institutional fabric.

If the current population growth rate continues for several decades, no stopgap expedient of agricultural employment will be able to provide enough jobs to accommodate the burgeoning work force.[b] And only a completely unprecedented rate of economic growth will be able to provision it.

Even if the birth rate should fall in the seventies or eighties, if little or no land reform takes place in the meantime, it is likely that by the nineties or even sooner social scientists will be studying ways to reconstruct after a complete institutional breakdown in Latin American cities.

Notes

1. Benjamin Higgins, "The City and Economic Development," in *The Urban Explosion in Latin America: A Continent in Process of Modernization*, ed. Glenn H. Beyer (Ithaca: Cornell University Press, 1967), p. 120.

2. Ibid., p. 136.

3. Arthur Domike, "Industrial and Agricultural Employment Prospects in Latin America," prepared for the Second Conference on Urbanization and Work in Modernizing Areas, St. Thomas, Virgin Islands, Nov. 2-4, 1967, p. 61.

4. Robert J. Alexander, "The Import-Substitution Strategy of Economic Development," *Journal of Economic Issues*, Dec. 1967, pp. 305 and 307.

5. *United Nations Economic Survey of Latin America*, 1966, E/CN.12/767, presented at the Twelfth Session ECLA meetings, Caracas, Venezuela, May 2-13, 1967, pp. 63 and 37 respectively.

6. Ibid., p. 37.

7. United Nations, *The Process of Industrial Development in Latin America*, E/CN.12/716/Rev. 1, New York, 1966, p. 36.

8. Domike, "Industrial and Agricultural Employment," p. 4. Both Manaster and Mangin estimate the number of urban squatters alone at 25% of the population of Lima in 1966. In Rio de Janeiro the comparable 'favela' percentage is about 16%. Similar percentages could be cited for most Latin American cities; Kenneth A. Manaster, "The Problem of Urban Squatters in Developing Countries: Peru," *Wisconsin Law Review*, 1968, p. 25; William

---

[b]Absorbing labor until industry was ready to provide employment was one avowed goal of the Mexican reform. Even though the Mexican industrial sector is now the most dynamic in Latin America, population growth continues high. Numbers of landless workers are increasing rapidly and there is little more land available to accommodate them. In this context, one cannot fall back on the agricultural sector for additional stopgap employment. *Continued high rates of population growth, it seems, will eventually thwart all possibilities of providing the work force with jobs.*

Mangin, "Squatter Settlements," *Scientific American*, Oct. 1967, p. 21; Richard M. Morse, "Recent Research on Latin American Urbanization: A Selective Survey with Commentary," *Latin American Research Review*, Fall, 1965, p. 50.

9. T. Lynn Smith, "The Growth of Population in Central and South America, 1940 to 1970," prepared for the Select Commission on Western Hemisphere Immigration, June 1967, mimeo.

10. Compare: Smith, "Growth of Population," Table III, p. 21 with United Nations, *Statistical Bulletin for Latin America*, IV, No. 1: 31-32, Feb. 1967.

11. Computed from the reference in Note 10.

12. Donald J. Bogue, "The End of the Population Explosion," *The Public Interest*, Spring 1967, p. 11.

13. Gunnar Myrdal, "The United Nations, Agriculture, and the World Economic Revolution," *Journal of Farm Economics*, Nov. 1965, pp. 894-95.

14. United Nations, *The Process of Industrial Development in Latin America*, p. 35.

15. Myrdal, "UN Agriculture," p. 895.

16. Marshall Wolf, "Social Trends in Latin America," Economic Commission for Latin America, Social Affairs Division, June 1967, draft, pp. 28 and 29; United Nations, *Economic Survey of Latin America 1966*, E/CN.12/767 presented at the Twelfth Session ECLA meetings, Caracas, Venezuela, May 2-13, 1967, Table 1-13, p. 63.

17. United Nations, *The Process of Industrial Development in Latin America*, p. 35.

18. Wolf, "Social Trends," p. 26.

19. United Nations, *The Process of Industrial Development in Latin America*, p. 26.

20. Computed from *United Nations Economic Survey 1966*, Tables 1-2, 1-13, pp. 50 and 63.

21. See also Solon Barraclough, "Rural Development and Employment Prospects in Latin America," prepared for the Second Conference on Urbanization and Work in Modernizing Areas, St. Thomas, Virgin Islands, Nov. 2-4, 1967, mimeo, p. 19.

22. United Nations Economic Commission for Latin America, *Economic Survey of Latin America, 1964*, E/CN.12/711/Rev. 1, 1966, p. 46.

23. Wolf, "Social Trends," p. 29; United Nations Economic Commission for Latin America, *Economic Survey of Latin America, 1965*, E/CN.12/752/Rev. 1, 1967, p. 62 and Tables 1-13, p. 63.

24. Ibid., pp. 30-31.

25. Ibid., pp. 32-35; United Nations Economic Commission for Latin America, "Structural Changes in Employment within the Context of Latin America's Economic Development," *Economic Bulletin for Latin America*, 10: 163-87, Oct. 1965.

26. Inter-American Committee for Agricultural Development, *Land Tenure Conditions and Socio-Economic Development of the Agricultural Sector for Argentina, Brazil, Chile, Colombia, Guatemala, Ecuador and Peru*, Washington, D.C., 1966.

27. Wyn F. Owen, "The Double Developmental Squeeze on Agriculture," *American Economic Review*, Mar. 1966, p. 62.

28. President's National Advisory Commission on Rural Poverty, *The People Left Behind*, Washington, D.C., 1967.

29. John F. Kain, and Joseph J. Persky, "The North's Stake in Southern Rural Poverty," Harvard University-M.I.T. Joint Center for Urban Studies, Program on Regional and Urban Economics, Discussion Paper No. 18, May 1967, pp. 73 and 74.

30. James M. McPherson, "Land for the Landless," in *The Negro's Civil War* (New York: Random House, 1965), pp. 293-300. Any description of the plantation-sharecropping system sounds strikingly like that of a hacienda in, say, Peru or Chile. See, for example, Rubin, and compare this description to one of a latifundia: Morton Rubin, *Plantation County* (Chapel Hill: The University of North Carolina Press, 1951). Inter-American Committee for Agricultural Development, *Land Tenure*.

31. James G. Maddox, et al., *The Advancing South: Manpower Prospects and Problems* (New York: The Twentieth Century Fund, 1967), p. 11.

32. Charles A. Beard, and Mary R. Beard, *The Rise of American Civilization* (New York: The MacMillan Company, 1930), p. 26.

33. Calvin L. Beale, "The Negro in American Agriculture," in *The American Negro Reference Book*, ed. John P. David, (Englewood Cliffs, N.J.: Prentice-Hall, Inc., 1966), p. 164.

34. Ibid.

35. Richard H. Day, "The Economics of Technological Change and the Demise of the Sharecropper," *American Economic Review*, 57, pp. 427-49, June 1967.

36. U.S. Department of Agriculture, *Rural People in the American Economy*, ERS Agricultural Economic Report, 101, Washington, D.C., Oct. 1966, p. 52.

37. President's National Advisory Commission on Rural Poverty, *The People Left Behind*, p. 22.

38. John Tebbel, "People and Jobs," *Saturday Review*, Dec. 30, 1967, p. 8.

39. Beale, "Negro in American Agriculture," p. 188.

40. William H. Nicholls, *Southern Tradition and Regional Progress*, (Chapel Hill: University of North Carolina Press, 1960), pp. 110-11, and 113.

41. Will Lissner, "The Negro as a Victim," in *The City in Crisis*, ed. Irwin Isenberg (New York: The H.W. Wilson Co., 1968), pp. 42-44.

42. For the statistical basis for these statements see Table I, p. 745 in the *American Journal of Agricultural Economics* (Vol. 51, No. 4, Nov. 1969) publication of this paper.

43. U.S. Department of Agriculture, *Rural People in the American Economy*, pp. 52-53.

44. See Table 2, in Nicholls, *Southern Tradition*.

45. U.S. Department of Agriculture, *Rural People in the American Economy*, p. 51.

46. Inter-American Committee for Agricultural Development, *Land Tenure*,

summarized in United Nations Economic Commission for Latin America, *Economic Survey of Latin America 1966*, E/CN. 12/767, presented at the Twelfth Session ECLA meetings, Caracas, Venezuela, May 2-13, 1967. Add. 4.

47. Nicholls, *Southern Tradition*.

48. Marshall Wolf, "Education, Social Structure and Development in Latin America," IV World Congress of Sociology, Evian, Sept. 1966, Mimeo; Marshall Wolf, "Social Trends in Latin America," op. cit.

49. *O Globo*, "Noventa Mil Profesôres Não Concluiram Primário," Rio de Janeiro, Dec. 22, 1967, p. 15.

50. A. Eugene Havens, "Education in Rural Colombia: An Investment in Human Resources," Research Paper No. 8, Madison, Land Tenure Center, Feb. 1965, mimeo.

51. Wolf Ladejinsky, "Traditional Agriculture and the *Ejido*," unpublished manuscript, Washington, D.C., Oct. 1966, p. 52.

52. E.J. Hobsbawm, "Peasants and Rural Migrants in Politics," in *The Politics of Conformity in Latin America*, ed. Claudio Veliz (London: Oxford University Press, 1967), pp. 54-55.

53. United Nations Economic Commission for Latin America, *Economic Survey of Latin America*, 1965, E/CN.12/752/Rev. 1, 1967, p. 39.

54. Max F. Millikan, and David Hapgood, *No Easy Harvest* (Boston: Little Brown & Co., 1967), pp. 64-66.

55. William C. Thiesenhusen, and Marion R. Brown, "Problems of Agriculture," a study prepared at the request of the Subcommittee on American Republics Affairs of the Committee on Foreign Relations, U.S. Senate, Dec. 1967; William C. Thiesenhusen, Marion R. Brown, and Peter Dorner, Testimony, before the Subcommittee on American Republics Affairs, "Survey of the Alliance for Progress," Hearings before the Committee on Foreign Relations, U.S. Senate, February 27, 1968, pp. 3-57.

56. Joseph R. Thome, "Title Problems in Rural Areas of Colombia," Centro Inter-americano de Reforma Agraria, Mimeo., No. 3, Bogotá, Oct. 1965.

57. M.J. Sternberg, "Agrarian Reform and Employment, with Special Reference to Latin America," *International Labour Review*, 95: 1-26, Jan.-June, 1967.

14 The Minifundia Dilemma: A Colombian Case Study

Emil B. Haney, Jr.

One of the most important contributions of peasant agriculture to capitalistic development is its capacity to employ rural masses at near subsistence levels of living until more remunerative employment opportunities are created in the non-agricultural sectors of the economy. Through continued land fragmentation, informal tenancy arrangements, land use intensification, and in some instances, declining levels of living, many countries have kept burgeoning peasant populations "on ice" for generations, while industrial development and urbanization gradually undermined their traditional economic and social order.

Like most developing countries, Colombia is experiencing an increased crowding of peasants onto the land. Notwithstanding an annual flow of 200,000 rural-urban migrants,[1] the rural population continues to grow at the rate of at least 1,000 new farm families per week.[2] While some of these families were undoubtedly among the nearly 60,000 beneficiaries of INCORA's title registration and land redistribution programs during the first six years of its operation,[3] the overwhelming majority obviously were not. Most of INCORA's efforts have focused upon the creation and strengthening of those family farms which have a high potential for increasing marketable surpluses. Meanwhile, more than 800,000 families—40 percent of the country's farm families—are landless or own too little land to provide even the barest subsistence.[4]

The fact is that neither the productive segment of the Colombian agricultural sector nor the incipient industrial sector seems to be providing sufficient income-earning opportunities to absorb the growing rural labor force. The only alternative for most of the annual increment in the rural labor force appears to be underemployment in the nearly saturated service sector of the cities, or peasant agriculture in already densely populated rural areas.[5] In view of the unprecedented national population growth rate of 3.2 percent per year and the backwash effects created by the mechanization of formerly labor intensive operations (especially family handicrafts), it seems likely that minifundia agriculture will be the only escape valve available to many rural people during the next few decades. Hence, the country faces the difficult task of expanding employment opportunities in both the agricultural and non-agricultural sectors of the economy without sacrificing the level of productivity required to meet its internal and external commitments.

This paper documents some of the important demographic and technological changes in a peasant community of the Colombian highlands. It suggests that in

265

order to increase the employment capacity of the minifundia and improve peasant participation in the greater society, an entirely new developmental approach must be employed in the already settled rural areas.

Fómeque: History

A case in point is the densely populated Río Negro Valley located in the eastern part of Cundinamarca between the Federal District of Bogotá and the Llanos Orientales. Excluding the sparsely inhabited areas above the timber line, the average population density of six *municipios* studied in this region is nearly 300 persons per square mile.[6] During the past decade, the population of the region increased at an average annual rate of about 1 percent[7] in spite of heavy out-migration to Bogotá and the Llanos Orientales. The effective fertility rates (the number of children under five years of age per 100 females in the childbearing age group) have risen from 66.7 in 1938, to 69.3 in 1951, to 77.8 in 1964.[8]

The predominant settlement pattern of the region is one of small service and trade centers surrounded by dispersed minifundia. Eighty percent of the agricultural production units have fewer than three hectares of land.[9] Most of the minifundia are located on steeply sloped and highly erodible soils and are fragmented into two or more separate parcels.

An intensive study was conducted in one of the municipios, Fómeque, to learn more about the demographic and agricultural adjustments occurring in the community and the possibilities for improving the agricultural production and levels of living on the minifundia. Most of Fómeque's 11,500 inhabitants live on scattered minifundia in the temperate and cold climate zones in the western third of the municipio.[10] The other two-thirds of the land area lies above the timber line in extensive pastoral estates. The administrative and political seat of the municipio has about 400 resident families, most of whom own land in the rural hinterland. Between the landlords residing in the village and those living in Bogotá, more than three-fourths of Fómeque's total land area is held by absentee owners.

According to sketchy census data and local informants, Fómeque has sustained a dense rural population since the latter part of the 19th century. This evidence is substantiated by the migratory movements from the municipio. From the end of the last century until 1932, when the first road was completed to Villavicencio, Fómeque was an important intermediate trade center between Bogotá and the Llanos Orientales. Many local peasants worked as muleteers or cattle drivers during the dry seasons. Even after the road was opened, bypassing the municipio to the south, an impetus was given to crop production in the Llanos, many Fómenqueños—predominantly the younger males—worked as seasonal laborers during the planting and harvest. There was also some permanent migration from Fómeque to the Llanos during this time. But because of malaria and other dreaded diseases of the tropics, most peasants preferred to raise their families in the cooler climate of the Río Negro Valley.

By the late 1940s and early 1950s, when DDT had reduced the threat of malaria, "la violencia" (Colombia's little publicized but prolonged and bloody era of civil unrest) had erupted in the Llanos. With the majority of its inhabitants oriented toward the traditional Liberal Party, the Llanos became politically inhospitable to most potential migrants from Fómeque, whose residents are predominantly Conservative Party followers. Indeed, there was some reversal in the migration flow during this period as many families escaped to the relatively peaceful Río Negro Valley from the Llanos and other hostile regions of the country. Nearly 10 percent of the households in the rural sample indicated that one or more of its members had in-migrated or returned to Fómeque because of civil unrest elsewhere.[a]

By the time the turbulence had been suppressed in the late 1950s, the influx of mostly Liberal migrants into the Llanos from the violence-torn provinces of Tolima, Huila, Caldas, and Valle—coupled with an accelerated population growth rate—had created a labor surplus in the region, and mechanization had been introduced on many larger farms. Consequently, seasonal migration to the Llanos declined steadily during the past decade. In the sample of rural households, one-fifth of the male household heads had worked in the Llanos as seasonal laborers. However, two-thirds of these respondents were over 40 years of age and had not worked there during the past decade.

Likewise, the opportunities for permanent migration to the Llanos seem to be diminishing as accessible areas of fertile bottom land become densely settled. A recent soil survey indicates that less than 10 percent of the foothill region is suitable for intensive cultivation or peasant agriculture, and most of this land is already occupied.[11] The rest of the region, as well as the vast plains east of the foothills, is suitable only for extensive grazing and irrigated agriculture under careful management.

Only 20 percent of the migrant siblings and 15 percent of the migrant children of the sampled household heads and spouses in Fómeque were living in the Llanos in 1966. Eighty-three percent of the rural respondents indicated that they had never seriously considered moving to the Llanos. Their rationale usually included one of three factors: they considered the climate to be unhealthy, they perceived the social environment to be undesirable for raising a family, or they felt the services to be inadequate. On the other hand, 35 percent of the interviewees said that they would be interested in moving to the Llanos if they had an opportunity to acquire land near a population center.

During the early part of the century, permanent and seasonal migration to the coffee zone of Quindío also provided an important "escape valve" for the peasants of Fómeque. But, like the Llanos, heavy in-migration into the region eventually reduced the supply of available land and the demand for migratory labor. Outbreaks of "la violencia," which began here in 1946, apparently dealt a final blow to the half-century migratory movement. Fifteen percent of the male

[a]The rural data is based upon a probability area sample which included approximately 10 percent of the total number of rural households in the municipio. A census of the village households was completed in a separate phase of the study.)

household heads in the Fómeque sample had worked in the coffee zone, but three-fourths of these respondents were over 40 years old. Only 14 percent of the migrant siblings and 6 percent of the migrant children of the sampled household heads and spouses were living in the Quindío region in 1966.

While permanent and seasonal migration of Fómequeños (especially peasant families of the lower socioeconomic strata) to other rural areas of Colombia continues at a pace much retarded from earlier in the century, the dominant migratory pattern today is toward the cities. This migration appears to be increasing. Whereas 47 percent of the migrant siblings of the sampled household heads and spouses went to Bogotá, this city has attracted 60 percent of the migrant children of the rural respondents. Three-fourths of the migrant children from the village have gone to Bogotá. Of these, only one-fourth were employed in manual occupations compared to three-fourths of the migrant children from the rural part of the municipio. When asked whether they had ever considered moving to Bogotá, the majority of the rural respondents replied affirmatively. Nearly all of the interviewees had traveled to the capital city and virtually everyone has relatives living there. In most of these peasant families, however, the threats of unemployment and personal insecurity in the city apparently outweigh the disadvantages of a deteriorating peasant agriculture.

A sharp decline in the fifteen to twenty-nine year age groups for rural males and the fifteen to twenty-four year age groups for rural females suggests a heavy out-migration of young adults. The population is very young, especially in the rural portion of the municipio where the birth rate tends to be higher. Children under five years of age comprise 15 percent of the rural population, and 44 percent are under fifteen years of age. The effective fertility ratio is 71.8 for the rural area compared to 47.0 for the village.

In comparison to the national population, the municipio's population tends to be older. With the exception of the fifteen to nineteen year age group for males, all age groups under thirty-five years for both sexes are proportionately smaller for Fómeque than those for the national population. Nearly 47 percent of the national population are under fifteen years of age. The country's effective fertility ratio is 77.9.

While the crude birth rate for Fómeque has risen slowly from 31 in 1938 to 34 in 1964, the crude death rate has declined from 14.5 to 10.7 during the same time span.[12] The decrease in infant mortality as a result of improved medical facilities has been particularly notable. In 1938 over 12 percent of the infants died before reaching one year of age, compared to only 5 percent in 1966.[13]

The intense demographic pressure on the land as a result of limited opportunities outside the community has manifested itself in numerous ways. Land conflicts in other parts of the country, which began in the late 1920s and continued at an accelerated rate, and the passage of Law 200 of 1936 with its security of tenure clause, triggered a pervasive land fragmentation which still continues.[b] During the past decade, the number of additional legally created land parcels in Fómeque averaged 168 per year while the average number of reported consolidations was only 24 per year.[14] Meanwhile, land prices have increased to as high as U.S. $1,000 per acre for good agricultural land close to the village. The restricted alternatives for peasant families, coupled with cumbersome transfer procedures and inheritance patterns, have also fostered de facto land fragmentation—the stacking up of two or three generations on a single family property.

A whole array of informal contractual arrangements have evolved to circumvent legal roadblocks and to provide a means of subsistence for new peasant families. More than one-fifth of the agricultural production units operated by families in the rural sample included land owned by non-nuclear family relatives; one-fourth of the respondents operated some land owned by non-relatives living in the rural hinterland; and, over one-fourth operated some land owned by village residents. The extreme fragmentation of properties and the paucity of income-earning opportunities on the minifundia are further exemplified by the fact that 83 percent of the sample households reported income from either off-farm or non-farm employment.

The shortage of land and capital among the peasant families has forced most of them into informal tenancy and credit arrangements with the merchants, middlemen, and professionals of the village who, in turn, extract an economic surplus from the peasants to underwrite their own positions of power. Eighty-five percent of the rural respondents had obtained credit in cash or kind from village proprietors within the past two years. Such alliances between the peasants and villagers are important in the production of commercial enterprises and the diffusion of new technology in the community. Typically, the villagers provide the land and the physical inputs while the peasants, known as *sembradores* or *partijeros*, in this case supply the human and animal labor inputs. The value of purchased factors is usually prorated among the two parties and the product is shared equally. More than one-third of the rural respondents produced tomatoes under these sharecropping (*compañía*) arrangements in 1966.[c] Fifteen percent of

---

[b]After three years of congressional haggling over earlier drafts, Law 200 of 1936—Colombia's first major legal instrument of land reform—was passed during the relatively progressive administration of Alfonso Lopez. Precipitated by a growing number of land conflicts and rural unrest, the law attempted to provide a judicial basis for (1) clearing up uncertain titles and existing land occupancy rights, and (2) predicating ownership on the "economic use" of land. See Albert O. Hirschman, *Journeys Toward Progress* (New York: The Twentieth Century Fund, 1963), pp. 95-116.

[c]*Compañía* is an informal sharecropping arrangement wherein two or more parties combine their resources for production and share the output accordingly. More than one-half of the families in the rural sample were involved in such agreements for producing crops or raising livestock.

the rural respondents combined sharecropping with service tenancy agreements (*arrendamiento*) with village residents and hence were obligated to perform other services as well.[d]

The landlords or creditors often purchase the producer's share of the output at a price somewhat less than the going market rate. As a result of tightly organized informal horizontal and vertical associations of local middlemen with those in the consuming centers, market margins between producer and wholesale levels usually exceed 50 percent for most commodities, and often are as high as 100 percent.

Such asymmetrical linkages between the peasants and the dominant community groups mean that most rural families are effectively excluded from the major decision-making processes of the community and they have little or no recourse to the actions taken by their superordinates. Except for members of the municipal council, Colombian local government officials are appointed. The municipal council itself has the prerogative of nominating a list of candidates from whom their successors are elected by the public. They, in turn, appoint the other local officials except for the mayor who is appointed by the departmental governor. Throughout the past decade, no fewer than five out of the ten council members have resided outside Fómeque, and most of the mayors have been short-termed outsiders. Fómeque has never had an elected or appointed peasant representative in the local government. Small wonder that only 14 percent of the 1967 municipal budget, equal to approximately U.S. $47,000, was designated specifically for projects in the rural portion of the municipio where 80 percent of the people live.

Fómeque-Current Structure

In general, the peasant families are locked into a chronic state of poverty on land which is condemned to a short life through the persistent use of exploitative production techniques. As a result of heavy demographic pressure, the cloud forest zones of the municipio are being threatened by rapid fragmentation and intensive cultivation. The destruction of these natural reservoirs, in turn, severely disrupts the normal hydrological cycle of the community—especially the populous lower areas of the municipio—by accentuating the wet and dry seasons.

Intensive commercial crops have provided additional slack in the delicate balance between the community's population and its natural resource base. But they have also injected new perils into the system. Clean cultivated crops such as tomatoes, which are produced in vertical rows on steep slopes, deplete the soils

---

[d]The *sistema de arrendamiento*, as it is known locally, consists of informal land tenancy contracts involving service obligations on the part of the tenants (*agregados*). Typically, tenants are supplied a house and a subsistence plot of land for their usufruct in exchange for services such as tending livestock, harvesting permanent crops, and delivering produce to the landlord. Landlords and tenants operating under this arrangement quite commonly enter into *compañía* agreements, as well, for producing annual crops or livestock enterprises.

at a much more rapid pace than the traditional intercultivated subsistence crops (such as maize, parsnips, broad beans, and squashes). With this accelerated rate of depletion, it is becoming impractical and even impossible to produce commercial crops without improved fertility practices. But the increasing amounts of chemical fertilizers which are used are not being applied with complementary soil and water conservation practices.

Although the introduction of intensive commercial enterprises (such as green beans, peppers, onions, flowers, as well as tomatoes) has resulted in a greater output per unit of land, population pressures have caused a continual decline in the average farm size. Much of the land formerly planted to subsistence crops has been shifted to commercial crop production; however, the depletive techniques used in the cultivation of these intensive enterprises reduce the capacity of the soil to produce subsistence crops which are traditionally grown without improved fertility practices. Increasing amounts of chemical fertilizers and pesticides are required to maintain constant yields, to say nothing of improving them. Because of a diminished land base for the production of subsistence enterprises and because of a decline in former artisan crafts, peasant families must purchase a greater portion of their family needs. But because they also must purchase more inputs than before at increasingly disfavorable costs in relation to the prices received for their products, the peasants are caught in an accelerating technological squeeze.

Yield-increasing technology such as improved livestock breeds, new crop varieties, chemical fertilizers and pesticides has generated additional employment opportunities in the past. Yet the Fómeque case illustrates that there are limitations to increases in employment which can be brought about by such technological change. In densely populated rural areas like Fómeque, it is unlikely that the existing types of technology and institutional arrangements will permit a further absorption of people into agriculture and an improvement in levels of living for the rural masses without causing irreversible damage in the natural resource base.

Case studies and programming analyses of selected minifundia indicate that a great potential exists for a further expansion of production and employment through an extended usage of agricultural chemicals and genetic improvements in combination with improved soil and water management techniques. Labor-intensive conservation practices and irrigation schemes are presently used to great advantage on the more progressive farms of the community. For most commercial crops, yield differentials between the lowest and highest producers are greater than tenfold. Most of this variation may be explained by differences in technology and management.

Unless changes are made in the institutional structure, however, the possibilities for augmenting the productivity of the community's human and physical resources are not bright. On the one hand, the effective demand for new inputs is reduced by heavy liens against the peasants' production, unstable product prices, a high incidence of natural calamities, and restricted opportunities for acquiring new knowledge and skills. Under these constraints, incentives for seeking out and adopting relevant high pay-off combinations of new technology are dampened. On the other hand, the development and supply of new technology is dependent upon a grossly inadequate and outmoded agricultural service structure. Unlike the more progressive farmers of the community who have access to the country's major agricultural research stations, supply agencies, and financial institutions, peasants must rely upon local sources of information and physical inputs. In the absence of effective instrumental organizations through which peasants can formulate collective goals and devise plans for achieving them, there is little inclination on the part of the community's dominant groups to improve the agricultural infrastructure.

At the same time, there is little reason to anticipate massive commitments from the national government for minifundia communities. Under the present national political system, priorities are given to projects in the urban areas and in the more productive segment of the agricultural sector. However, if a larger portion of local resources were channelled into infrastructural investments such as roads, schools, health facilities, markets, and technical information systems for which the rural masses manifest a need, the employment and production capacities of the minifundia and their operators could be increased substantially.

Some of the resources required for these projects could conceivably be diverted from public funds now used to support local bureaucracies and conspicuous projects in the villages. But because of the narrow spectrum of local political power, the peasants are unable to effectively challenge such expenditures. Land taxes are the principal source of revenue for most local governments in Colombia. But because of low property assessments complicated by cumbersome reappraisal procedures, inflation, and a high incidence of noncompliance, the actual amount of funds collected falls far short of the potential. In 1966, Fómeque collected U.S. $7,838 in current and delinquent property taxes—only one-fifth of the total revenue of the local government. Most of the local government revenue consisted of participation funds and transfer payments from the departmental and national governments. A reassessment program just completed increased the potential land tax collections of the municipio by more than five times in real terms. But in context of the existing local political structure, peasants will have little incentive or justification for paying the additional taxes. In other minifundia communities, reassessment programs have apparently resulted in an expansion of local bureaucracies and higher rates of noncompliance.[15]

The local church has been more successful than the government in extracting resources from the peasantry. In 1966, it collected more than U.S. $25,000 in the community through Sunday collections, paid masses, bazaars, and fund campaigns for a new cemetery and rectory. It is estimated that nearly an equivalent amount of revenue was contributed in the form of labor, food, and building supplies. Formerly, a portion of the religious funds was returned to the rural neighborhoods for the construction of schools and roads. But in recent years, the growing village bureaucracy (teachers, municipal officials, and employees of public agencies) has effectively controlled the disbursement of these church funds into village projects including a complete elementary, secondary, and vocational school system, a consumer cooperative, a credit union, an experimental farm, a hospital, a market plaza, and a theater.

Meanwhile, peasant participation in the church's community development program has remained essentially that of contributing generously to a one-way flow of resources from the rural hinterland to the village. Few peasant children are enrolled in the village school system, for example. A bulldozer owned by the local church-sponsored development corporation is rented to a neighboring municipal government instead of being used to improve local penetration roads. In these cases and many others, effective pressure from the peasants could produce many benefits through extended usage of existing facilities and a better allocation of current revenues.

Implications

The dilemma, then, is not simply a matter of dismantling peasant agriculture and assimilating a burgeoning rural population into the cities as Laughlin Currie suggested in his "Operación Colombia" plan of 1961.[16] There is also the concomitant task of increasing the absorptive capacity of the agricultural sector so that growing numbers of rural people can be absorbed in remunerative employment during the early stages of industrialization. The challenge is rendered particularly difficult by the necessity to favor employment maximization subject to the physical and political constraints of providing adequate supplies of agricultural products for domestic consumption and foreign exchange earnings.

The capacity of peasant agriculture to increase the absorption of labor and the production of marketable surpluses has been constrained by structural barriers which impede the mobilization of relatively abundant low opportunity cost resources in this segment of the agricultural sector. The Fómeque case demonstrates that a continuing source of flexibility for increased employment and production on the minifundia can be achieved through a further application of agricultural chemicals and genetic improvements in combination with labor-intensive soil and water management practices. However, a continuous supply of improved inputs and services at remunerative prices is contingent upon an effective organization of the peasants through which they can present their demands to the community and the greater society.

Such technological and institutional changes in minifundia agriculture are, of course, only transitory steps in the overall development effort. Unless these changes are accompanied by pervasive structural modifications in the national economy, sustained high population growth rates will continue to generate unemployable rural masses. Indeed, the creation of remunerative employment opportunities for the existing backlog of rural youth constitutes a very formidable challenge to the nation, to say nothing of the future generations.

Increased employment and improved levels of living in peasant communities are consistent with the national goals of greater agricultural productivity and increased transfers of productive resources to the non-agricultural sectors of the economy. The costs of inaction will be quite high in terms of prolonged violence and destitution in both rural and urban areas as well as the continued destruction and waste of human and physical resources at an accelerating rate.

Notes

1. Dale W. Adams, "Rural Migrants and Agricultural Development in Colombia," Paper presented at the 13th Conference of the International Association of Agricultural Economists, Sydney, Australia, August 1967.

2. Speech to a Senate Commission by Enrique Peñalosa, director of the Colombian Agrarian Reform Institute (INCORA), quoted in *El Tiempo*, April 12, 1967, p. 23.

3. Inter-American Development Bank, *Socio-Economic Progress in Latin America*, Seventh Annual Report (Washington, D.C.: IDB, 1967), p. 114.

4. Interview with Enrique Peñalosa in *El Tiempo*, January 2, 1967, p. 17.

5. Ibid. According to Peñalosa, the number of rural families is projected to increase by 500,000 during the next decade, while an estimated 300,000 rural families are expected to migrate to the urban areas. Also see Marco F. Reyes C., "Estudio Socio-económico del Fenómeno de la Inmigración a Bogotá: Segunda Parte," *Economía Colombiana*, 22:21-29, November 1964. Reyes' study of a representative sample of in-migrants to Bogotá shows that 62 percent of those employed listed manual occupations—sales, operatives, artisan, day and wage labor, and personal and other services. Nearly 60 percent were absorbed in the service and commercial sectors, while 20 percent were employed in the industrial sector. Of the nearly one-third who moved to Bogotá for reasons of employment, only 36 percent had a definite position prior to migration.

6. Departamento Administrativo Nacional de Estadística (DANE), *Mapa Estadístico de Cundinamarca* (Bogotá: Imprenta Nacional, 1966).

7. From DANE, *Censo General de Población de 5 de Julio de 1938*, Tomo VII, Departamento de Cundinamarca (Bogotá: Imprenta Nacional, 1941); DANE, *Censo General de Población de 1951*, Departamento de Cundinamarca (Bogotá: Imprenta Nacional, 1954); and DANE, *XIII Censo Nacional de Población de 1964* (Bogotá: Multilith Estadinal, 1965).

8. Ibid., and DANE (unpublished statistics from the 1964 census).

9. Comité Interamericano de Desarrollo Agrícola (CIDA), *Tenencia de la Tierra y Desarrollo Socio-Económico del Sector Agrícola: Colombia* (Washington, D.C.: Pan American Union, 1966), p. 88.

10. DANE, *XIII Censo Nacional de Población, 1964*. On the basis of the data collected and reviewed during the study, it appears that the census figure may be understated by as much as 20 percent, especially in the rural sector.

11. Food and Agriculture Organization of the United Nations, *Reconocimiento Edafológico de los Llanos Orientales: Colombia* (Rome: United Nations Special Fund, 1965).

12. DANE, *Censo General de Población, 1938*; DANE, *XIII Censo Nacional de Población, 1964*; and local church records.

13. Records from the local church and notary.

14. Cadastral records of Fómeque.

15. L. Harlan Davis, "Economics of the Property Tax in Rural Colombia," (unpublished Ph.D. dissertation, University of Wisconsin, Madison, 1968).

16. Laughlin Currie, *Accelerating Development: The Necessity and the Means* (New York: McGraw-Hill, 1966). The basic ideas of the plan were originally presented by Professor Currie in a paper entitled *Operación, Colombia: Un Programa Nacional de Desarrollo Económico y Social* (Bogotá: Departamento Administrativo de Planeación y Servicios Técnicos, 1961).

About the Contributors

Joseph J. Spengler (Ph.D., Economics, Ohio State University) is James B. Duke Professor of Economics at Duke University. He has published widely on demography, economic development, and the history of economic thought. He is author of *France Faces Depopulation* and *French Predecessors of Malthus*; co-author and editor (with Ralph Braibanti) of *Tradition, Values and Socio-Economic Development* and *Administration and Economic Development in India*; (with William R. Allen), *Essays in the History of Economic Thought: Aristotle to Marshall*; (with Otis Dudley Duncan), *Demographic Analysis: Selected Readings* and *Population Theory and Policy: Selected Readings*. His current interests are population problems, economic development, and the history of socio-economic ideas, on which areas of inquiry most of his papers focus.

Lincoln H. Day (Ph.D., Sociology, 1957, Columbia) is chief of the United Nations Demographic and Social Statistics Branch. He has published (with Alice Taylor Day) *Too Many Americans*, Houghton Mifflin, 1964 and (with A.J. Jaffee and W. Adams) *Disabled Workers in the Labor Market*, Bedminster 1964, as well as numerous articles including "Natality and Ethnocentrism: Some Conclusions Based on an Analysis of Catholic-Protestant Differentials in Industrialized Countries," *Population Studies*, March 1968. He is currently continuing with research into the socio-cultural setting of low fertility in industrialized countries.

Kingsley Davis (Ph.D., 1936, Sociology, Harvard) is Professor of Sociology in the Department of Sociology and Lecturer in the Department of Demography at the University of California (Berkeley). He is also Director of International Population and Urban Research at Berkeley, a research office which has been especially concerned with the comparative demography of Latin America. Among the publications of IPUR are Andrew Collver, *Birth Rates in Latin America: New Estimates of Historical Trends and Fluctuations* (1965), Eduardo Arriaga, *New Life Tables for Latin American Populations in the Nineteenth and Twentieth Centuries* (1968), and José Hernández, *Return Migration to Puerto Rico* (1967).

Bernard Berelson (Ph.D., Sociology, University of Chicago), former Director of the Bureau of Applied Social Research at Columbia University, is now the President of the Population Council. He has published *Graduate Education in the United States*, McGraw-Hill, 1960, *Human Behavior: an Inventory of Scientific Findings* with Gary A. Steiner, Harcourt Brace and World, 1964, and, as editor and contributor, *Family Planning Programs: an International Study*, Basic Books, 1969.

J. Mayone Stycos (Ph.D., Sociology, Columbia) is senior consultant on Latin America to the Population Council, Director of the International Population

Program at Cornell University and Chairman of Cornell's Department of Sociology. He is the author of many articles on fertility and several books, the most recent of which is *Human Fertility in Latin America*, Cornell University Press, Ithaca, 1968.

Vivian Epstein is a doctoral candidate in Political Science at the University of Wisconsin and a Woodrow Wilson fellow. She has completed field research on the policy aspects of family planning programs in Costa Rica and Chile as a fellow of the Population Council and Dougherty Foundation. She has contributed a paper on "Population Policy in Costa Rica" to a forthcoming volume on *Multidisciplinary Analyses of Transportation in Costa Rica* edited by Warren J. Bilkey.

Ivan D. Illich (Ph.D., History, Salzburg and Munich) is one of the founders of the *Centro Intercultural de Documentación* (CIDOC) in Cuernavaca, Mexico, which serves as an orientation center for foreigners going to work in Latin America as well as a social policy research institute. He was the acting president of the University of Ponce in Puerto Rico and a member of the governing board of the State University (1956-60). Since 1960 he has been a faculty member in Political Science at Fordham. Among his publications are: "The Futility of Schooling in Latin America," *Saturday Review*, April 20, 1968; "The Seamy Side of Charity," *America*, January 21, 1967; "Violence: A Mirror for Americans," *America*, April 27, 1968; and *Celebration of Awareness*, Doubleday, 1970.

William P. Glade (Ph.D., 1955, Economics, University of Texas), professor of Economics and Business at the University of Wisconsin, is currently Associate Director of the Institute of Latin American Studies at the University of Texas. He is the co-author (with Charles Anderson) of *The Political Economy of Mexico*, University of Wisconsin Press, 1963, and *The Latin American Economies: A Study of Their Institutional Evolution*, D. Van Nostrand, 1969.

Richard U. Miller (Ph.D., Industrial Relations, Cornell, 1966), "Labor Relations and Status Symbols in a Developing Country: Comment," in Bhal Bhatt (editor), *Manpower Problems in Socio-Economic Development of Emerging Nations*. (Proceedings of a Conference sponsored by the Center for Comparative Industrial Studies, State University of New York at Buffalo, New York, April 15-16, 1969) forthcoming. "Executive Training Programs, Their Role in Development: Comment," in F.T. Bachmura (editor), *Human Resources in Latin America*, Bureau of Business Research, Graduate School of Business, Indiana University, 1968. "Labor Legislation and Mexican Industrial Relations," *Industrial Relations*, Vol. 7, No. 2, February 1968.

David Chaplin (Ph.D., 1963, Sociology, Princeton) is an Associate Professor of Sociology at the University of Wisconsin. He is the author of *The Peruvian Industrial Labor Force*, Princeton University Press, 1967, and numerous articles on labor problems, social stratification and politics in Peru. He is currently pursuing an historical and comparative study of household and family structure and the female labor force during industrialization in Peru, the United States, Spain and England.

Lehman B. Fletcher (Ph.D., Economics, University of California, Berkeley, 1960), Professor of Economics at Iowa State University. He is doing research in Guatemala and Mexico on alternative policies and programs to accelerate agricultural development. His publications include *Latin American Agricultural Development and Policies*, Monograph 8, I.S.U., International Studies in Economics, 1968. "Pricing and Allocative Efficiency in Agricultural Development," *American Journal of Agricultural Economics*, December 1968. "A Generalization of the CES Production Function," *Review of Economics and Statistics*, November 1968.

William C. Thiesenhusen (Ph.D., Agricultural Economics, University of Wisconsin, 1965) is an Associate Professor of Agricultural Economics and Agricultural Journalism and director of the Land Tenure Center at the University of Wisconsin. He has done field research in Venezuela, Mexico and Chile. He has published numerous articles on agrarian reform and the "Brain Drain" in Latin America which include *Chile's Experiments in Agrarian Reform*, Land Economics Monograph No. 1, University of Wisconsin Press, 1966; "Latin America's Employment Problem," *Science*, Vol. 171, March 5, 1971; "A Suggested Policy for Industrial Reinvigoration in Latin America," *Journal of Latin American Studies*, May 1972.

Emil B. Haney, Jr. (Ph.D., Agricultural Economics, University of Wisconsin, 1969) is Assistant Professor of Modernization Processes (Economics) at the University of Wisconsin-Green Bay. In addition to a major commitment to curriculum development and teaching in problems of environmental quality, he has continued a longitudinal study of a peasant community in the Colombian highlands. During the 1970-71 academic year, he was a Fulbright-Hays lecturer in Regional Economic Development at the Universidad Veracruzana in Xalapa, Mexico. His doctoral thesis is "The Economic Reorganization of Minifundia in a Highland Community of Colombia."

Index

Index

Abandoned children. *See also* Motivation
  as the Venezuelan rationale for family
    planning, 12
Abortion
  high efficacy of, 53-91
  limits to, 78
  as a population control policy, 65
  primary birth control techniques in Latin
    America, 54, 177
  rates in Argentina and Uruguay, 13
  rates in Lima and Santiago, 12
Absorption of labor in agriculture, 256. *See*
    also Agriculture, labor
  in Colombia, 265 passim
    technological limits to, 271
  not feasible in Mexico, 260
Administrative feasibility
  of birth control techniques beyond family
    planning, 82 passim
  of generating capital from savings or taxa-
    tion in agriculture, 234
Adult education. *See also* Freire, Paulo
  and family planning in Latin America, 16,
    17, 177 passim, 183-186
Age, distribution. *See also* Dependency
    Burden
  at marriage, 225
  and productivity, 30
  in currently developing areas, 33
  in Europe, 29
"Agrarian dualism" in the U.S.
  and self-finance farm social welfare, 252
Agrarian reform. *See* Land reform
Agriculture. *See also* Land reform, Coloniza-
    tion, Family farms, Farm, "Contrived
    dualism," "Agrarian dualism"
  declining productivity in, 215
  employment levels in, 200
  needed technical reforms in, 244-246
  neglect of and contribution of, 233
  and population growth, 237
AID population programs, 5, 16, 112, 118,
    124 passim
    See also U.S. aid for Family Planning
Aid, economic. *See also* U.S. aid, AID
  reduction of U.S. to Latin America, 8,
    114
Argentina, 139
  wage structure in, 213
Arrendamiento (tenancy) in Colombia, 270
ASCOFAME (Colombian Association of

Medical Faculties), 143-144, 162
Asentamiento cooperatives in Chile, 259
Asian population policies
  critique of, 58

BENFAM (Family Welfare Society) Brazil,
    141, 160
Birth control programs, 12 passim. *See also*
    Family planning, Population control,
    Population policies
  among Catholics, 39
  in Latin America—failure of, 178
Birth rates in Latin America
  recent rise in, 57, 223
Blacks in the U.S.
  and birth control, 5, 113
  compared to Latin Americans, 182, 253-
    254
Bolivia, 140
  education and agrarian reform, 258
Brazil, 141, 159
  reaction to U.S. birth control programs,
    120, 159

Capital intensive bias in development plans,
    191, 197-198
Catholic church. *See also* church, *Humanae*
    Vitae, Pope Paul
  decreased opposition to birth control, 114
  in Costa Rica, 166-167
  recent changes in Latin America, 5
  worldwide efficacy of its pronatalist doc-
    trine, 37 passim
  worldwide natality differentials—causes
    of, 40 passim
CELADE (Latin American Demographic
    Center), 142, 143, 144, 163
Chile, 142, 168
  cost of welfare benefits, 3
  decline in growth rate, 1
  institutionalization of family planning, 19,
    123
  wage structure in, 211
Church fund raising. *See also* Catholic
    church
  as a drain on peasant capital in Colombia,
    270
Colombia, 143, 161 passim, 265
  Catholic church in, 162
  family planning in, 123

283